NARUTO

VOL. 61
UCHIHA BROTHERS UNITED FRONT

CONTENTS

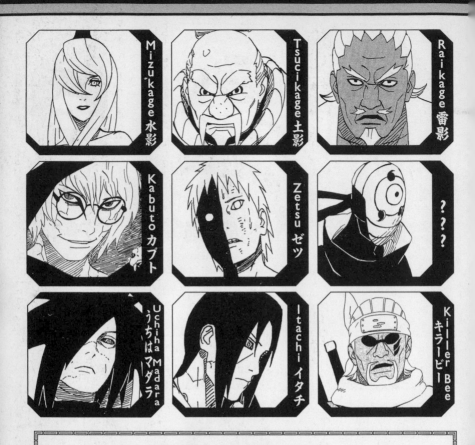

Raikage 雷影
Tsucikage 土影
Mizukage 水影
???
Zetsu ゼツ
Kabuto カブト
Killer Bee キラービー
Itachi イタチ
Uchiha Madara うちはマダラ

THE STORY SO FAR...

Naruto, the biggest troublemaker at the Ninja Academy in the Village of Konohagakure, finally becomes a ninja along with his classmates Sasuke and Sakura. They grow and mature through countless trials and battles. However, Sasuke, unable to give up his quest for vengeance, leaves Konohagakure to seek Orochimaru and his power.

Two years pass. Naruto grows up and engages in fierce battles against the Tailed Beast-targeting Akatsuki. Elsewhere, after winning the heroic battle against Itachi and learning his older brother's true intentions, Sasuke allies with the Akatsuki and sets out to destroy Konoha.

The Fourth Great Ninja War against the Akatsuki begins. The Allied Shinobi Forces begin to rally back after a series of unfavorable battles early on and have the Five Shadows assemble on the battlefield in order to stop the Edotensei-revived Madara! Naruto deepens his bond with Nine Tails and the other jinchûriki during his battle against the masked man. Meanwhile, Sasuke encounters a revived Itachi!

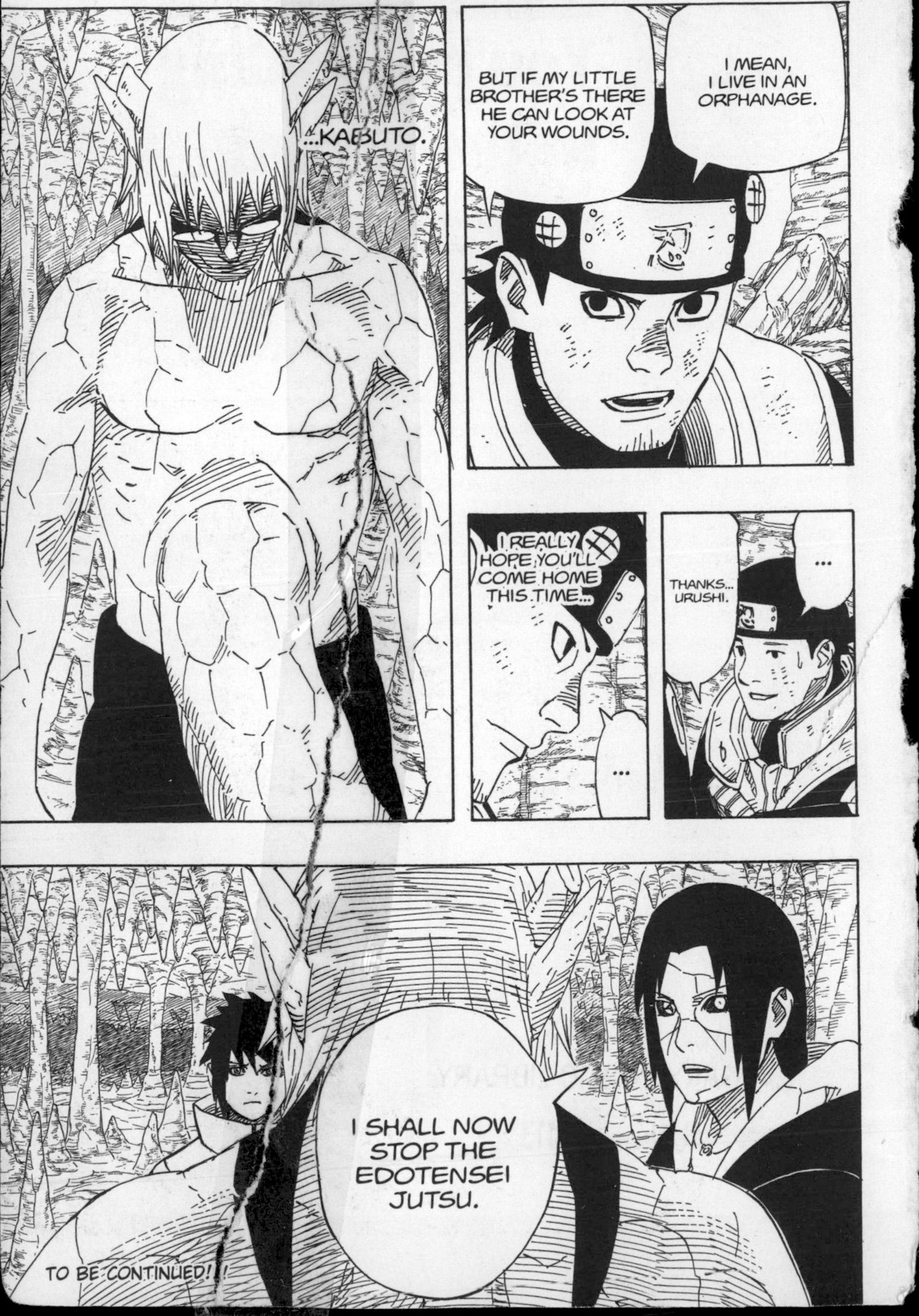
I MEAN, I LIVE IN AN ORPHANAGE.
BUT IF MY LITTLE BROTHER'S THERE HE CAN LOOK AT YOUR WOUNDS.
...
THANKS... URUSHI.
I REALLY HOPE YOU'LL COME HOME THIS TIME...
...
...KABUTO.
I SHALL NOW STOP THE EDOTENSEI JUTSU.
TO BE CONTINUED!!

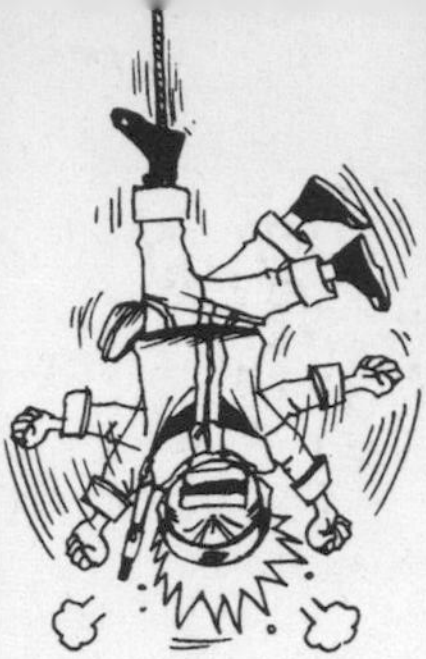

You're Reading in the Wrong Direction!!

Whoops! Guess what? You're starting at the wrong end of the comic!

...It's true! In keeping with the original Japanese format, **Naruto** is meant to be read from right to left, starting in the upper-right corner.

Unlike English, which is read from left to right, Japanese is read from right to left, meaning that action, sound effects and word-balloon order are completely reversed... something which can make readers unfamiliar with Japanese feel pretty backwards themselves. For this reason, manga or Japanese comics published in the U.S. in English have sometimes been published "flopped"—that is, printed in exact reverse order, as though seen from the other side of a mirror.

By flopping pages, U.S. publishers can avoid confusing readers, but the compromise is not without its downside. For one thing, a character in a flopped manga series who once wore in the original Japanese version a T-shirt emblazoned with "M A Y" (as in "the merry month of") now wears one which reads "Y A M"! Additionally, many manga creators in Japan are themselves unhappy with the process, as some feel the mirror-imaging of their art alters their original intentions.

We are proud to bring you Masashi Kishimoto's **Naruto** in the original unflopped format. For now, though, turn to the other side of the book and let the ninjutsu begin...!

—Editor

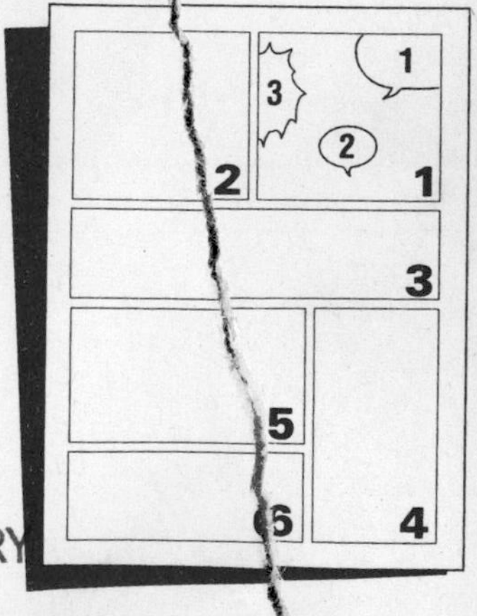
1
2
3
1
2
3
4
5
6

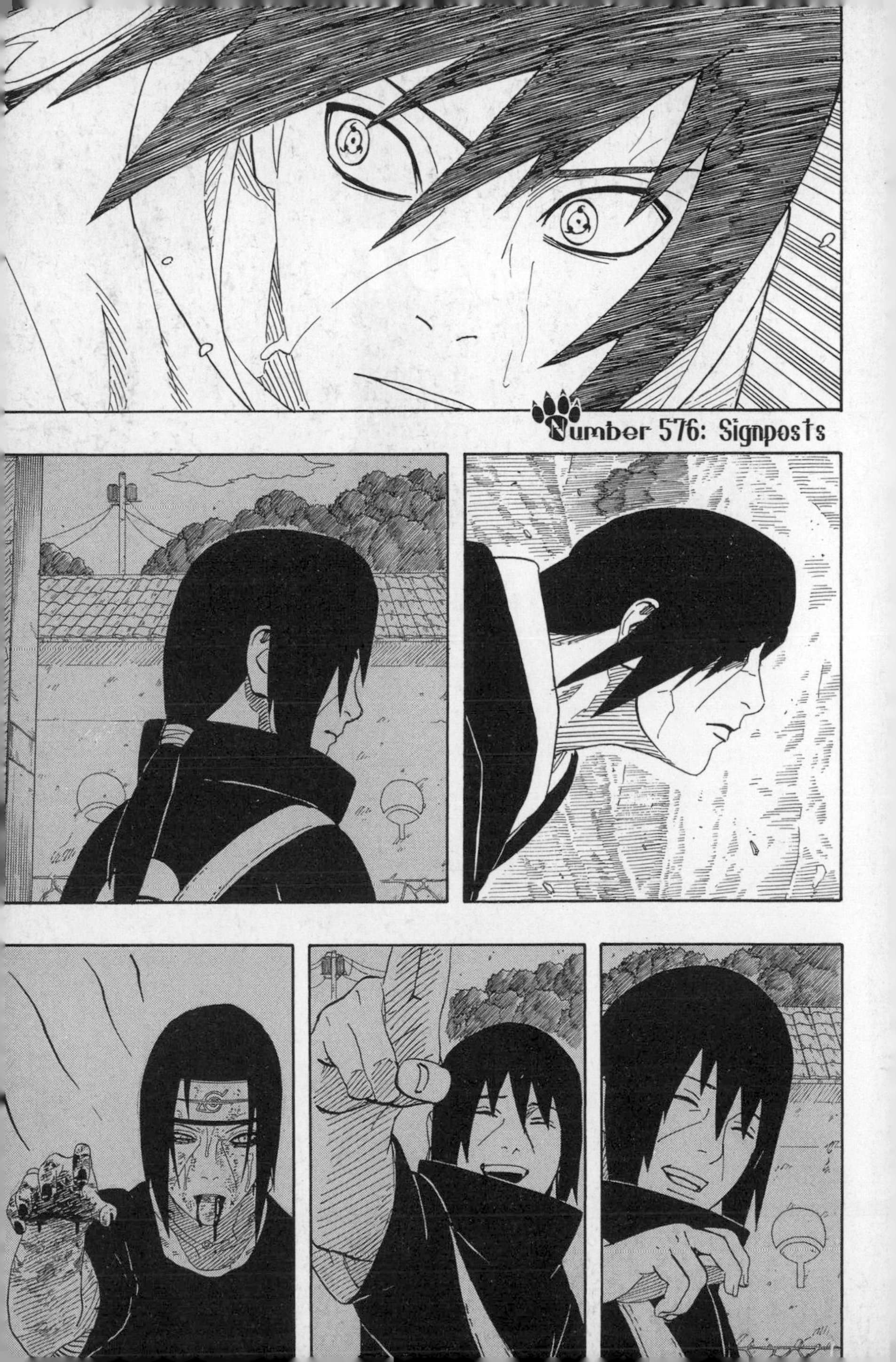
Number 576: Signposts

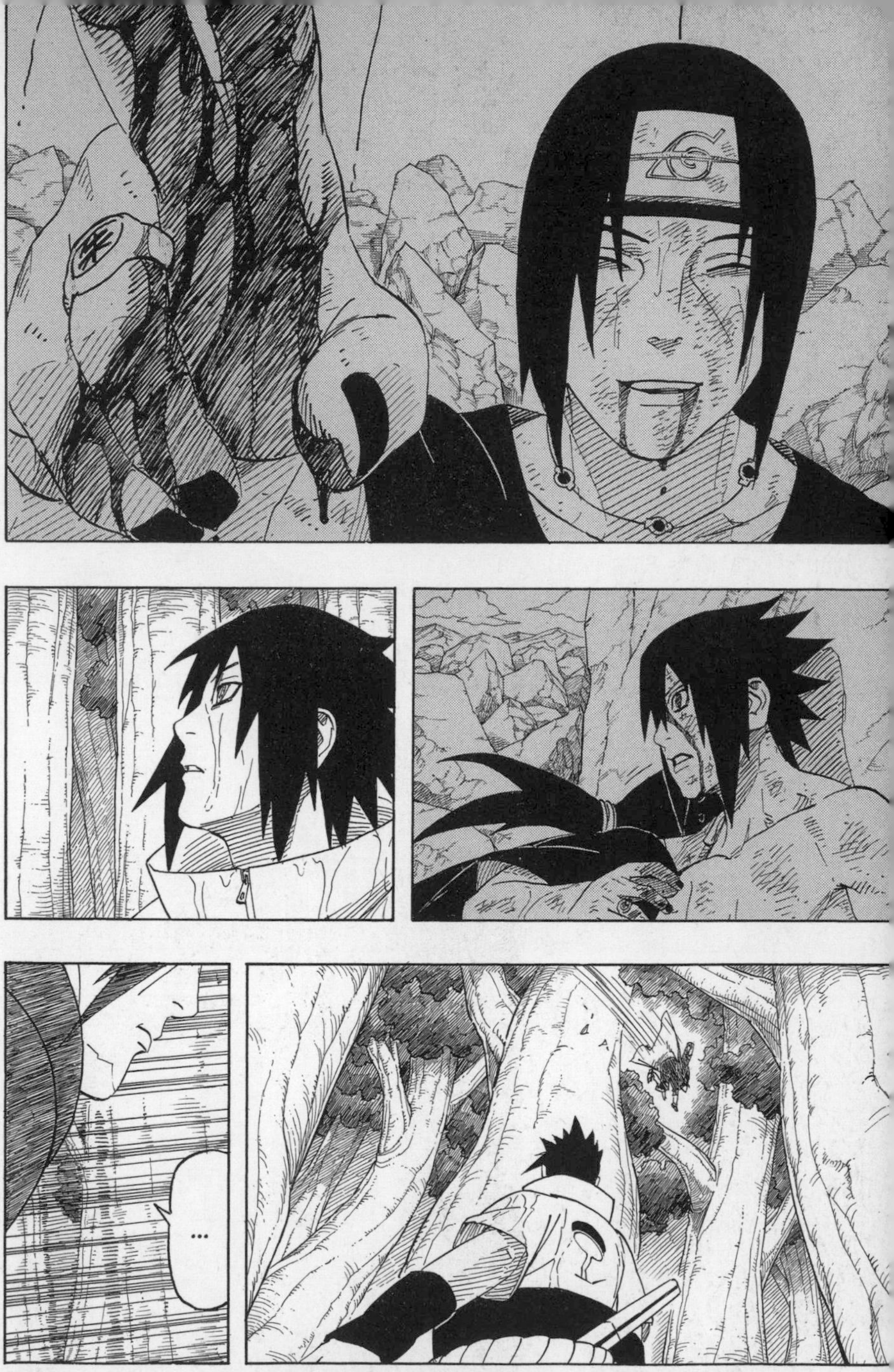
...

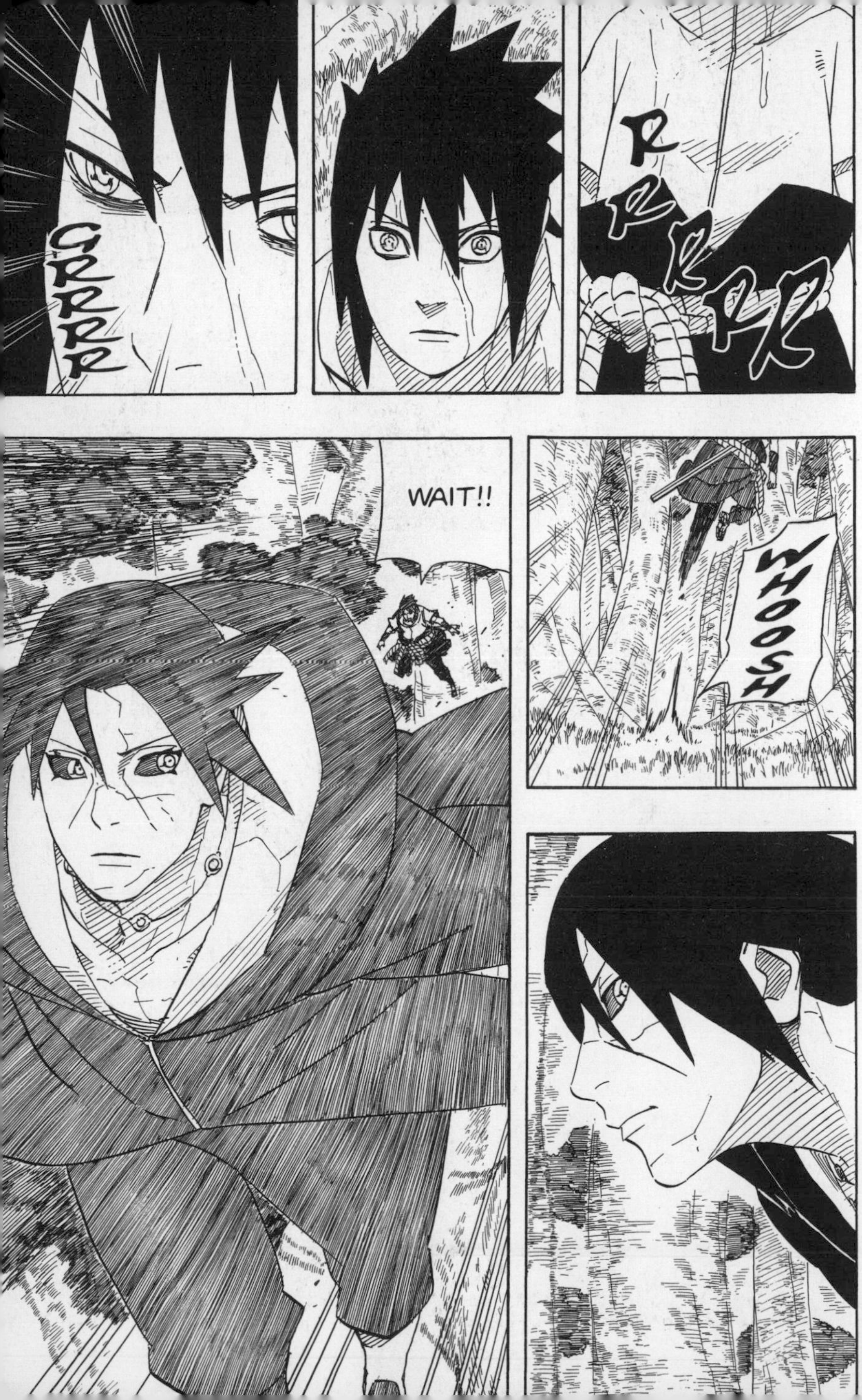
RRRRR
GRRRR
WHOOOSH
WAIT!!

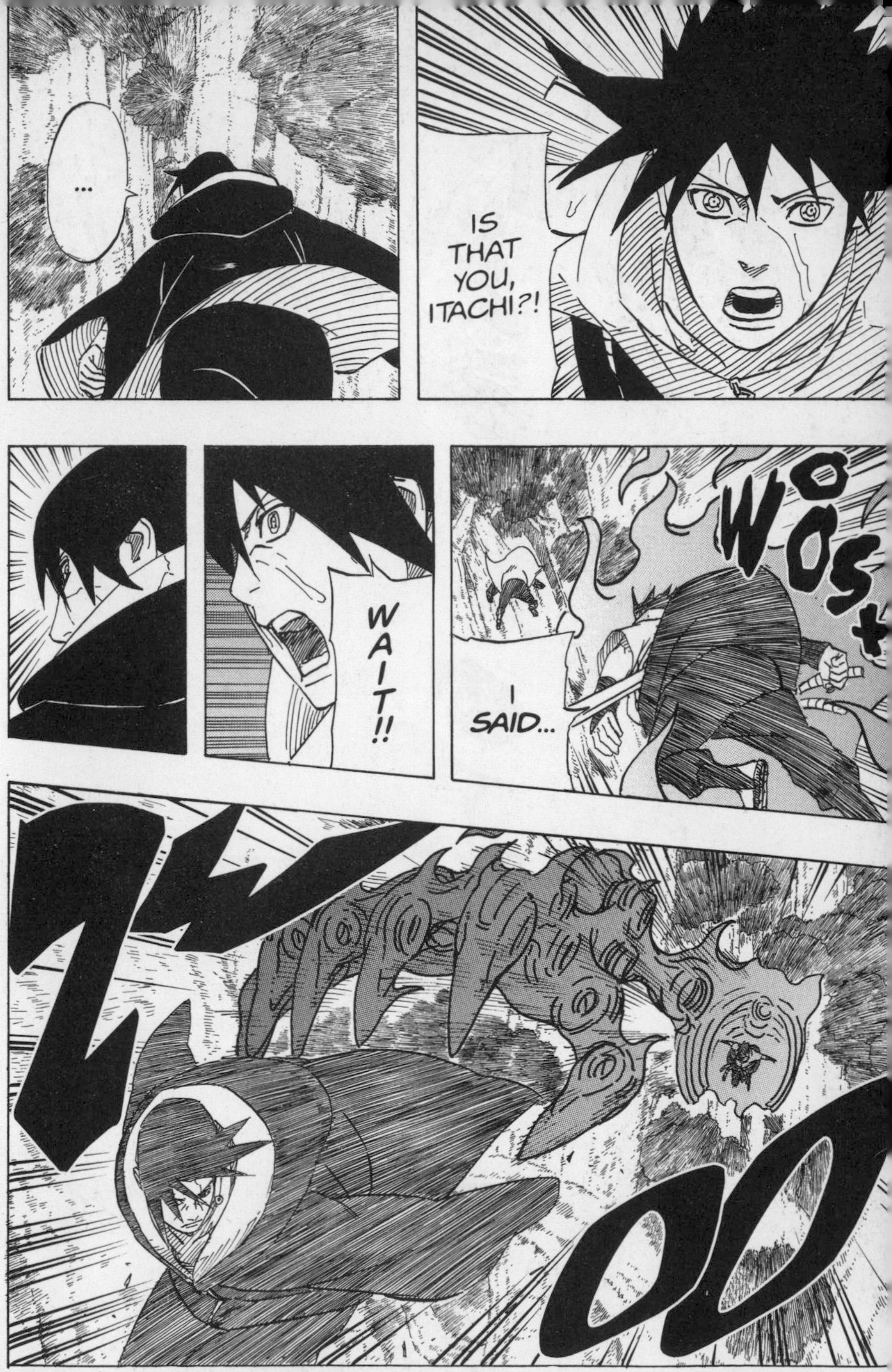
IS THAT YOU, ITACHI?!
...
I SAID...
WAIT!!

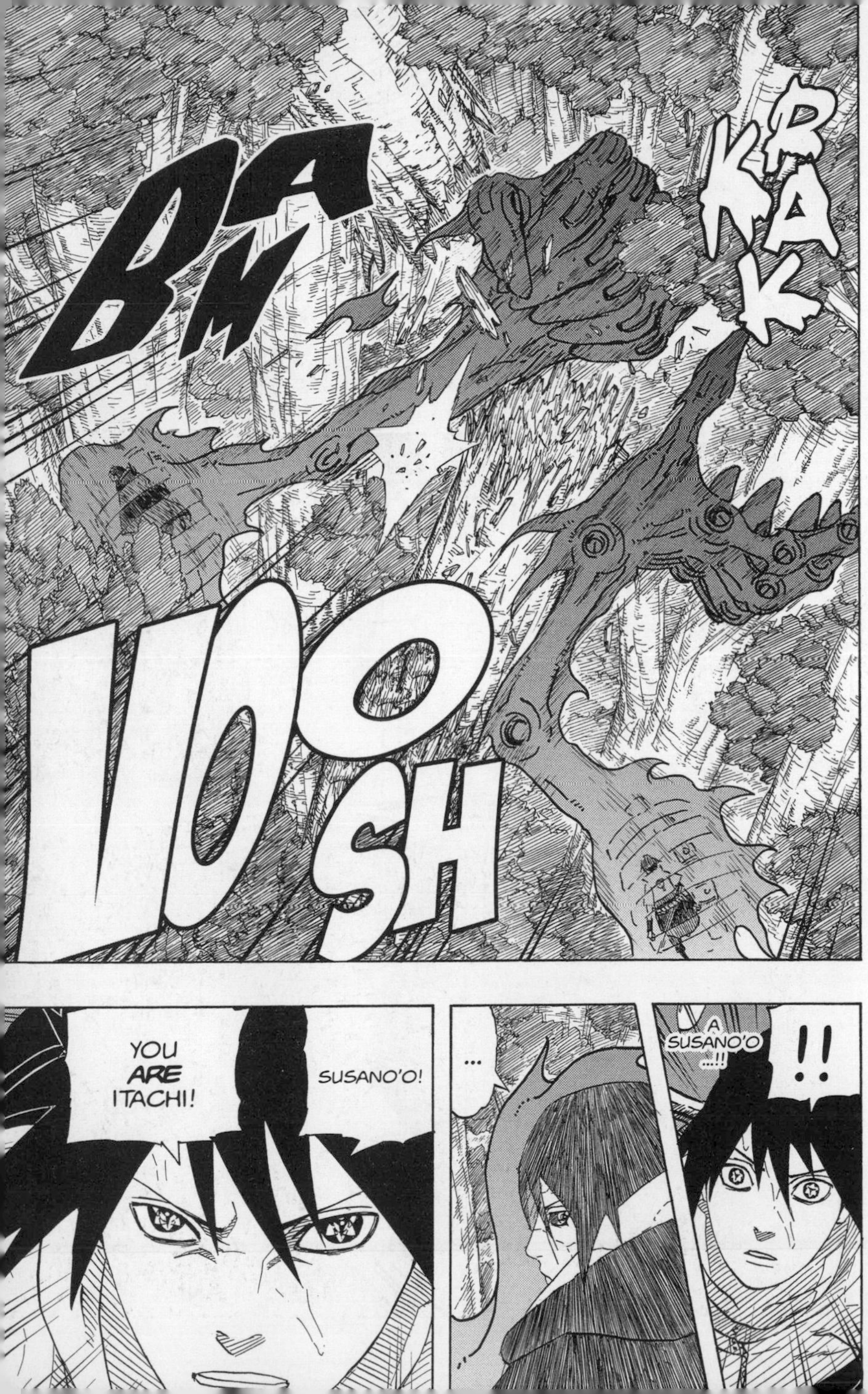
KRAK
BAM
WOOSH
!!
A SUSANO'O ...!!
...
SUSANO'O!
YOU ARE ITACHI!

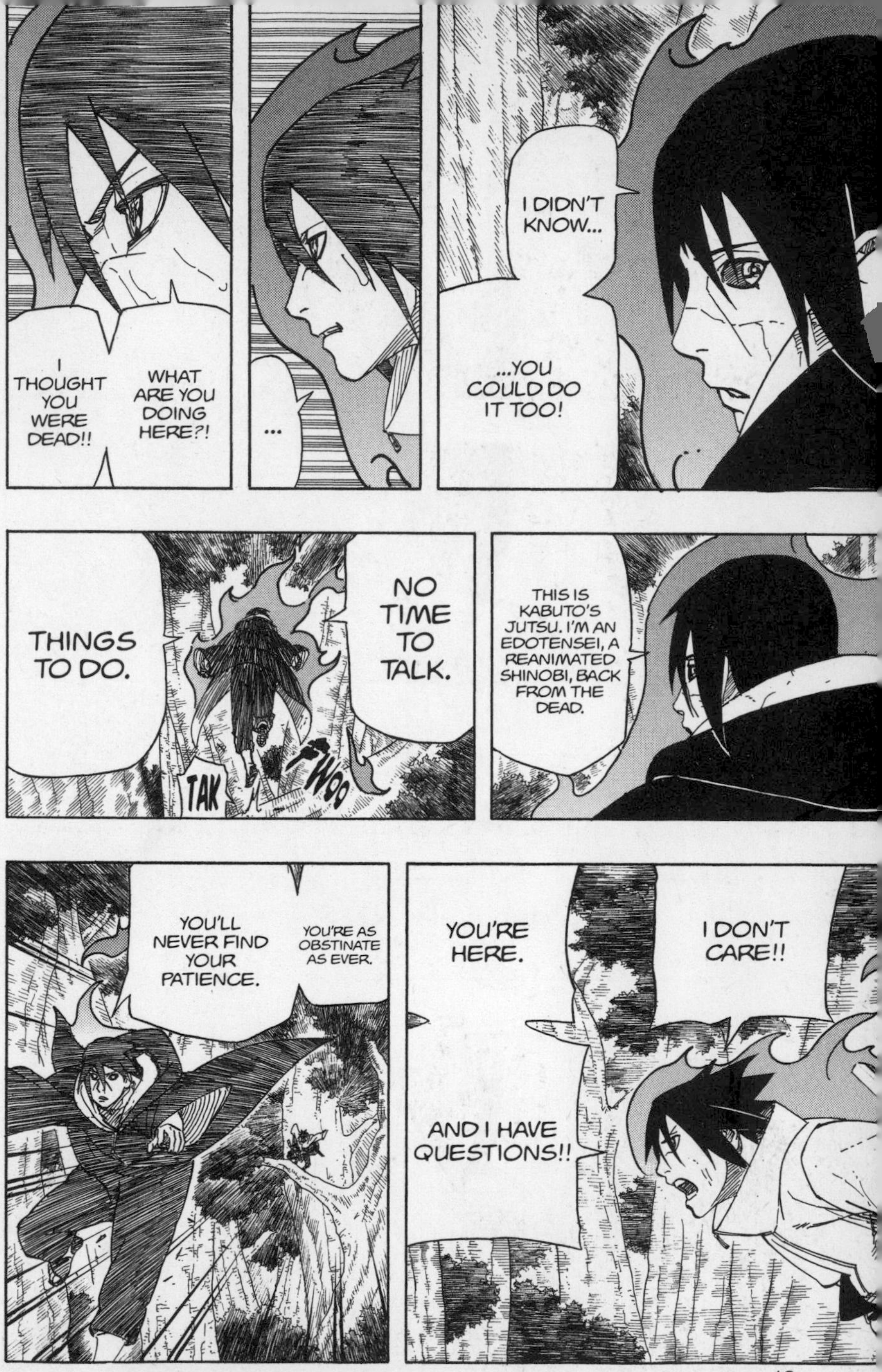
I DIDN'T KNOW...
...YOU COULD DO IT TOO!
...
WHAT ARE YOU DOING HERE?!
I THOUGHT YOU WERE DEAD!!
THIS IS KABUTO'S JUTSU. I'M AN EDOTENSEI, A REANIMATED SHINOBI, BACK FROM THE DEAD.
NO TIME TO TALK.
THINGS TO DO.
FWOO
TAK
I DON'T CARE!!
YOU'RE HERE.
AND I HAVE QUESTIONS!!
YOU'RE AS OBSTINATE AS EVER.
YOU'LL NEVER FIND YOUR PATIENCE.

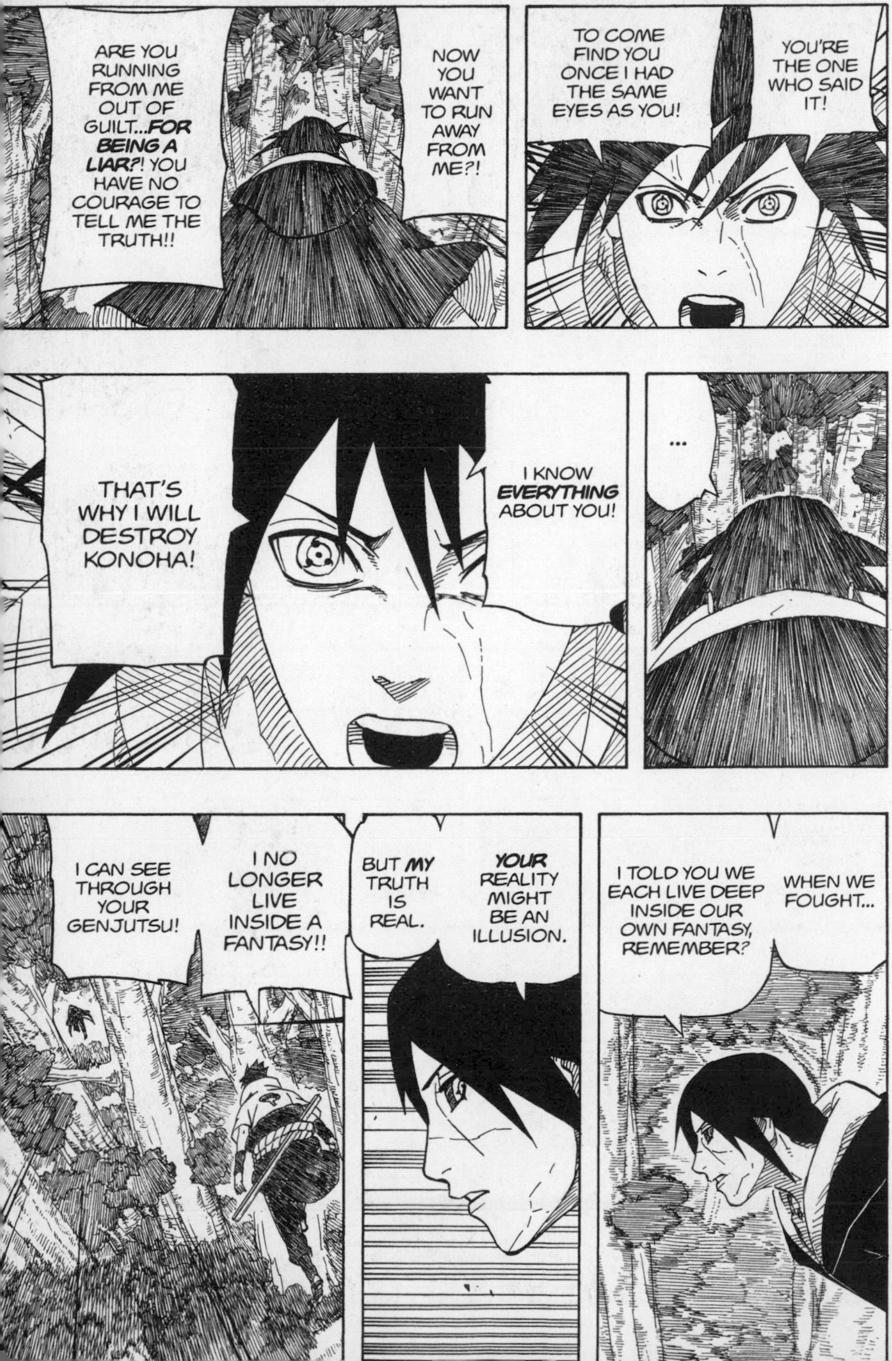
YOU'RE THE ONE WHO SAID IT!
TO COME FIND YOU ONCE I HAD THE SAME EYES AS YOU!
NOW YOU WANT TO RUN AWAY FROM ME?!
ARE YOU RUNNING FROM ME OUT OF GUILT...**FOR BEING A LIAR?!** YOU HAVE NO COURAGE TO TELL ME THE TRUTH!!
...
I KNOW ***EVERYTHING*** ABOUT YOU!
THAT'S WHY I WILL DESTROY KONOHA!
WHEN WE FOUGHT...
I TOLD YOU WE EACH LIVE DEEP INSIDE OUR OWN FANTASY, REMEMBER?
YOUR REALITY MIGHT BE AN ILLUSION.
BUT ***MY*** TRUTH IS REAL.
I NO LONGER LIVE INSIDE A FANTASY!!
I CAN SEE THROUGH YOUR GENJUTSU!

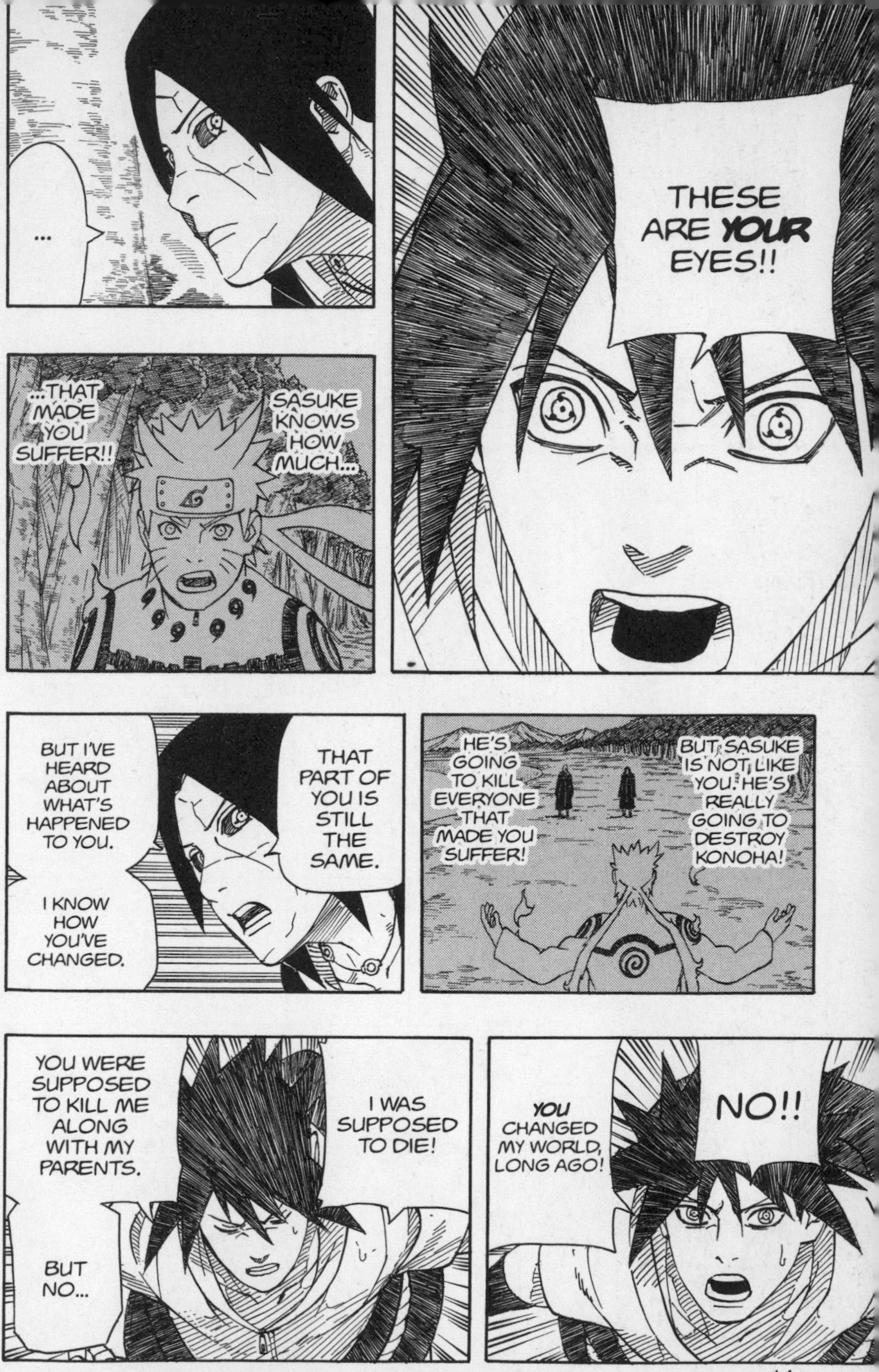
THESE ARE **YOUR** EYES!!
...
SASUKE KNOWS HOW MUCH...
...THAT MADE YOU SUFFER!!
BUT SASUKE IS NOT LIKE YOU! HE'S REALLY GOING TO DESTROY KONOHA!
HE'S GOING TO KILL EVERYONE THAT MADE YOU SUFFER!
THAT PART OF YOU IS STILL THE SAME.
BUT I'VE HEARD ABOUT WHAT'S HAPPENED TO YOU.
I KNOW HOW YOU'VE CHANGED.
NO!!
YOU CHANGED MY WORLD, LONG AGO!
I WAS SUPPOSED TO DIE!
YOU WERE SUPPOSED TO KILL ME ALONG WITH MY PARENTS.
BUT NO...

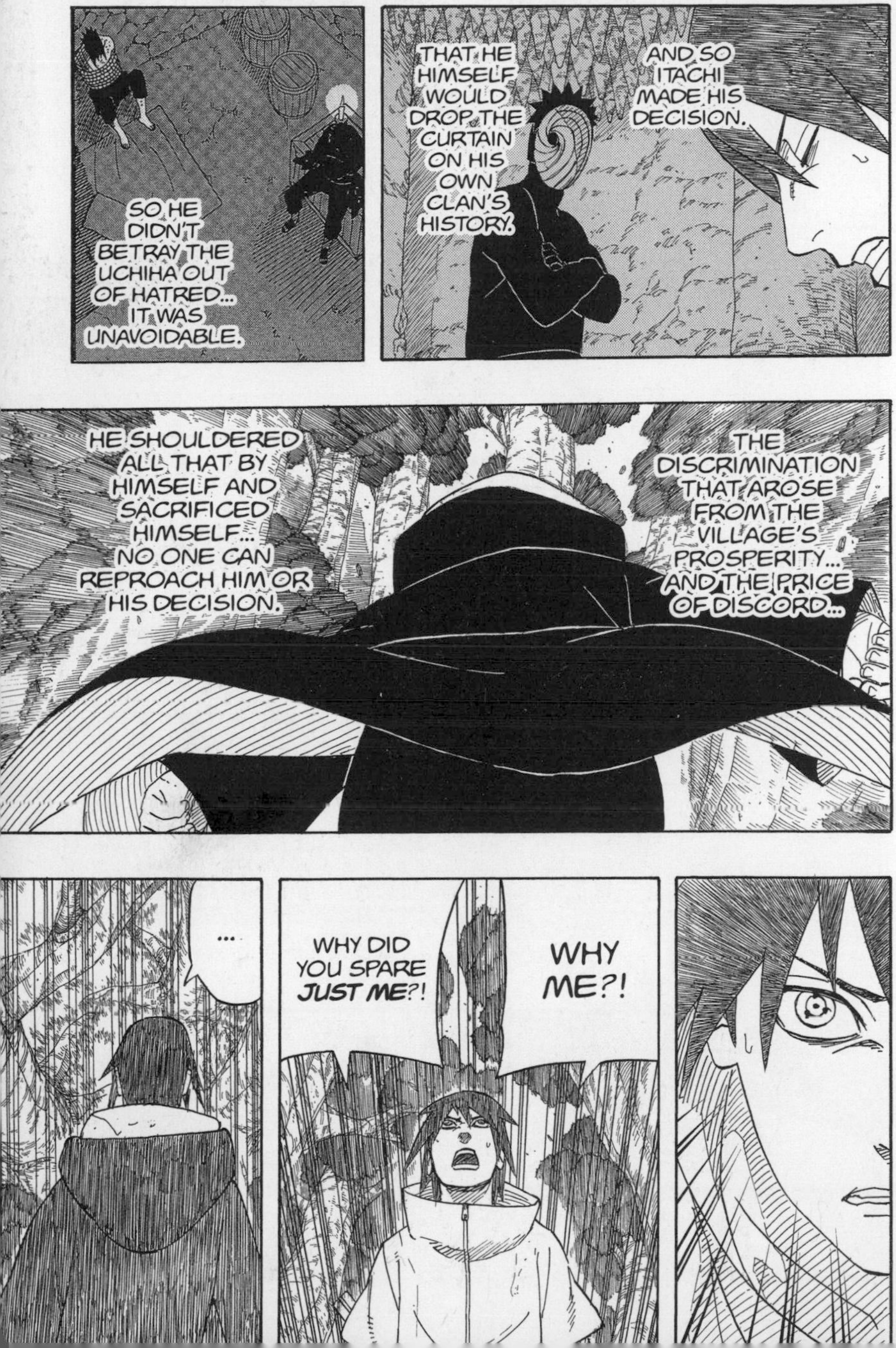
AND SO ITACHI MADE HIS DECISION.
THAT HE HIMSELF WOULD DROP THE CURTAIN ON HIS OWN CLAN'S HISTORY.
SO HE DIDN'T BETRAY THE UCHIHA OUT OF HATRED... IT WAS UNAVOIDABLE.
THE DISCRIMINATION THAT AROSE FROM THE VILLAGE'S PROSPERITY... AND THE PRICE OF DISCORD...
HE SHOULDERED ALL THAT BY HIMSELF AND SACRIFICED HIMSELF... NO ONE CAN REPROACH HIM OR HIS DECISION.
WHY ME?!
WHY DID YOU SPARE **JUST ME**?!
...

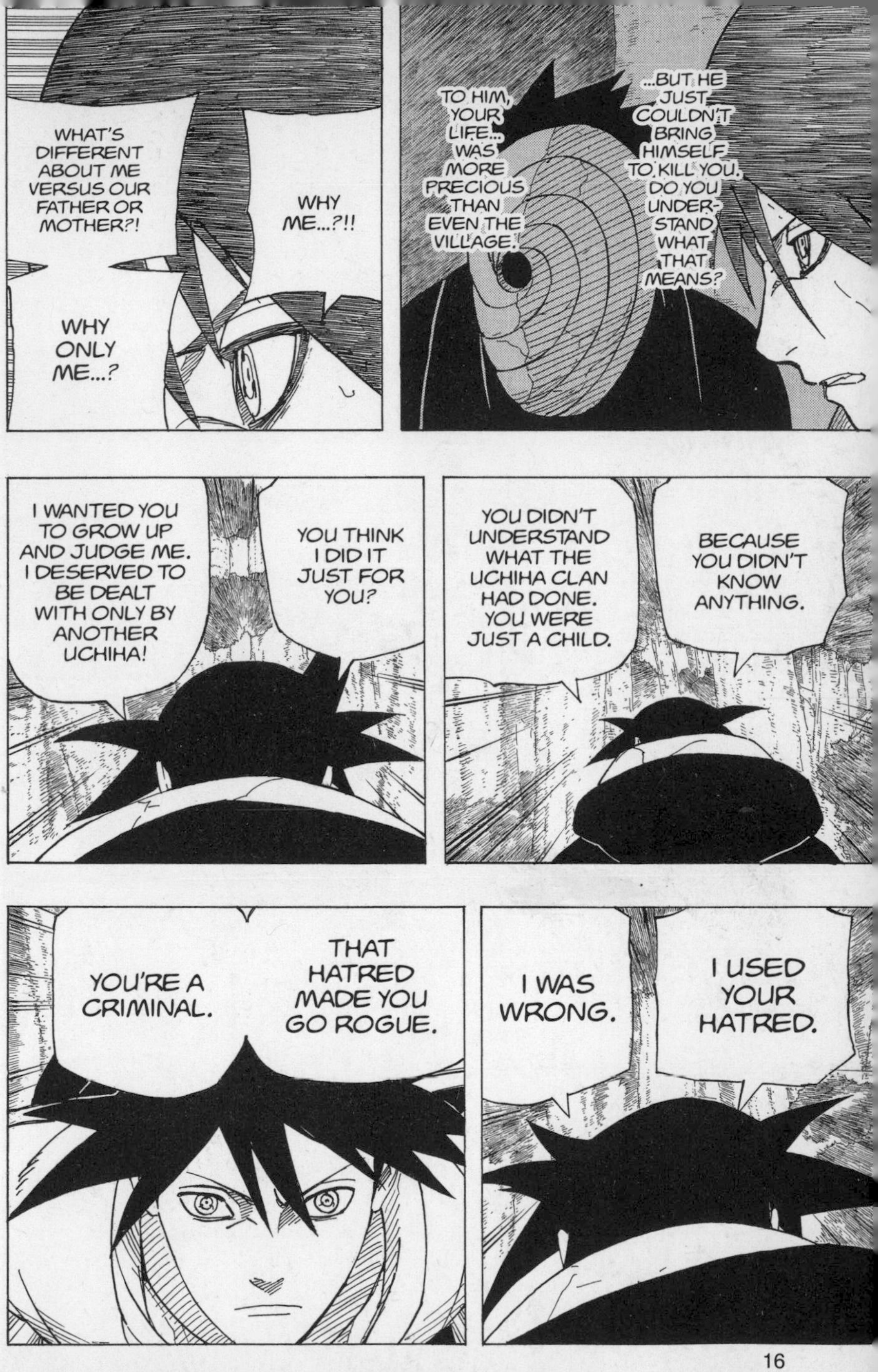
...BUT HE JUST COULDN'T BRING HIMSELF TO KILL YOU. DO YOU UNDERSTAND WHAT THAT MEANS?
TO HIM, YOUR LIFE... WAS MORE PRECIOUS THAN EVEN THE VILLAGE.
WHY ME...?!!
WHAT'S DIFFERENT ABOUT ME VERSUS OUR FATHER OR MOTHER?!
WHY ONLY ME...?
BECAUSE YOU DIDN'T KNOW ANYTHING.
YOU DIDN'T UNDERSTAND WHAT THE UCHIHA CLAN HAD DONE. YOU WERE JUST A CHILD.
YOU THINK I DID IT JUST FOR YOU?
I WANTED YOU TO GROW UP AND JUDGE ME. I DESERVED TO BE DEALT WITH ONLY BY ANOTHER UCHIHA!
I USED YOUR HATRED.
I WAS WRONG.
THAT HATRED MADE YOU GO ROGUE.
YOU'RE A CRIMINAL.

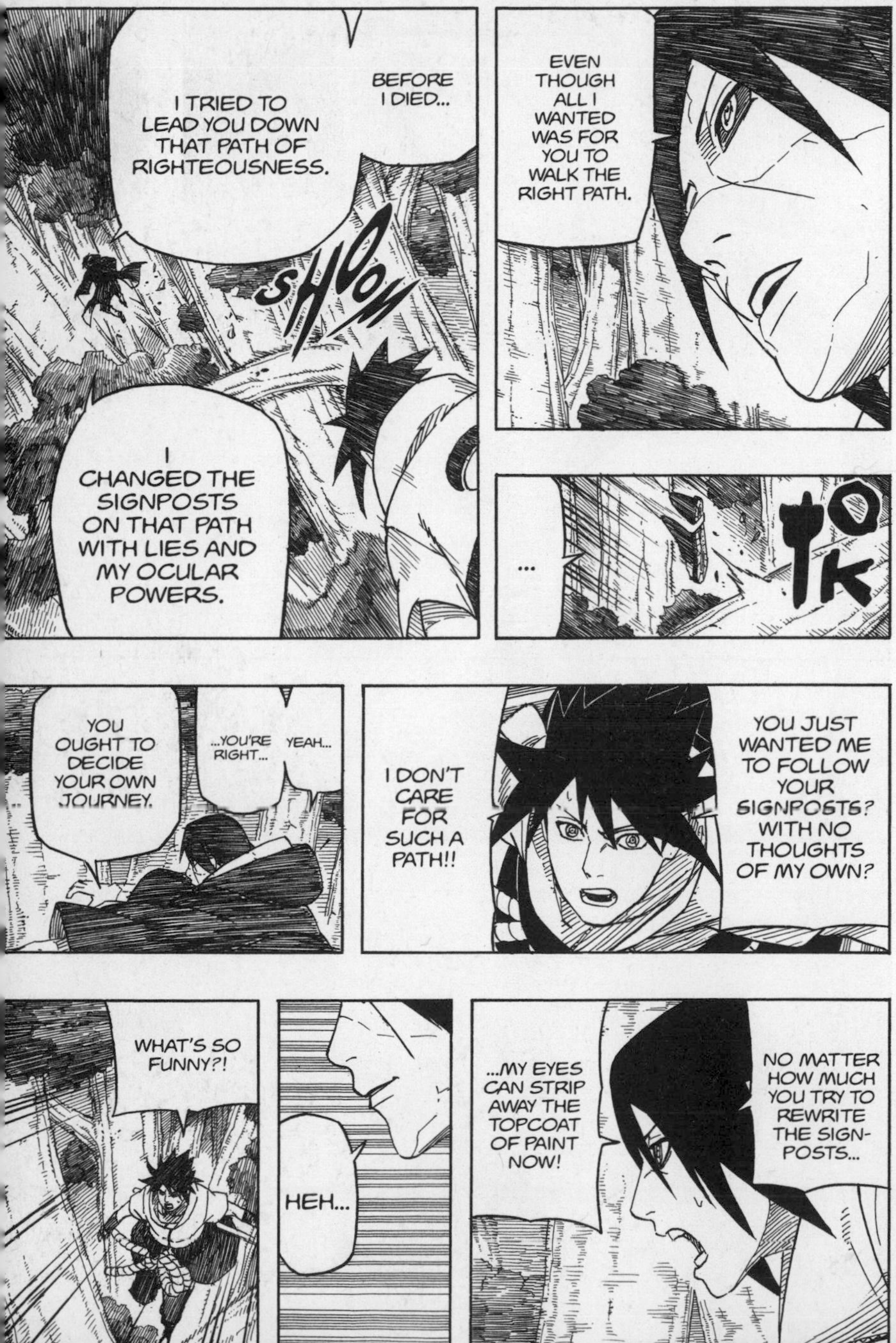
EVEN THOUGH ALL I WANTED WAS FOR YOU TO WALK THE RIGHT PATH.
...
TOK
BEFORE I DIED...
I TRIED TO LEAD YOU DOWN THAT PATH OF RIGHTEOUSNESS.
SHOOM
I CHANGED THE SIGNPOSTS ON THAT PATH WITH LIES AND MY OCULAR POWERS.
YOU JUST WANTED ME TO FOLLOW YOUR SIGNPOSTS? WITH NO THOUGHTS OF MY OWN?
I DON'T CARE FOR SUCH A PATH!!
YEAH...
...YOU'RE RIGHT...
YOU OUGHT TO DECIDE YOUR OWN JOURNEY.
NO MATTER HOW MUCH YOU TRY TO REWRITE THE SIGN-POSTS...
...MY EYES CAN STRIP AWAY THE TOPCOAT OF PAINT NOW!
HEH...
WHAT'S SO FUNNY?!

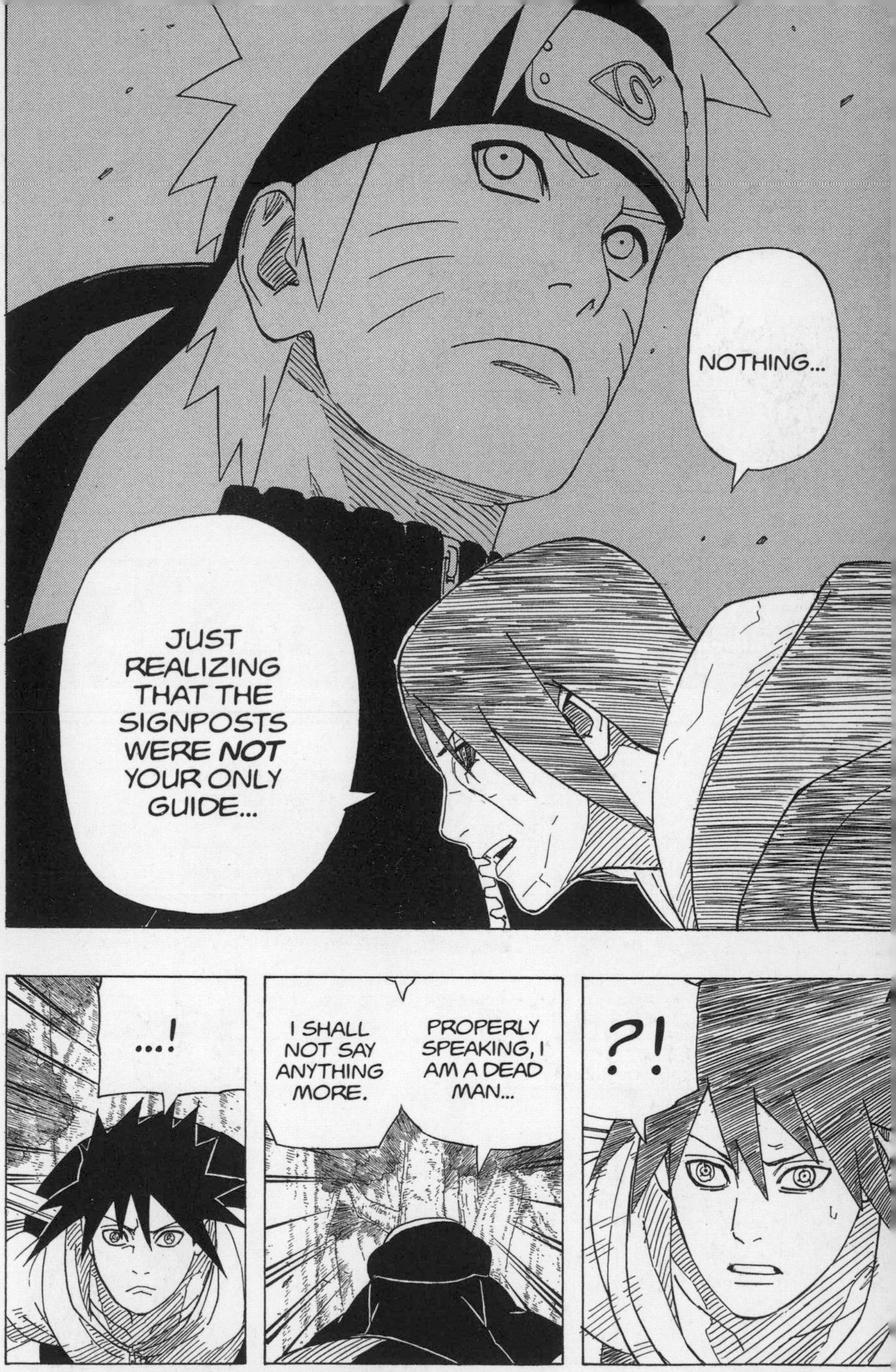
NOTHING...
JUST REALIZING THAT THE SIGNPOSTS WERE **NOT** YOUR ONLY GUIDE...
?!
PROPERLY SPEAKING, I AM A DEAD MAN...
I SHALL NOT SAY ANYTHING MORE.
...!

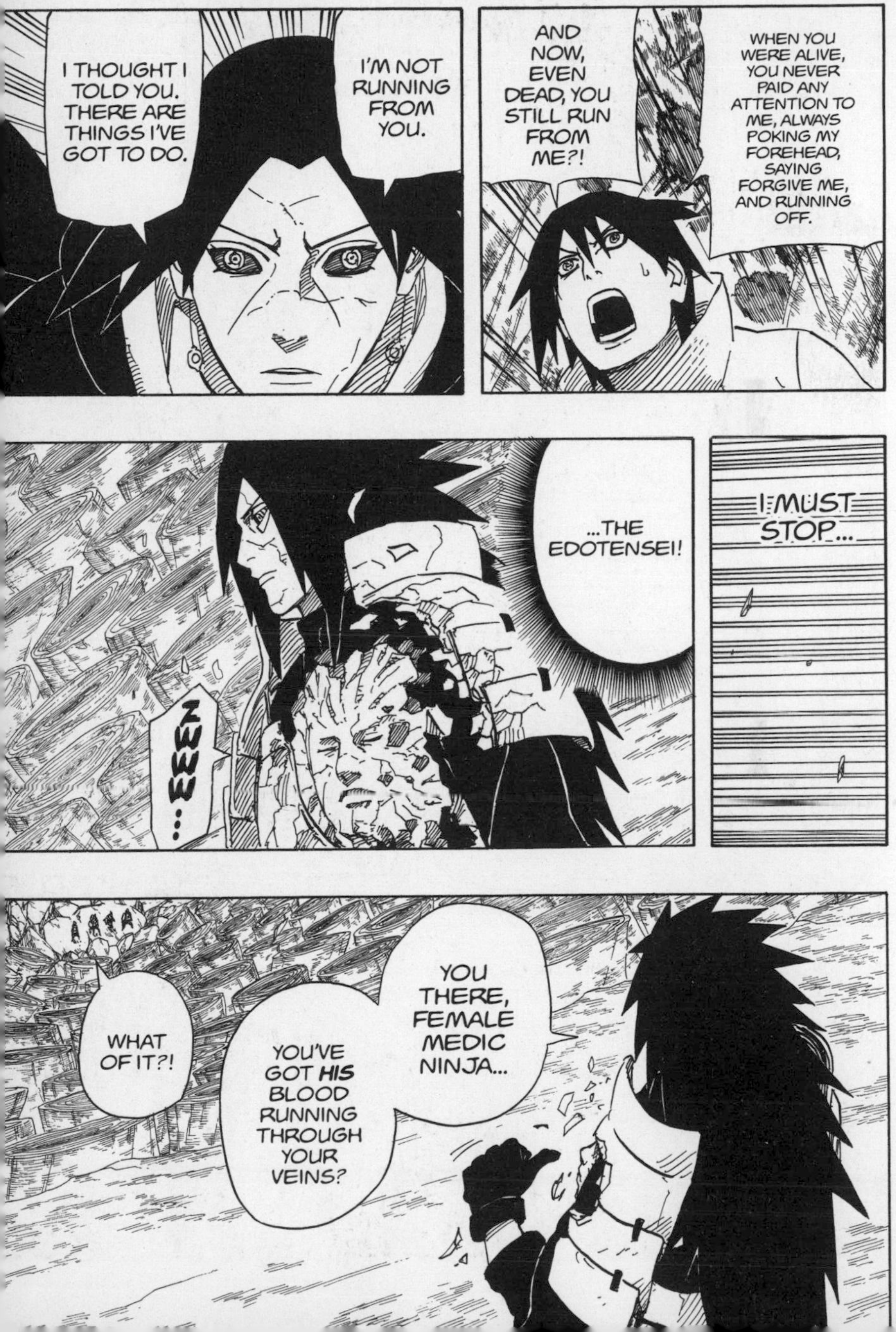
WHEN YOU WERE ALIVE, YOU NEVER PAID ANY ATTENTION TO ME, ALWAYS POKING MY FOREHEAD, SAYING FORGIVE ME, AND RUNNING OFF.
AND NOW, EVEN DEAD, YOU STILL RUN FROM ME?!
I'M NOT RUNNING FROM YOU.
I THOUGHT I TOLD YOU. THERE ARE THINGS I'VE GOT TO DO.
I MUST STOP...
...THE EDOTENSEI!
ZWWW...
YOU THERE, FEMALE MEDIC NINJA...
YOU'VE GOT **HIS** BLOOD RUNNING THROUGH YOUR VEINS?
WHAT OF IT?!

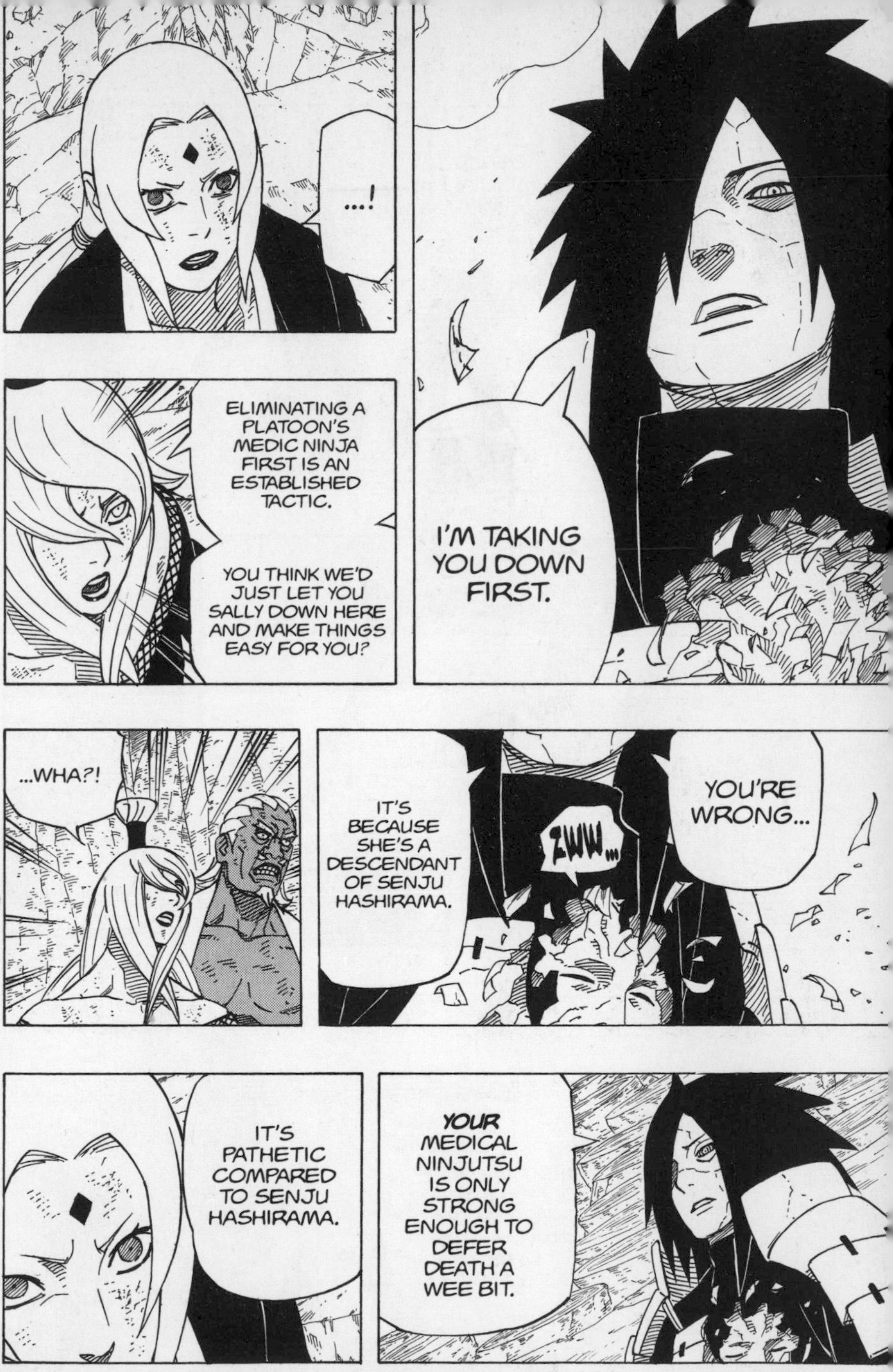
I'M TAKING YOU DOWN FIRST.
...!
ELIMINATING A PLATOON'S MEDIC NINJA FIRST IS AN ESTABLISHED TACTIC.
YOU THINK WE'D JUST LET YOU SALLY DOWN HERE AND MAKE THINGS EASY FOR YOU?
YOU'RE WRONG...
ZWW...
IT'S BECAUSE SHE'S A DESCENDANT OF SENJU HASHIRAMA.
...WHA?!
YOUR MEDICAL NINJUTSU IS ONLY STRONG ENOUGH TO DEFER DEATH A WEE BIT.
IT'S PATHETIC COMPARED TO SENJU HASHIRAMA.

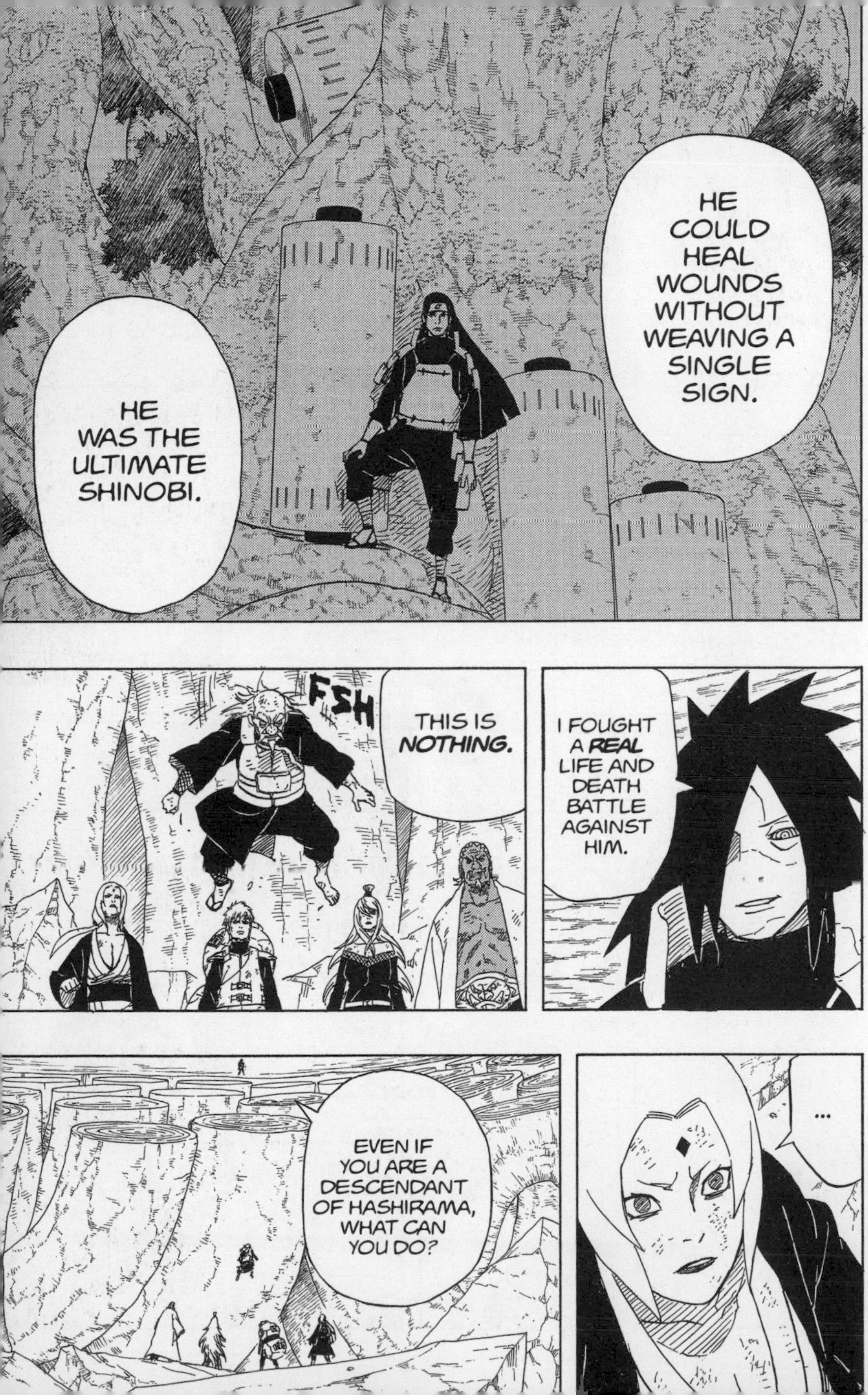
HE COULD HEAL WOUNDS WITHOUT WEAVING A SINGLE SIGN.
HE WAS THE ULTIMATE SHINOBI.
I FOUGHT A REAL LIFE AND DEATH BATTLE AGAINST HIM.
THIS IS NOTHING.
FSH
...
EVEN IF YOU ARE A DESCENDANT OF HASHIRAMA, WHAT CAN YOU DO?

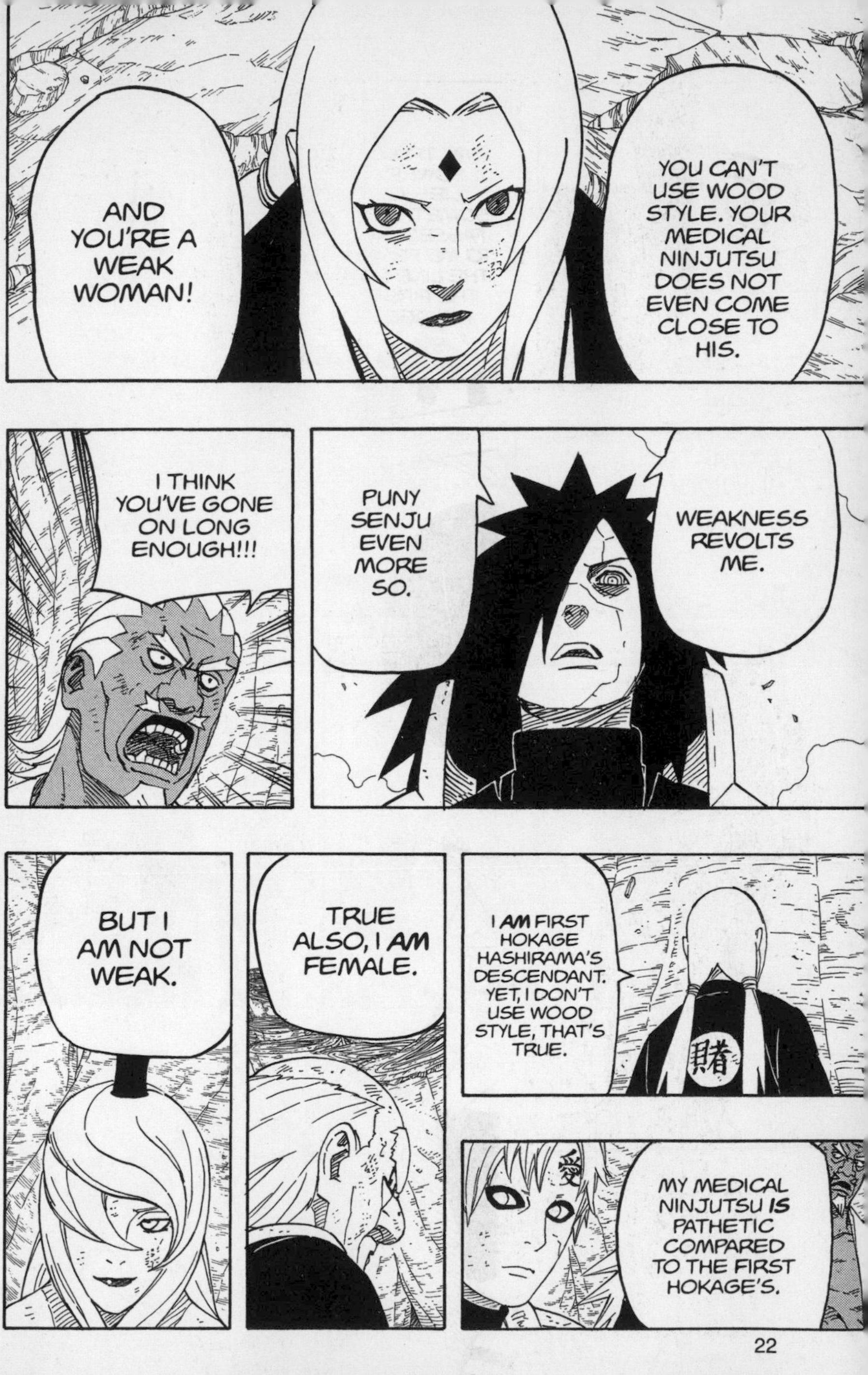
YOU CAN'T USE WOOD STYLE. YOUR MEDICAL NINJUTSU DOES NOT EVEN COME CLOSE TO HIS.
AND YOU'RE A WEAK WOMAN!
WEAKNESS REVOLTS ME.
PUNY SENJU EVEN MORE SO.
I THINK YOU'VE GONE ON LONG ENOUGH!!!
I AM FIRST HOKAGE HASHIRAMA'S DESCENDANT. YET, I DON'T USE WOOD STYLE, THAT'S TRUE.
MY MEDICAL NINJUTSU IS PATHETIC COMPARED TO THE FIRST HOKAGE'S.
TRUE ALSO, I AM FEMALE.
BUT I AM NOT WEAK.

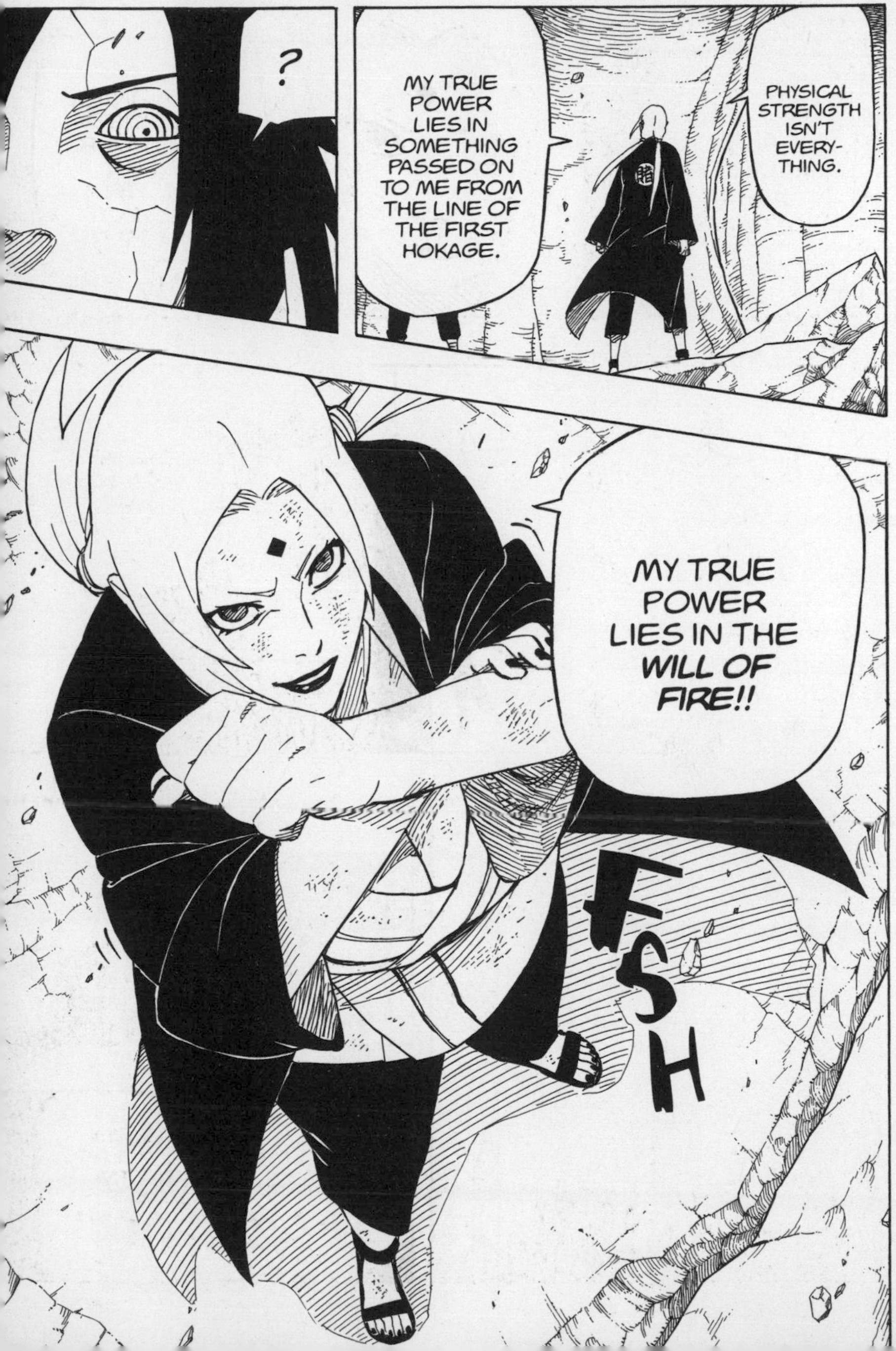
PHYSICAL STRENGTH ISN'T EVERY-THING.
MY TRUE POWER LIES IN SOMETHING PASSED ON TO ME FROM THE LINE OF THE FIRST HOKAGE.
?
MY TRUE POWER LIES IN THE *WILL OF FIRE!!*
FSH

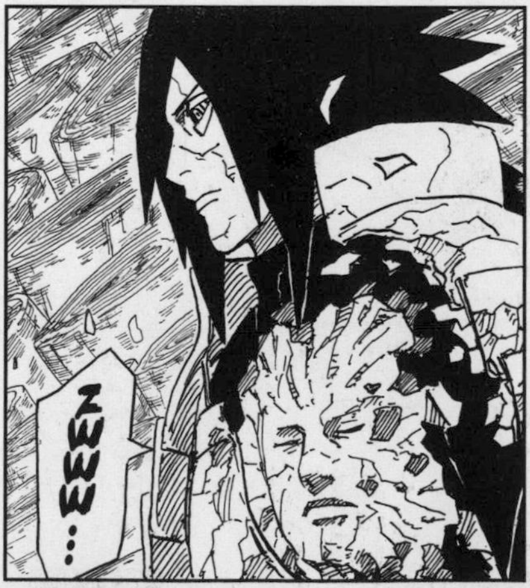
ZWWW...

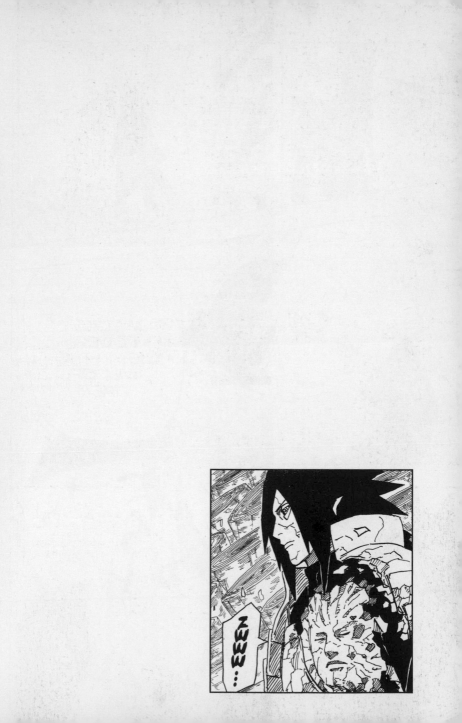

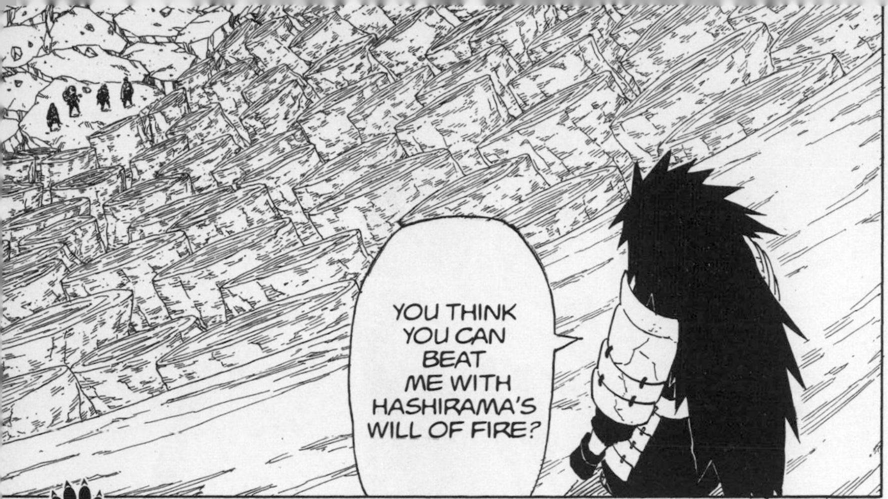
YOU THINK YOU CAN BEAT ME WITH HASHIRAMA'S WILL OF FIRE?

Number 577: Hate Blade

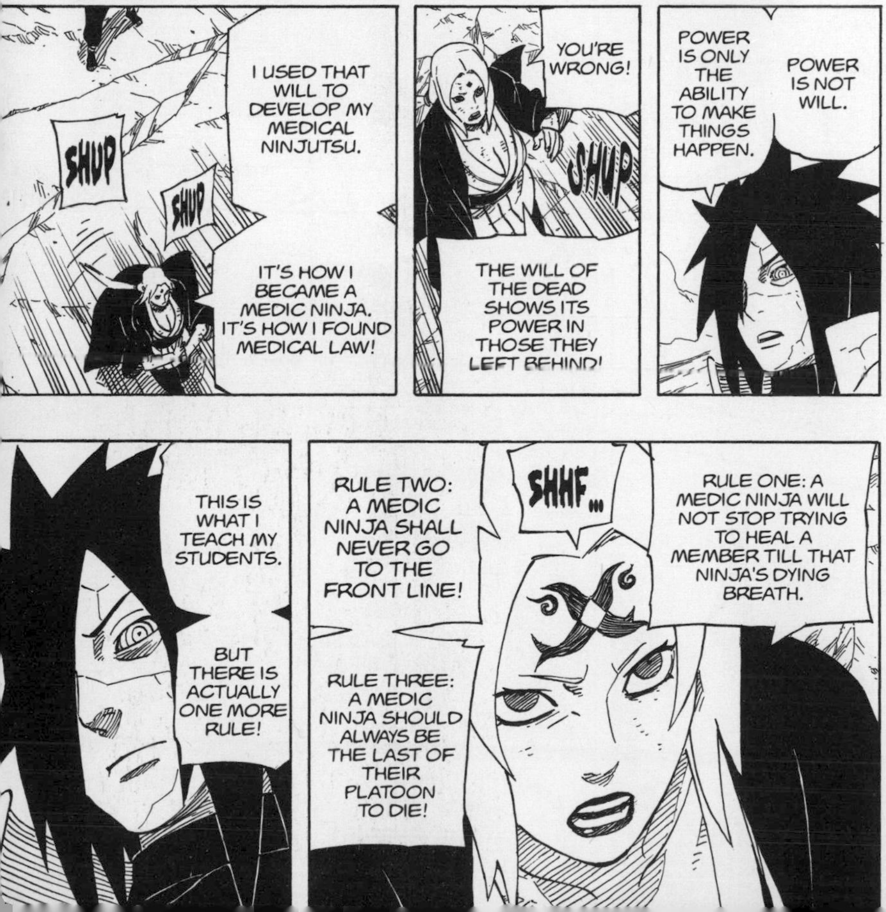
POWER IS NOT WILL.
POWER IS ONLY THE ABILITY TO MAKE THINGS HAPPEN.
YOU'RE WRONG!
SHUP
THE WILL OF THE DEAD SHOWS ITS POWER IN THOSE THEY LEFT BEHIND!
I USED THAT WILL TO DEVELOP MY MEDICAL NINJUTSU.
SHUP
SHUP
IT'S HOW I BECAME A MEDIC NINJA. IT'S HOW I FOUND MEDICAL LAW!
RULE ONE: A MEDIC NINJA WILL NOT STOP TRYING TO HEAL A MEMBER TILL THAT NINJA'S DYING BREATH.
SHHF...
RULE TWO: A MEDIC NINJA SHALL NEVER GO TO THE FRONT LINE!
RULE THREE: A MEDIC NINJA SHOULD ALWAYS BE THE LAST OF THEIR PLATOON TO DIE!
THIS IS WHAT I TEACH MY STUDENTS.
BUT THERE IS ACTUALLY ONE MORE RULE!

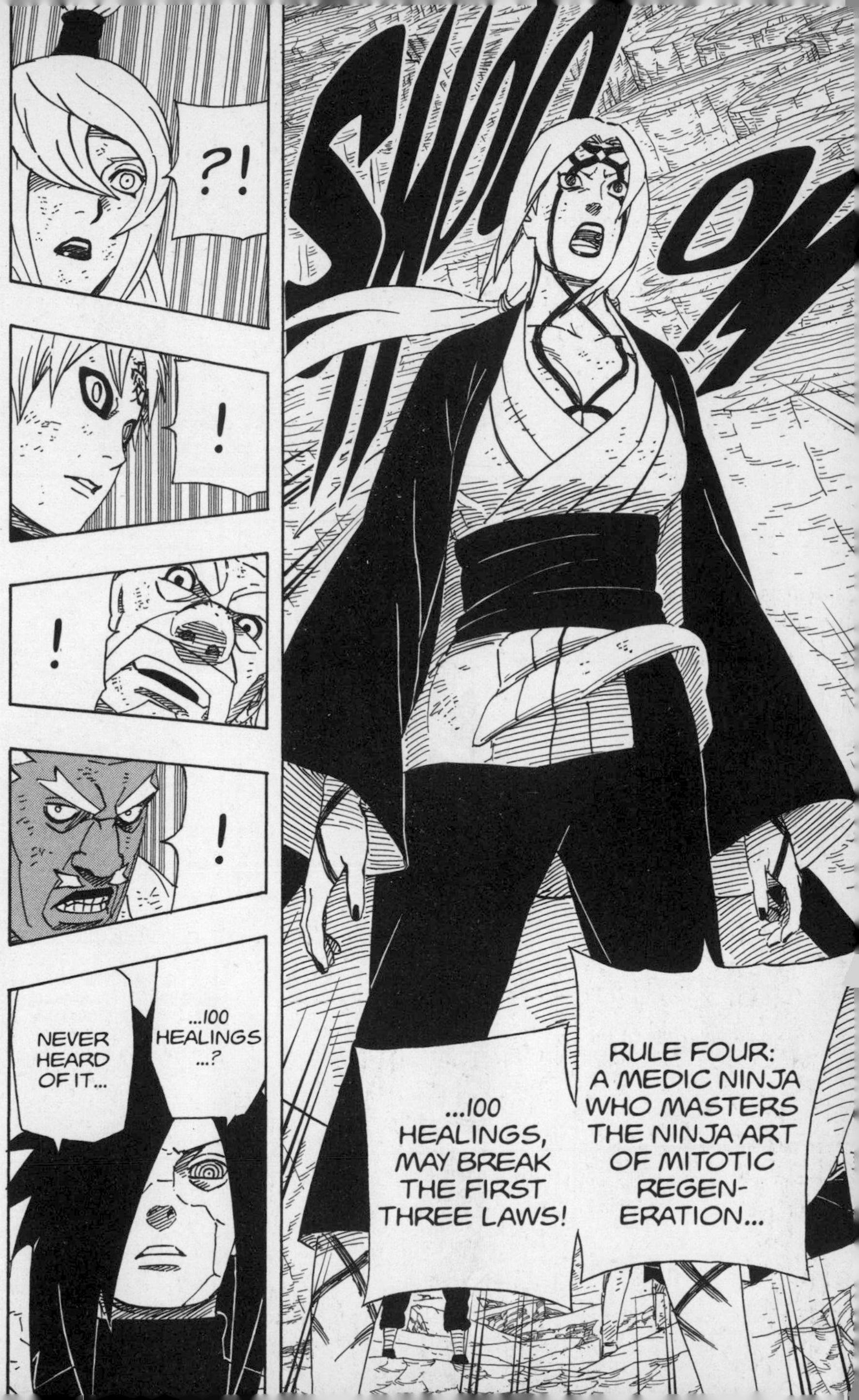
RULE FOUR: A MEDIC NINJA WHO MASTERS THE NINJA ART OF MITOTIC REGEN-ERATION...
...100 HEALINGS, MAY BREAK THE FIRST THREE LAWS!
?!
!
!
!
...100 HEALINGS ...?
NEVER HEARD OF IT...

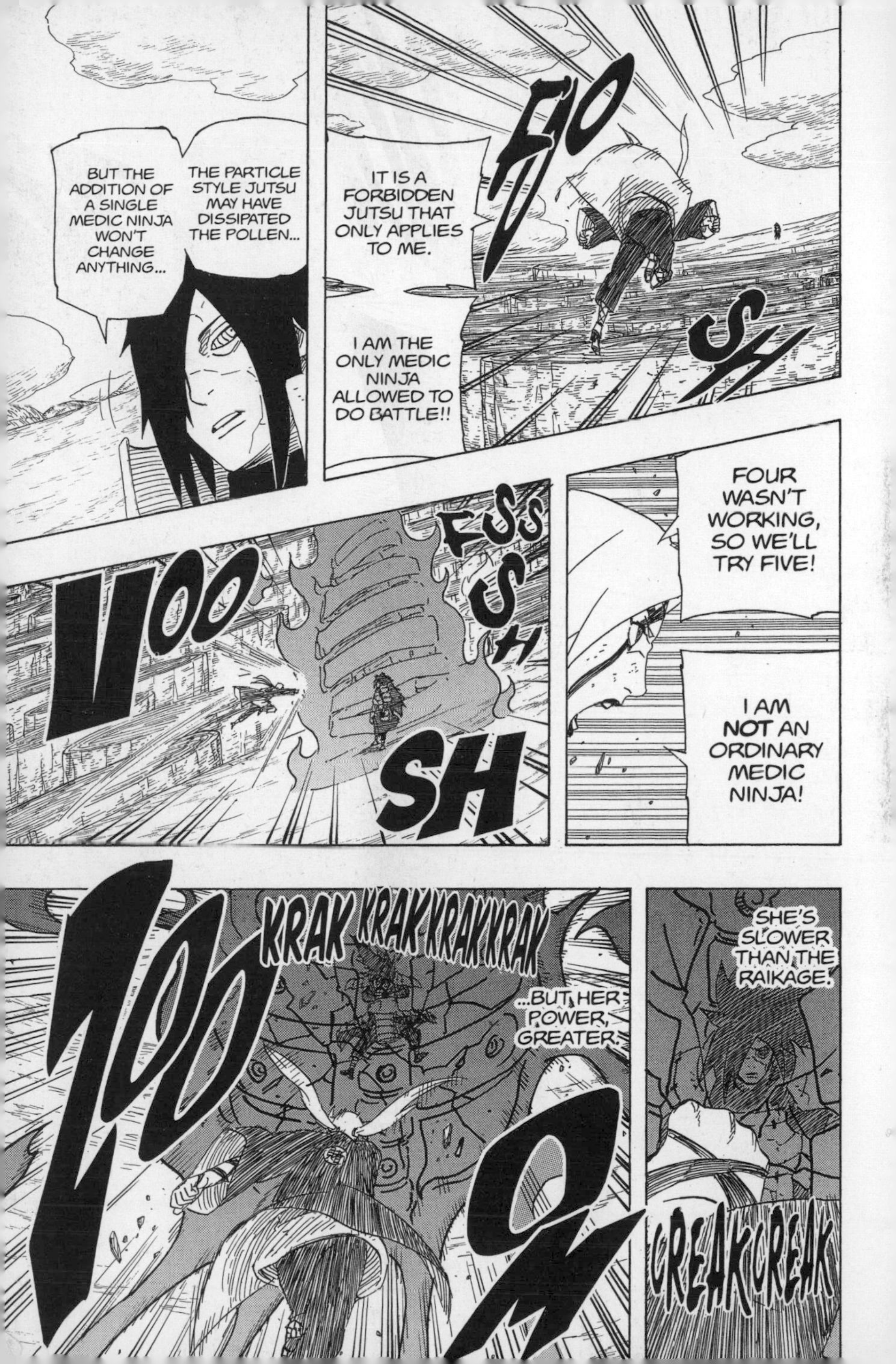
IT IS A FORBIDDEN JUTSU THAT ONLY APPLIES TO ME.
I AM THE ONLY MEDIC NINJA ALLOWED TO DO BATTLE!!
SH
THE PARTICLE STYLE JUTSU MAY HAVE DISSIPATED THE POLLEN...
BUT THE ADDITION OF A SINGLE MEDIC NINJA WON'T CHANGE ANYTHING...
FOUR WASN'T WORKING, SO WE'LL TRY FIVE!
I AM **NOT** AN ORDINARY MEDIC NINJA!
SH
SH
SHE'S SLOWER THAN THE RAIKAGE.
CREAKCREAK
KRAK KRAK KRAK KRAK
...BUT HER POWER, GREATER.

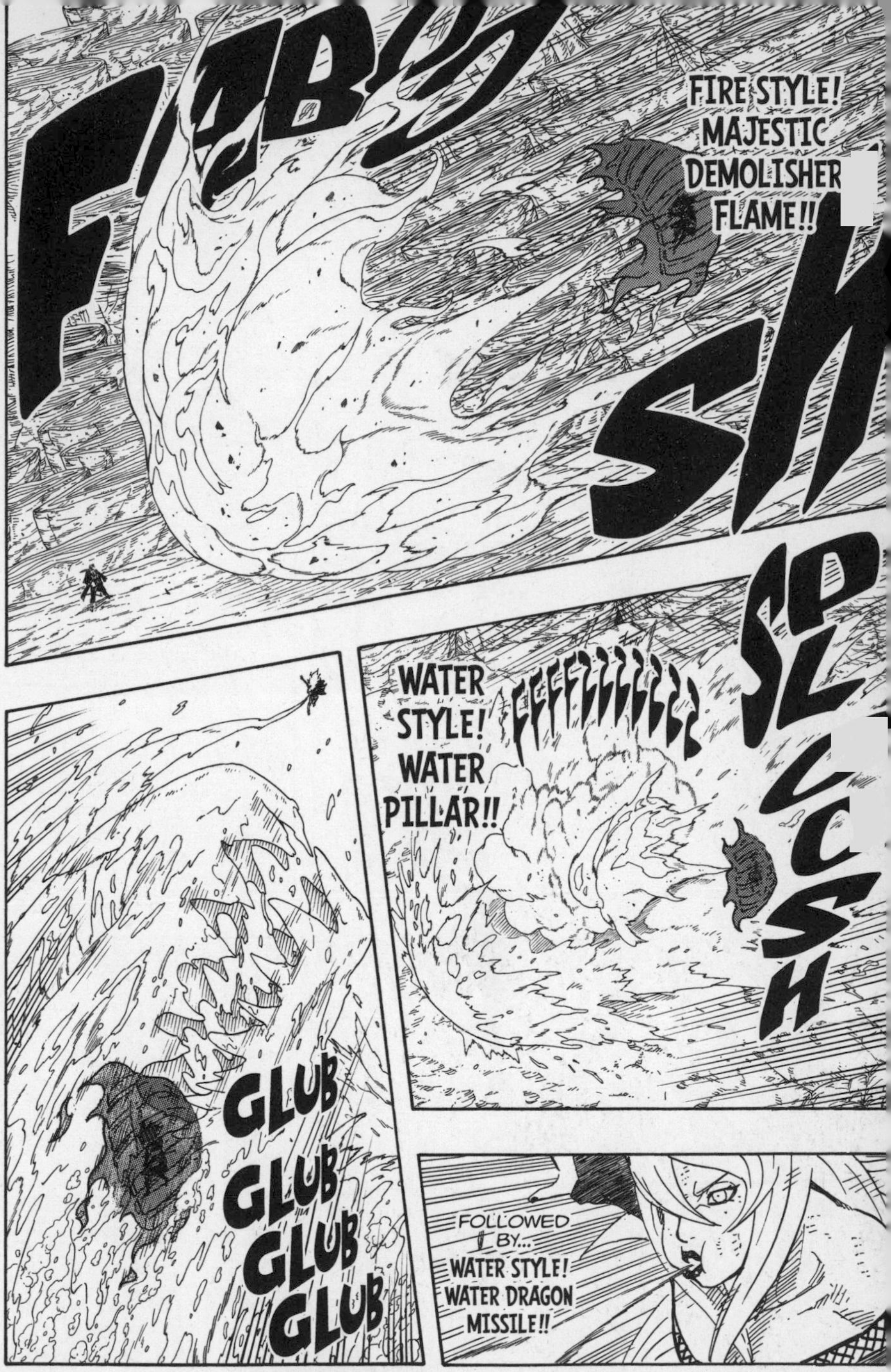
FIRE STYLE! MAJESTIC DEMOLISHER FLAME!!
WATER STYLE! WATER PILLAR!!
GLUB
GLUB
GLUB
GLUB
FOLLOWED BY... WATER STYLE! WATER DRAGON MISSILE!!

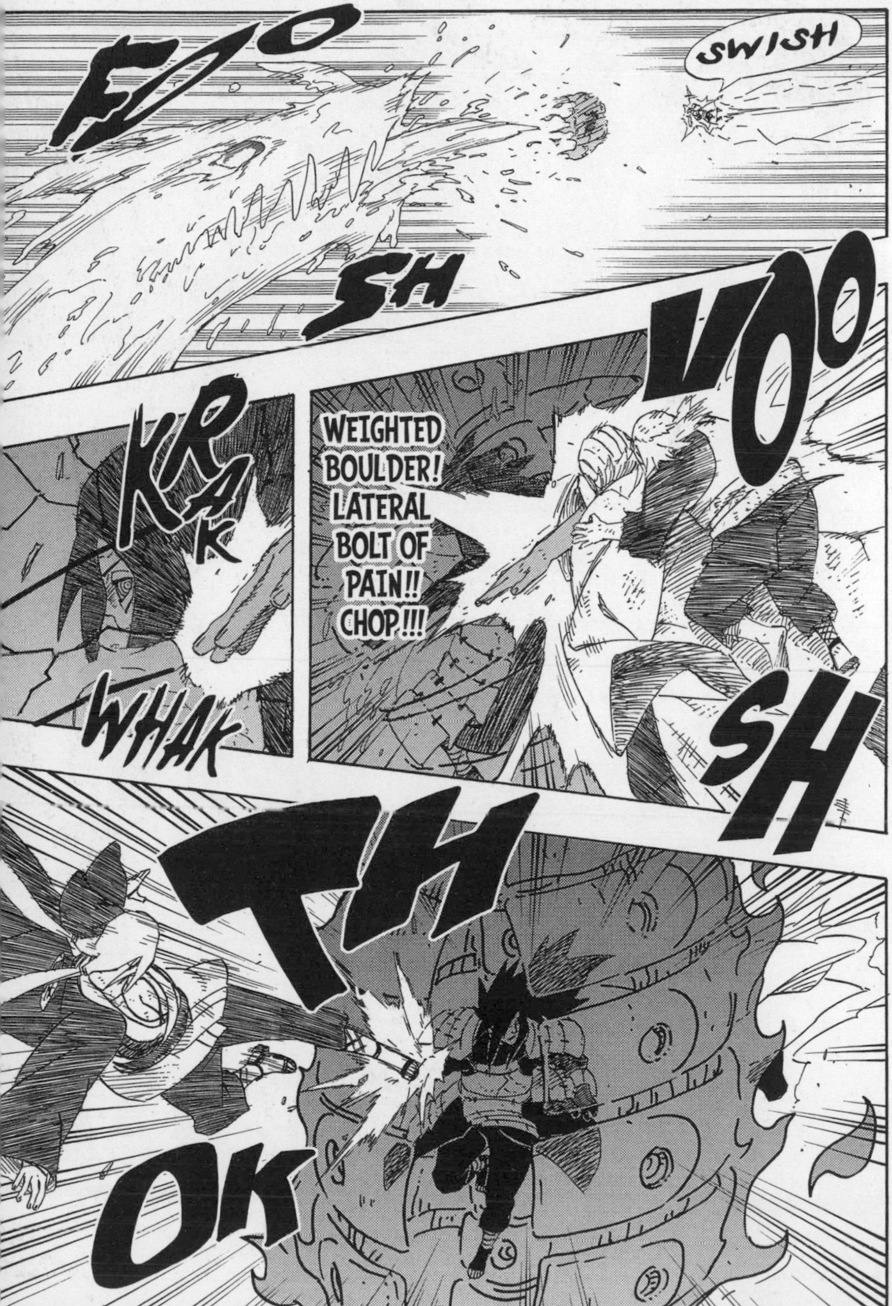
SWISH
FOO
SH
VOO
WEIGHTED BOULDER! LATERAL BOLT OF PAIN!! CHOP!!!
SH
KRAK
WHAK
TH
OK

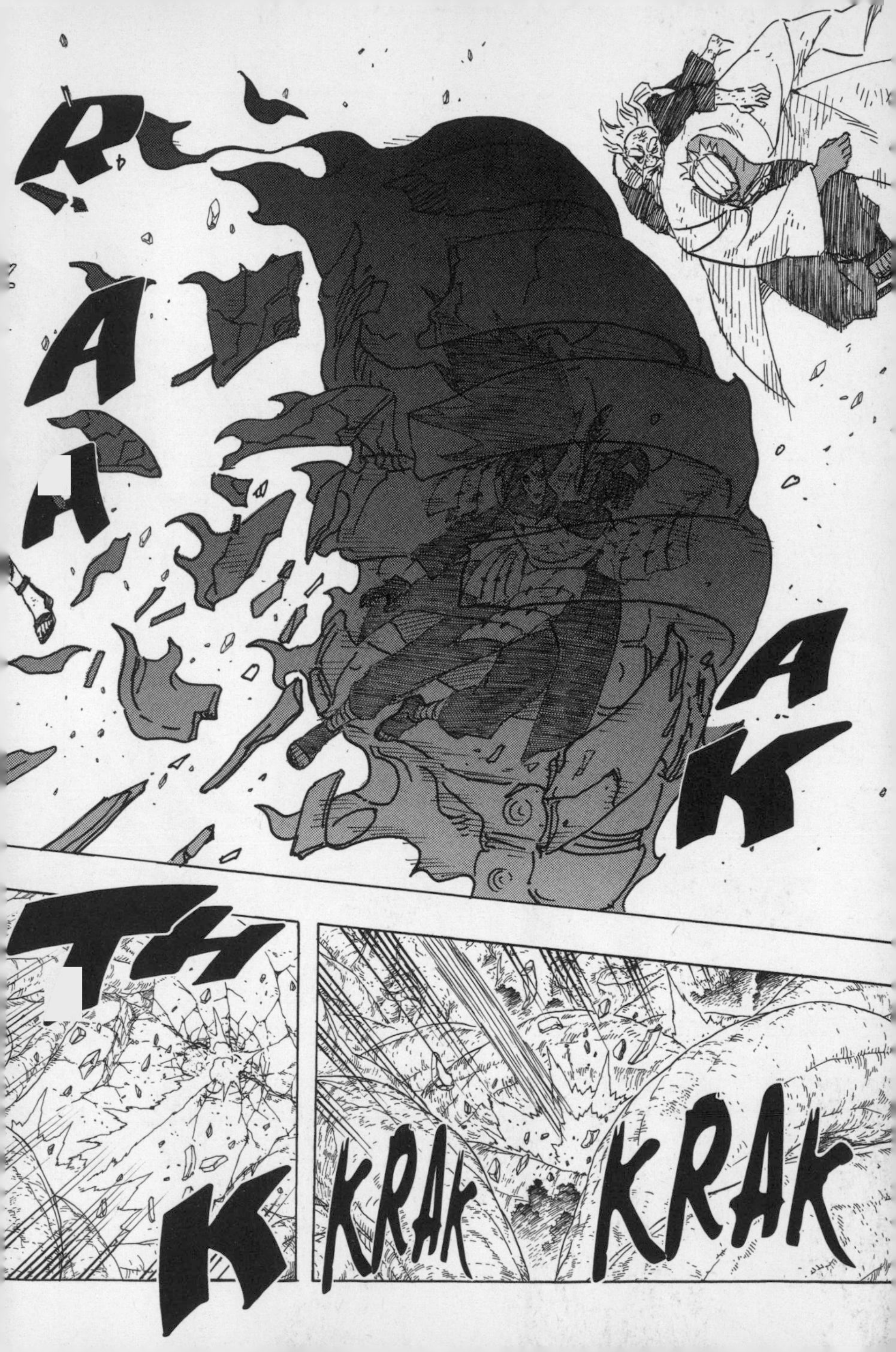
RAAA
AK
KRAK KRAK
THK

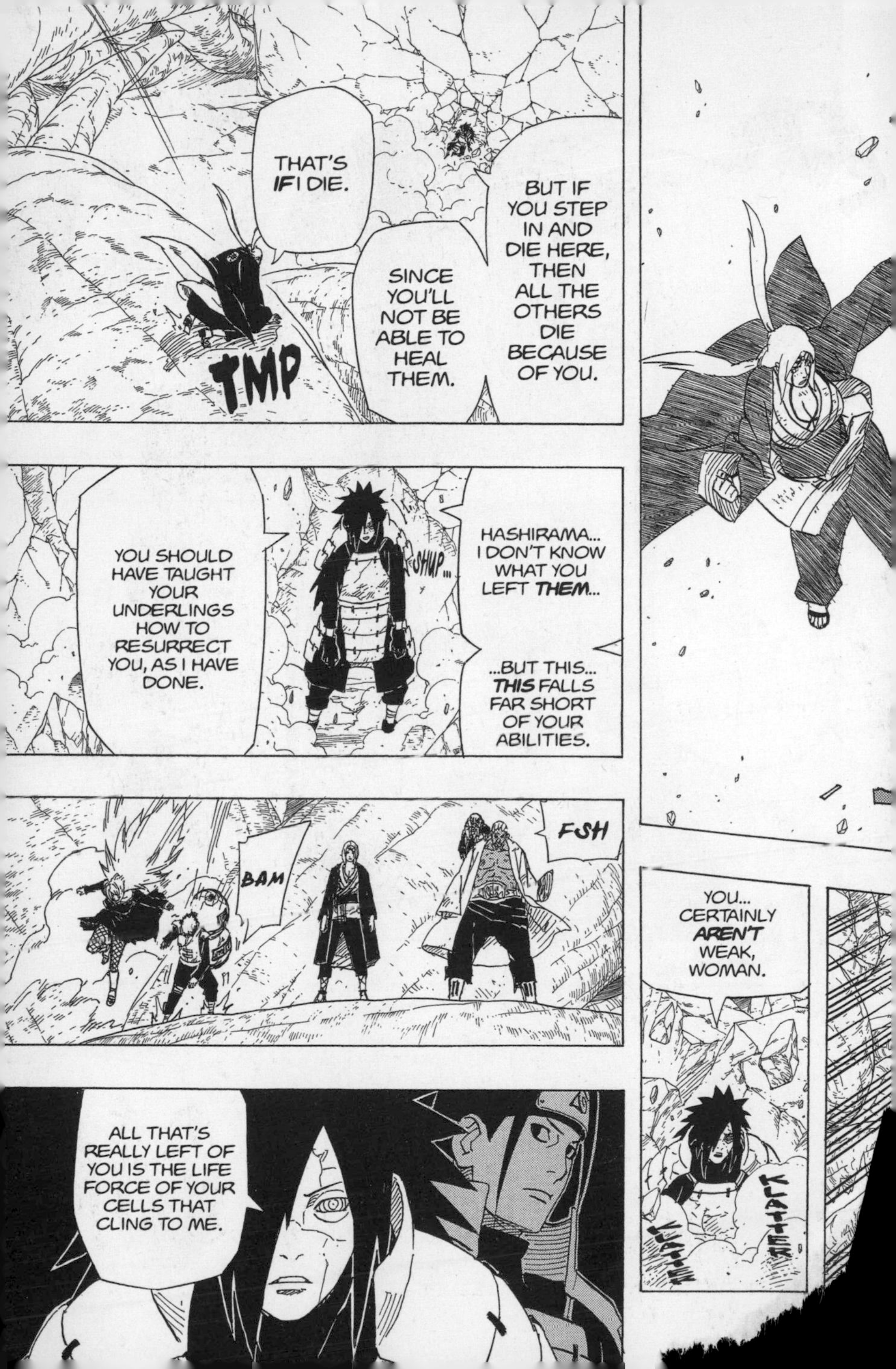
BUT IF YOU STEP IN AND DIE HERE, THEN ALL THE OTHERS DIE BECAUSE OF YOU.
SINCE YOU'LL NOT BE ABLE TO HEAL THEM.
THAT'S **IF** I DIE.
TMP
HASHIRAMA... I DON'T KNOW WHAT YOU LEFT **THEM**...
...BUT THIS... **THIS** FALLS FAR SHORT OF YOUR ABILITIES.
SHUP...
YOU SHOULD HAVE TAUGHT YOUR UNDERLINGS HOW TO RESURRECT YOU, AS I HAVE DONE.
FSH
BAM
YOU... CERTAINLY **AREN'T** WEAK, WOMAN.
KLATTER
KLATTER
ALL THAT'S REALLY LEFT OF YOU IS THE LIFE FORCE OF YOUR CELLS THAT CLING TO ME.

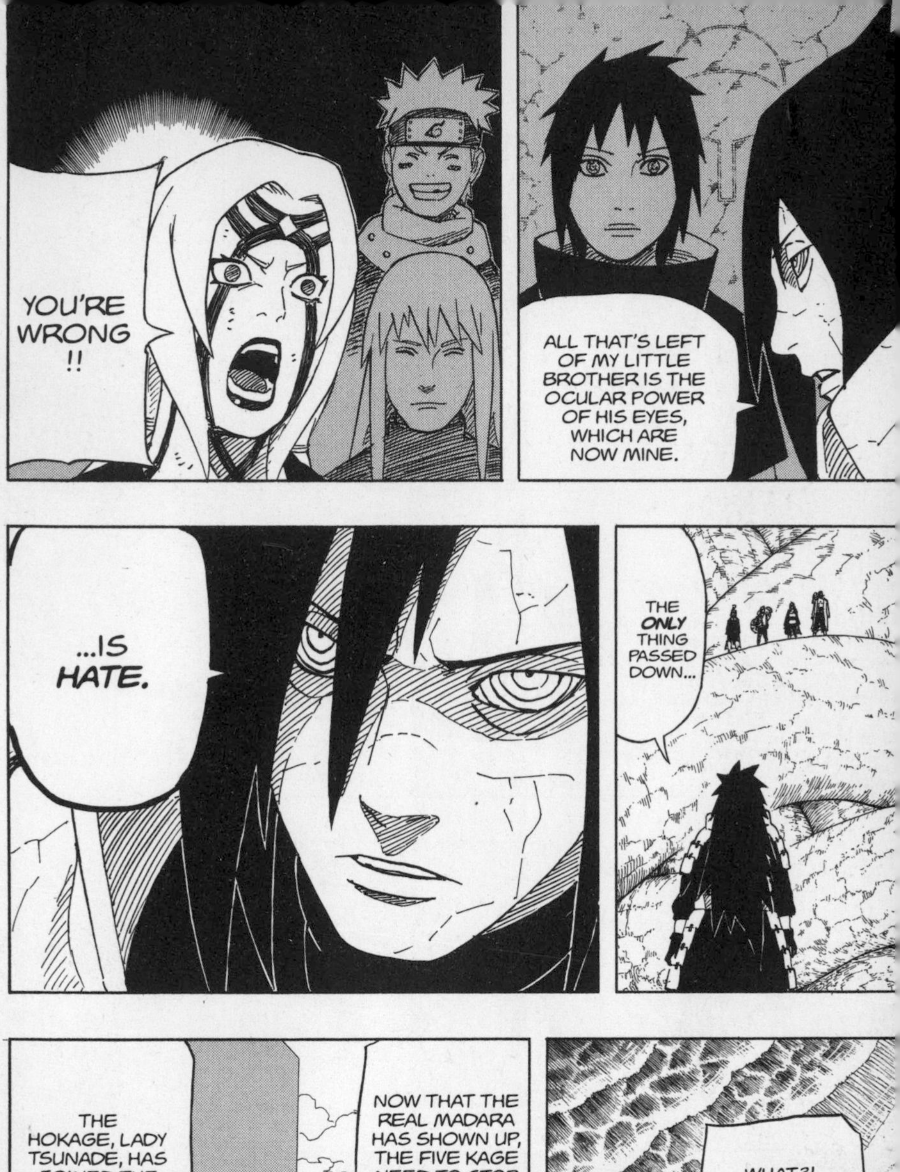
ALL THAT'S LEFT OF MY LITTLE BROTHER IS THE OCULAR POWER OF HIS EYES, WHICH ARE NOW MINE.
YOU'RE WRONG !!
THE *ONLY* THING PASSED DOWN...
...IS **HATE.**
WHAT?! ***MADARA*** WAS BROUGHT BACK WITH EDOTENSEI?!
NOW THAT THE REAL *MADARA* HAS SHOWN UP, THE FIVE KAGE NEED TO STOP MESSING AROUND.
THE HOKAGE, LADY TSUNADE, HAS JOINED THE BATTLE!

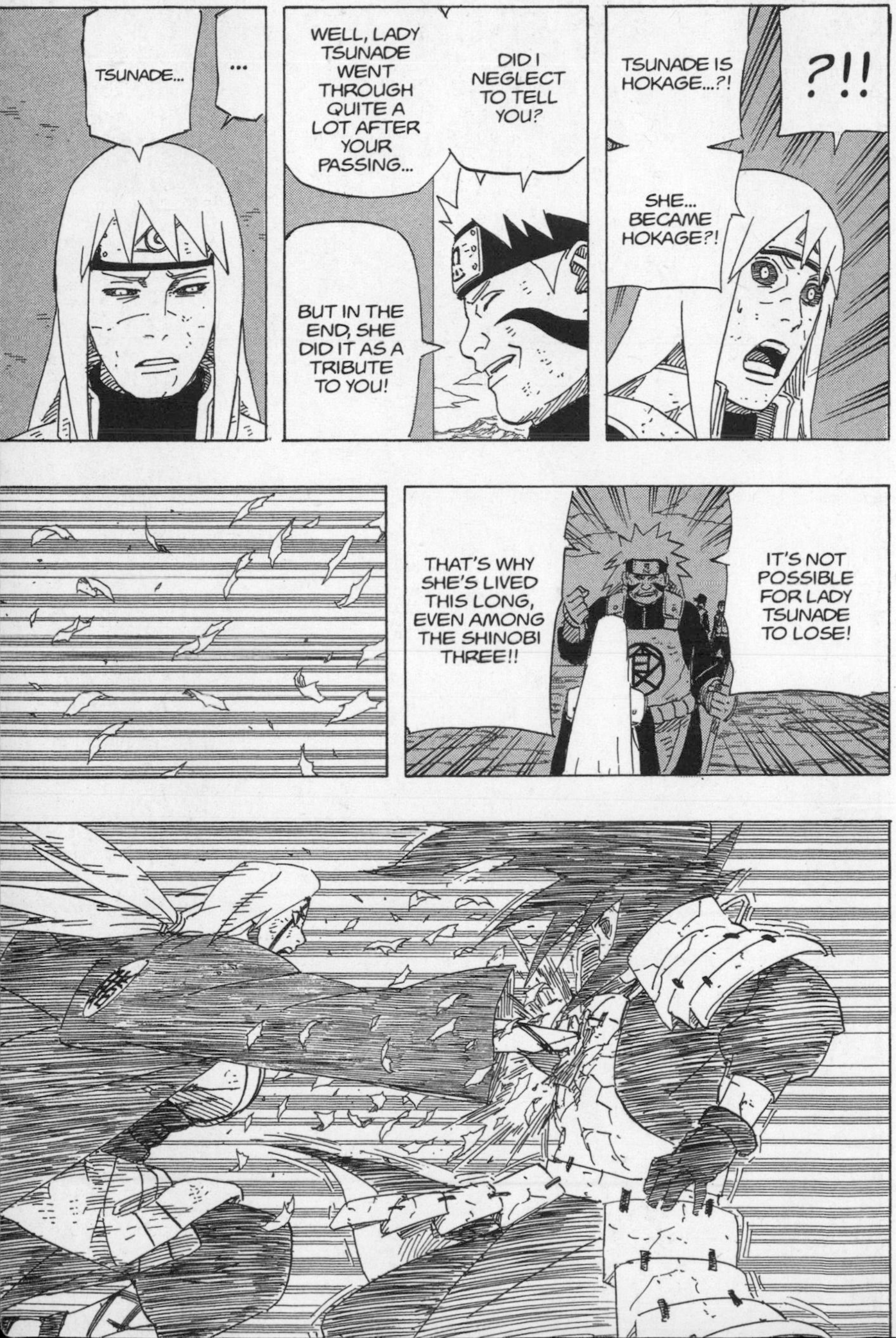
?!!
TSUNADE IS HOKAGE...?!
SHE... BECAME HOKAGE?!
DID I NEGLECT TO TELL YOU?
WELL, LADY TSUNADE WENT THROUGH QUITE A LOT AFTER YOUR PASSING...
BUT IN THE END, SHE DID IT AS A TRIBUTE TO YOU!
...
TSUNADE...
IT'S NOT POSSIBLE FOR LADY TSUNADE TO LOSE!
THAT'S WHY SHE'S LIVED THIS LONG, EVEN AMONG THE SHINOBI THREE!!

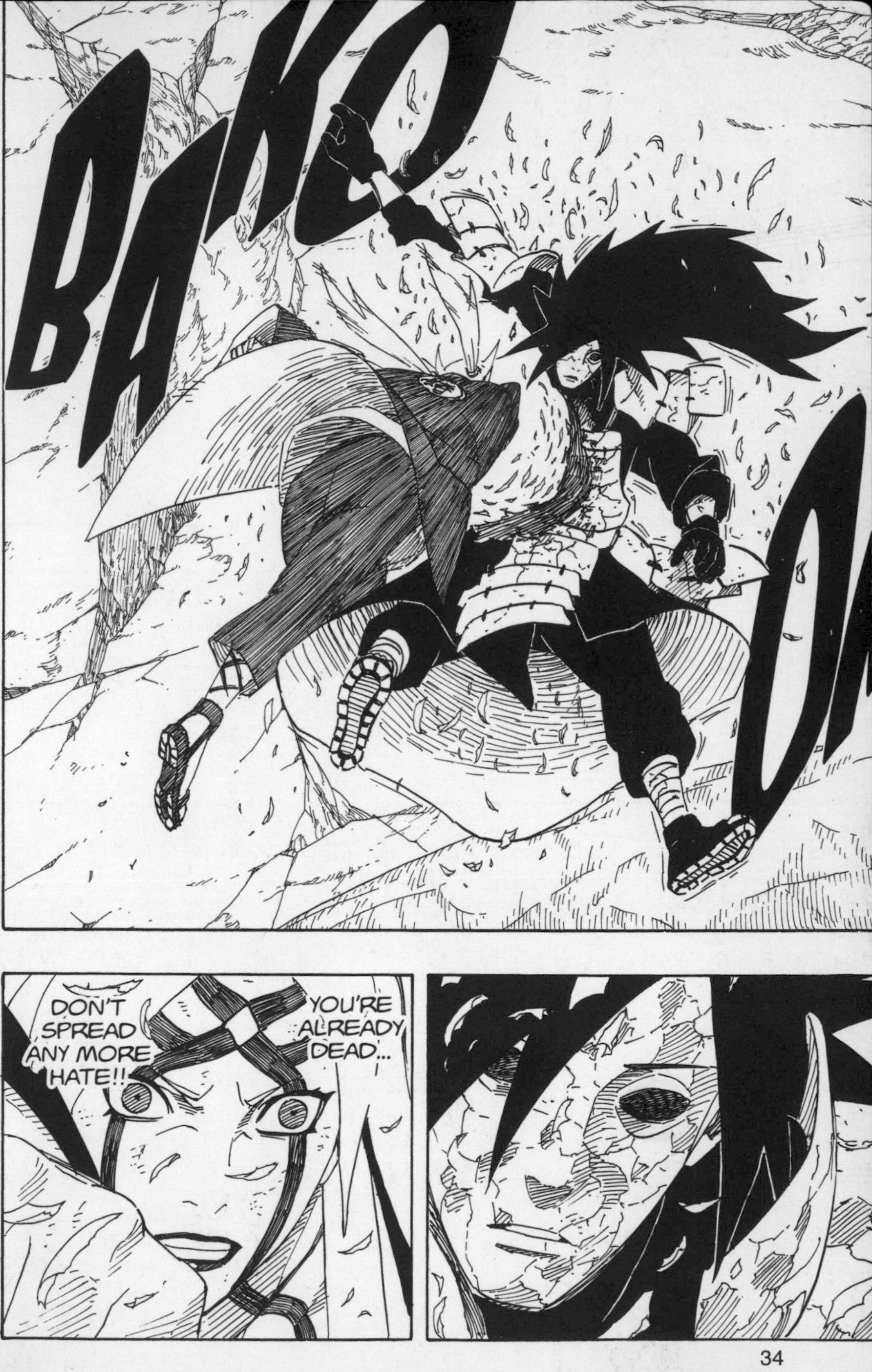
BAKO
YOU'RE ALREADY DEAD...
DON'T SPREAD ANY MORE HATE!!

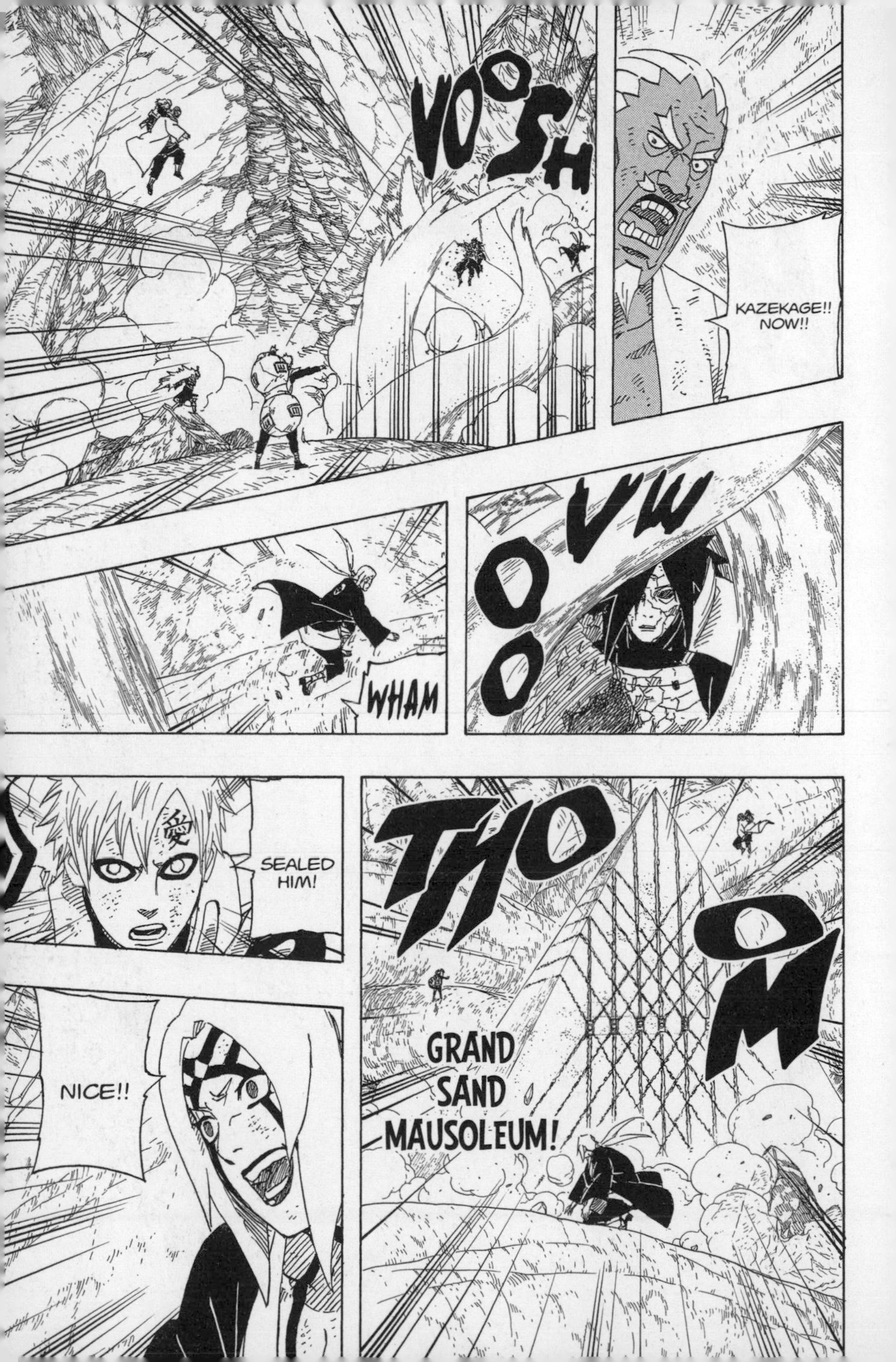
KAZEKAGE!! NOW!!
VOOSH
VWOO
WHAM
THOOM
GRAND SAND MAUSOLEUM!
SEALED HIM!
NICE!!

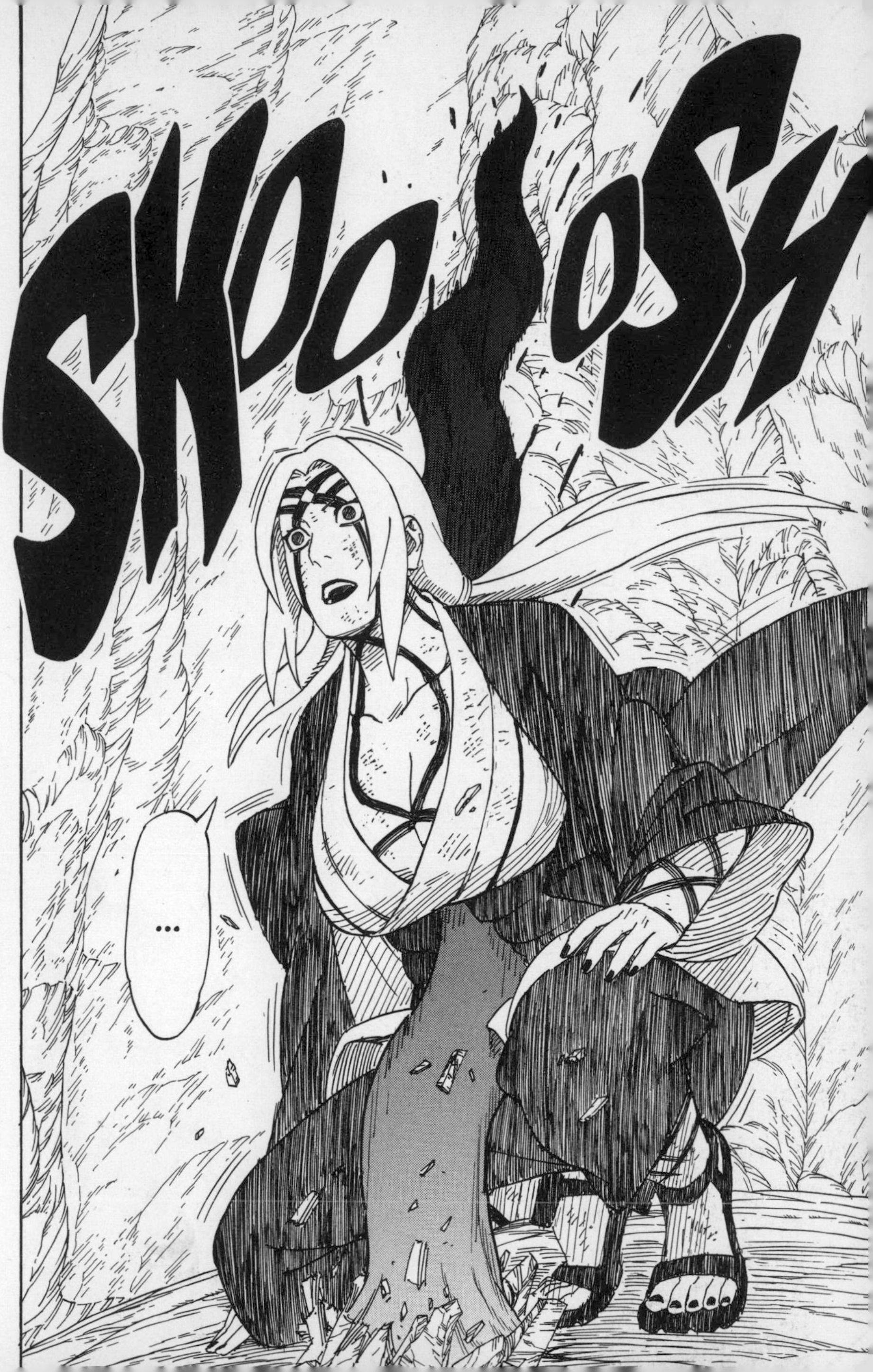
SHOOSOSH
...

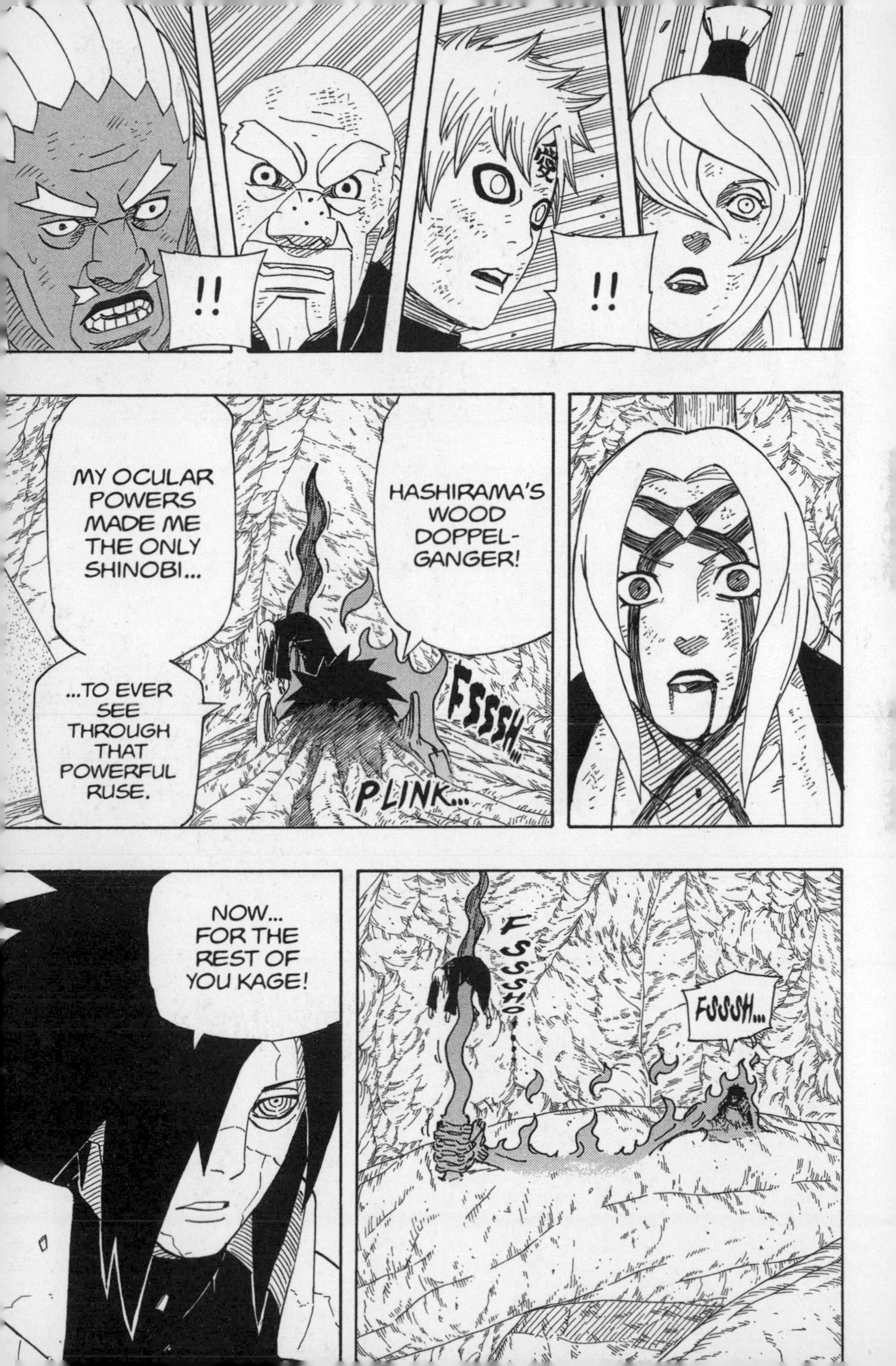
!!
!!
HASHIRAMA'S WOOD DOPPEL-GANGER!
MY OCULAR POWERS MADE ME THE ONLY SHINOBI...
...TO EVER SEE THROUGH THAT POWERFUL RUSE.
FSSSH...
PLINK...
FSSSH...
FSSSH...
NOW... FOR THE REST OF YOU KAGE!

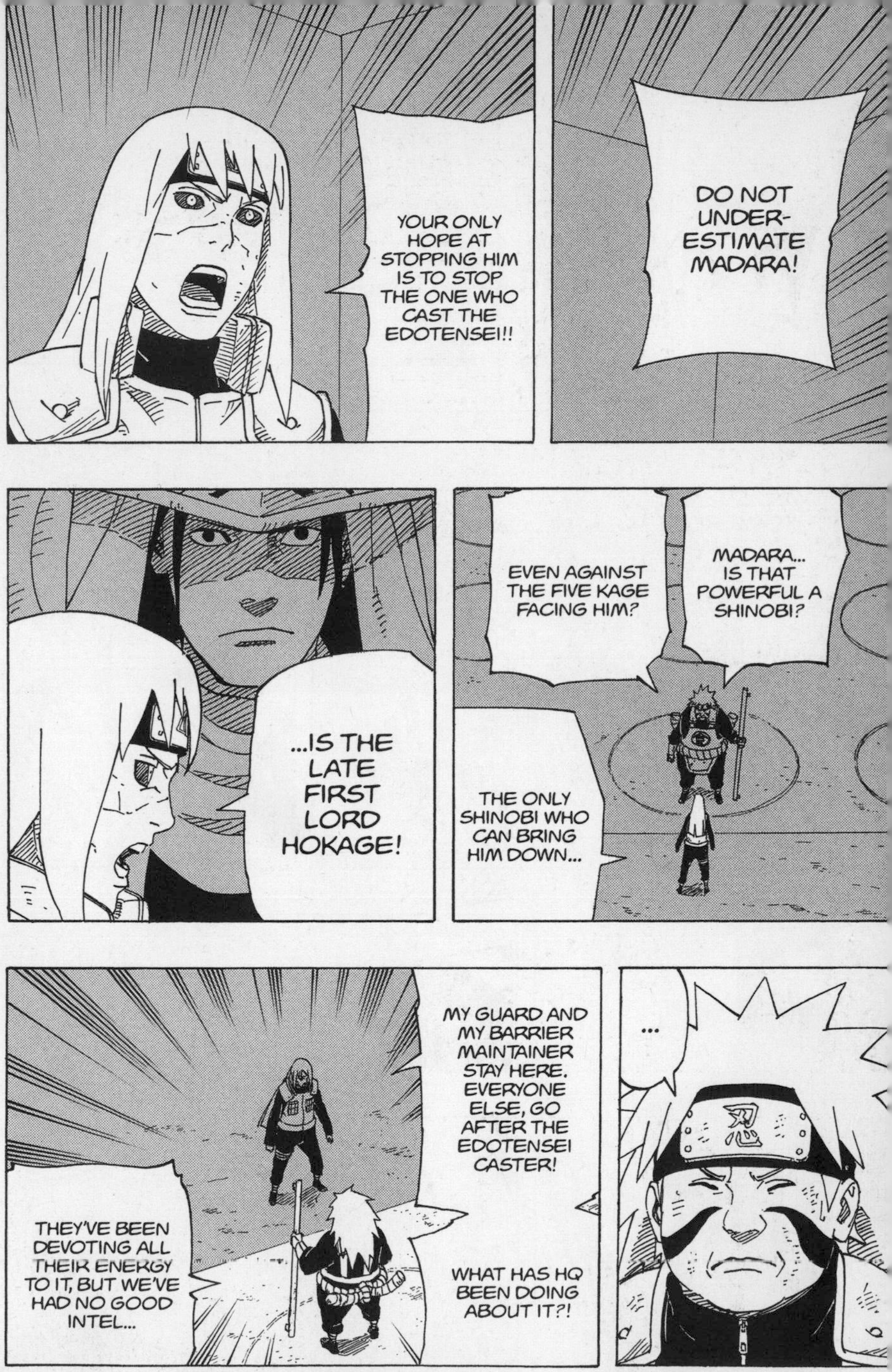
DO NOT UNDER-ESTIMATE MADARA!
YOUR ONLY HOPE AT STOPPING HIM IS TO STOP THE ONE WHO CAST THE EDOTENSEI!!
MADARA... IS THAT POWERFUL A SHINOBI?
EVEN AGAINST THE FIVE KAGE FACING HIM?
THE ONLY SHINOBI WHO CAN BRING HIM DOWN...
...IS THE LATE FIRST LORD HOKAGE!
...
MY GUARD AND MY BARRIER MAINTAINER STAY HERE. EVERYONE ELSE, GO AFTER THE EDOTENSEI CASTER!
WHAT HAS HQ BEEN DOING ABOUT IT?!
THEY'VE BEEN DEVOTING ALL THEIR ENERGY TO IT, BUT WE'VE HAD NO GOOD INTEL...

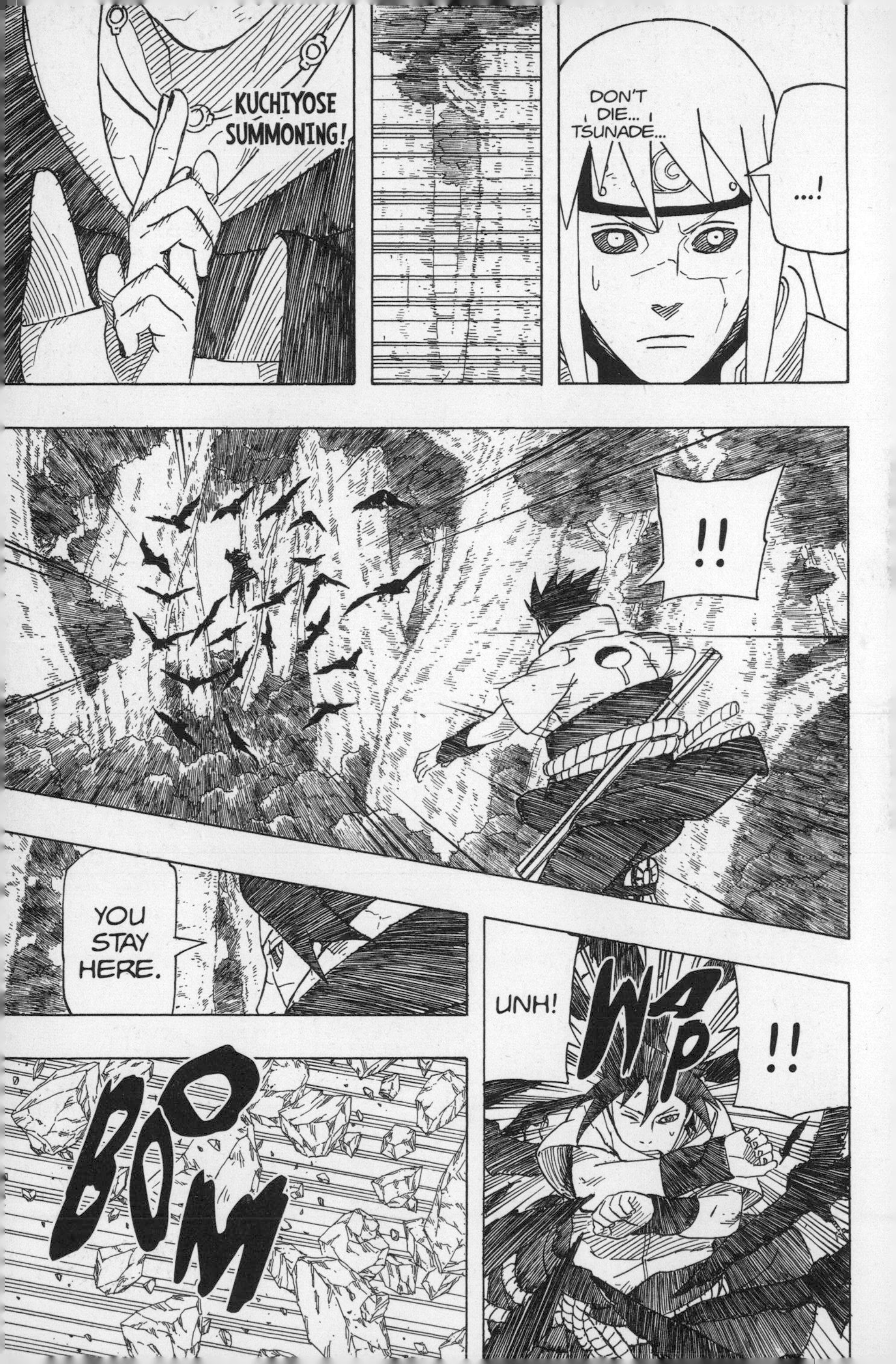
DON'T DIE... TSUNADE...
...!
KUCHIYOSE SUMMONING!
!!
UNH!
WAP
!!
YOU STAY HERE.
BOOM

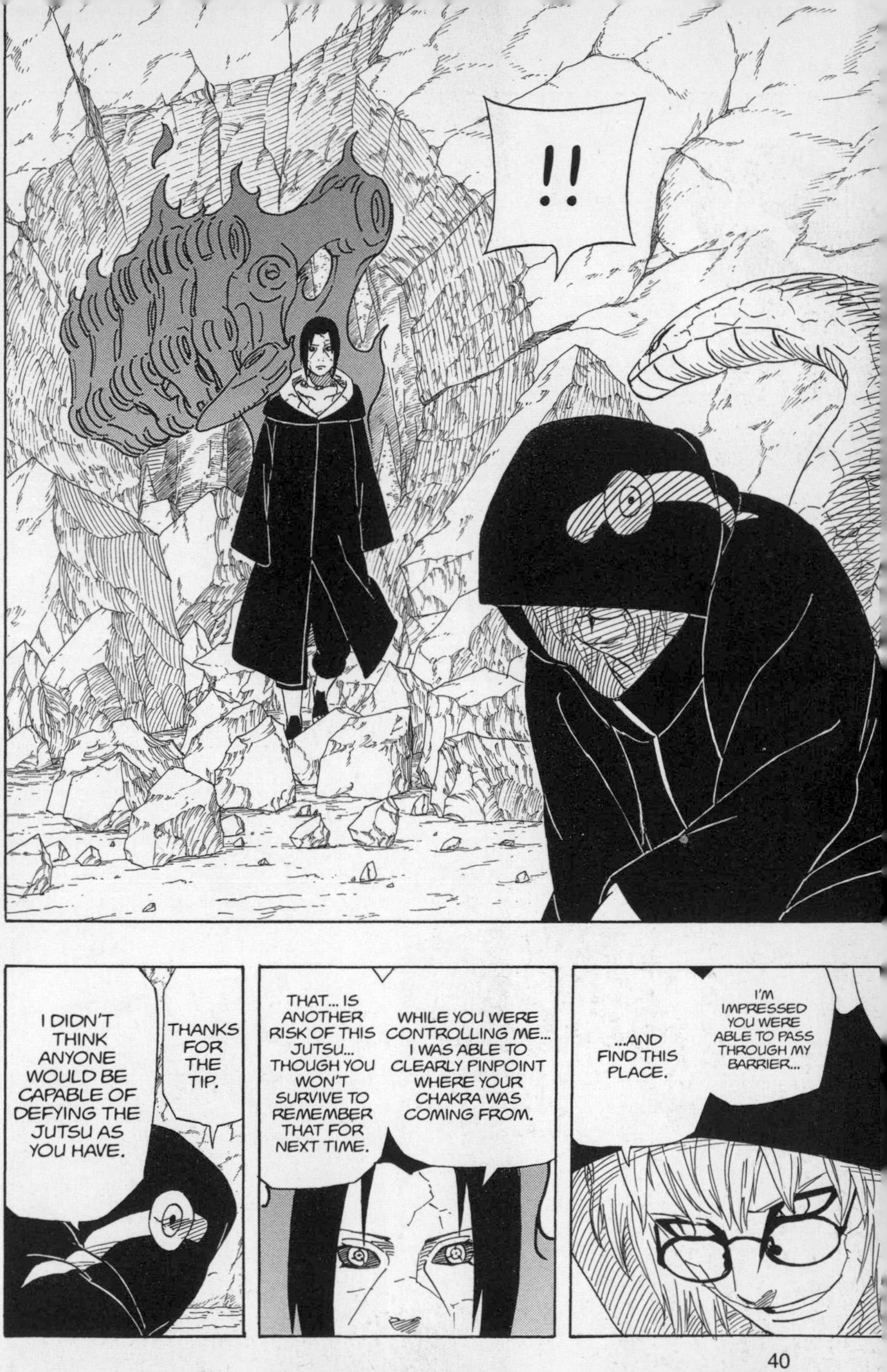
!!
I'M IMPRESSED YOU WERE ABLE TO PASS THROUGH MY BARRIER...
...AND FIND THIS PLACE.
WHILE YOU WERE CONTROLLING ME... I WAS ABLE TO CLEARLY PINPOINT WHERE YOUR CHAKRA WAS COMING FROM.
THAT... IS ANOTHER RISK OF THIS JUTSU... THOUGH YOU WON'T SURVIVE TO REMEMBER THAT FOR NEXT TIME.
THANKS FOR THE TIP.
I DIDN'T THINK ANYONE WOULD BE CAPABLE OF DEFYING THE JUTSU AS YOU HAVE.

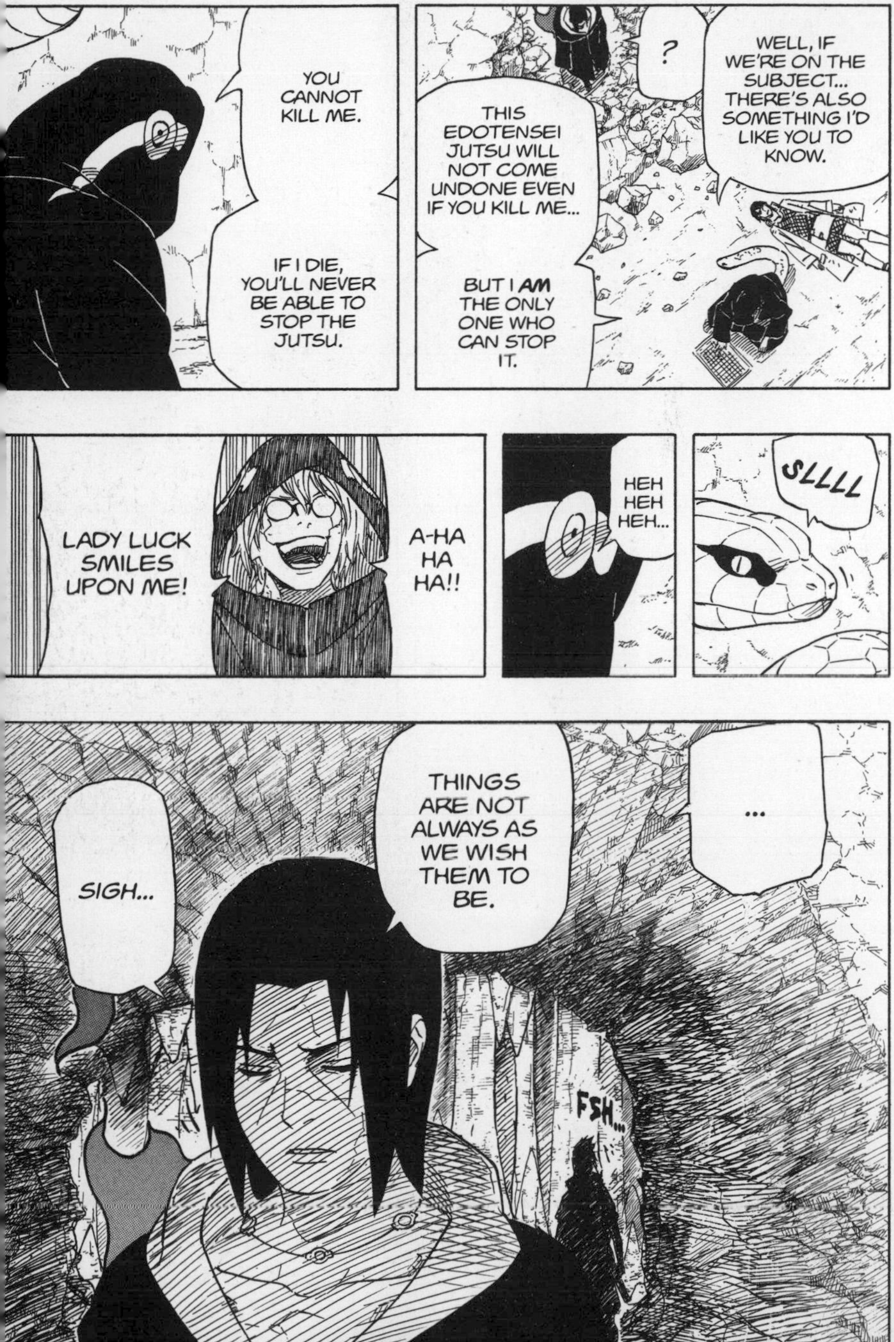
WELL, IF WE'RE ON THE SUBJECT... THERE'S ALSO SOMETHING I'D LIKE YOU TO KNOW.
?
THIS EDOTENSEI JUTSU WILL NOT COME UNDONE EVEN IF YOU KILL ME...
BUT I AM THE ONLY ONE WHO CAN STOP IT.
YOU CANNOT KILL ME.
IF I DIE, YOU'LL NEVER BE ABLE TO STOP THE JUTSU.
SLLLL
HEH HEH HEH...
A-HA HA HA!!
LADY LUCK SMILES UPON ME!
...
THINGS ARE NOT ALWAYS AS WE WISH THEM TO BE.
SIGH...
FSH...

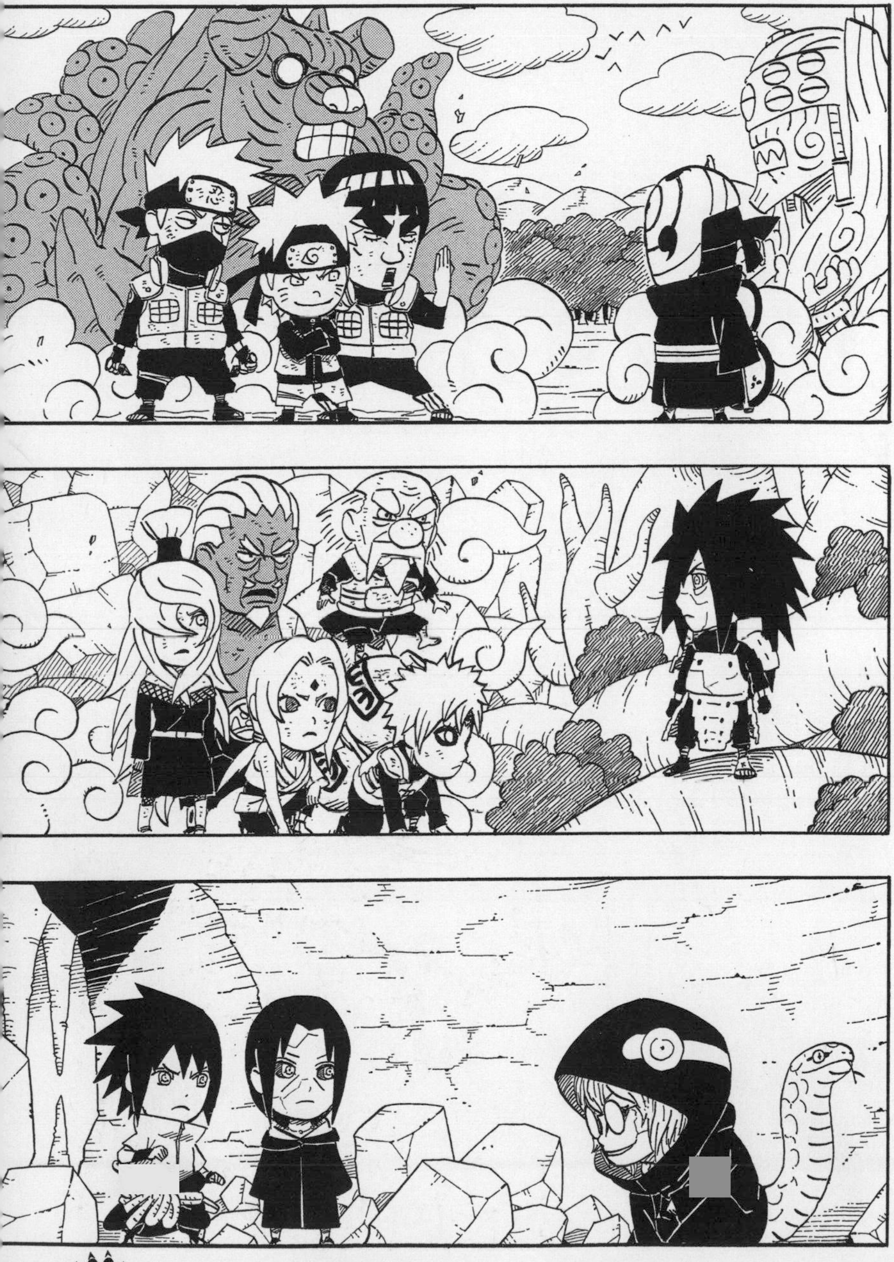

Number 578: The Weak Point of Despair!!

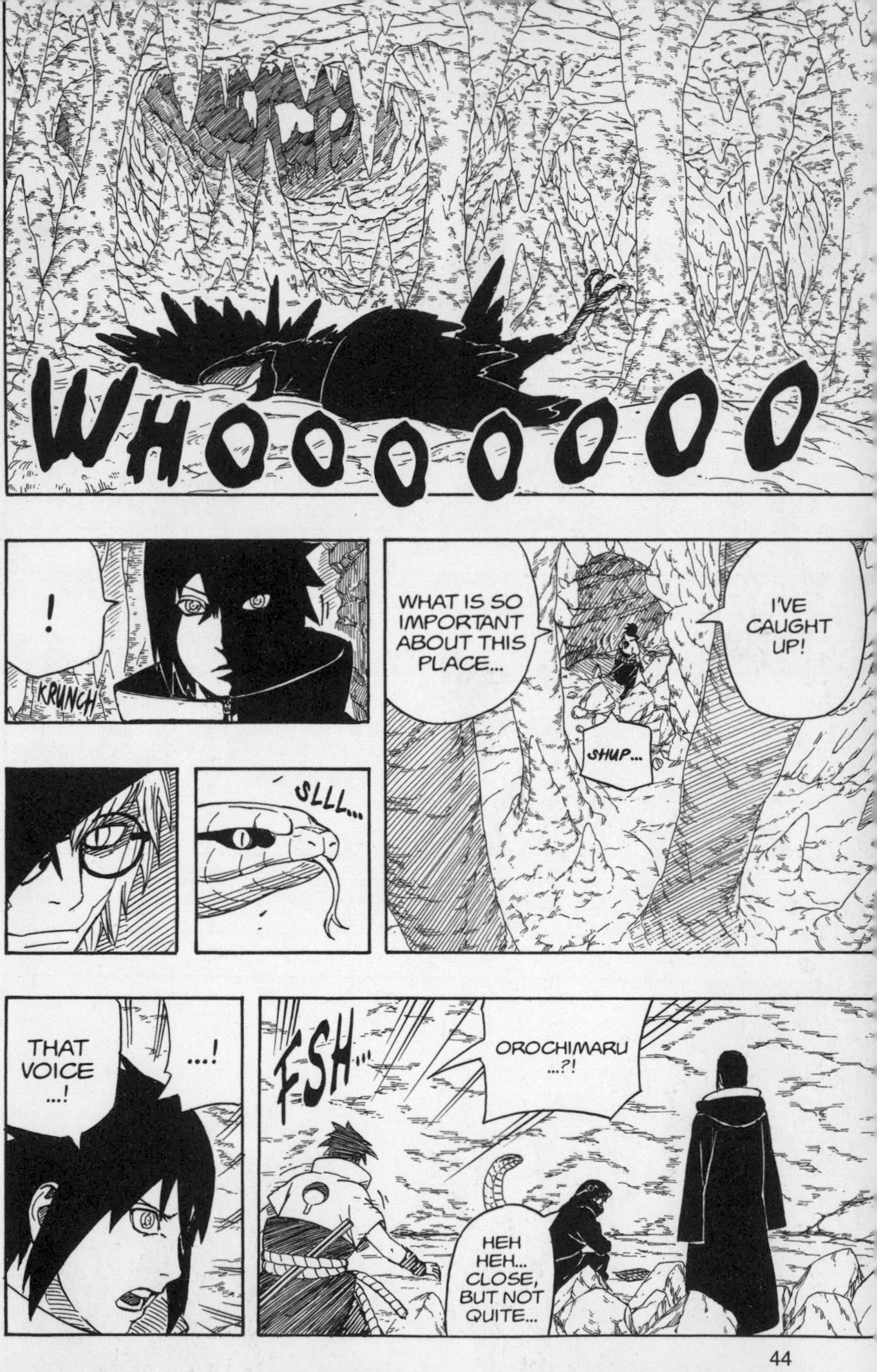
WHOOOOOOOO
I'VE CAUGHT UP!
WHAT IS SO IMPORTANT ABOUT THIS PLACE...
SHUP...
!
KRUNCH
SLLL...
OROCHIMARU ...?!
FSH...
HEH HEH... CLOSE, BUT NOT QUITE...
...!
THAT VOICE ...!

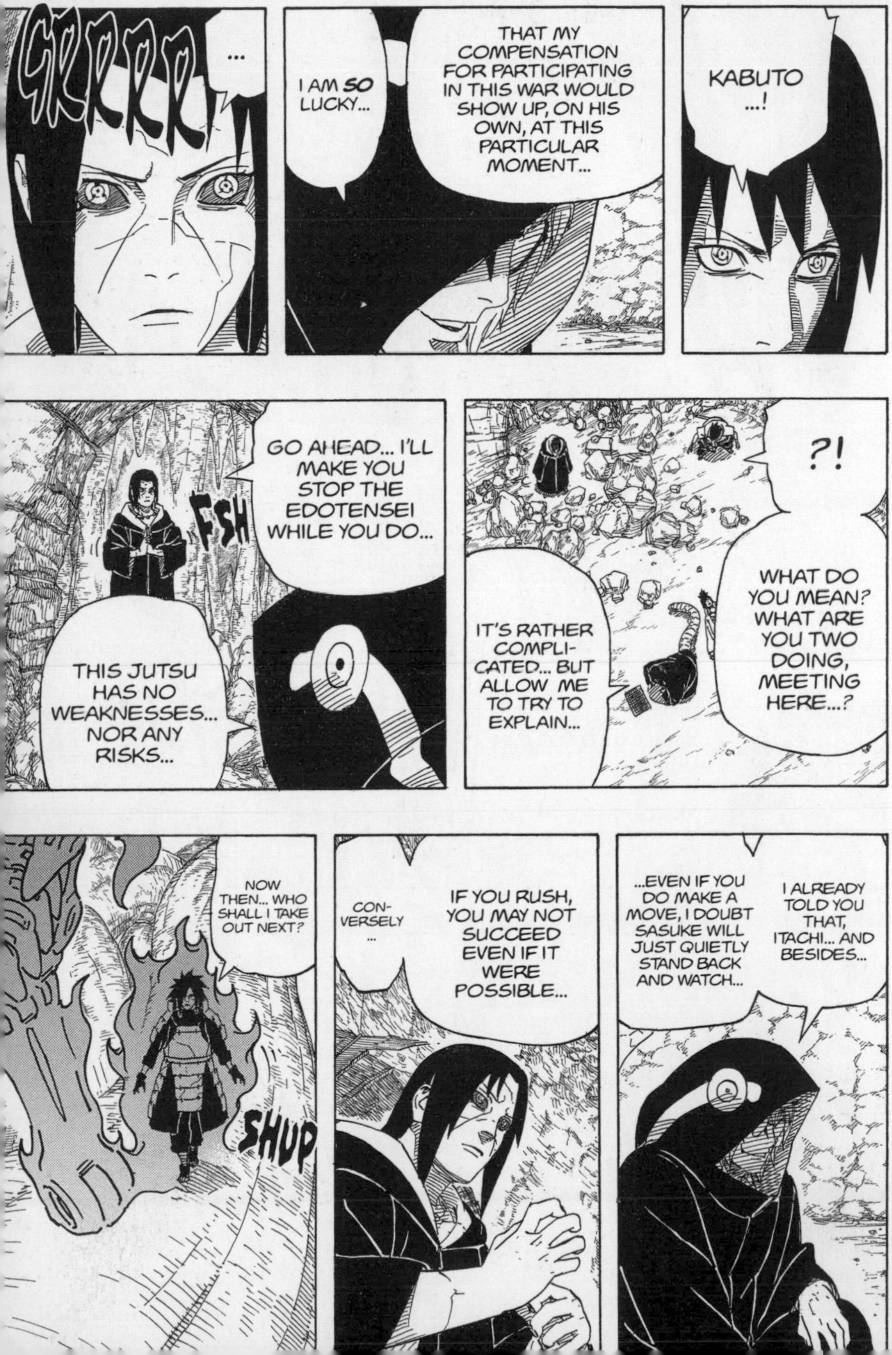
KABUTO ...!
THAT MY COMPENSATION FOR PARTICIPATING IN THIS WAR WOULD SHOW UP, ON HIS OWN, AT THIS PARTICULAR MOMENT...
I AM **SO** LUCKY...
...
GRRRR
?!
WHAT DO YOU MEAN? WHAT ARE YOU TWO DOING, MEETING HERE...?
IT'S RATHER COMPLICATED... BUT ALLOW ME TO TRY TO EXPLAIN...
GO AHEAD... I'LL MAKE YOU STOP THE EDOTENSEI WHILE YOU DO...
FSH
THIS JUTSU HAS NO WEAKNESSES... NOR ANY RISKS...
I ALREADY TOLD YOU THAT, ITACHI... AND BESIDES...
...EVEN IF YOU DO MAKE A MOVE, I DOUBT SASUKE WILL JUST QUIETLY STAND BACK AND WATCH...
IF YOU RUSH, YOU MAY NOT SUCCEED EVEN IF IT WERE POSSIBLE...
CON-VERSELY ...
NOW THEN... WHO SHALL I TAKE OUT NEXT?
SHUP

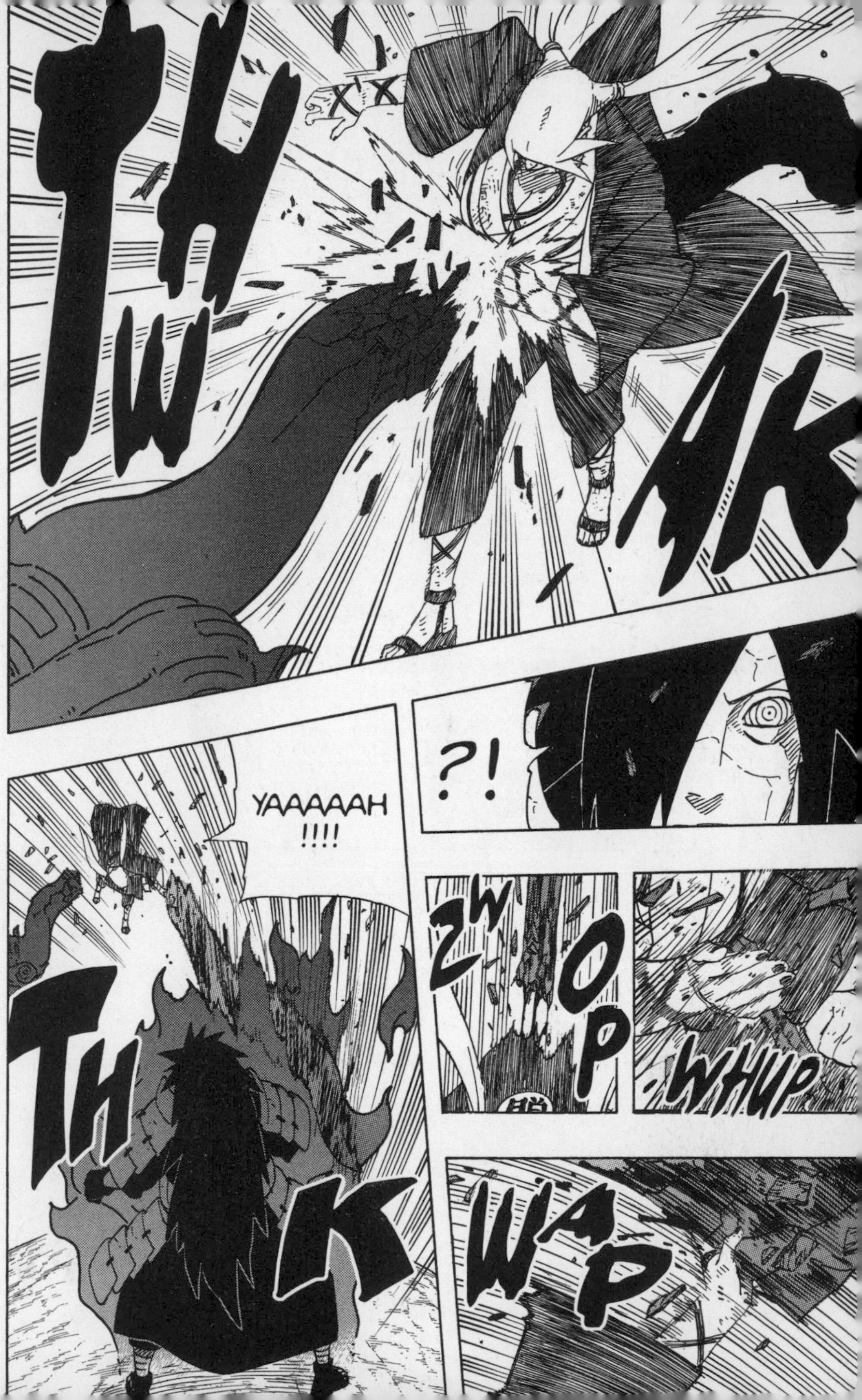
THWAK
?!
WHUP
ZWOOP
WAP
YAAAAAH !!!!
THK

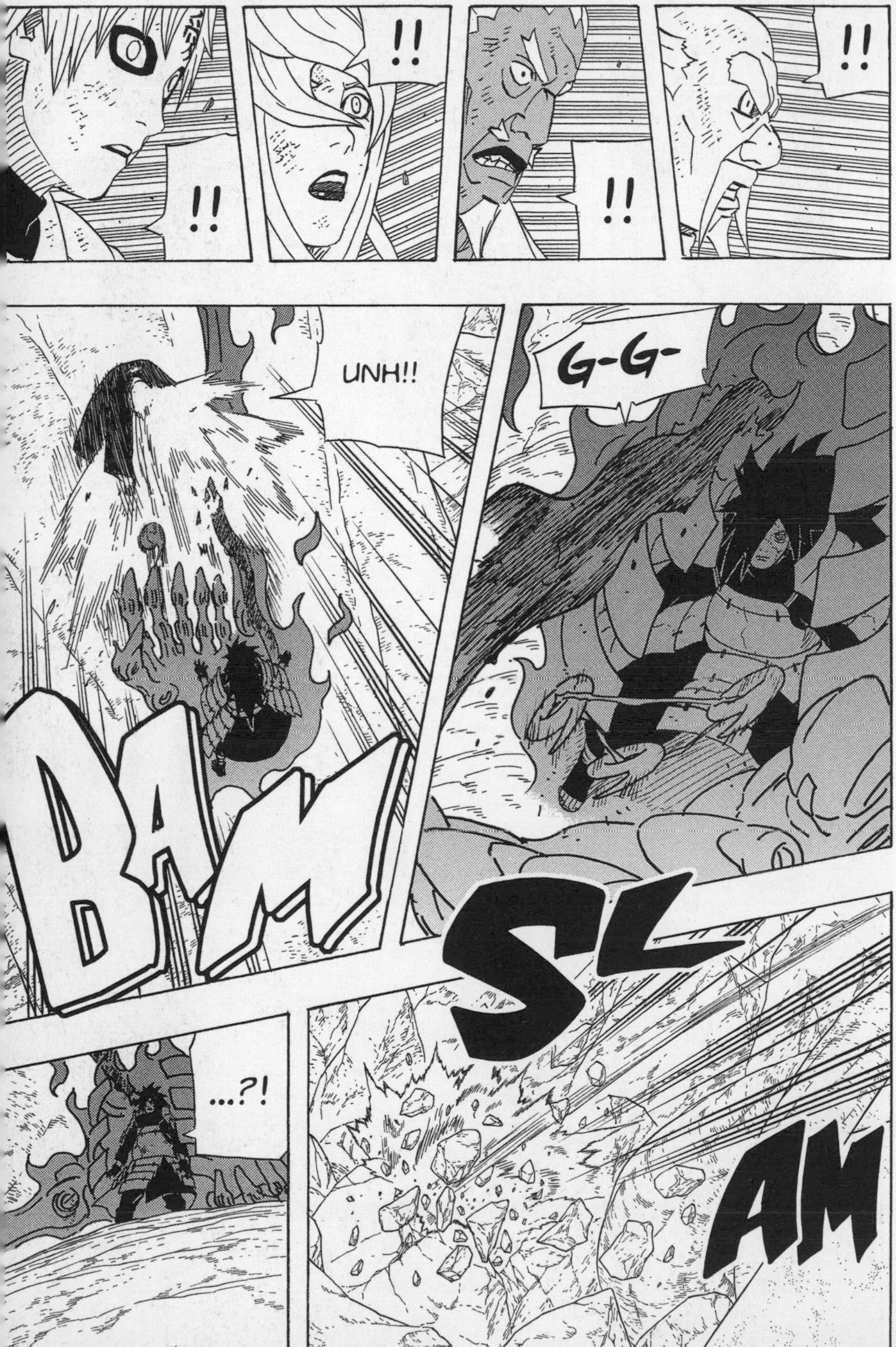

!!
!!
!!
!!
!!
!!
G-G-
UNH!!
BAM
SLAM
...?!

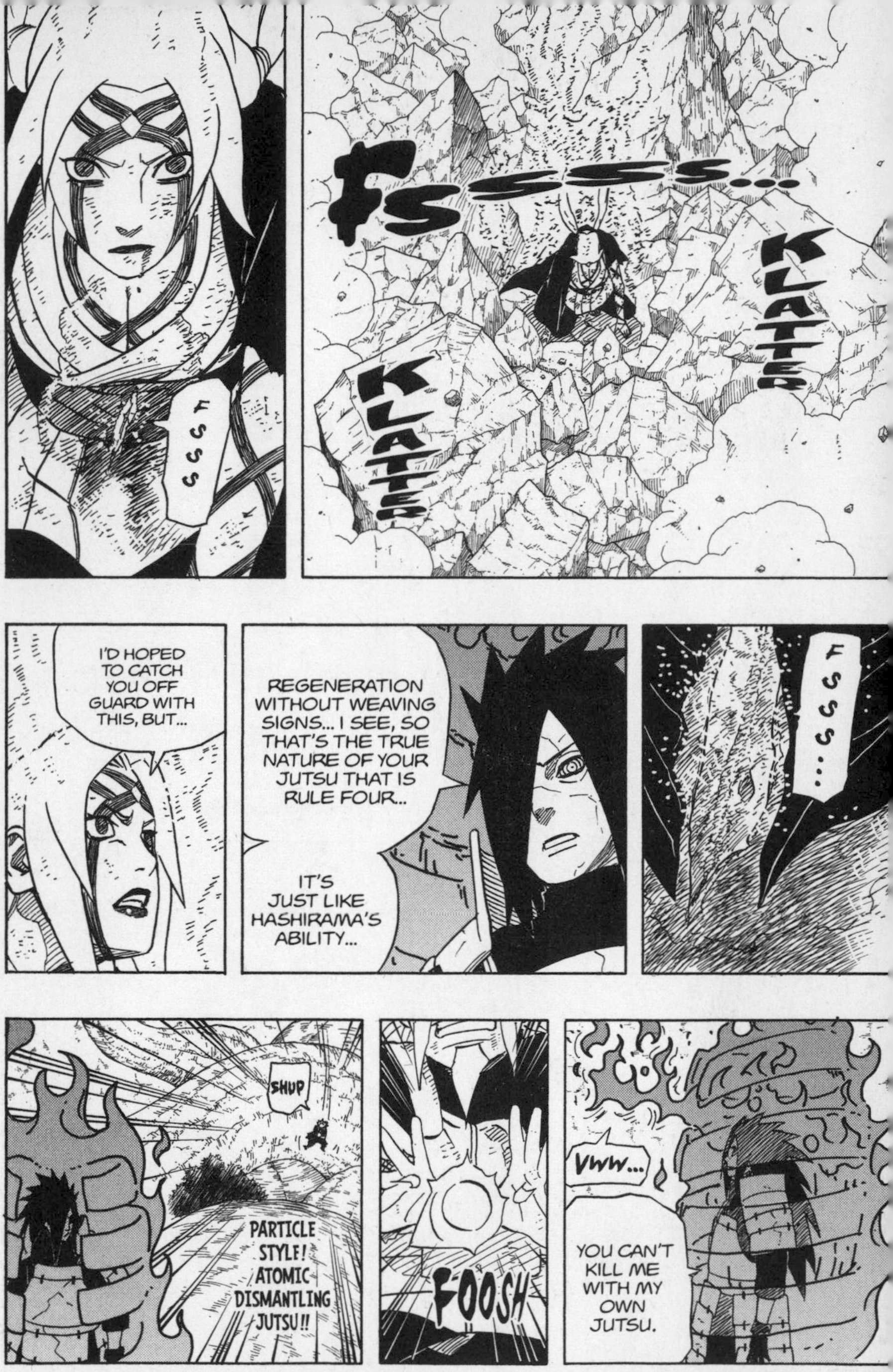
FSSSSS...
KLATTER
KLATTER
FSSS
FSSS...
REGENERATION WITHOUT WEAVING SIGNS... I SEE, SO THAT'S THE TRUE NATURE OF YOUR JUTSU THAT IS RULE FOUR...
IT'S JUST LIKE HASHIRAMA'S ABILITY...
I'D HOPED TO CATCH YOU OFF GUARD WITH THIS, BUT...
VWW...
YOU CAN'T KILL ME WITH MY OWN JUTSU.
FOOSH
SHUP
PARTICLE STYLE! ATOMIC DISMANTLING JUTSU!!

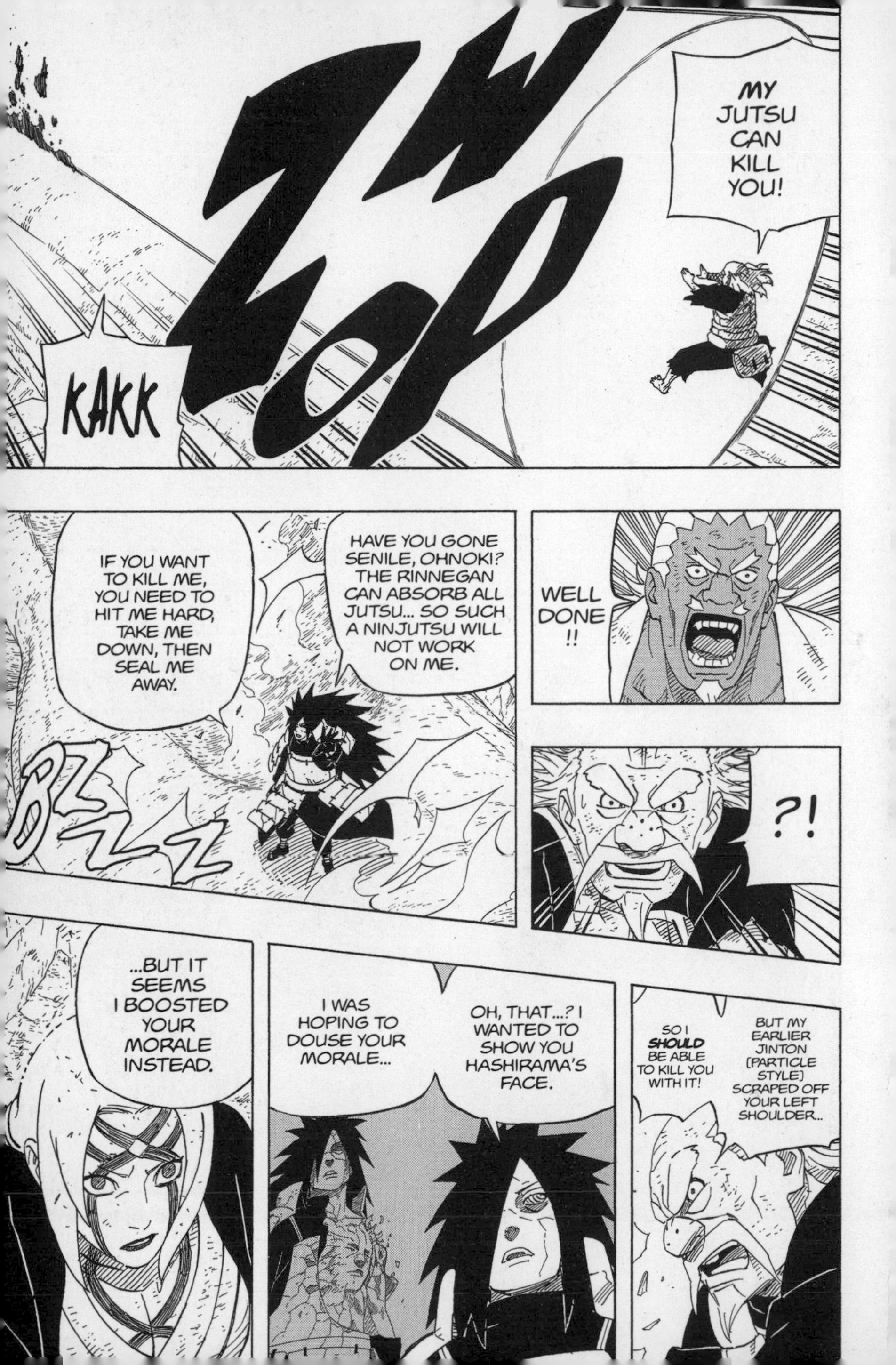
MY JUTSU CAN KILL YOU!
ZWOP
KAKK
WELL DONE !!
?!
HAVE YOU GONE SENILE, OHNOKI? THE RINNEGAN CAN ABSORB ALL JUTSU... SO SUCH A NINJUTSU WILL NOT WORK ON ME.
IF YOU WANT TO KILL ME, YOU NEED TO HIT ME HARD, TAKE ME DOWN, THEN SEAL ME AWAY.
BZZZ
BUT MY EARLIER JINTON [PARTICLE STYLE] SCRAPED OFF YOUR LEFT SHOULDER...
SO I **SHOULD** BE ABLE TO KILL YOU WITH IT!
OH, THAT...? I WANTED TO SHOW YOU HASHIRAMA'S FACE.
I WAS HOPING TO DOUSE YOUR MORALE...
...BUT IT SEEMS I BOOSTED YOUR MORALE INSTEAD.

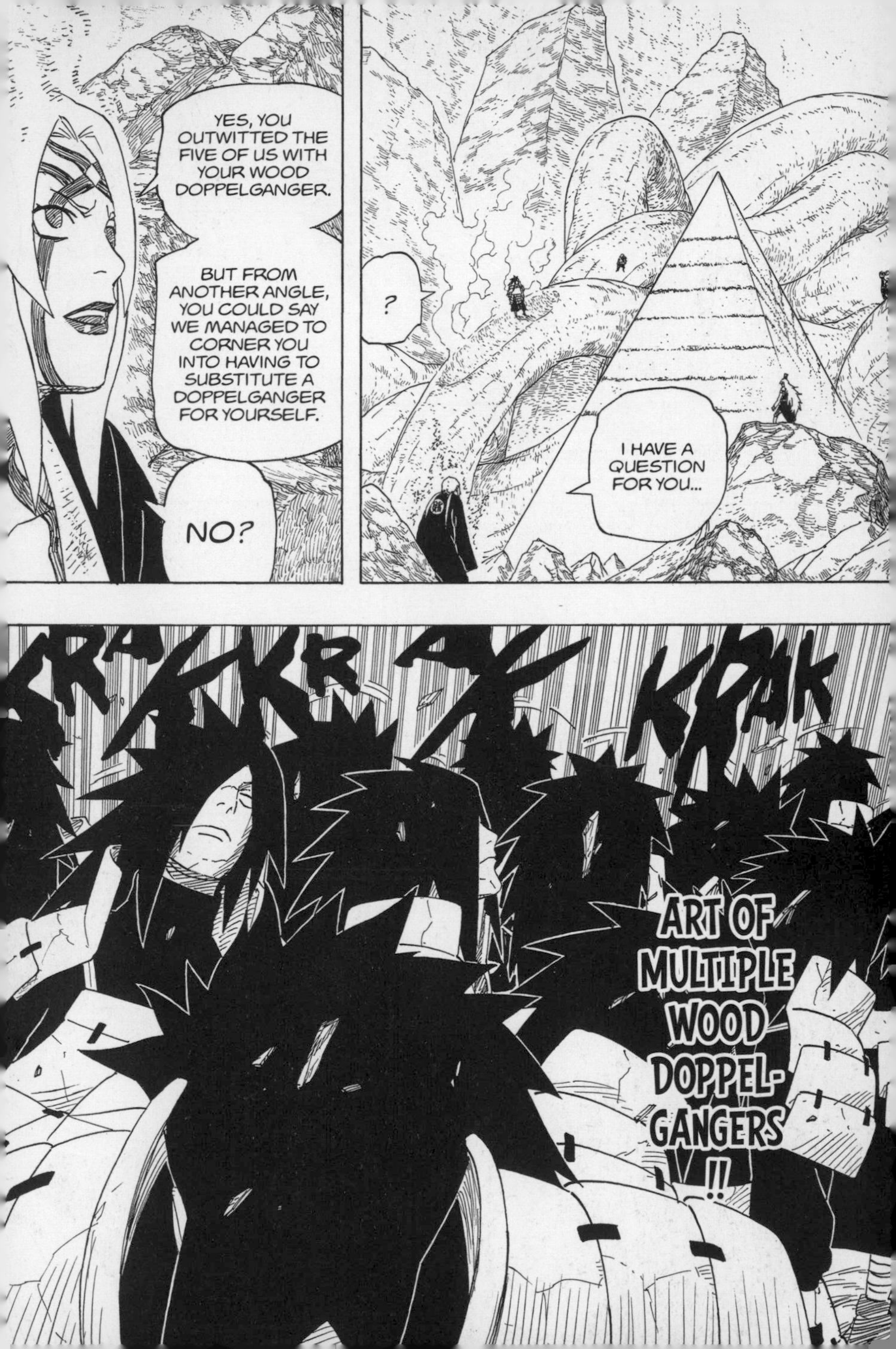
?
I HAVE A QUESTION FOR YOU...
YES, YOU OUTWITTED THE FIVE OF US WITH YOUR WOOD DOPPELGANGER.
BUT FROM ANOTHER ANGLE, YOU COULD SAY WE MANAGED TO CORNER YOU INTO HAVING TO SUBSTITUTE A DOPPELGANGER FOR YOURSELF.
NO?
KRAK
ART OF MULTIPLE WOOD DOPPEL-GANGERS!!

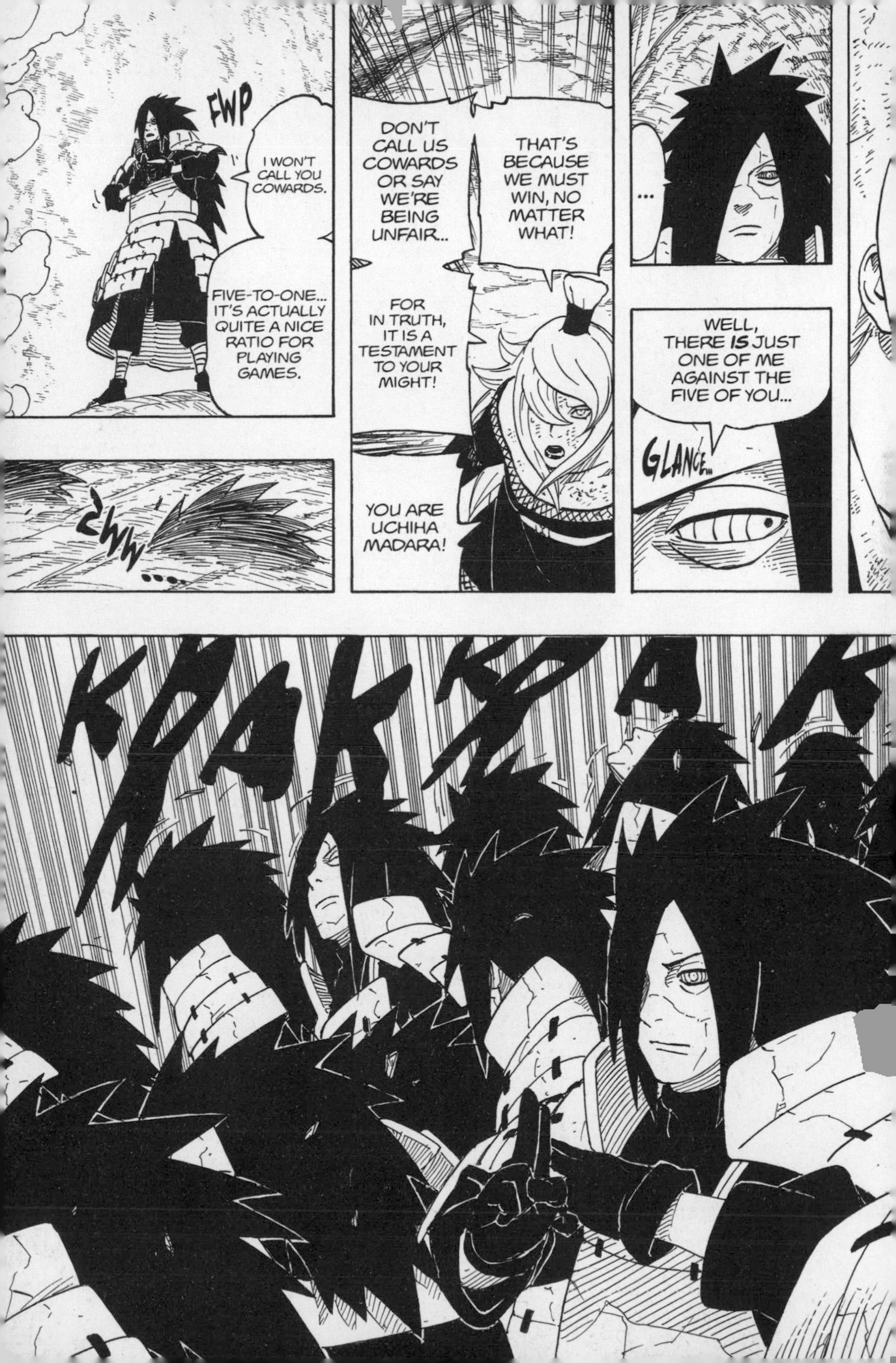

...
WELL, THERE IS JUST ONE OF ME AGAINST THE FIVE OF YOU...
GLANCE...
DON'T CALL US COWARDS OR SAY WE'RE BEING UNFAIR...
THAT'S BECAUSE WE MUST WIN, NO MATTER WHAT!
FOR IN TRUTH, IT IS A TESTAMENT TO YOUR MIGHT!
YOU ARE UCHIHA MADARA!
FWP
I WON'T CALL YOU COWARDS.
FIVE-TO-ONE... IT'S ACTUALLY QUITE A NICE RATIO FOR PLAYING GAMES.
ZWW...

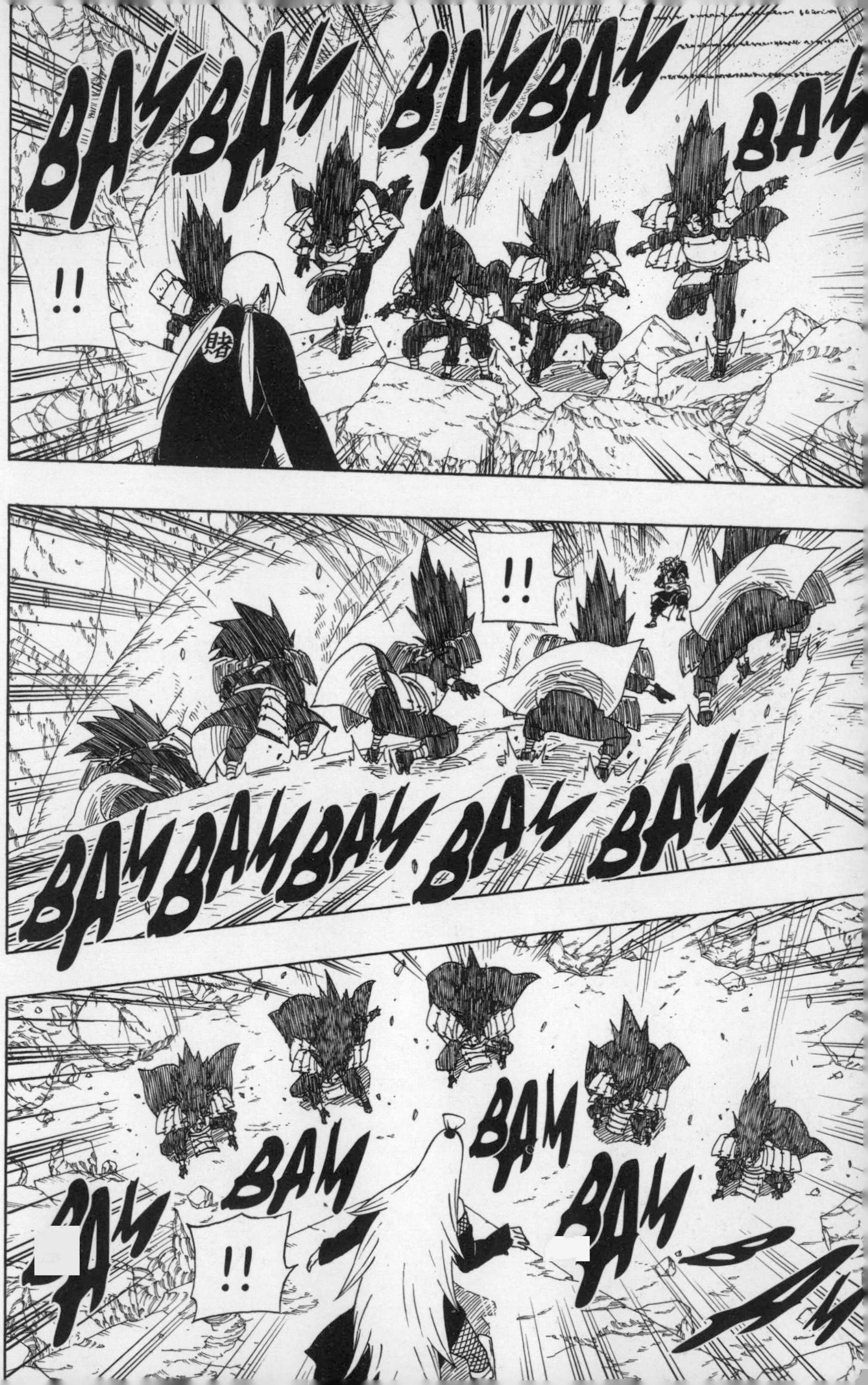

BAM BAM BAM BAM BAM
!!
!!
BAM BAM BAM BAM BAM
BAM
BAM
BAM
BAM
BAM
!!

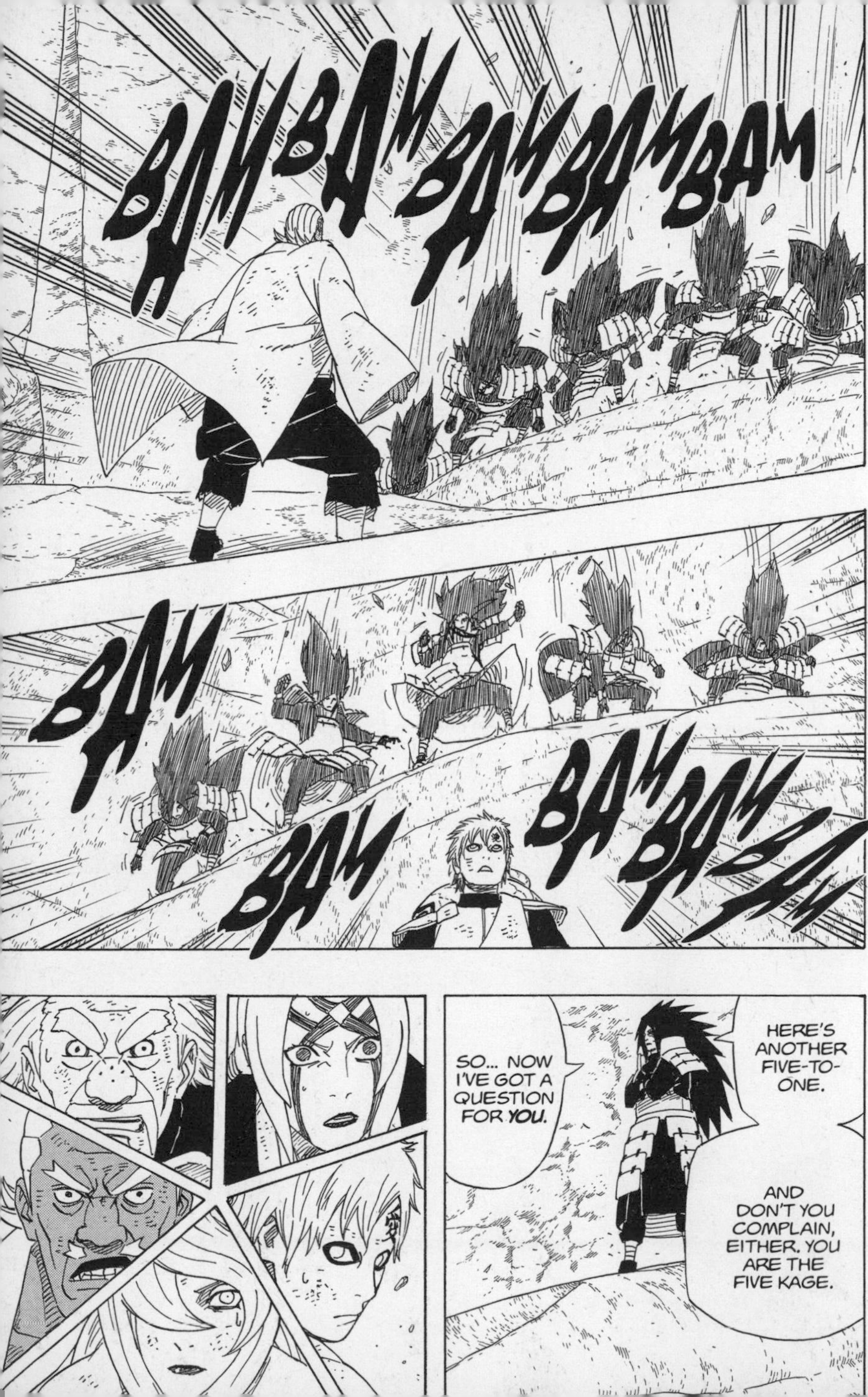
BAM BAM BAM BAM BAM
BAM
BAM
BAM BAM BAM
HERE'S ANOTHER FIVE-TO-ONE.
AND DON'T YOU COMPLAIN, EITHER. YOU ARE THE FIVE KAGE.
SO... NOW I'VE GOT A QUESTION FOR *YOU*.

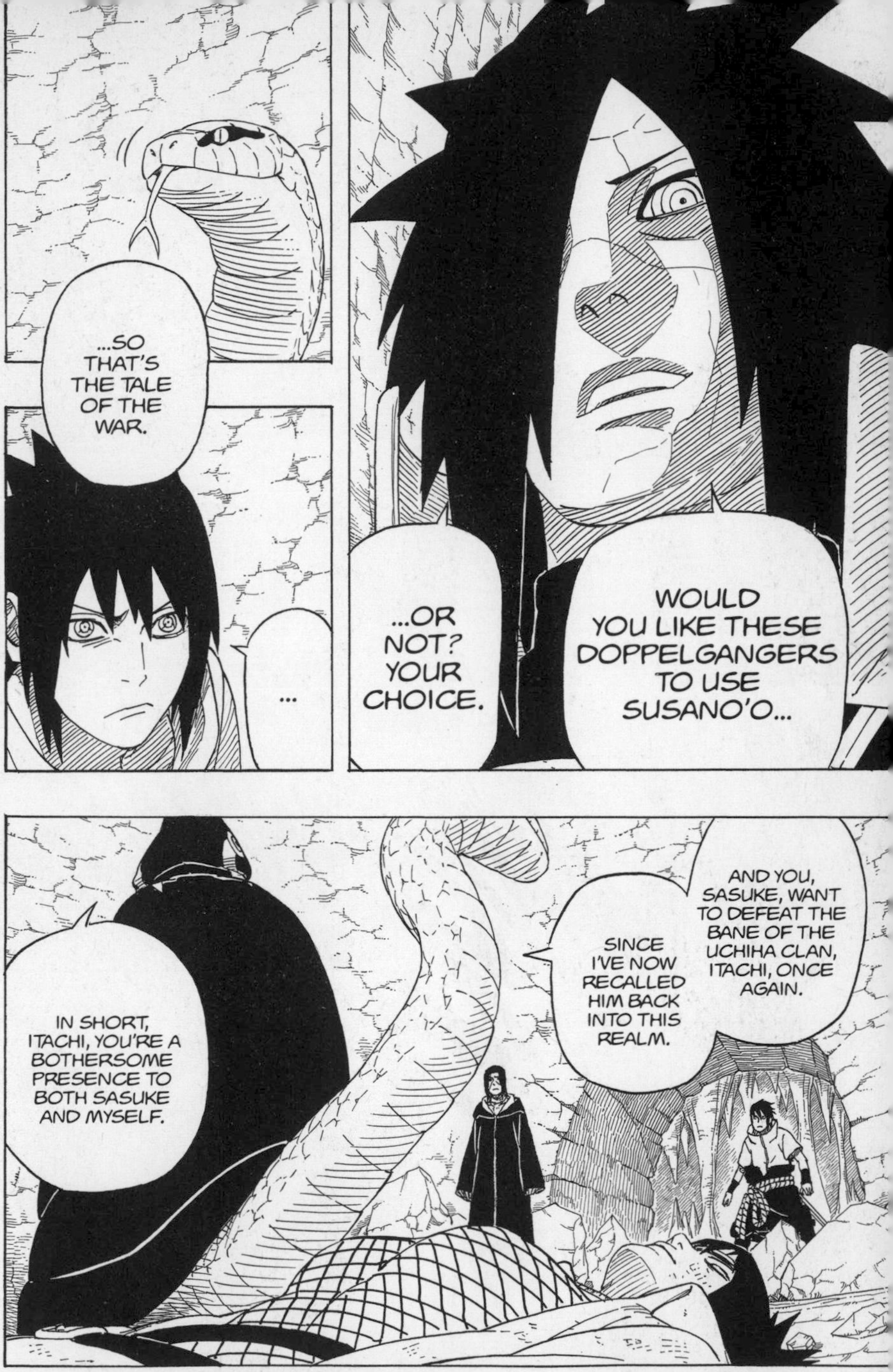
WOULD YOU LIKE THESE DOPPELGANGERS TO USE SUSANO'O...
...OR NOT? YOUR CHOICE.
...SO THAT'S THE TALE OF THE WAR.
...
AND YOU, SASUKE, WANT TO DEFEAT THE BANE OF THE UCHIHA CLAN, ITACHI, ONCE AGAIN.
SINCE I'VE NOW RECALLED HIM BACK INTO THIS REALM.
IN SHORT, ITACHI, YOU'RE A BOTHERSOME PRESENCE TO BOTH SASUKE AND MYSELF.

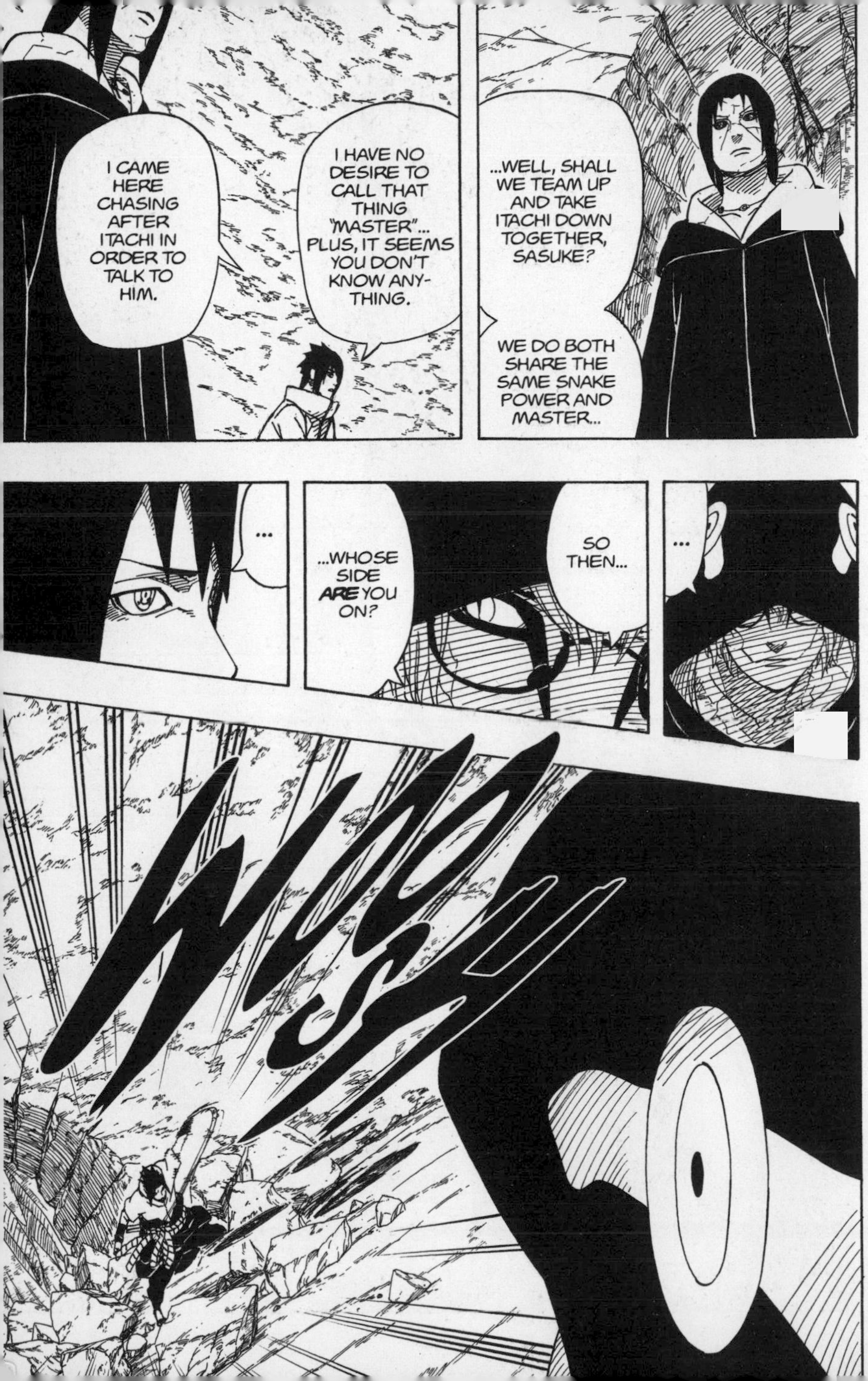
...WELL, SHALL WE TEAM UP AND TAKE ITACHI DOWN TOGETHER, SASUKE?
WE DO BOTH SHARE THE SAME SNAKE POWER AND MASTER...
I HAVE NO DESIRE TO CALL THAT THING "MASTER"... PLUS, IT SEEMS YOU DON'T KNOW ANYTHING.
I CAME HERE CHASING AFTER ITACHI IN ORDER TO TALK TO HIM.
...
SO THEN...
...WHOSE SIDE **ARE** YOU ON?
...

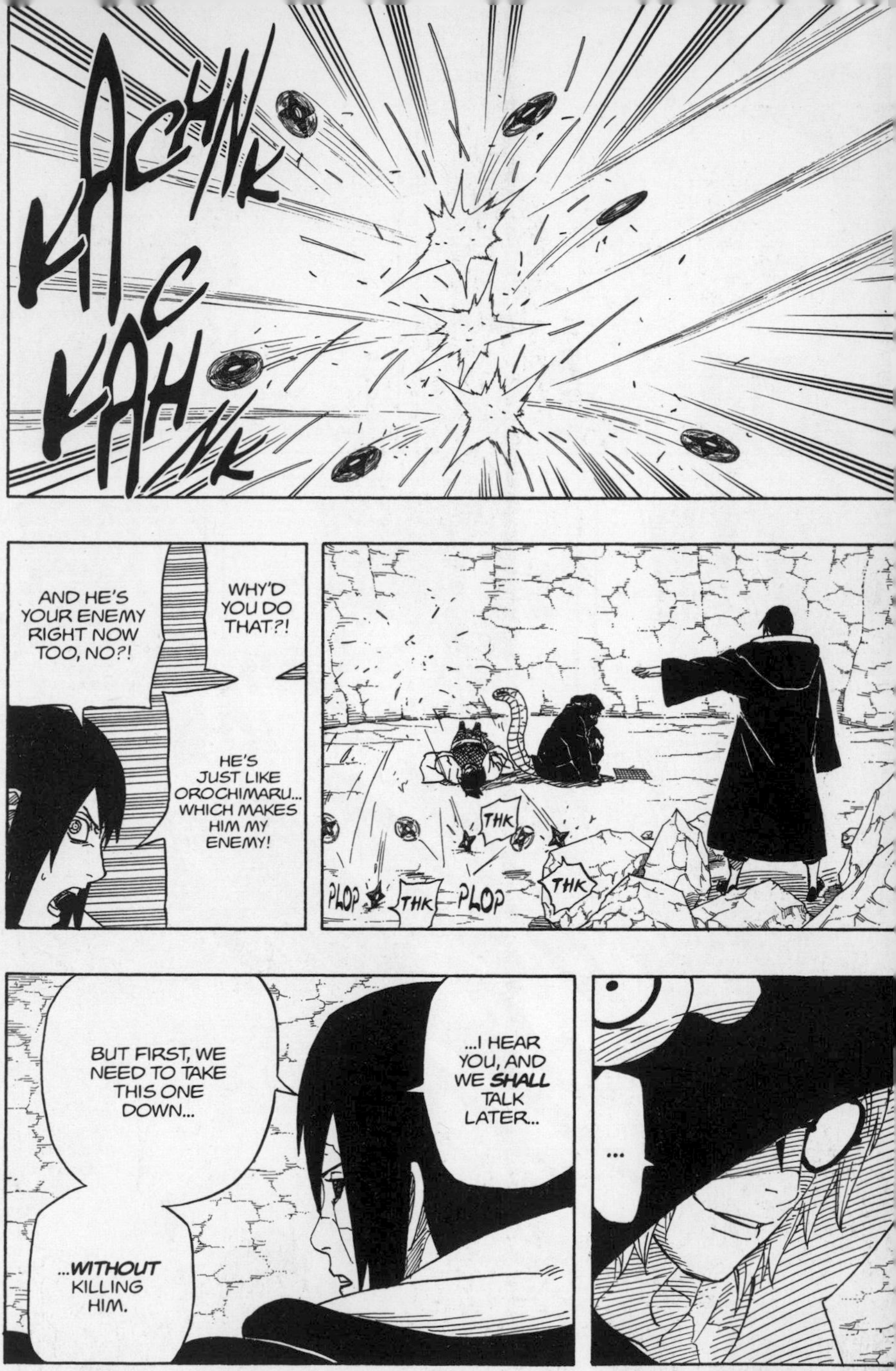
KACHNK
C KAHNK
THK
THK
PLOP
THK
PLOP
WHY'D YOU DO THAT?!
AND HE'S YOUR ENEMY RIGHT NOW TOO, NO?!
HE'S JUST LIKE OROCHIMARU... WHICH MAKES HIM MY ENEMY!
...
...I HEAR YOU, AND WE **SHALL** TALK LATER...
BUT FIRST, WE NEED TO TAKE THIS ONE DOWN...
...**WITHOUT** KILLING HIM.

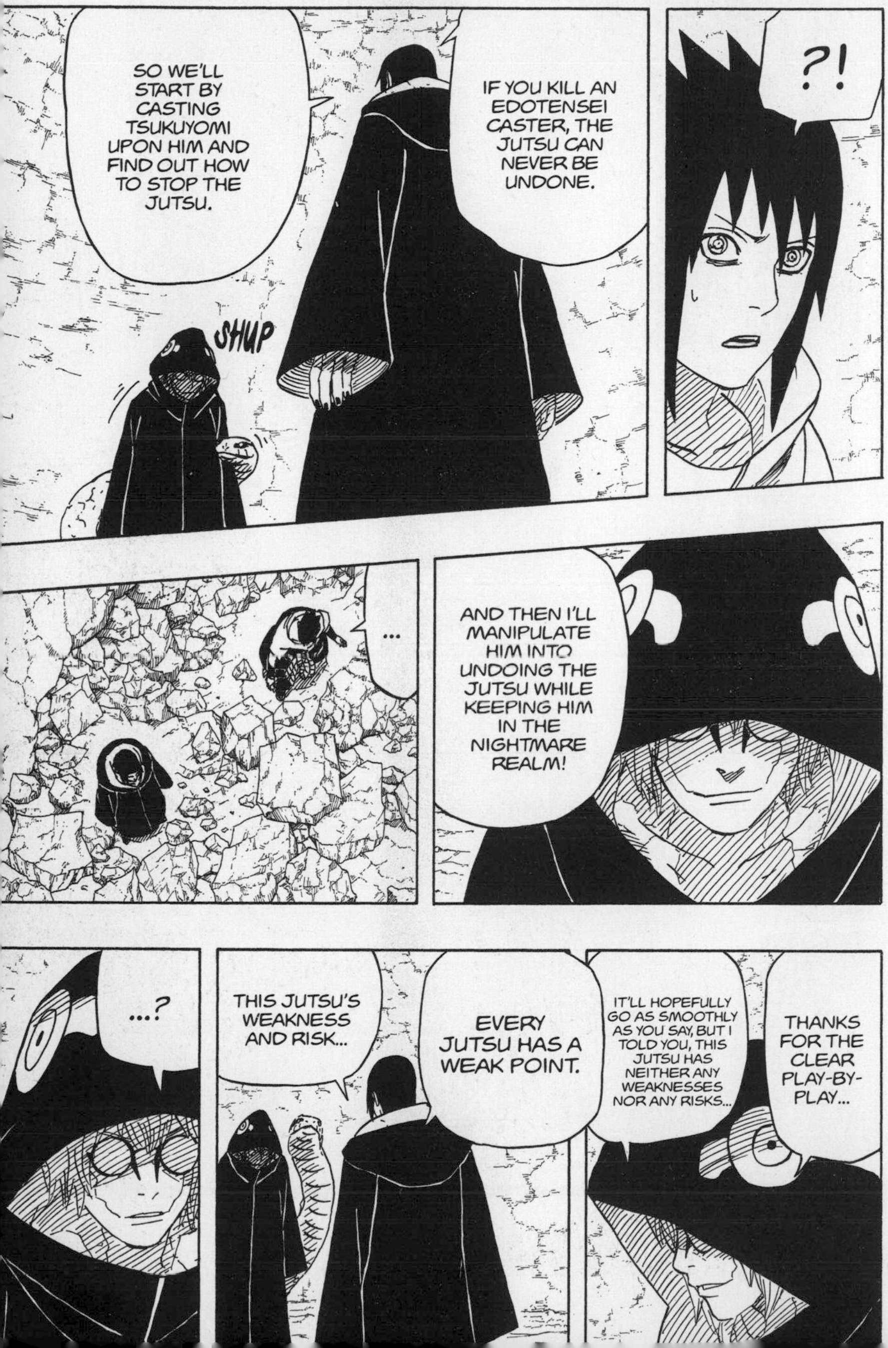
?!
IF YOU KILL AN EDOTENSEI CASTER, THE JUTSU CAN NEVER BE UNDONE.
SO WE'LL START BY CASTING TSUKUYOMI UPON HIM AND FIND OUT HOW TO STOP THE JUTSU.
SHUP
AND THEN I'LL MANIPULATE HIM INTO UNDOING THE JUTSU WHILE KEEPING HIM IN THE NIGHTMARE REALM!
...
THANKS FOR THE CLEAR PLAY-BY-PLAY...
IT'LL HOPEFULLY GO AS SMOOTHLY AS YOU SAY, BUT I TOLD YOU, THIS JUTSU HAS NEITHER ANY WEAKNESSES NOR ANY RISKS...
EVERY JUTSU HAS A WEAK POINT.
THIS JUTSU'S WEAKNESS AND RISK...
...?

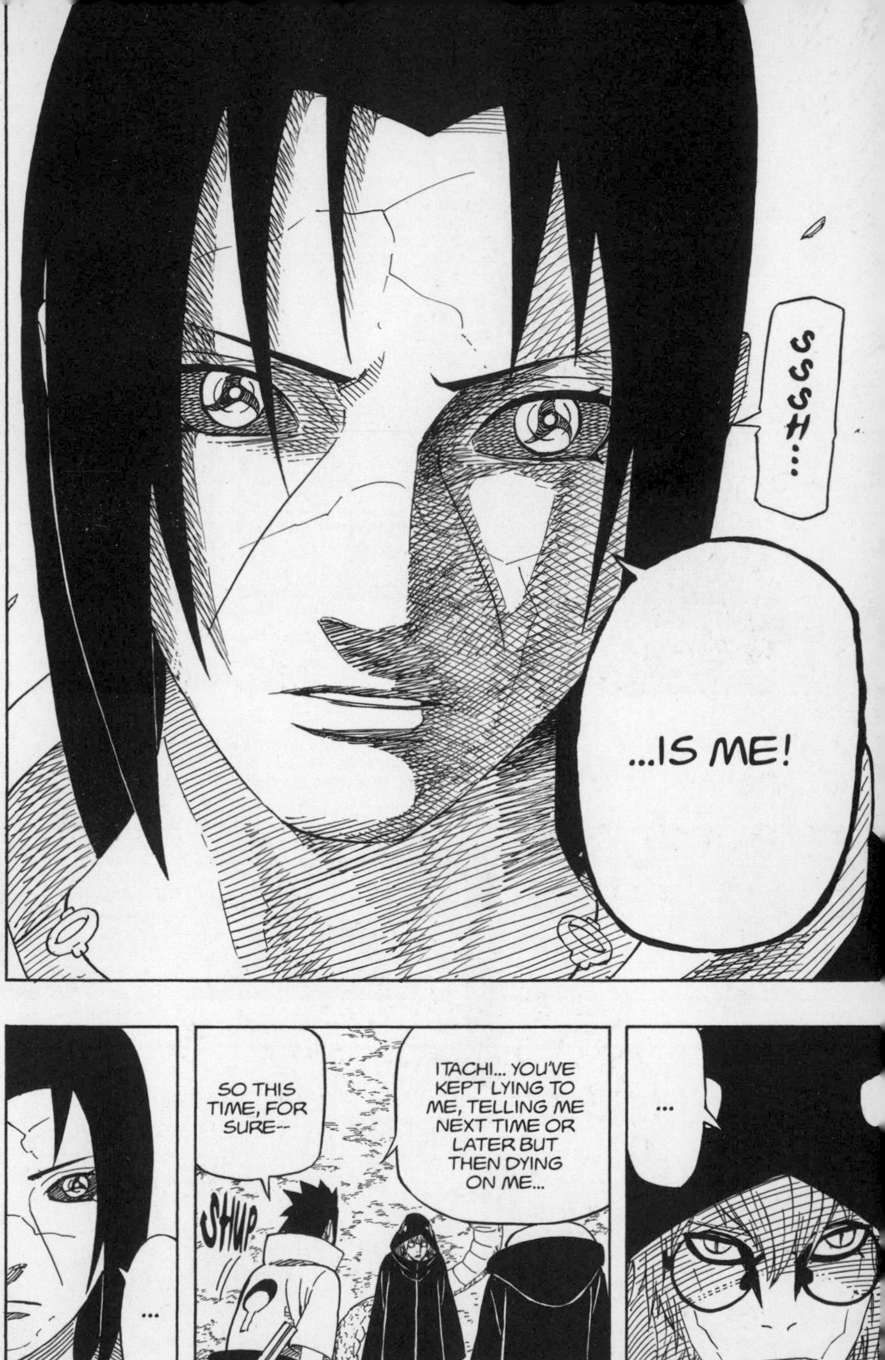
SSSH...
...IS ME!
...
ITACHI... YOU'VE KEPT LYING TO ME, TELLING ME NEXT TIME OR LATER BUT THEN DYING ON ME...
SO THIS TIME, FOR SURE--
SHUP
...

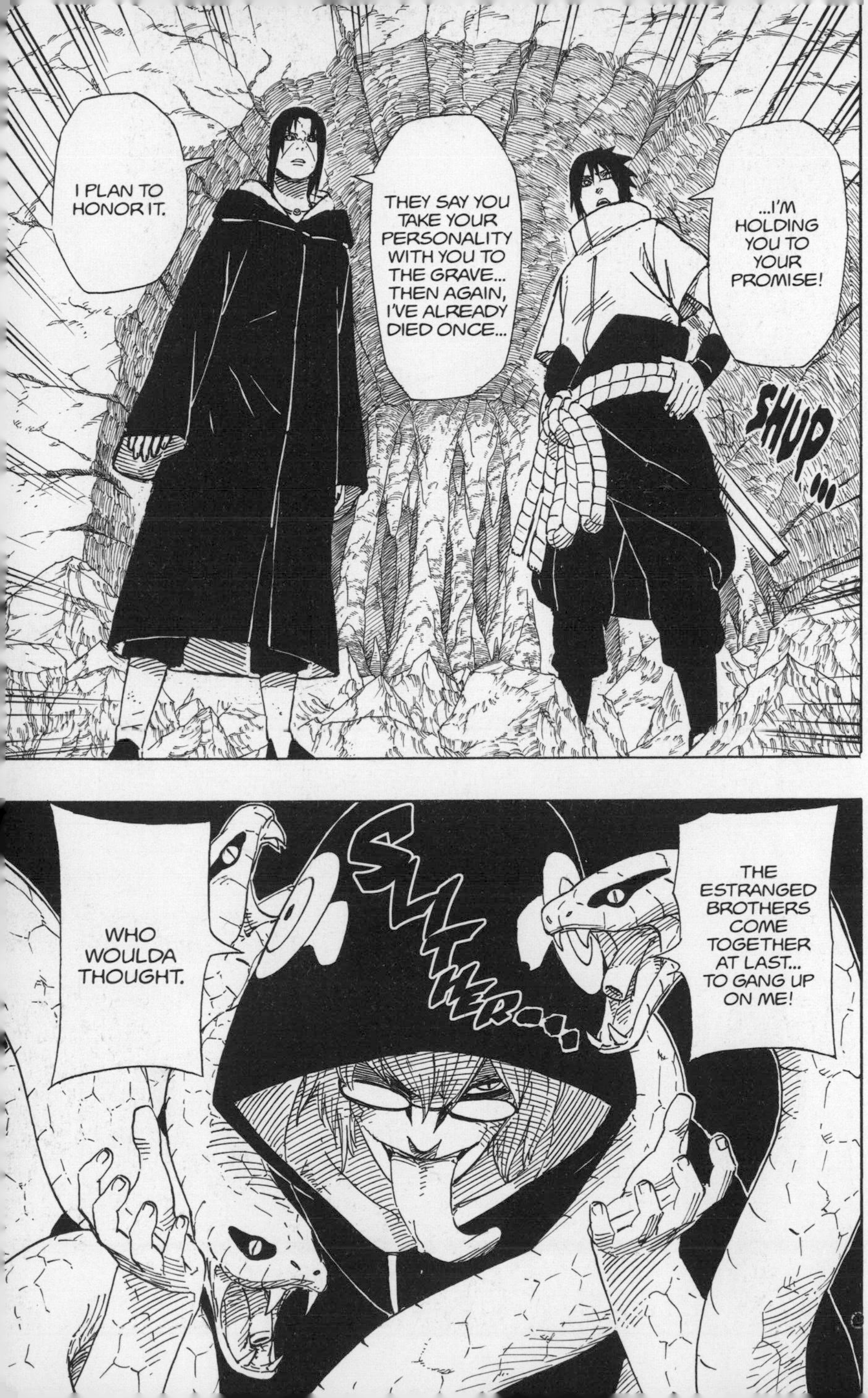
...I'M HOLDING YOU TO YOUR PROMISE!
SHUP...
THEY SAY YOU TAKE YOUR PERSONALITY WITH YOU TO THE GRAVE... THEN AGAIN, I'VE ALREADY DIED ONCE...
I PLAN TO HONOR IT.
THE ESTRANGED BROTHERS COME TOGETHER AT LAST... TO GANG UP ON ME!
SLITHER...
WHO WOULDA THOUGHT.

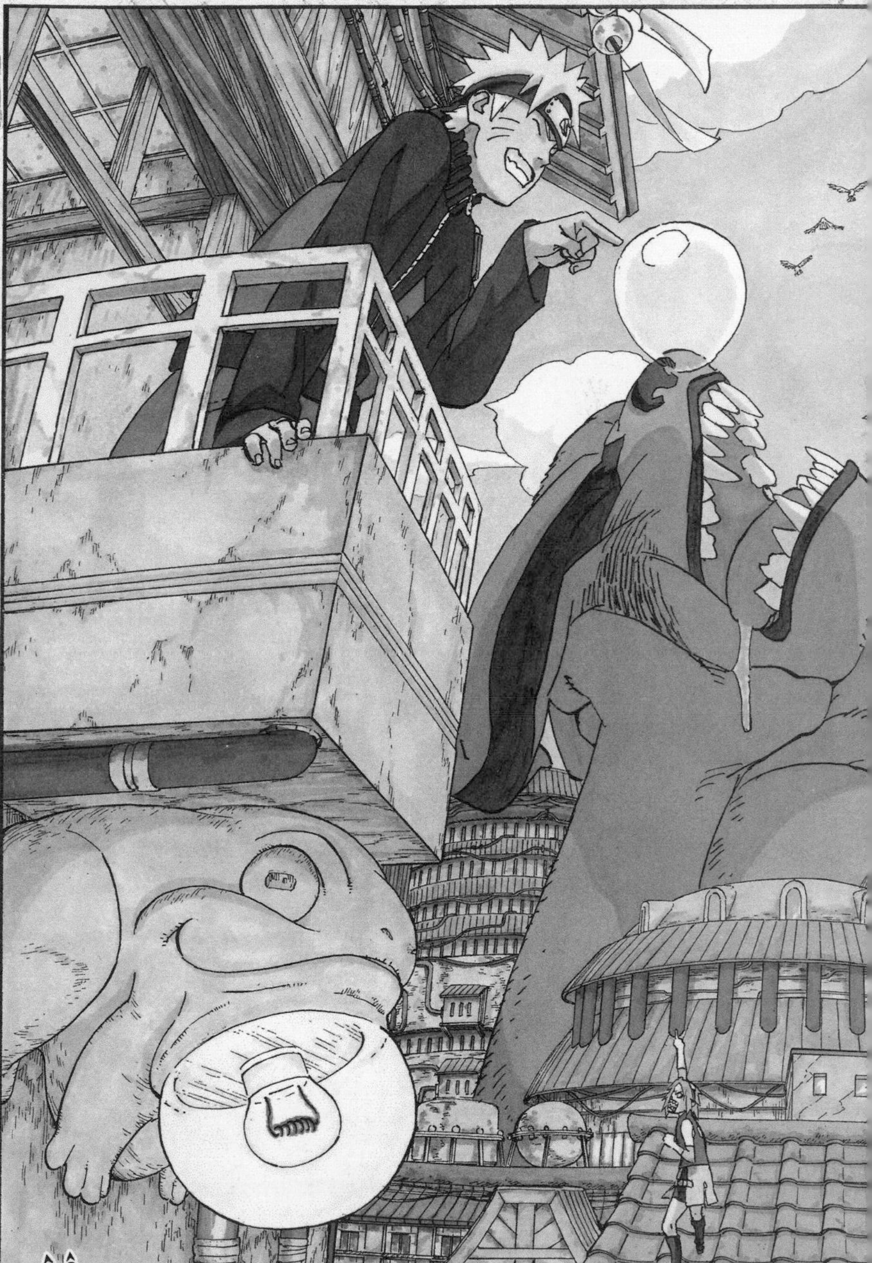

Number 579: Uchiha Brothers United Front!!

NARUTO
—ナルト—

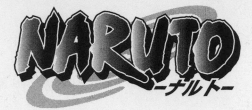

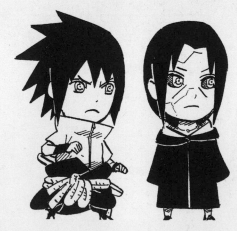

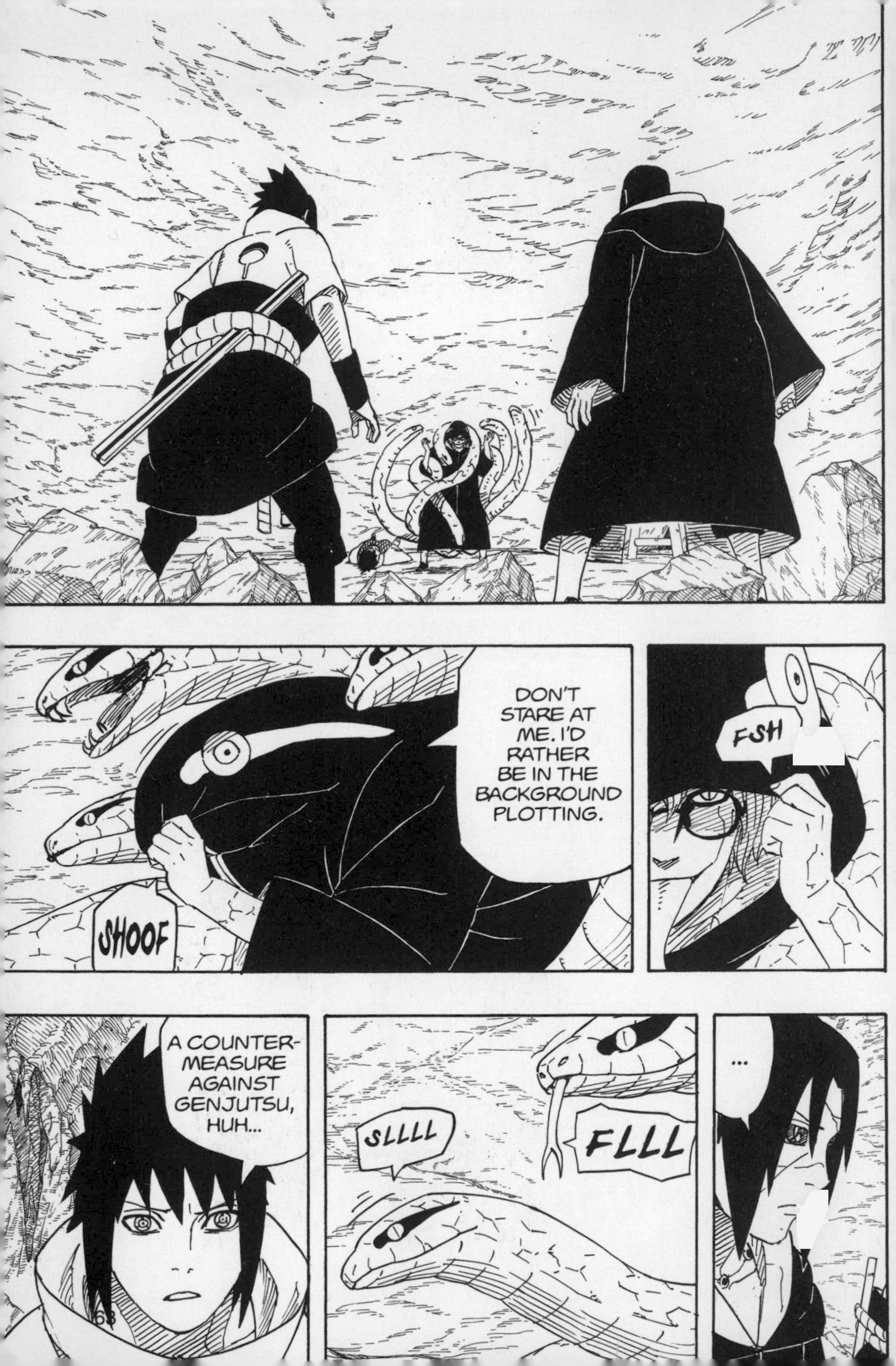
FSH
DON'T STARE AT ME. I'D RATHER BE IN THE BACKGROUND PLOTTING.
SHOOF
...
FLLL
SLLL
A COUNTER-MEASURE AGAINST GENJUTSU, HUH...

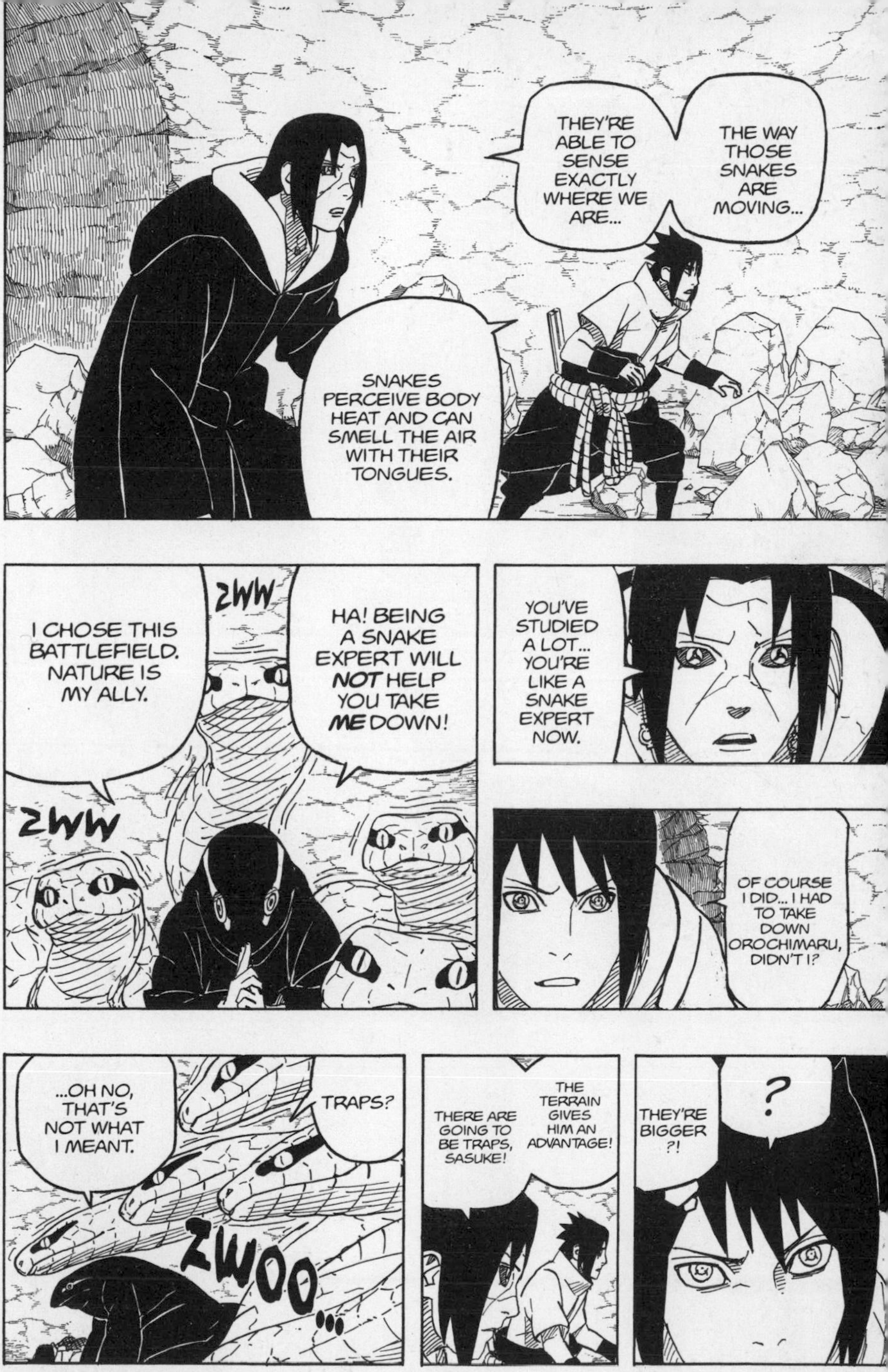
THE WAY THOSE SNAKES ARE MOVING...
THEY'RE ABLE TO SENSE EXACTLY WHERE WE ARE...
SNAKES PERCEIVE BODY HEAT AND CAN SMELL THE AIR WITH THEIR TONGUES.
YOU'VE STUDIED A LOT... YOU'RE LIKE A SNAKE EXPERT NOW.
OF COURSE I DID... I HAD TO TAKE DOWN OROCHIMARU, DIDN'T I?
HA! BEING A SNAKE EXPERT WILL **NOT** HELP YOU TAKE **ME** DOWN!
ZWW
I CHOSE THIS BATTLEFIELD. NATURE IS MY ALLY.
ZWW
?
THEY'RE BIGGER ?!
THE TERRAIN GIVES HIM AN ADVANTAGE!
THERE ARE GOING TO BE TRAPS, SASUKE!
TRAPS?
...OH NO, THAT'S NOT WHAT I MEANT.
ZWOO...

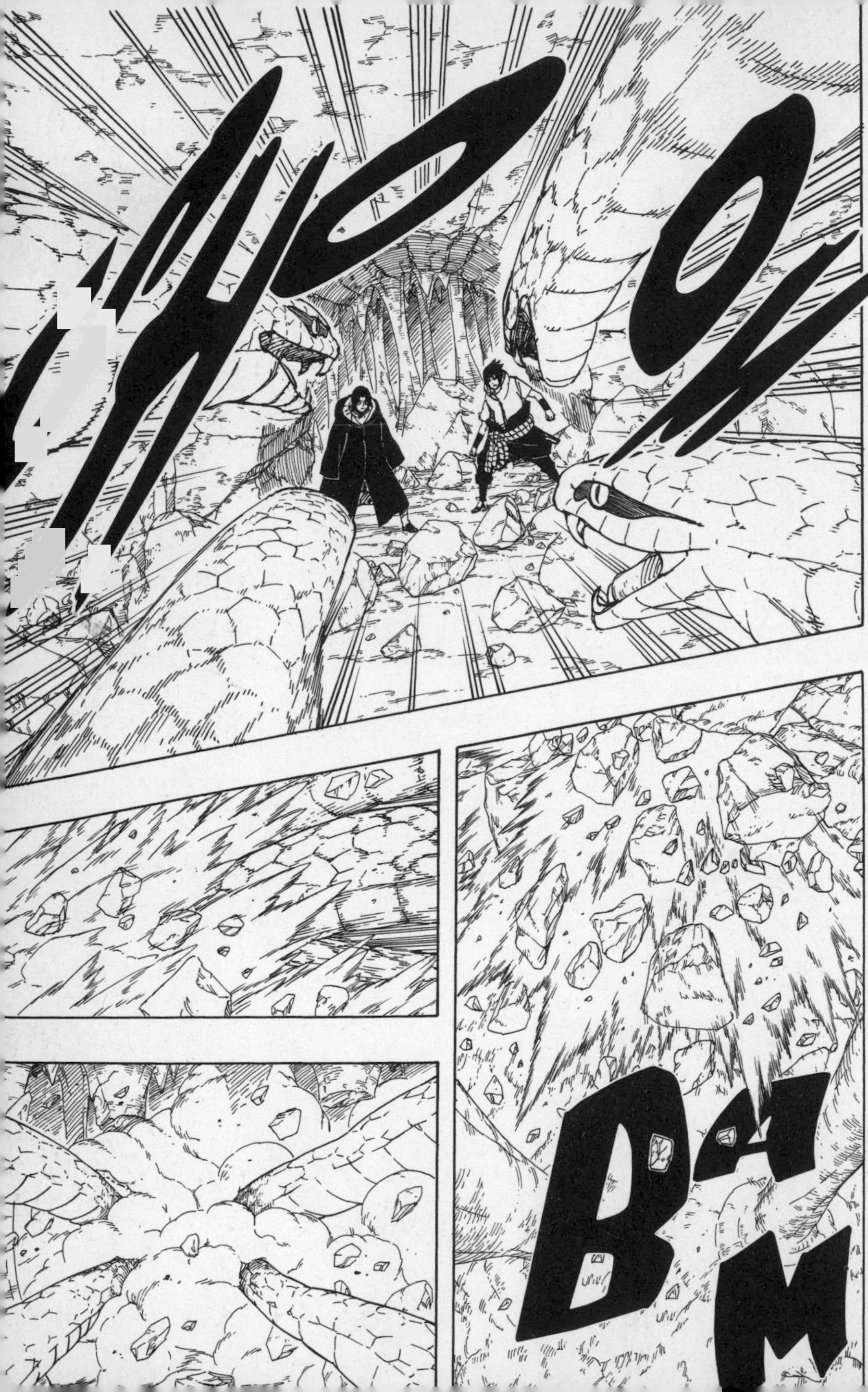

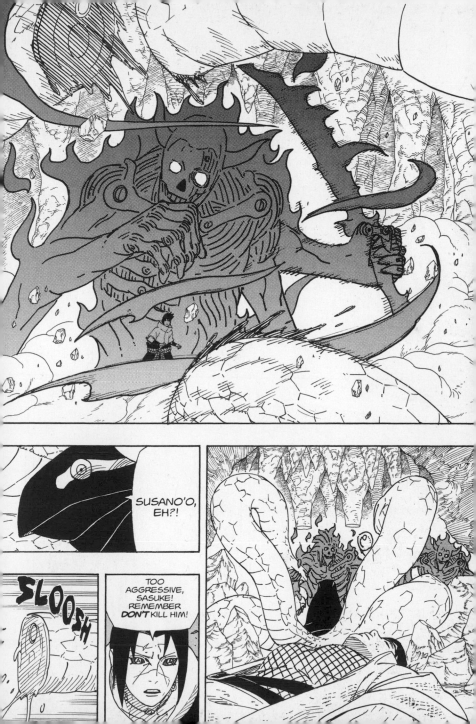

SUSANO'O, EH?!

SLOOSH

TOO AGGRESSIVE, SASUKE! REMEMBER **DON'T** KILL HIM!

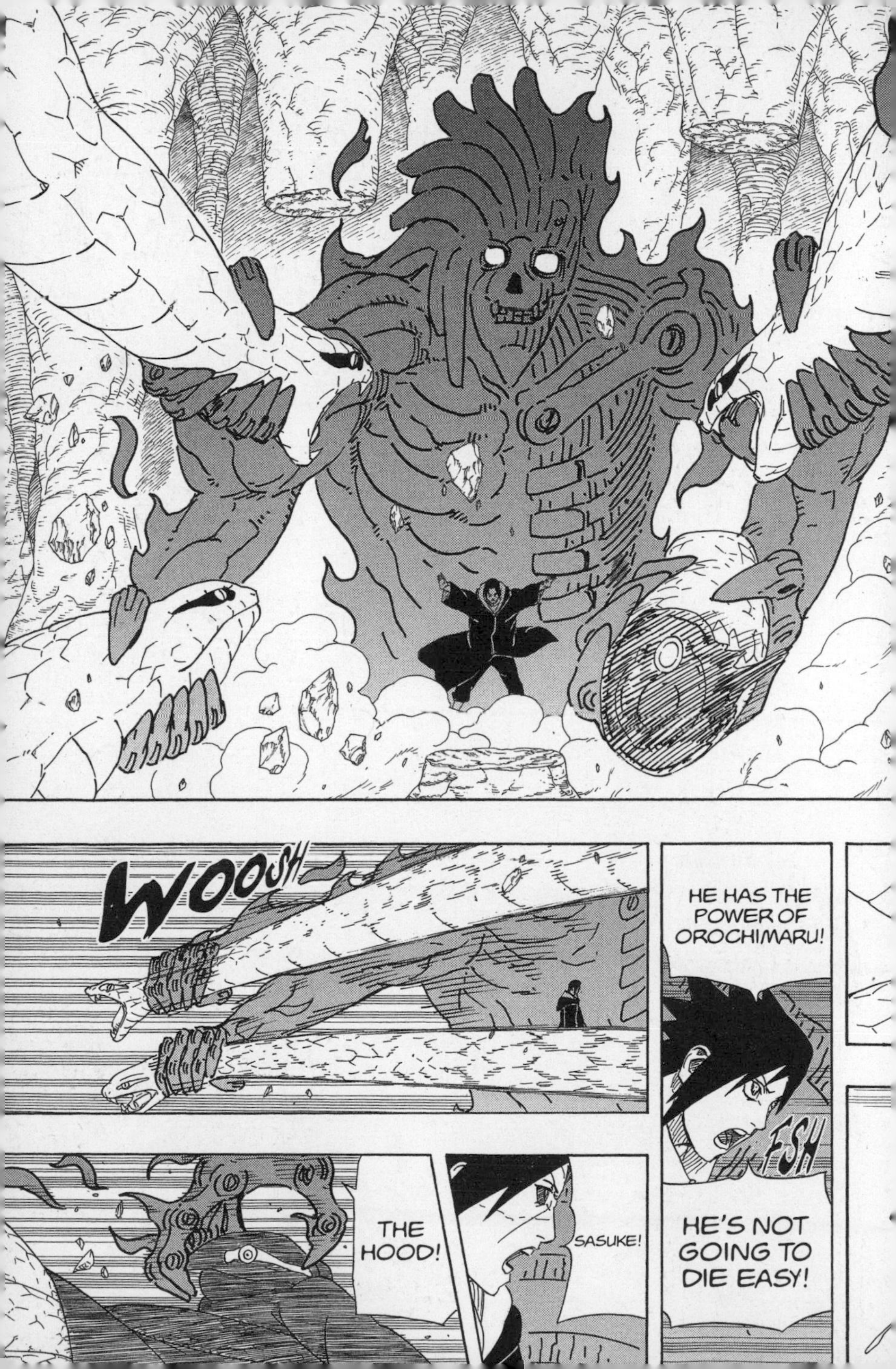
HE HAS THE POWER OF OROCHIMARU!
FSH
HE'S NOT GOING TO DIE EASY!
WOOSH
SASUKE!
THE HOOD!

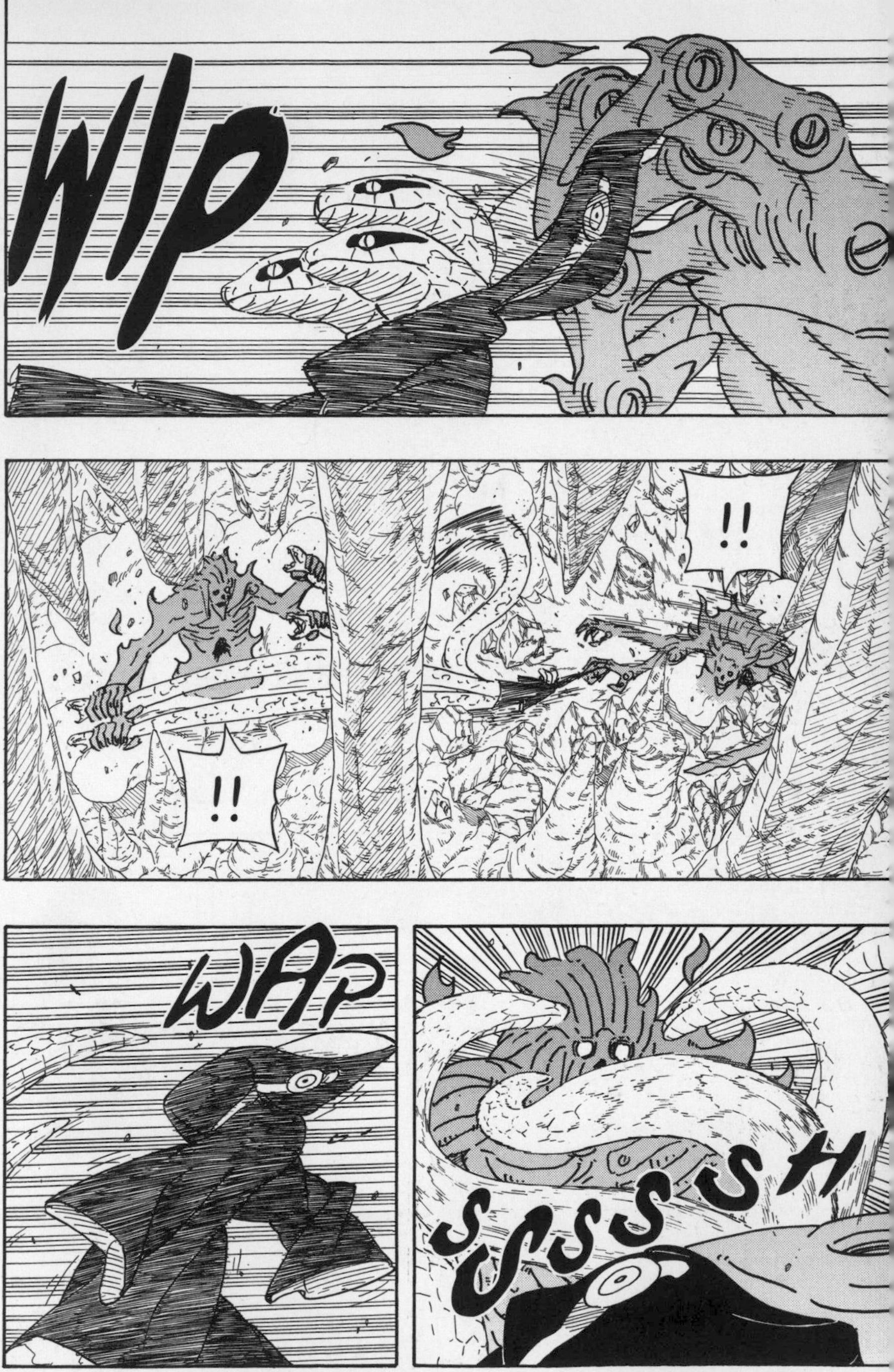
WIP
!!
!!
SSSSH
WAP

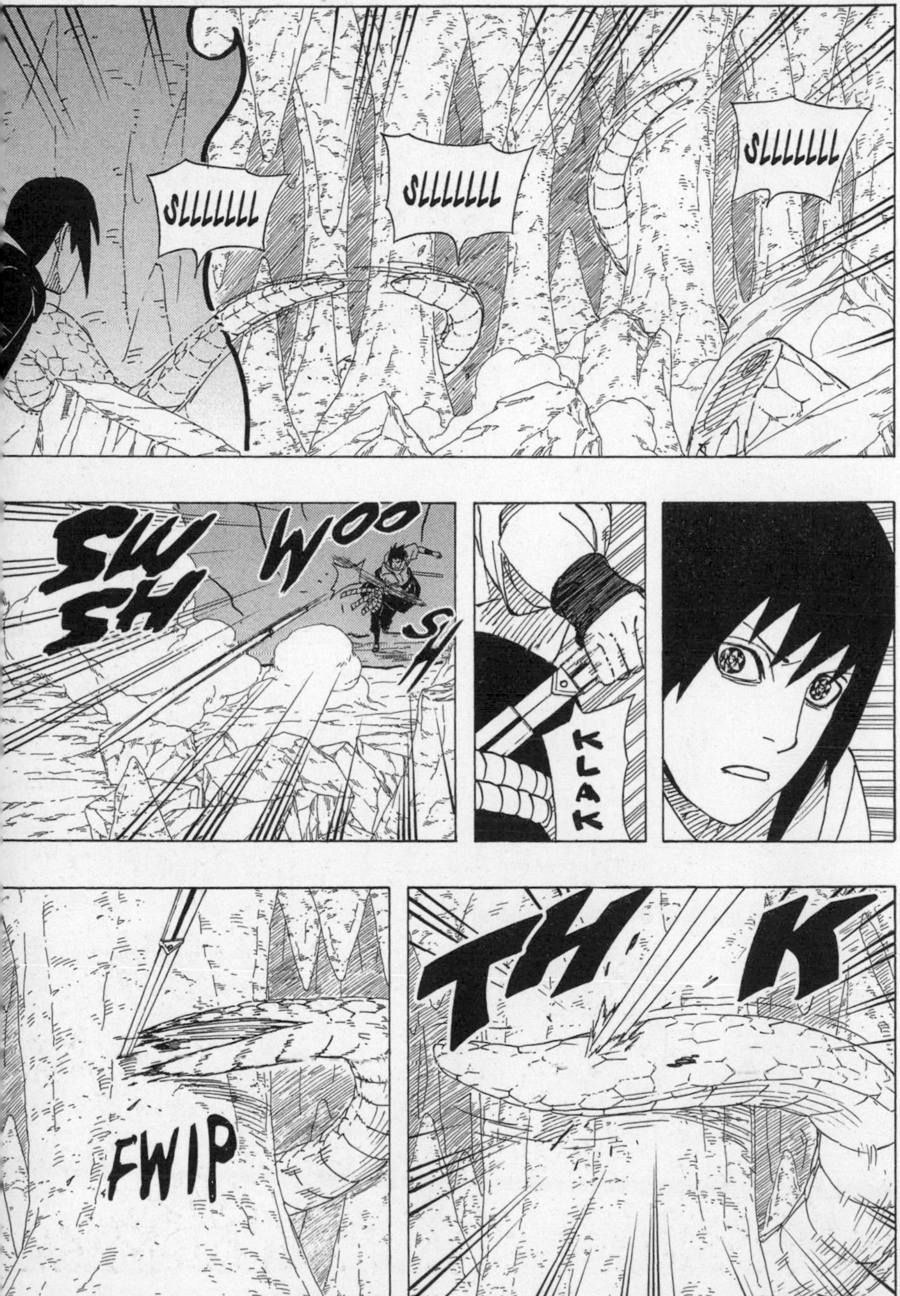
SLLLLLLL
SLLLLLLL
SLLLLLLL
KLAK
SWSH
WOO
SH
THK
FWIP

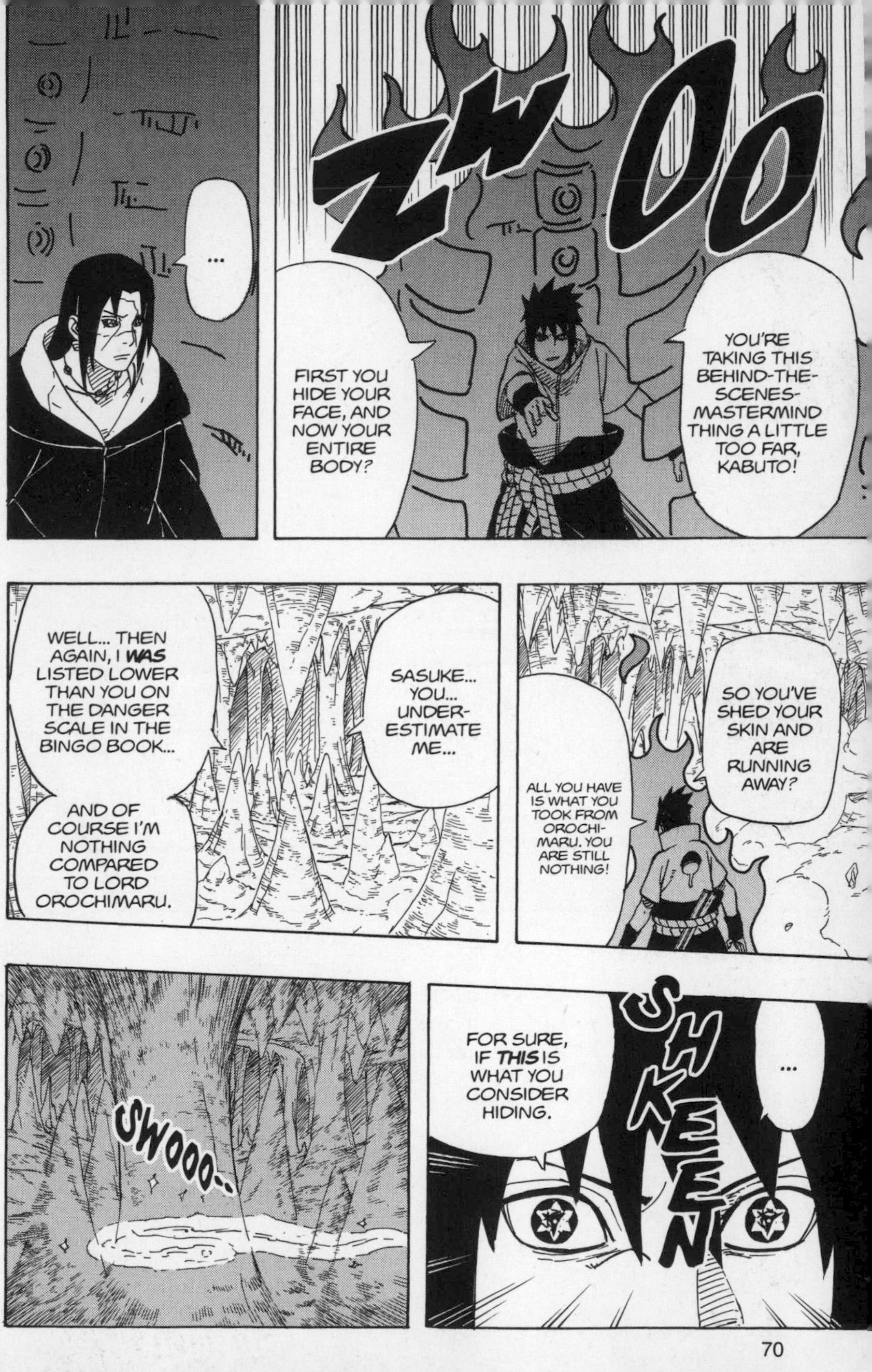
ZWOOO
YOU'RE TAKING THIS BEHIND-THE-SCENES-MASTERMIND THING A LITTLE TOO FAR, KABUTO!
FIRST YOU HIDE YOUR FACE, AND NOW YOUR ENTIRE BODY?
...
SO YOU'VE SHED YOUR SKIN AND ARE RUNNING AWAY?
ALL YOU HAVE IS WHAT YOU TOOK FROM OROCHI-MARU. YOU ARE STILL NOTHING!
SASUKE... YOU... UNDER-ESTIMATE ME...
WELL... THEN AGAIN, I **WAS** LISTED LOWER THAN YOU ON THE DANGER SCALE IN THE BINGO BOOK...
AND OF COURSE I'M NOTHING COMPARED TO LORD OROCHIMARU.
...
SHKEEN
FOR SURE, IF **THIS** IS WHAT YOU CONSIDER HIDING.
SWOOO..

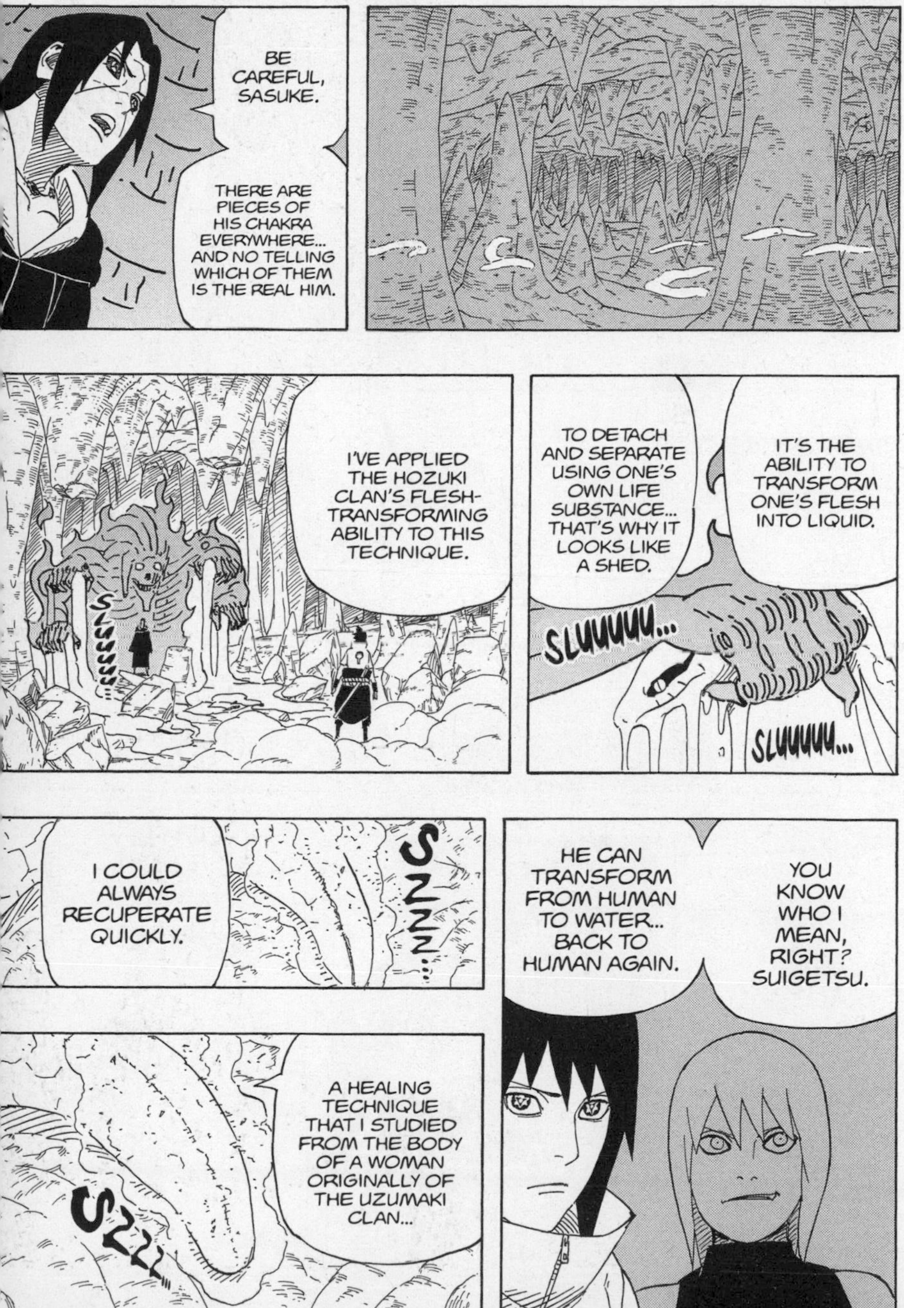
BE CAREFUL, SASUKE.
THERE ARE PIECES OF HIS CHAKRA EVERYWHERE... AND NO TELLING WHICH OF THEM IS THE REAL HIM.
IT'S THE ABILITY TO TRANSFORM ONE'S FLESH INTO LIQUID.
TO DETACH AND SEPARATE USING ONE'S OWN LIFE SUBSTANCE... THAT'S WHY IT LOOKS LIKE A SHED.
SLUUUUU...
SLUUUUU...
I'VE APPLIED THE HOZUKI CLAN'S FLESH-TRANSFORMING ABILITY TO THIS TECHNIQUE.
SLUUUUU...
YOU KNOW WHO I MEAN, RIGHT? SUIGETSU.
HE CAN TRANSFORM FROM HUMAN TO WATER... BACK TO HUMAN AGAIN.
I COULD ALWAYS RECUPERATE QUICKLY.
SZZZ...
A HEALING TECHNIQUE THAT I STUDIED FROM THE BODY OF A WOMAN ORIGINALLY OF THE UZUMAKI CLAN...
SZZZ

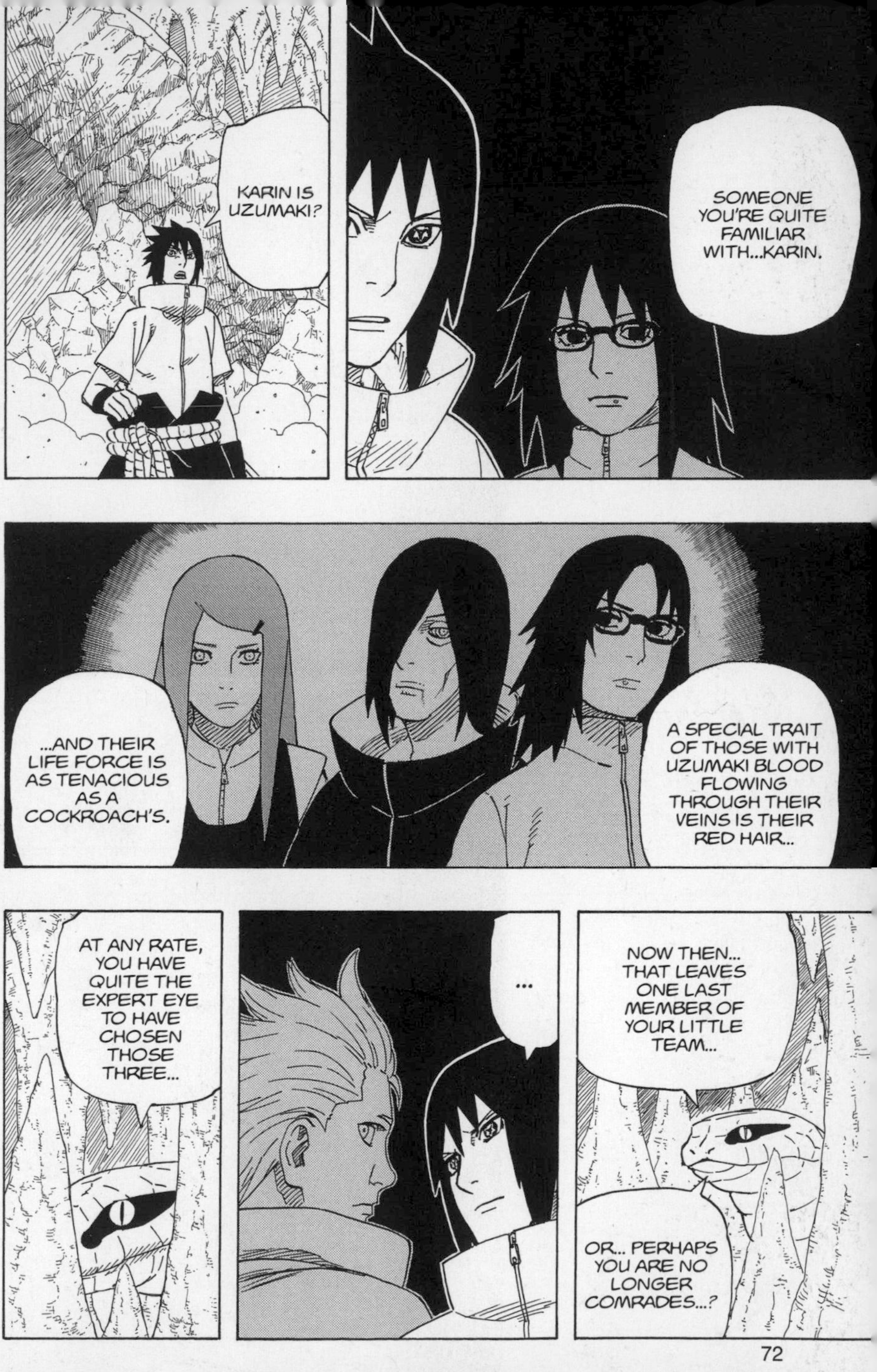
SOMEONE YOU'RE QUITE FAMILIAR WITH...KARIN.
KARIN IS UZUMAKI?
A SPECIAL TRAIT OF THOSE WITH UZUMAKI BLOOD FLOWING THROUGH THEIR VEINS IS THEIR RED HAIR...
...AND THEIR LIFE FORCE IS AS TENACIOUS AS A COCKROACH'S.
NOW THEN... THAT LEAVES ONE LAST MEMBER OF YOUR LITTLE TEAM...
OR... PERHAPS YOU ARE NO LONGER COMRADES...?
...
AT ANY RATE, YOU HAVE QUITE THE EXPERT EYE TO HAVE CHOSEN THOSE THREE...

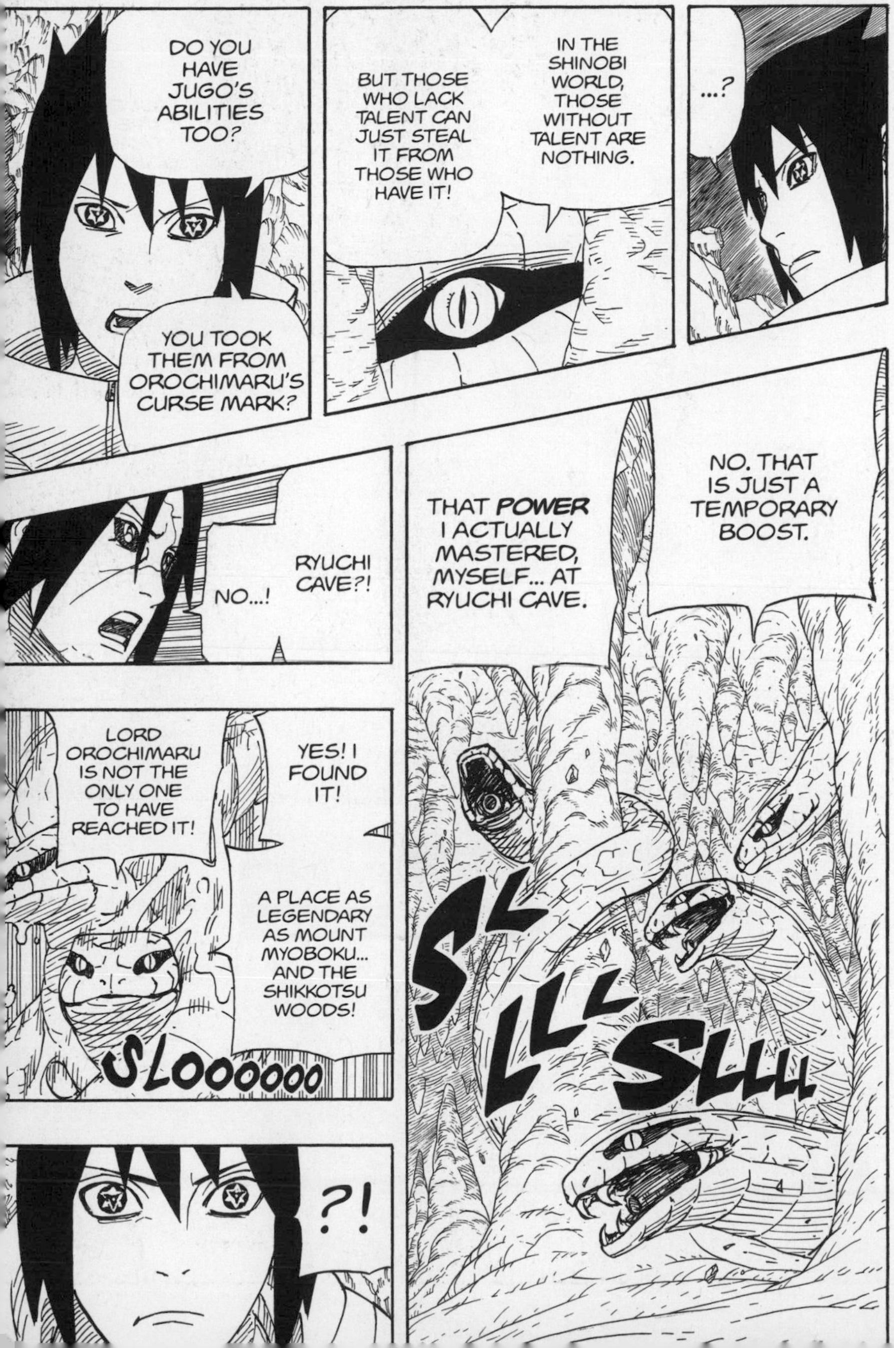
...?
IN THE SHINOBI WORLD, THOSE WITHOUT TALENT ARE NOTHING.
BUT THOSE WHO LACK TALENT CAN JUST STEAL IT FROM THOSE WHO HAVE IT!
DO YOU HAVE JUGO'S ABILITIES TOO?
YOU TOOK THEM FROM OROCHIMARU'S CURSE MARK?
NO. THAT IS JUST A TEMPORARY BOOST.
THAT ***POWER*** I ACTUALLY MASTERED, MYSELF... AT RYUCHI CAVE.
SLLLL
SLLLL
RYUCHI CAVE?!
NO...!
YES! I FOUND IT!
LORD OROCHIMARU IS NOT THE ONLY ONE TO HAVE REACHED IT!
A PLACE AS LEGENDARY AS MOUNT MYOBOKU... AND THE SHIKKOTSU WOODS!
SLOOOOOO
?!

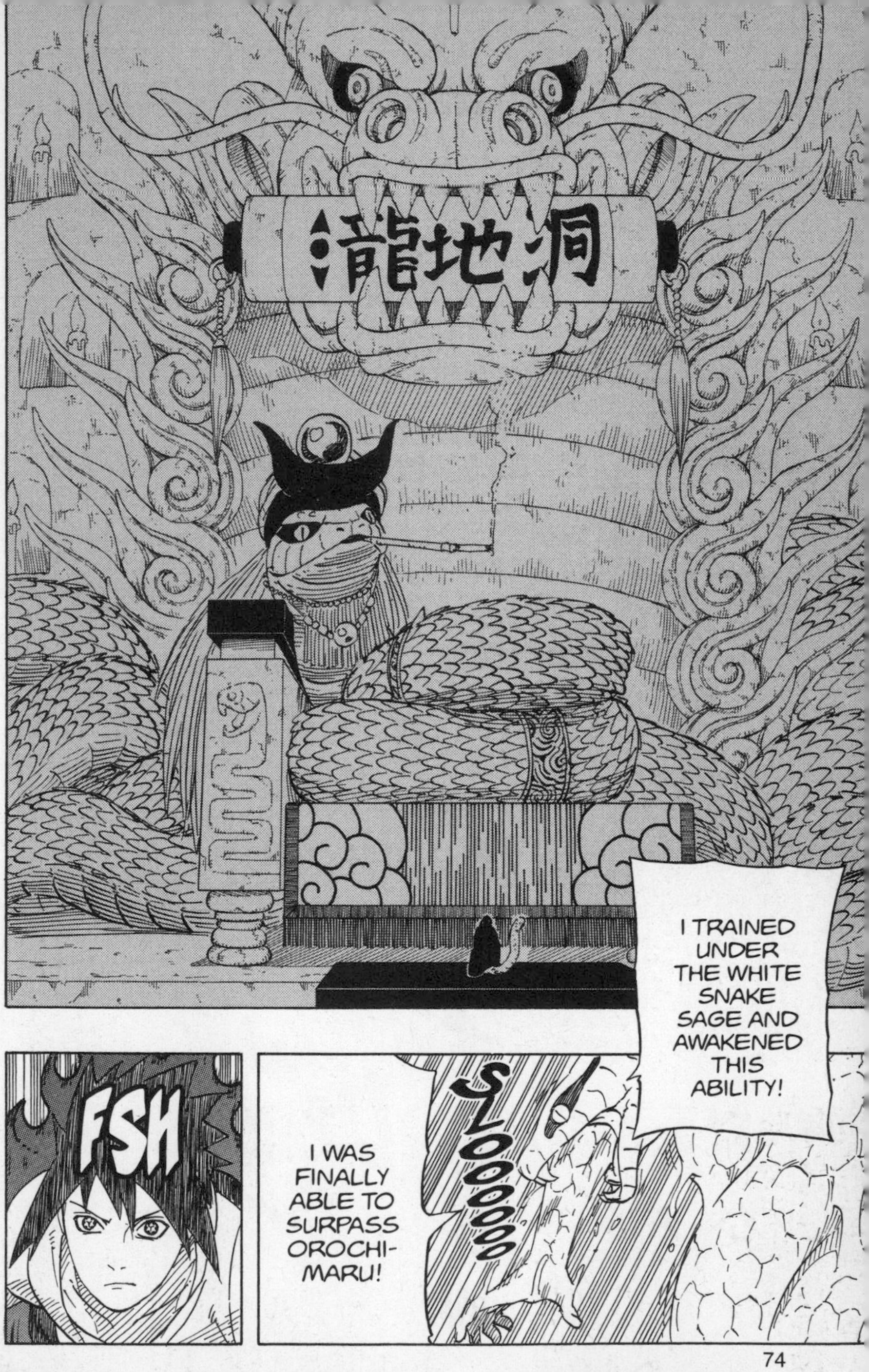
龍地洞
I TRAINED UNDER THE WHITE SNAKE SAGE AND AWAKENED THIS ABILITY!
SLOOOOOO
I WAS FINALLY ABLE TO SURPASS OROCHI-MARU!
FSH

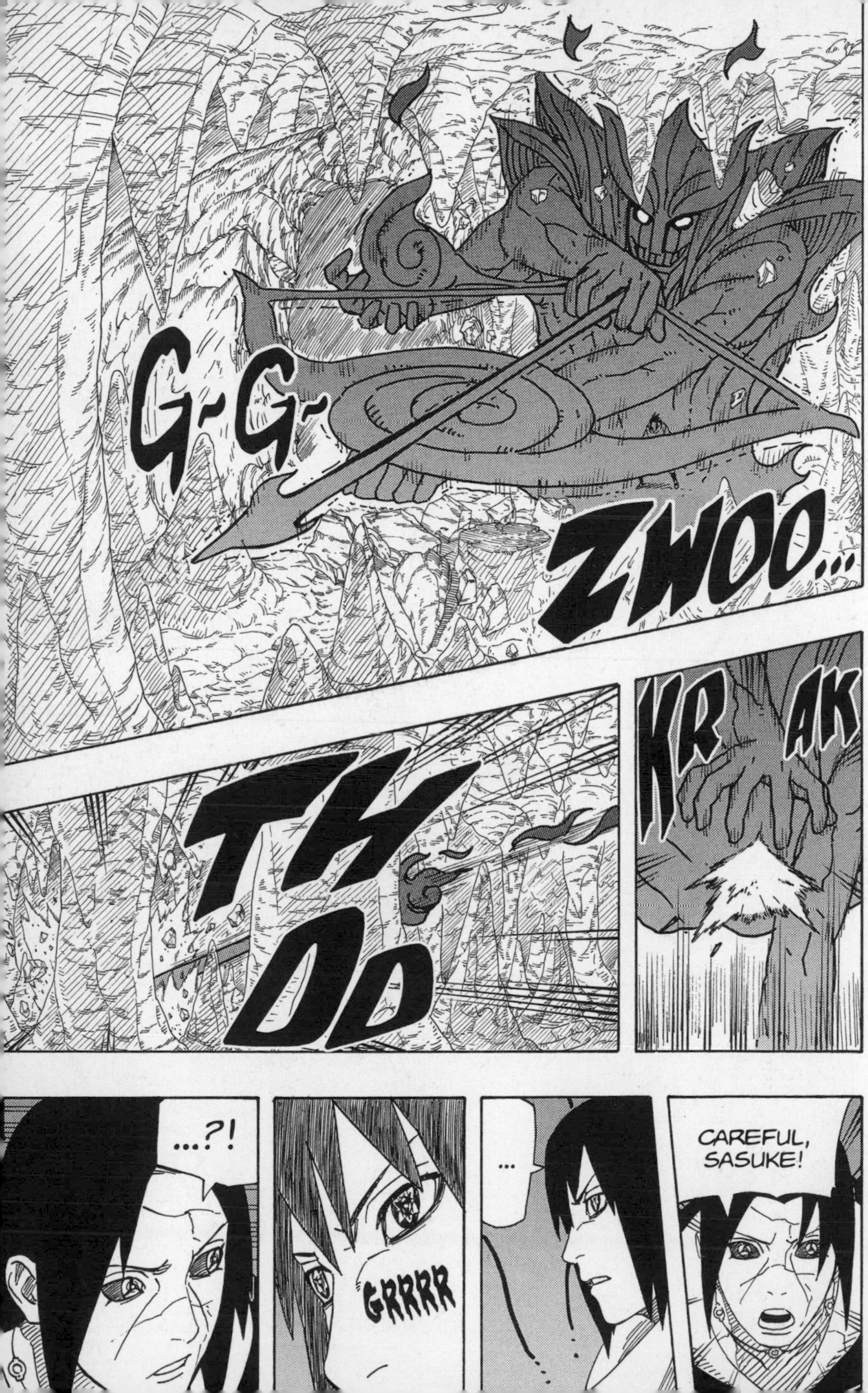
G-G-G-
ZWOO...
KR AK
THOD
CAREFUL, SASUKE!
...
GRRRR
...?!

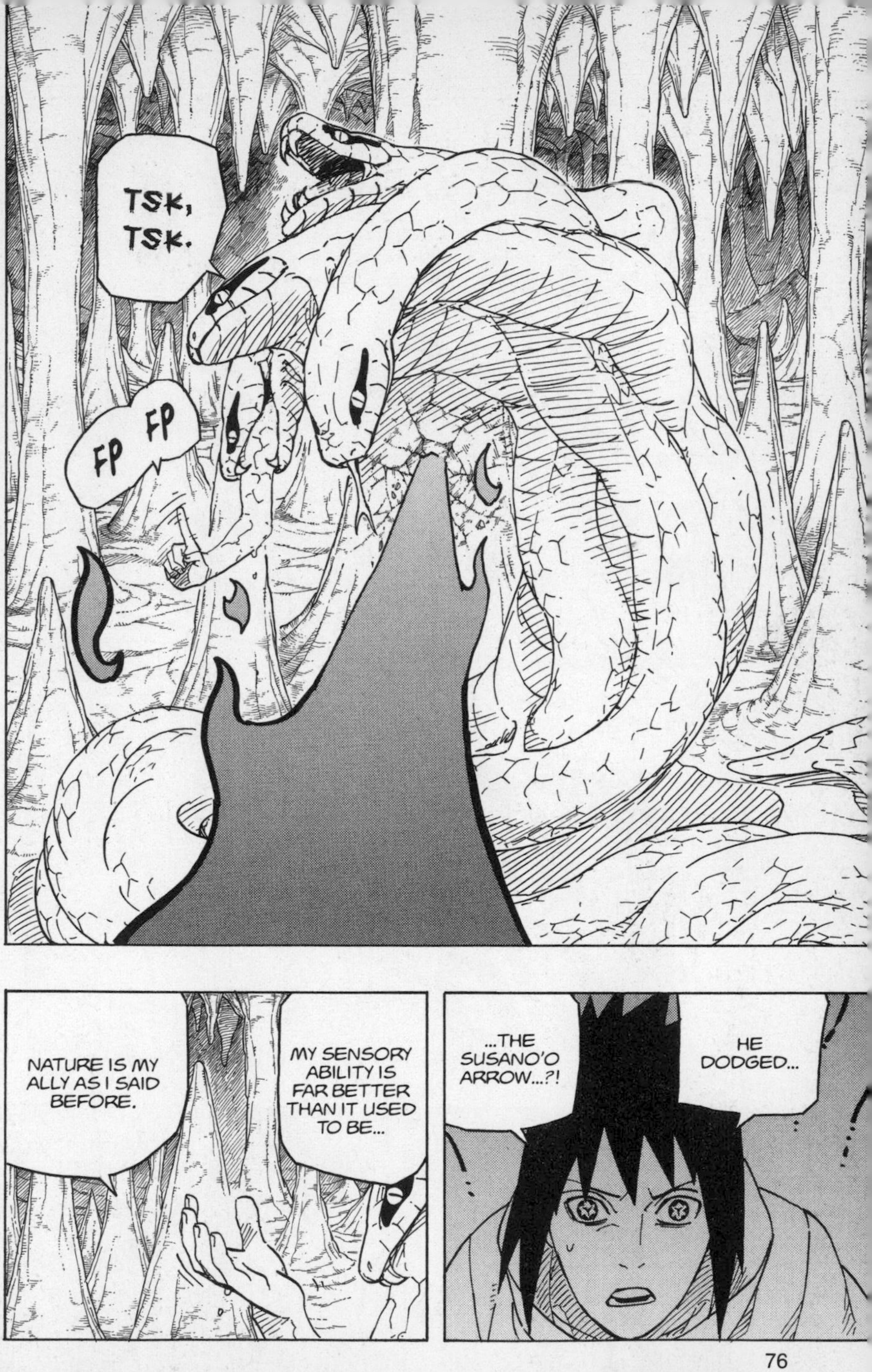
TSK, TSK.
FP FP
HE DODGED...
...THE SUSANO'O ARROW...?!
MY SENSORY ABILITY IS FAR BETTER THAN IT USED TO BE...
NATURE IS MY ALLY AS I SAID BEFORE.

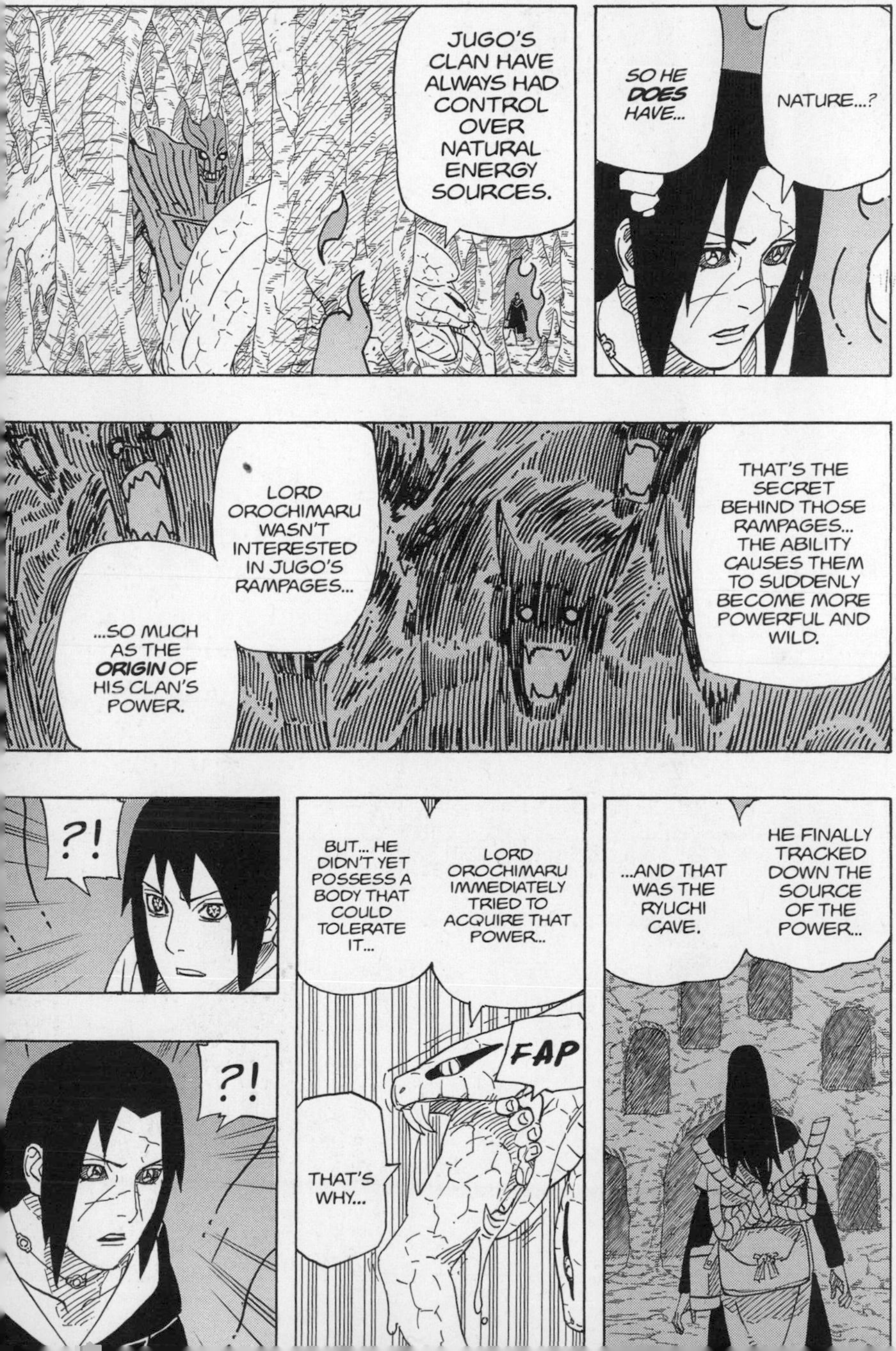

SO HE **DOES** HAVE...
NATURE...?
JUGO'S CLAN HAVE ALWAYS HAD CONTROL OVER NATURAL ENERGY SOURCES.
THAT'S THE SECRET BEHIND THOSE RAMPAGES... THE ABILITY CAUSES THEM TO SUDDENLY BECOME MORE POWERFUL AND WILD.
LORD OROCHIMARU WASN'T INTERESTED IN JUGO'S RAMPAGES...
...SO MUCH AS THE **ORIGIN** OF HIS CLAN'S POWER.
HE FINALLY TRACKED DOWN THE SOURCE OF THE POWER...
...AND THAT WAS THE RYUCHI CAVE.
LORD OROCHIMARU IMMEDIATELY TRIED TO ACQUIRE THAT POWER...
BUT... HE DIDN'T YET POSSESS A BODY THAT COULD TOLERATE IT...
FAP
THAT'S WHY...
?!
?!

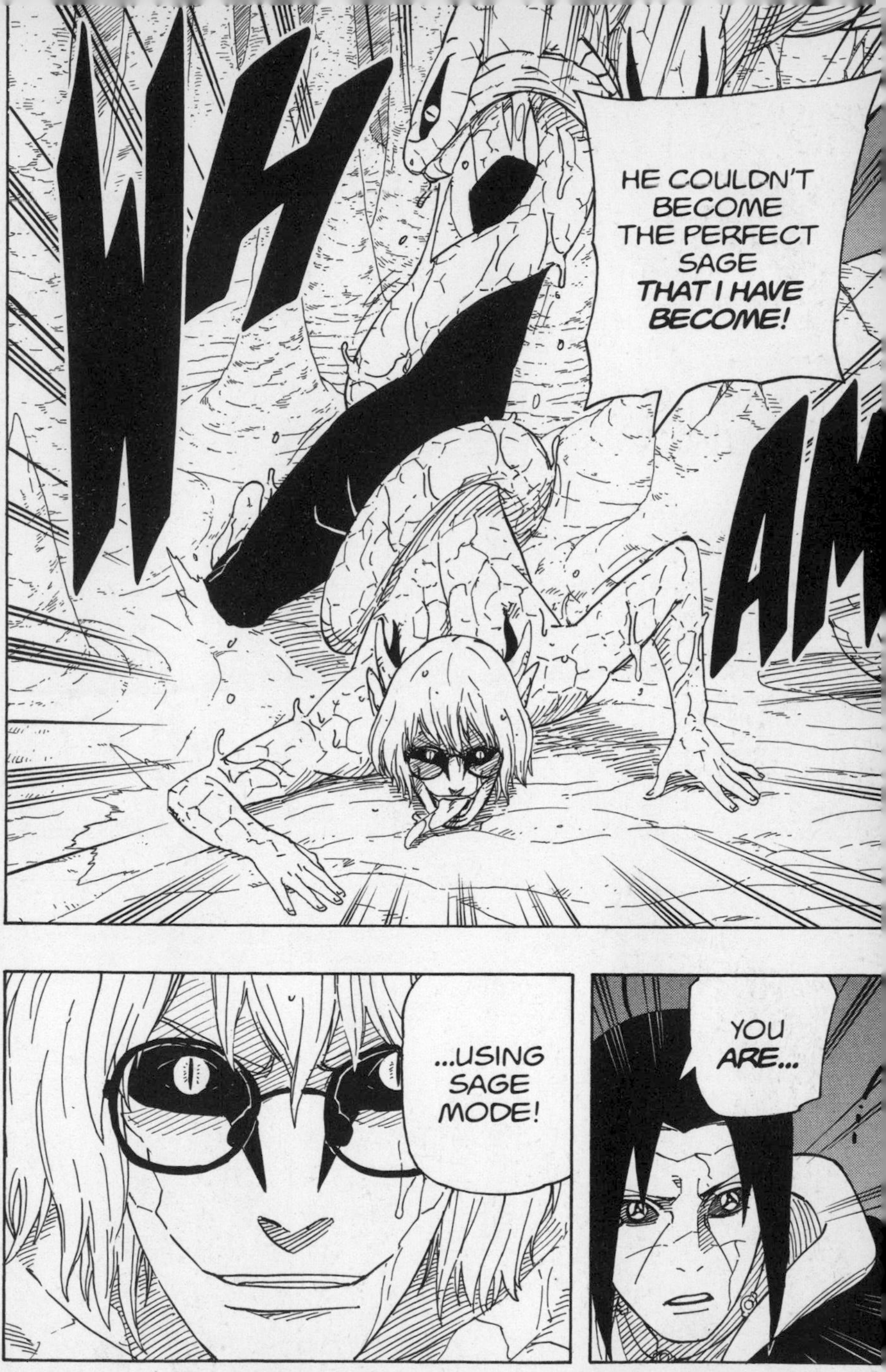
HE COULDN'T BECOME THE PERFECT SAGE THAT I HAVE BECOME!
WHAM
YOU ARE...
...USING SAGE MODE!

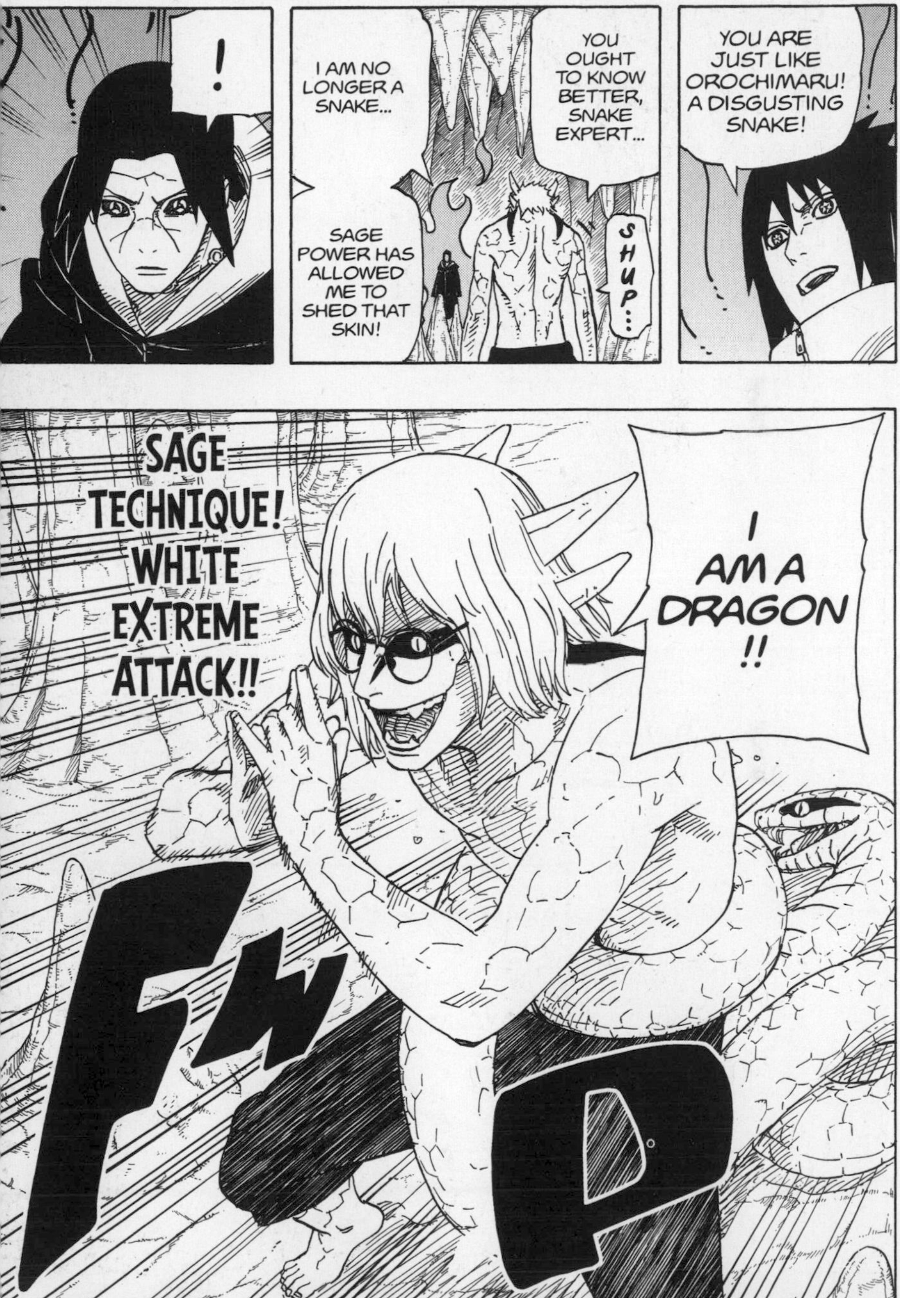
YOU ARE JUST LIKE OROCHIMARU! A DISGUSTING SNAKE!
YOU OUGHT TO KNOW BETTER, SNAKE EXPERT...
I AM NO LONGER A SNAKE...
SHUP...
SAGE POWER HAS ALLOWED ME TO SHED THAT SKIN!
!
I AM A DRAGON!!
SAGE TECHNIQUE! WHITE EXTREME ATTACK!!
FWP

FLLL
SLLLL

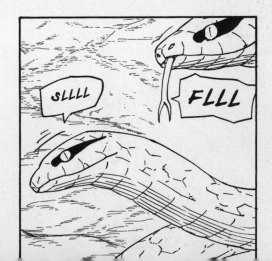

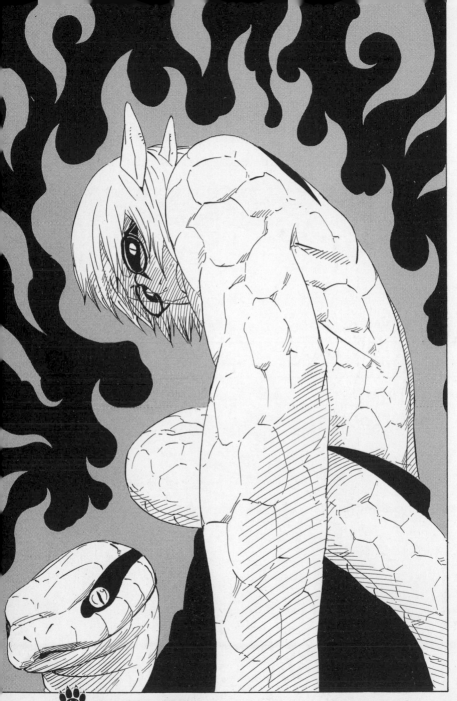

Number 580: Siblings

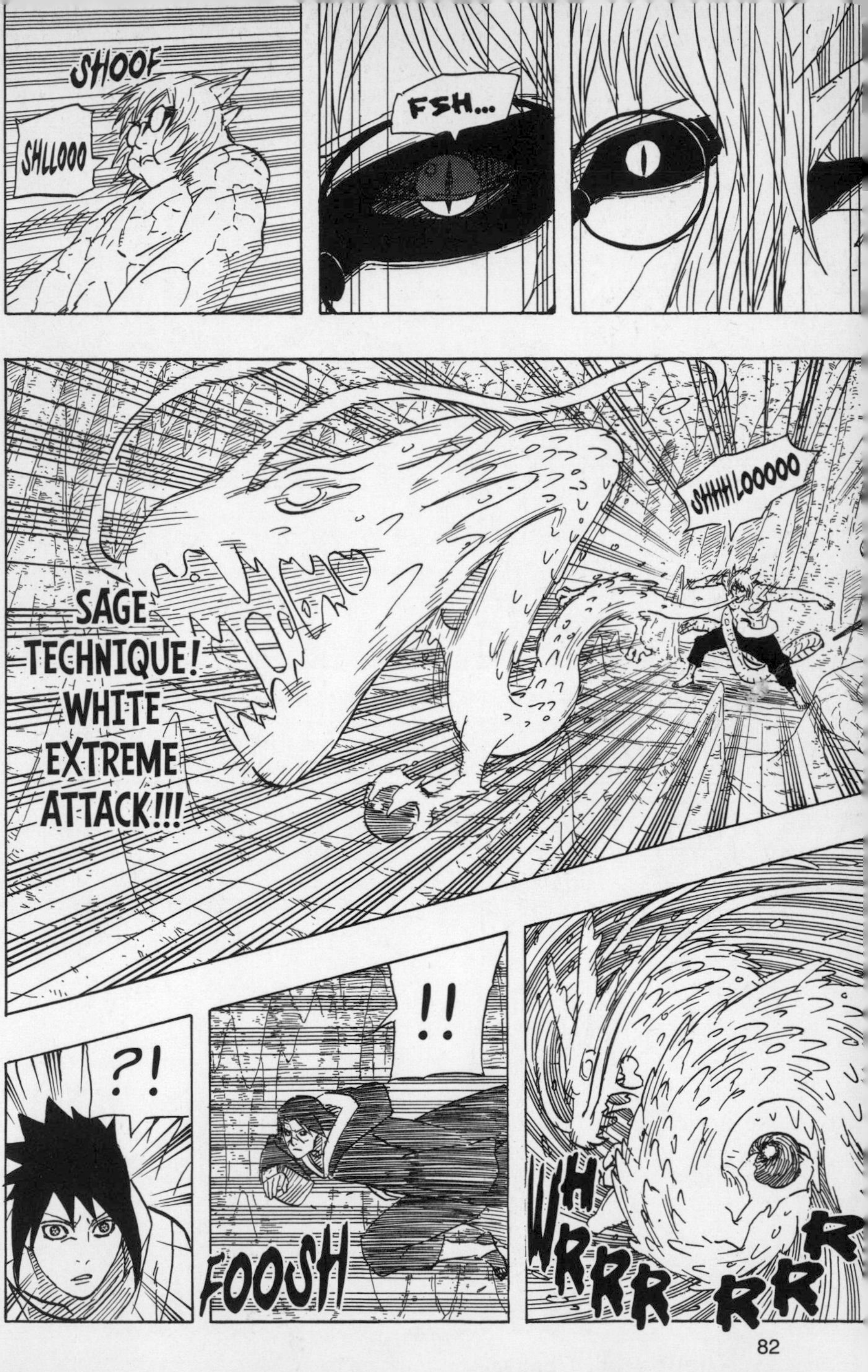
FSH...
SHOOF
SHLLOOO
SHHHLOOOOO
SAGE TECHNIQUE! WHITE EXTREME ATTACK!!!
WH
WRRRR RRRR
!!
FOOSH
?!

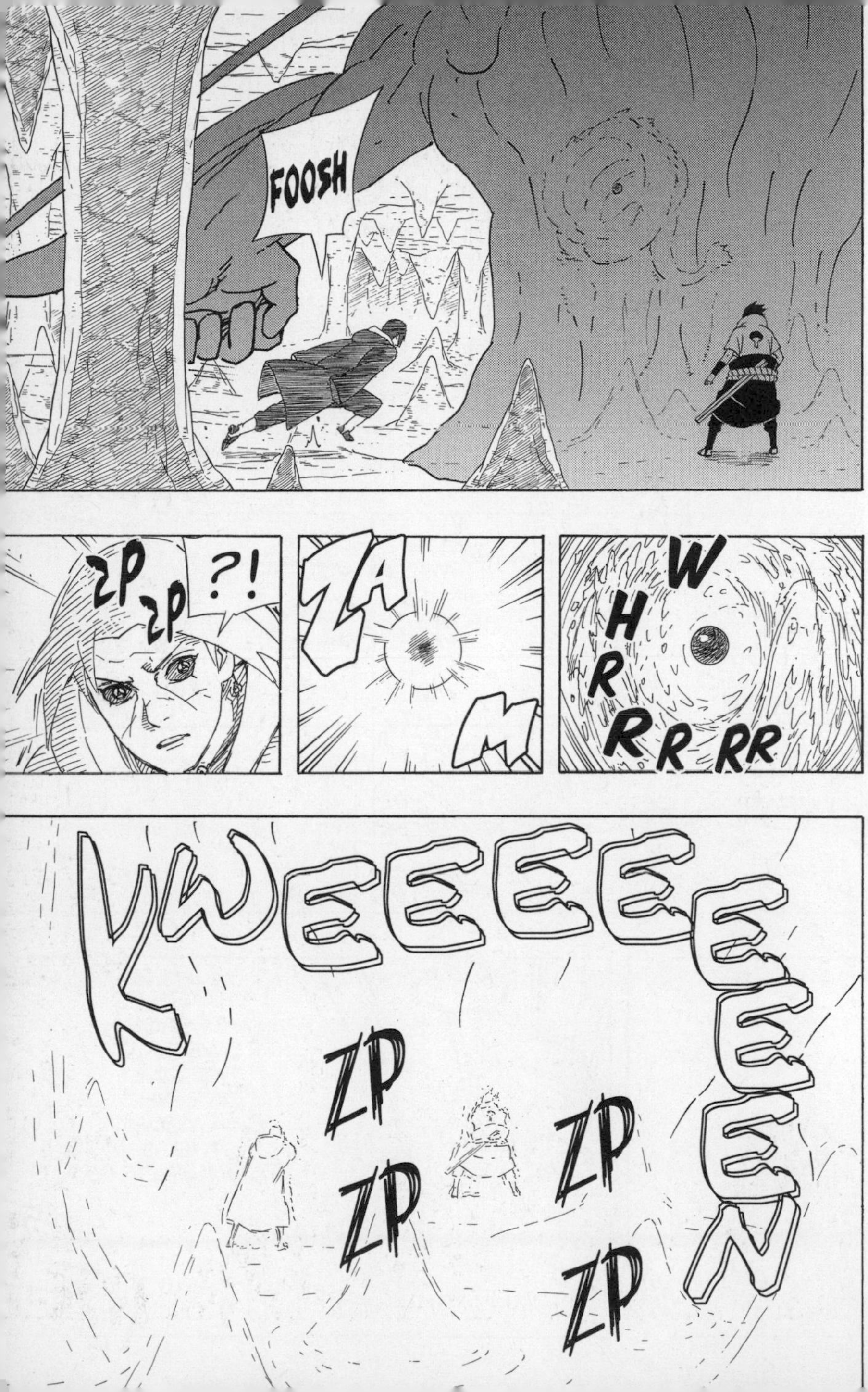
FOOSH
WHRRRRRRR
ZAM
?!
ZP ZP
KWEEEEEEEEEN
ZP ZP
ZP
ZP

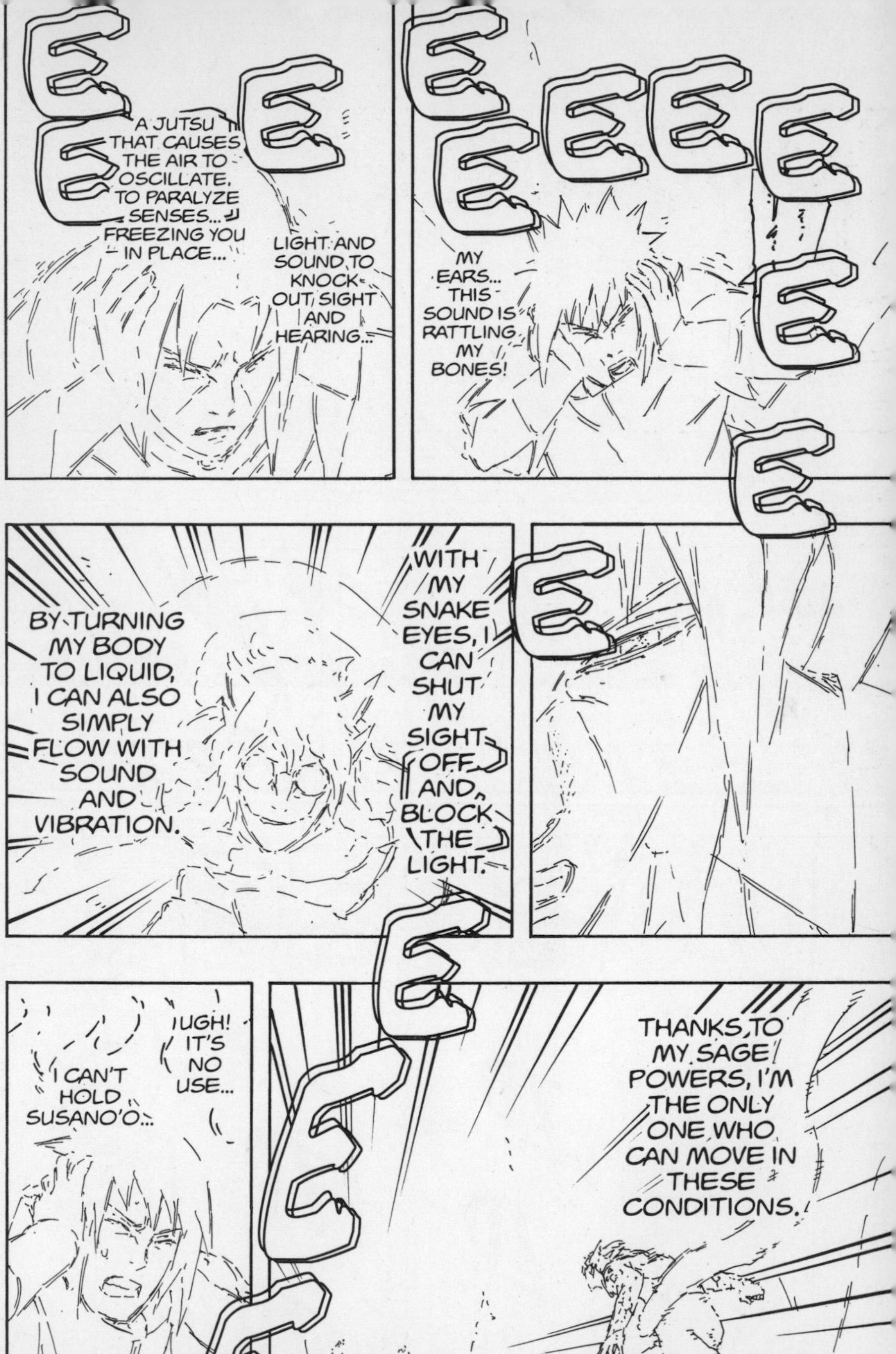
EEEEEE
MY EARS... THIS SOUND IS RATTLING MY BONES!
EEE
A JUTSU THAT CAUSES THE AIR TO OSCILLATE, TO PARALYZE SENSES... FREEZING YOU IN PLACE...
LIGHT AND SOUND TO KNOCK OUT SIGHT AND HEARING...
EE
WITH MY SNAKE EYES, I CAN SHUT MY SIGHT OFF AND BLOCK THE LIGHT.
BY TURNING MY BODY TO LIQUID, I CAN ALSO SIMPLY FLOW WITH SOUND AND VIBRATION.
EEE
THANKS TO MY SAGE POWERS, I'M THE ONLY ONE WHO CAN MOVE IN THESE CONDITIONS.
UGH! IT'S NO USE...
I CAN'T HOLD SUSANO'O...

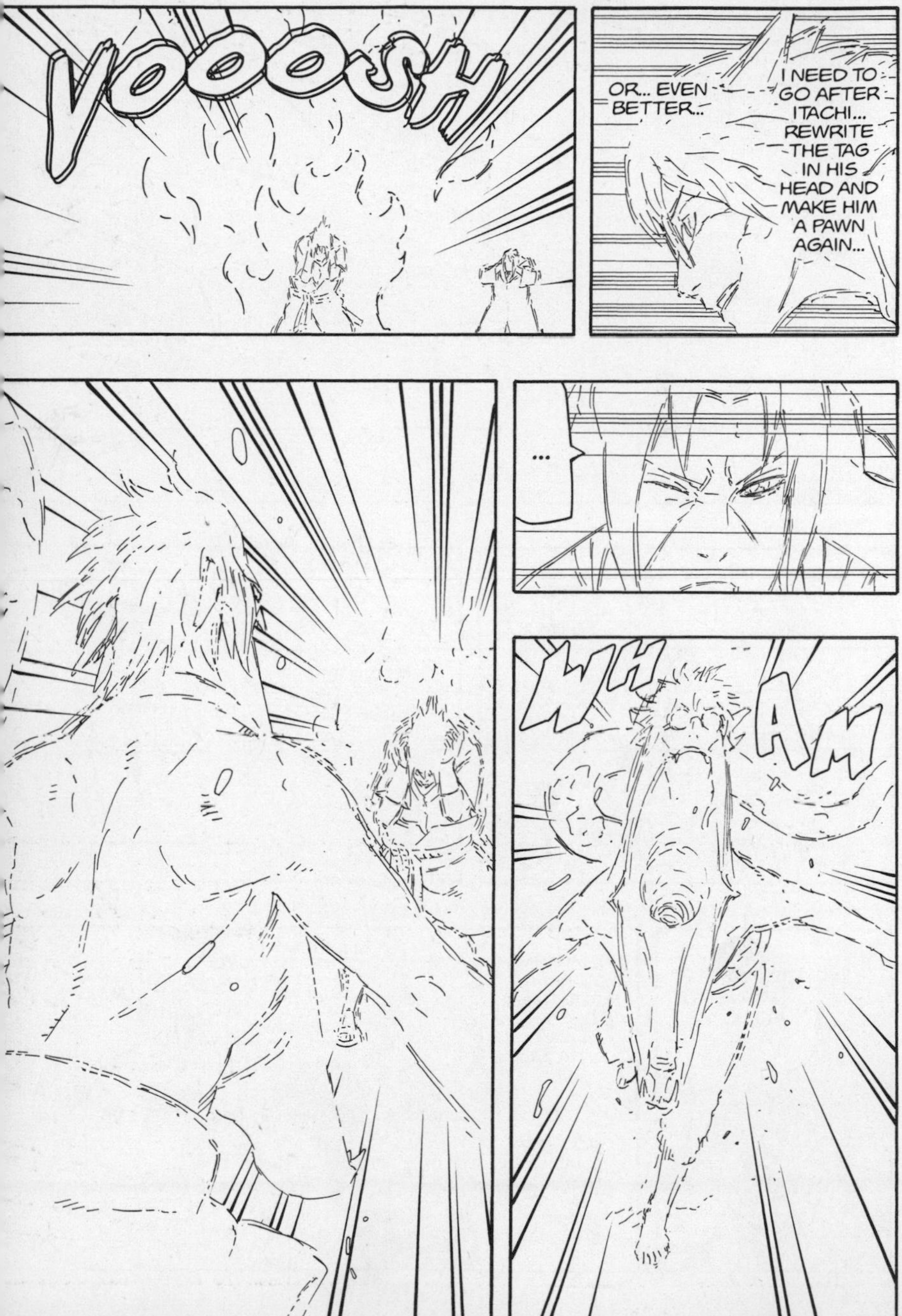
I NEED TO GO AFTER ITACHI... REWRITE THE TAG IN HIS HEAD AND MAKE HIM A PAWN AGAIN...
OR... EVEN BETTER...
VOOOSH
...
WHAM

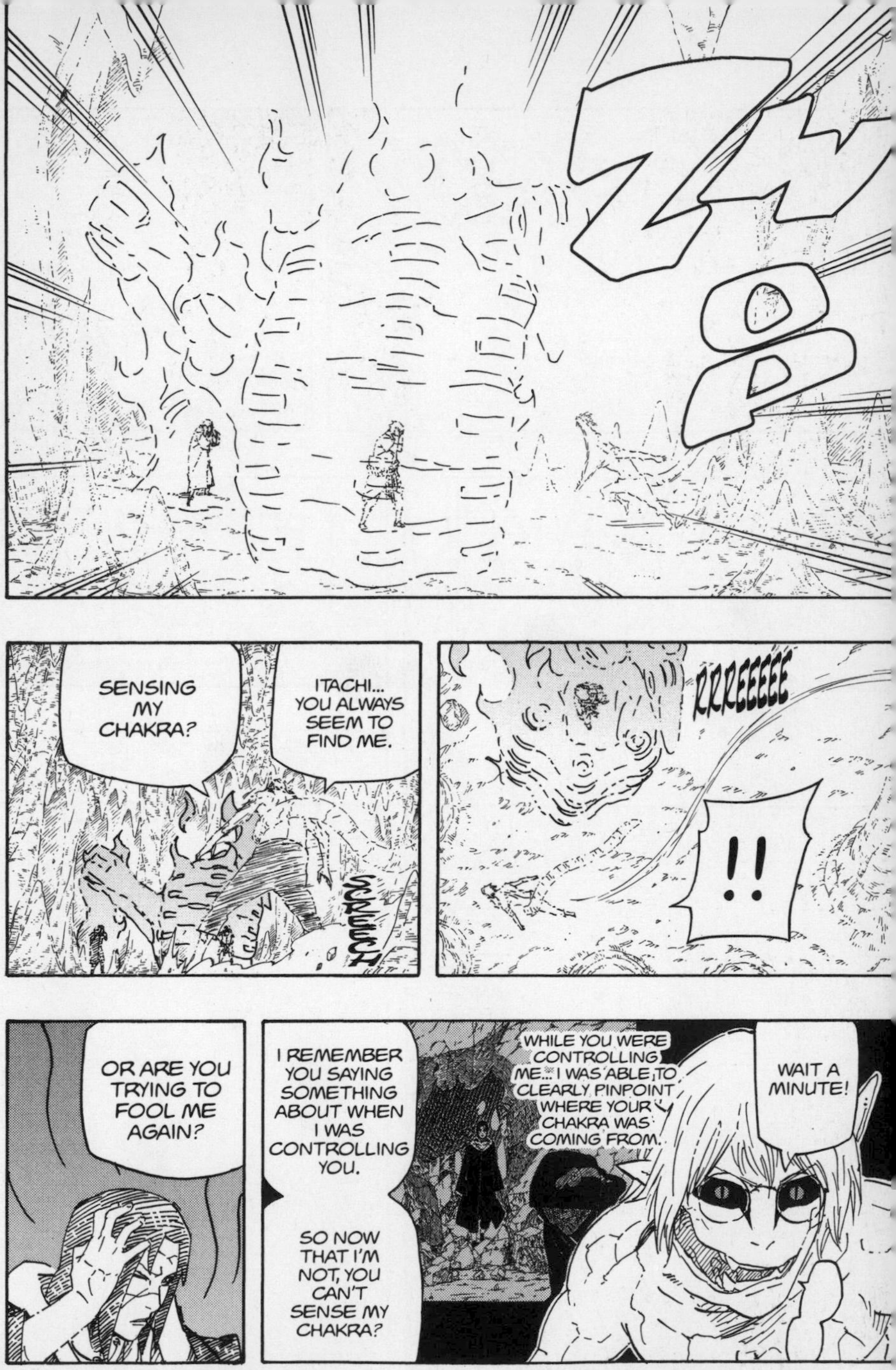
ZWOP
RRREEEEE
!!
ITACHI... YOU ALWAYS SEEM TO FIND ME.
SENSING MY CHAKRA?
SCREECH
WAIT A MINUTE!
WHILE YOU WERE CONTROLLING ME... I WAS ABLE TO CLEARLY PINPOINT WHERE YOUR CHAKRA WAS COMING FROM.
I REMEMBER YOU SAYING SOMETHING ABOUT WHEN I WAS CONTROLLING YOU.
SO NOW THAT I'M NOT, YOU CAN'T SENSE MY CHAKRA?
OR ARE YOU TRYING TO FOOL ME AGAIN?

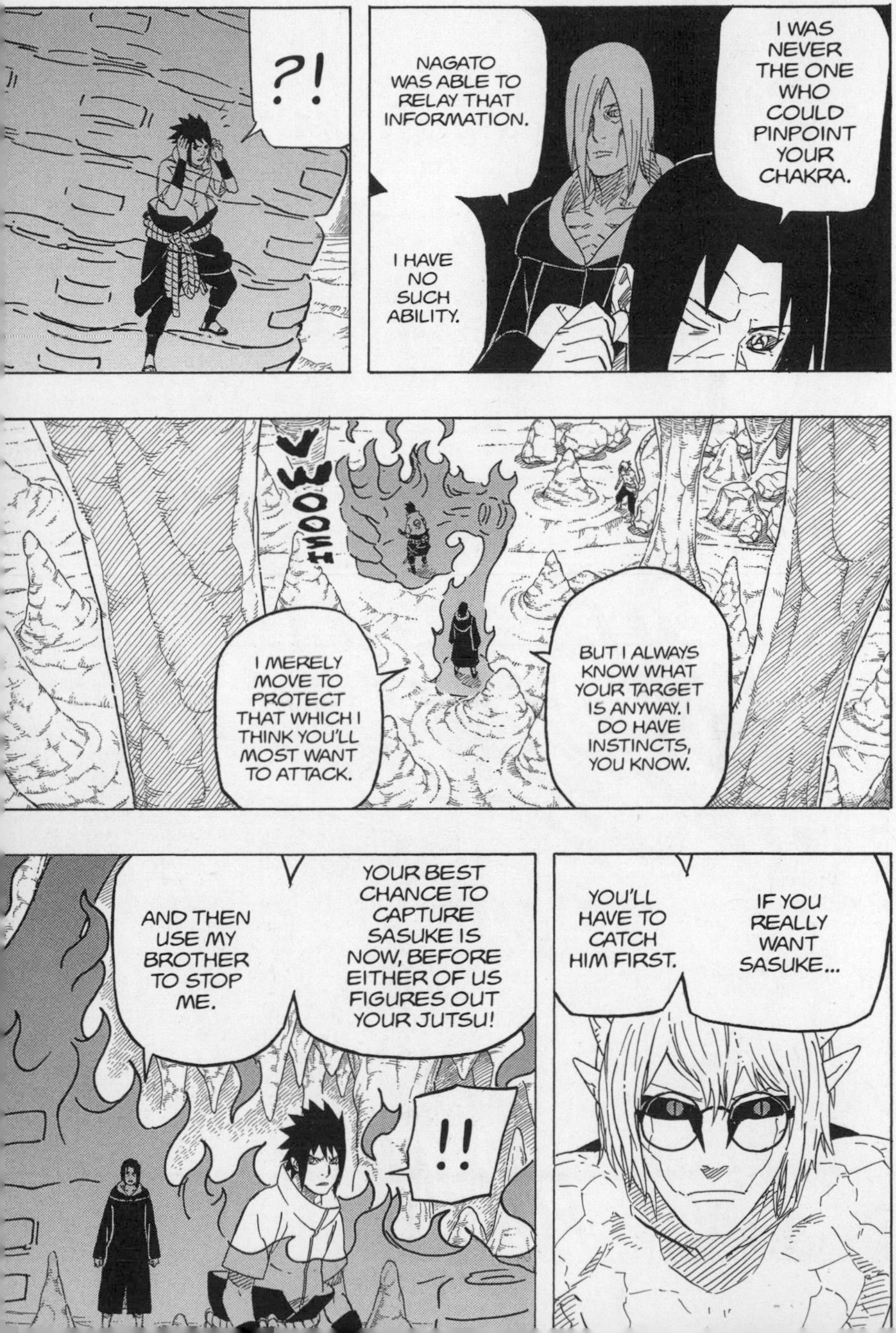
I WAS NEVER THE ONE WHO COULD PINPOINT YOUR CHAKRA.
NAGATO WAS ABLE TO RELAY THAT INFORMATION.
I HAVE NO SUCH ABILITY.
?!
VWOOSH
BUT I ALWAYS KNOW WHAT YOUR TARGET IS ANYWAY. I DO HAVE INSTINCTS, YOU KNOW.
I MERELY MOVE TO PROTECT THAT WHICH I THINK YOU'LL MOST WANT TO ATTACK.
IF YOU REALLY WANT SASUKE...
YOU'LL HAVE TO CATCH HIM FIRST.
YOUR BEST CHANCE TO CAPTURE SASUKE IS NOW, BEFORE EITHER OF US FIGURES OUT YOUR JUTSU!
AND THEN USE MY BROTHER TO STOP ME.
!!

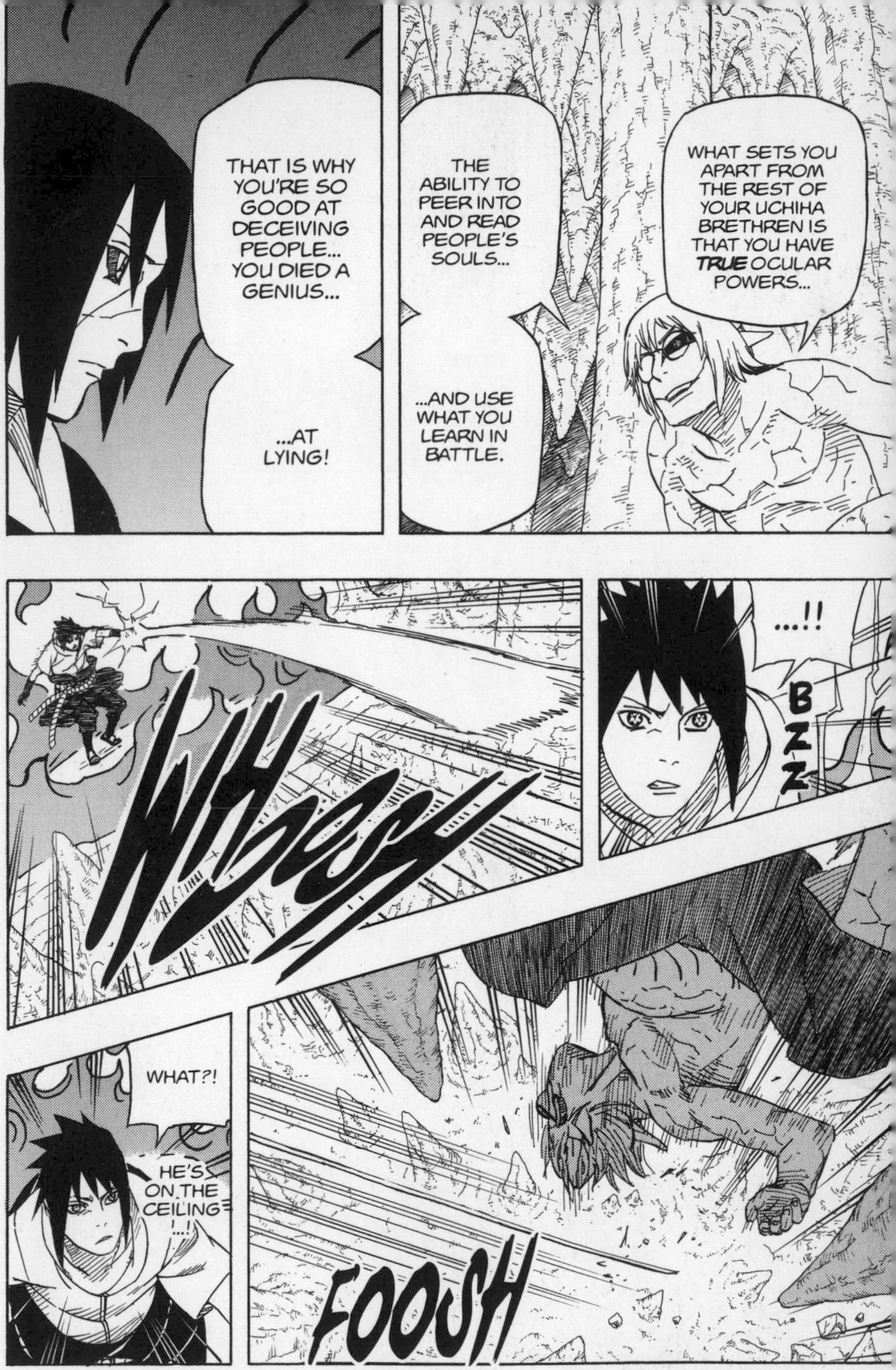

WHAT SETS YOU APART FROM THE REST OF YOUR UCHIHA BRETHREN IS THAT YOU HAVE ***TRUE*** OCULAR POWERS...
THE ABILITY TO PEER INTO AND READ PEOPLE'S SOULS...
...AND USE WHAT YOU LEARN IN BATTLE.
THAT IS WHY YOU'RE SO GOOD AT DECEIVING PEOPLE... YOU DIED A GENIUS...
...AT LYING!
...!!
BZZ
WHOOSH
FOOSH
WHAT?!
HE'S ON THE CEILING...!

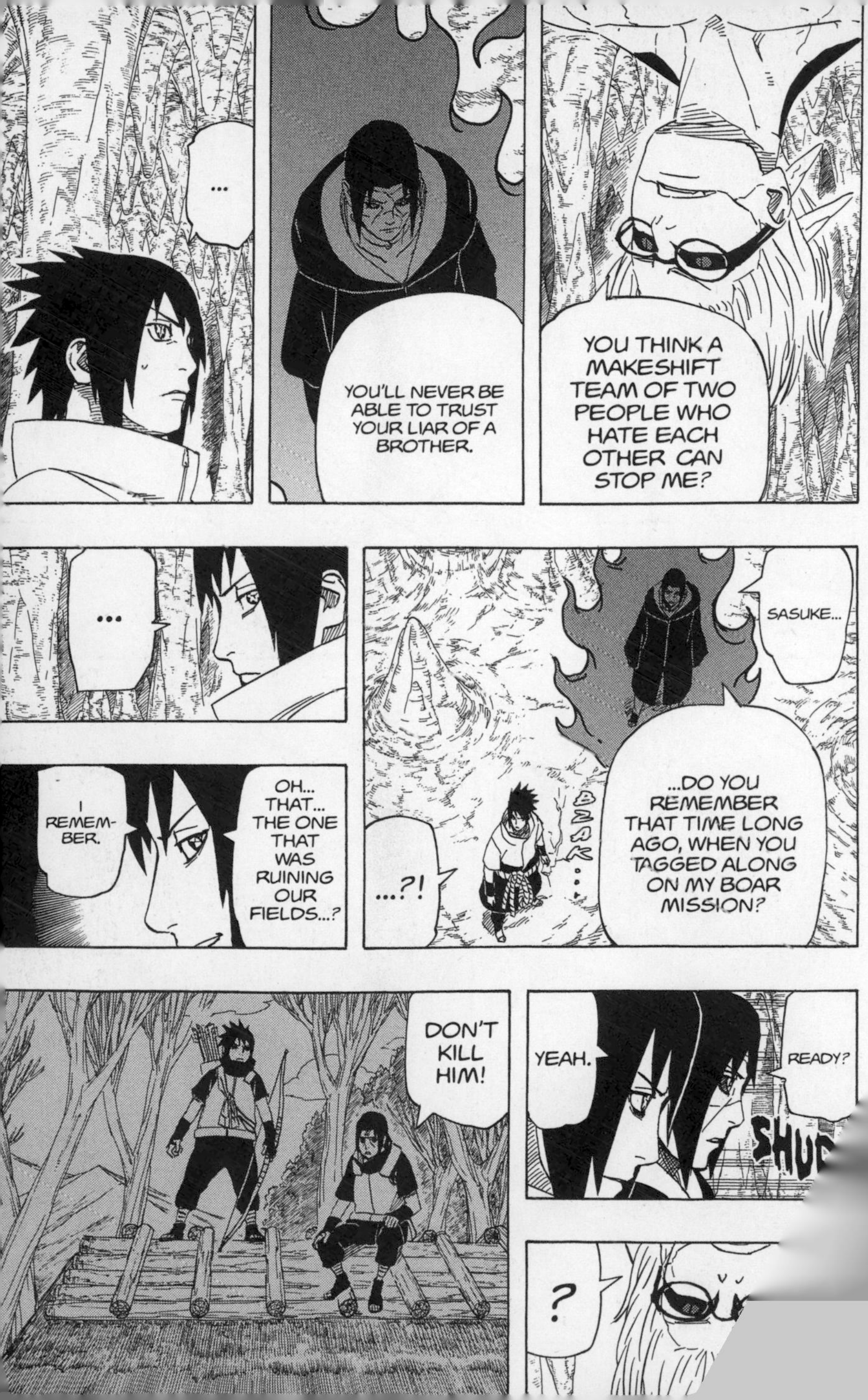
YOU THINK A MAKESHIFT TEAM OF TWO PEOPLE WHO HATE EACH OTHER CAN STOP ME?
YOU'LL NEVER BE ABLE TO TRUST YOUR LIAR OF A BROTHER.
...
SASUKE...
...DO YOU REMEMBER THAT TIME LONG AGO, WHEN YOU TAGGED ALONG ON MY BOAR MISSION?
BZAK...
...?!
...
OH... THAT... THE ONE THAT WAS RUINING OUR FIELDS...?
I REMEMBER.
READY?
YEAH.
SHU
?
DON'T KILL HIM!

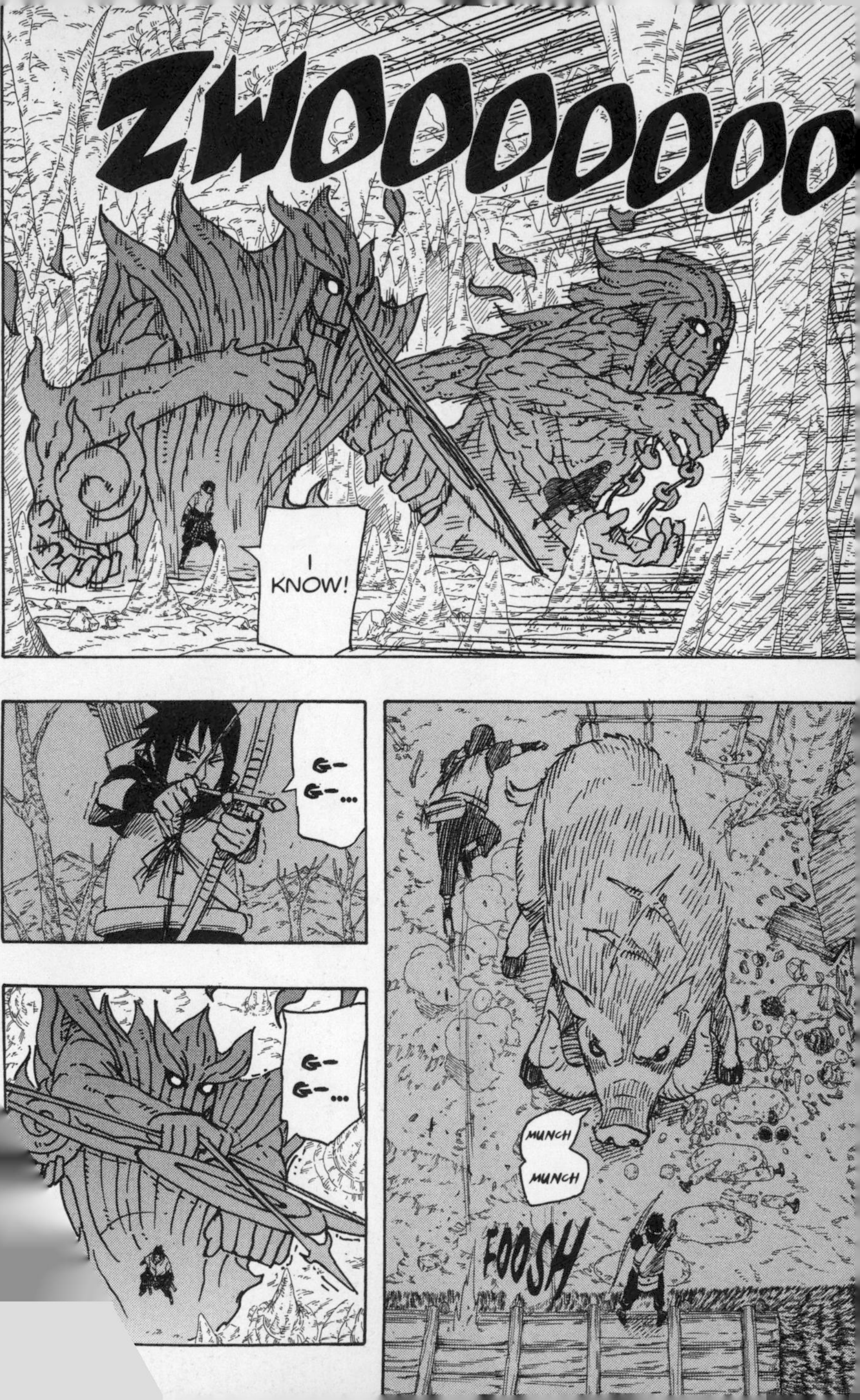
ZWOOOOOOOO
I KNOW!
MUNCH
MUNCH
FOOSH
G-
G-...
G-
G-...

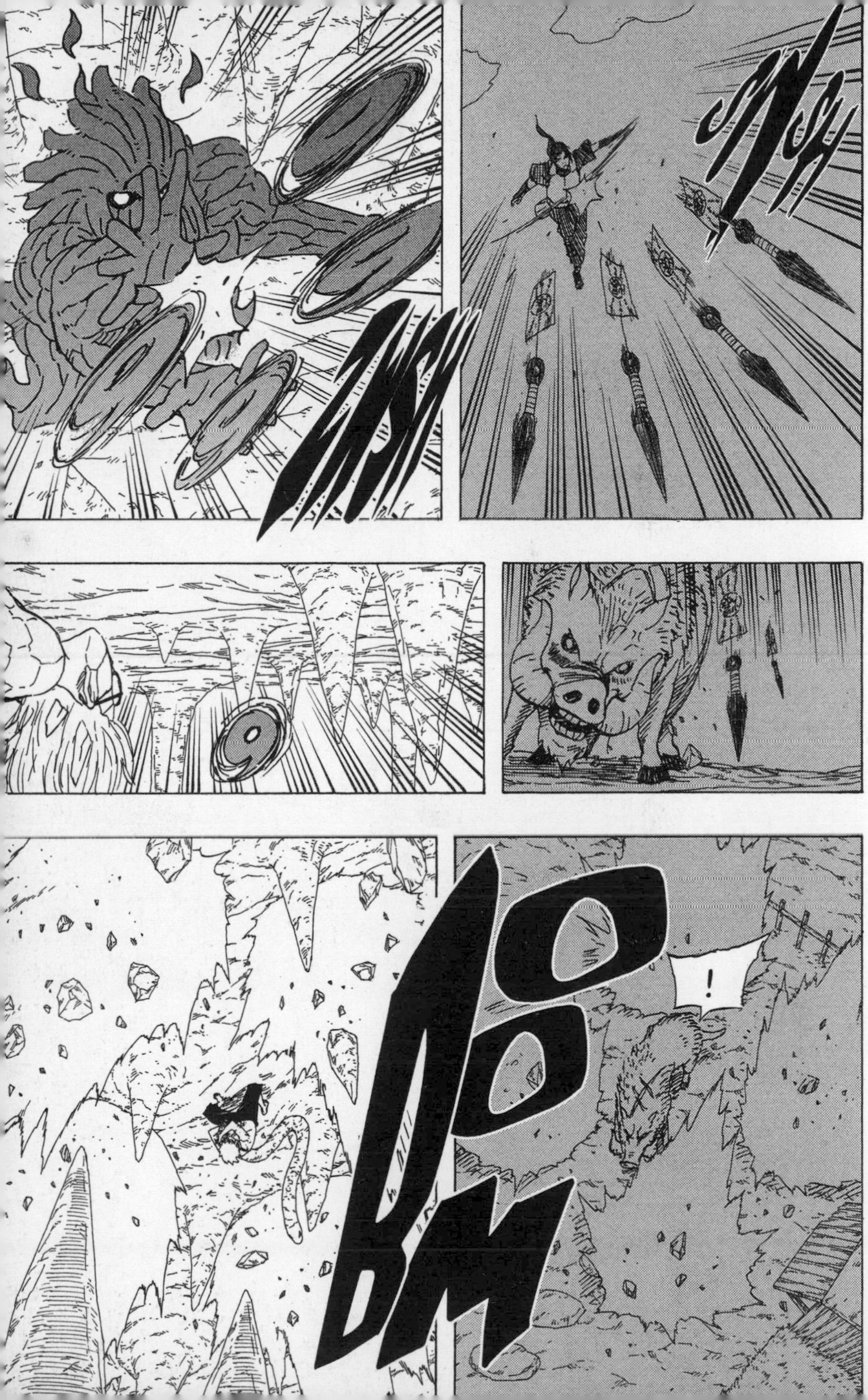
!

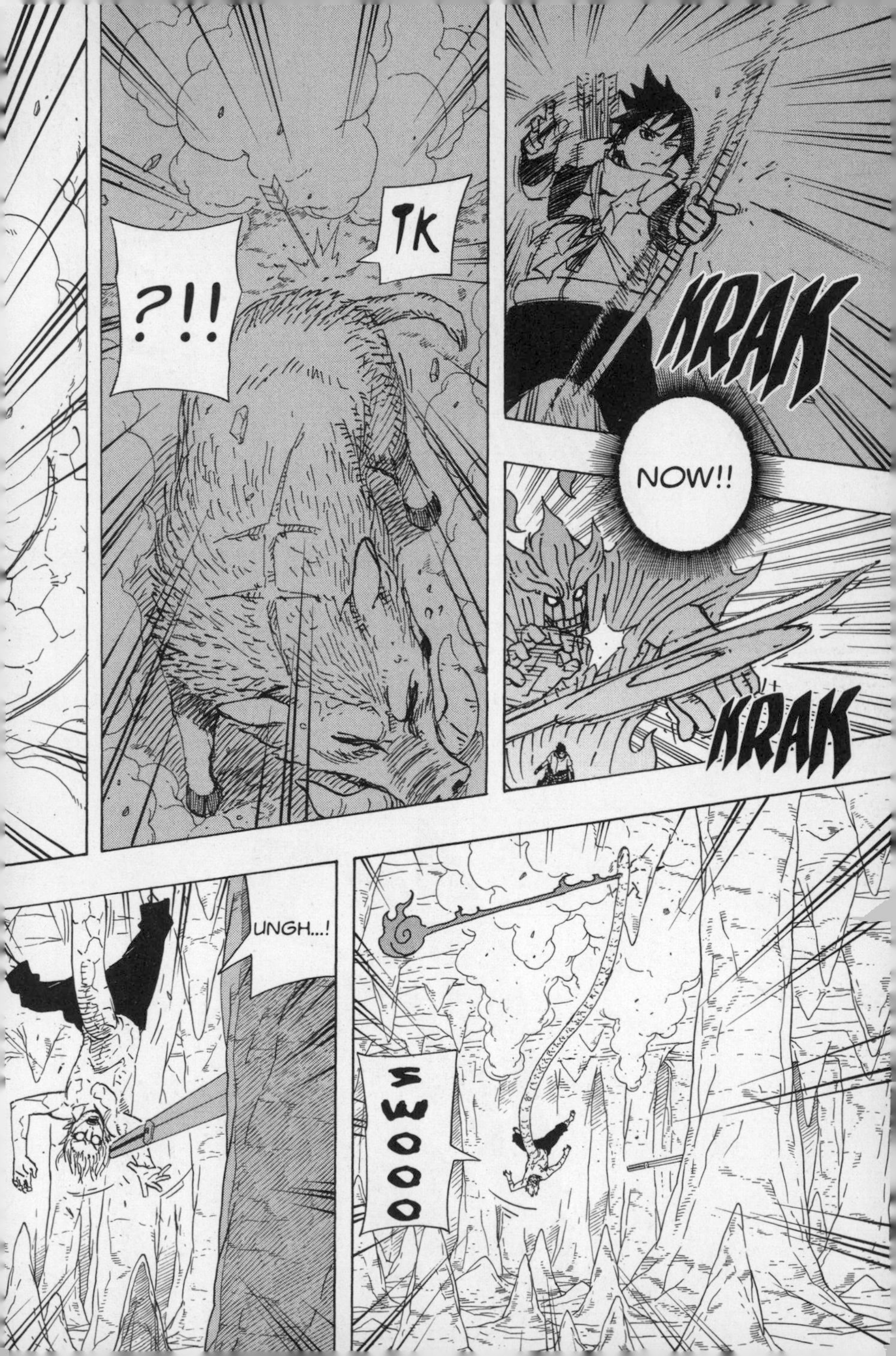
KRAK
NOW!!
KRAK
TK
?!!
SWOOO
UNGH...!

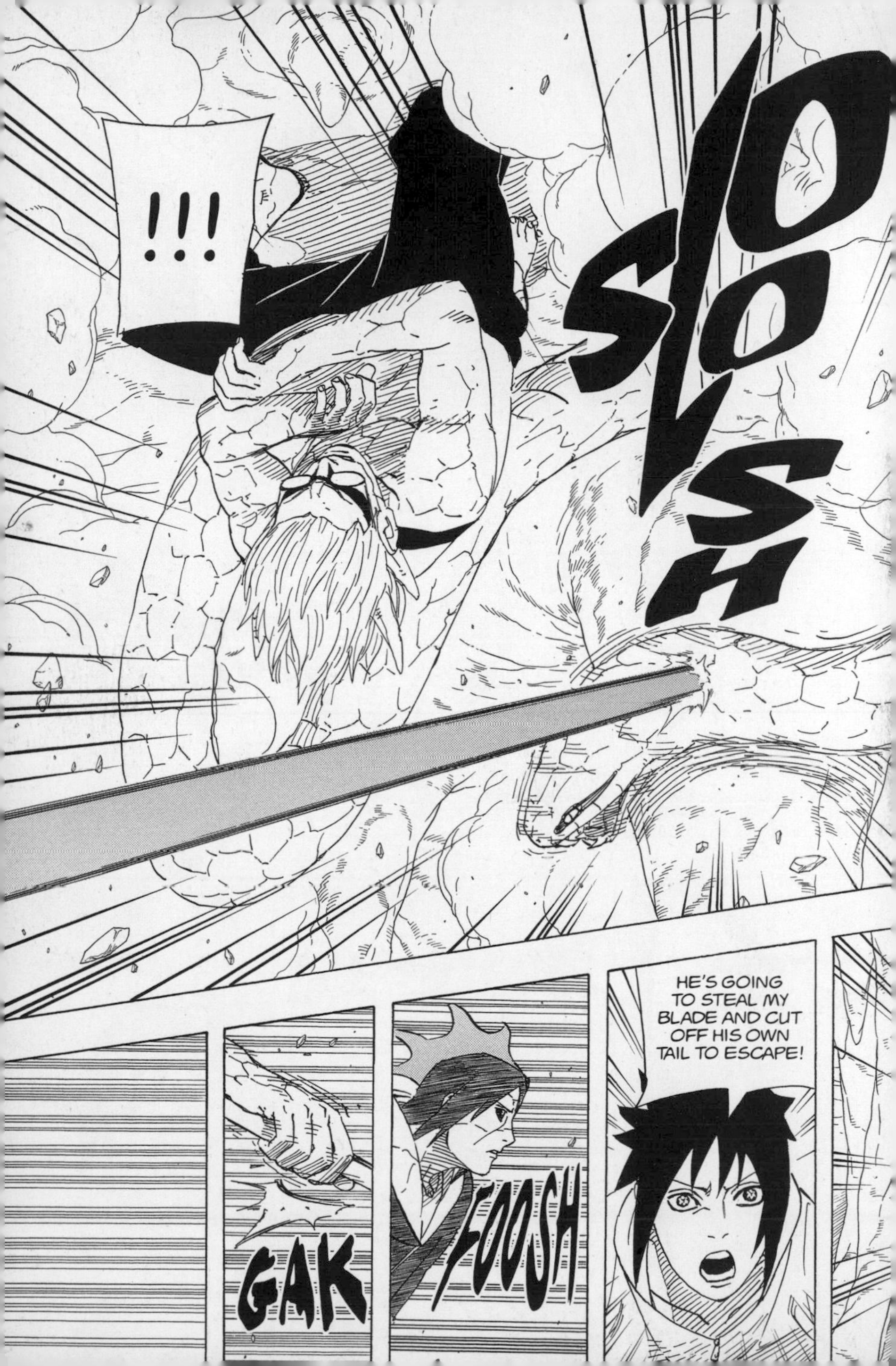
SLOOSH
!!!
HE'S GOING TO STEAL MY BLADE AND CUT OFF HIS OWN TAIL TO ESCAPE!
FOOSH
GAK

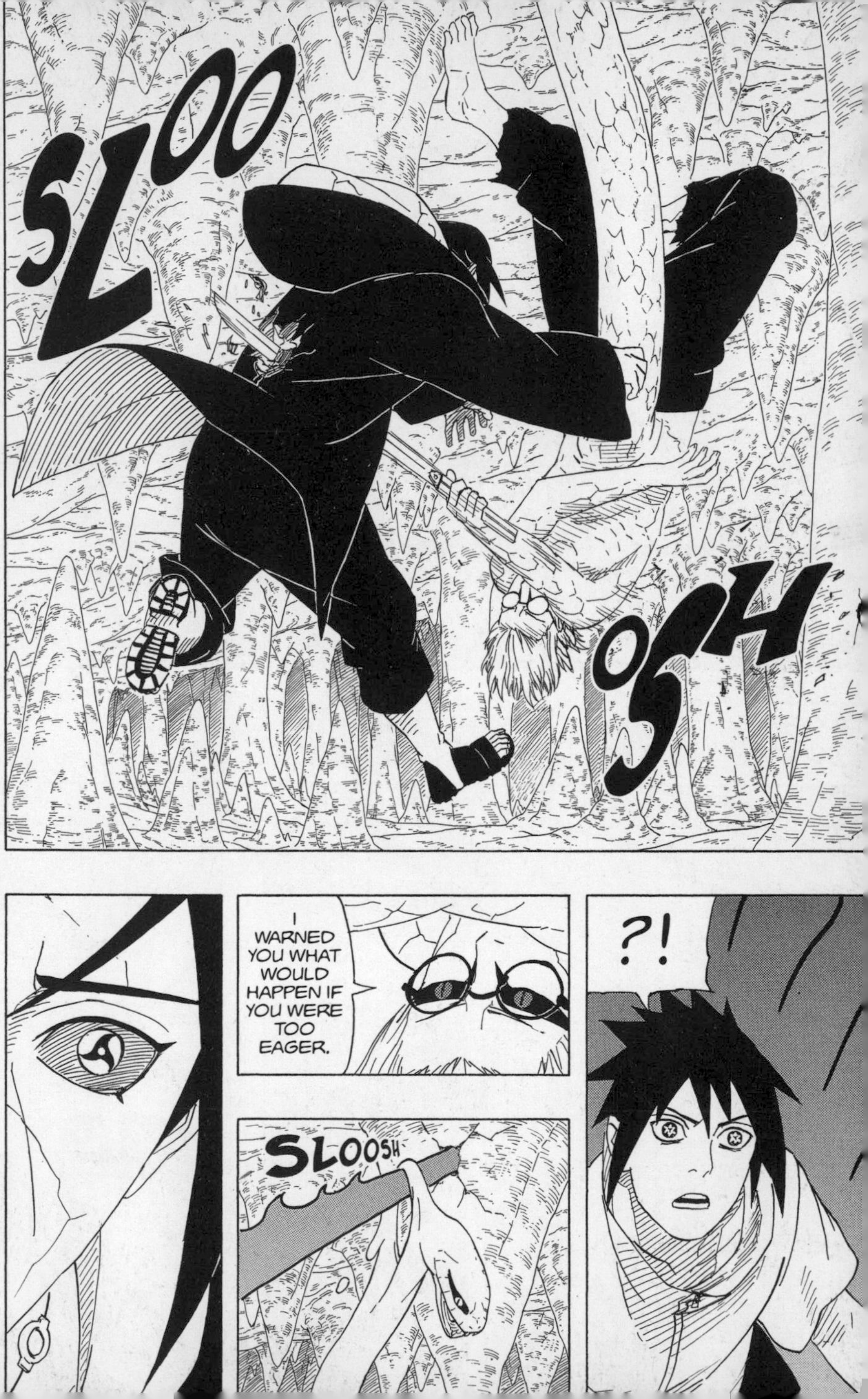
SLOO
OSH
?!
I WARNED YOU WHAT WOULD HAPPEN IF YOU WERE TOO EAGER.
SLOOSH

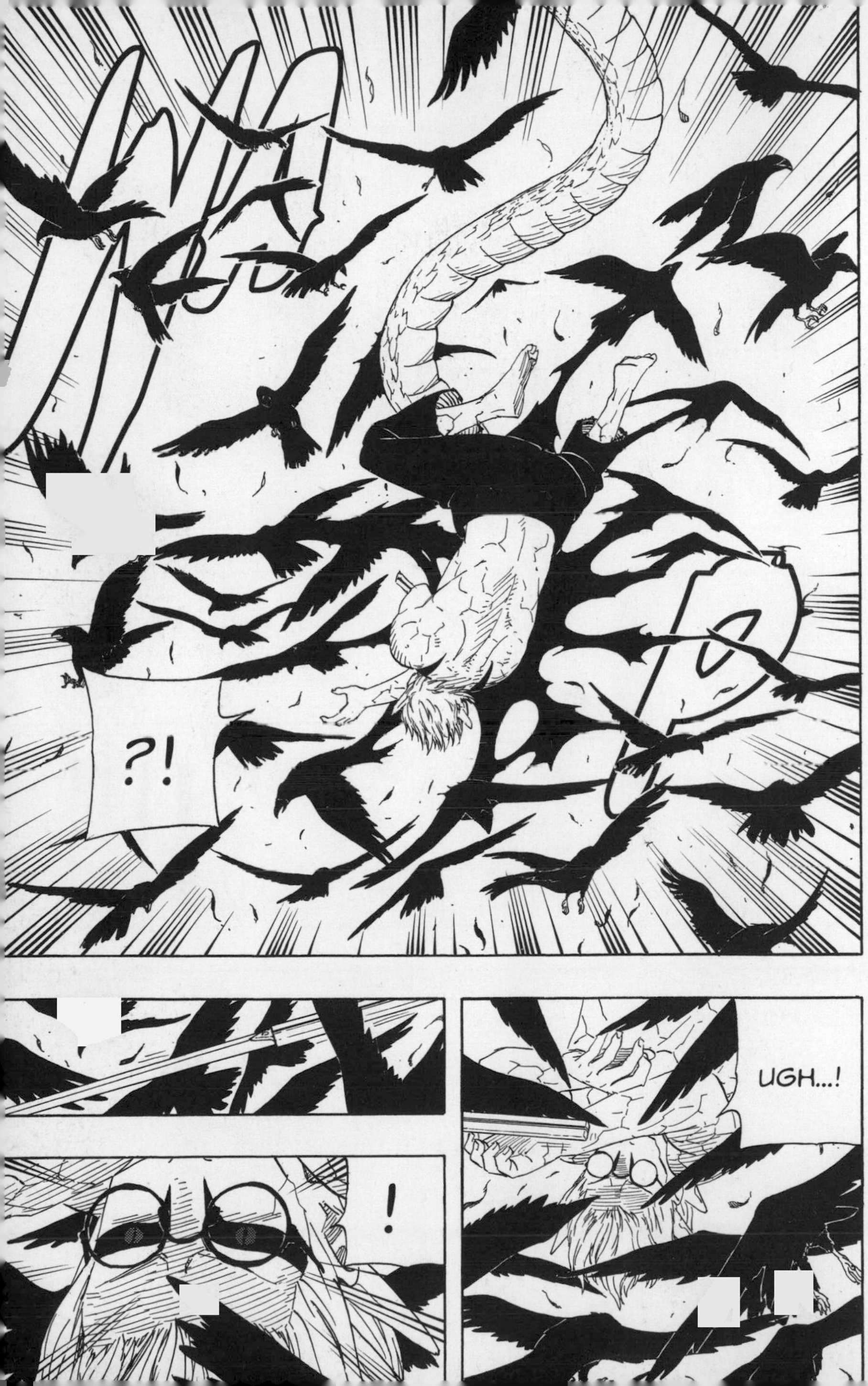
?!
UGH...!
!

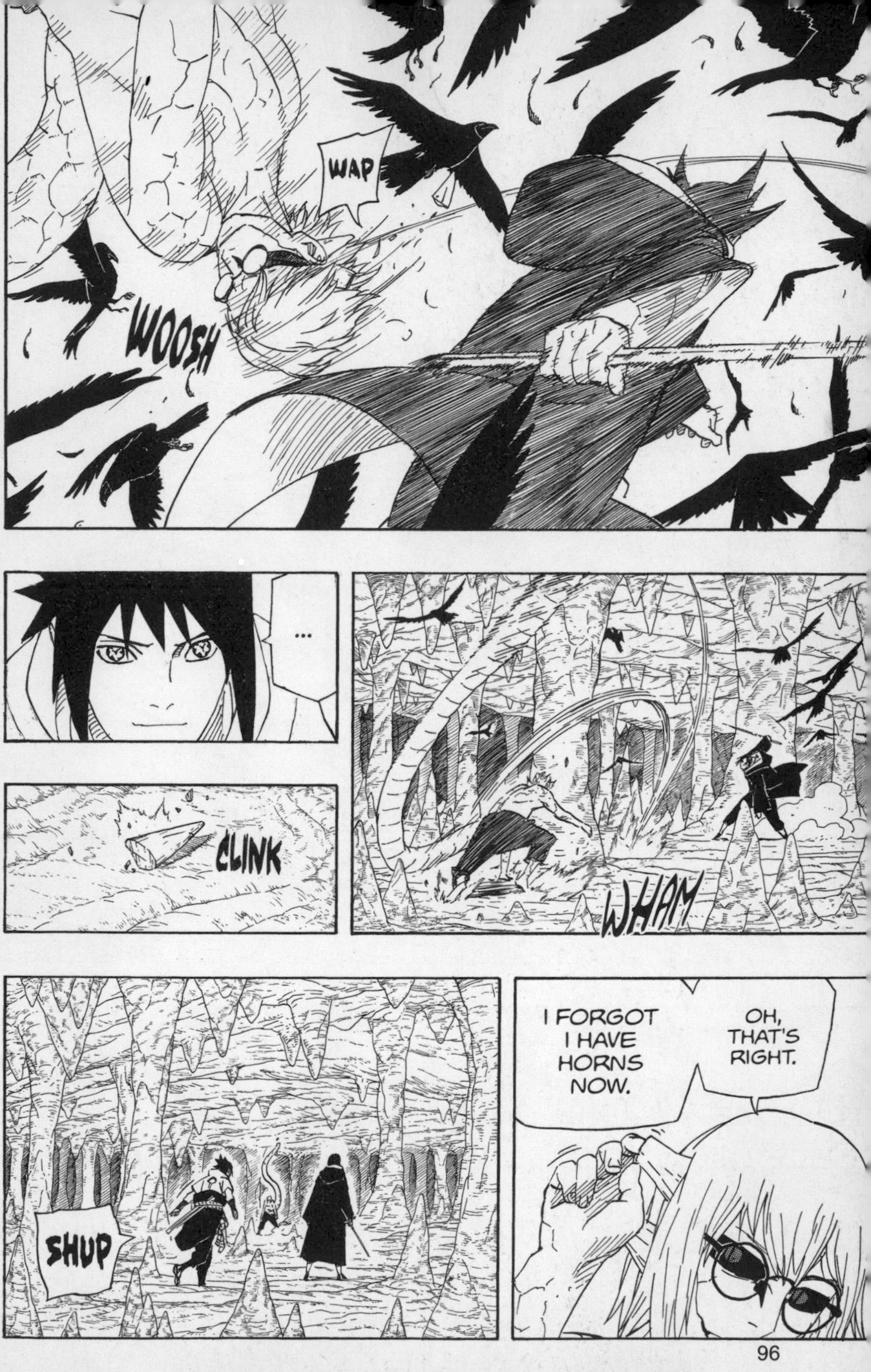
WAP
WOOSH
WHAM
...
CLINK
OH, THAT'S RIGHT.
I FORGOT I HAVE HORNS NOW.
SHUP

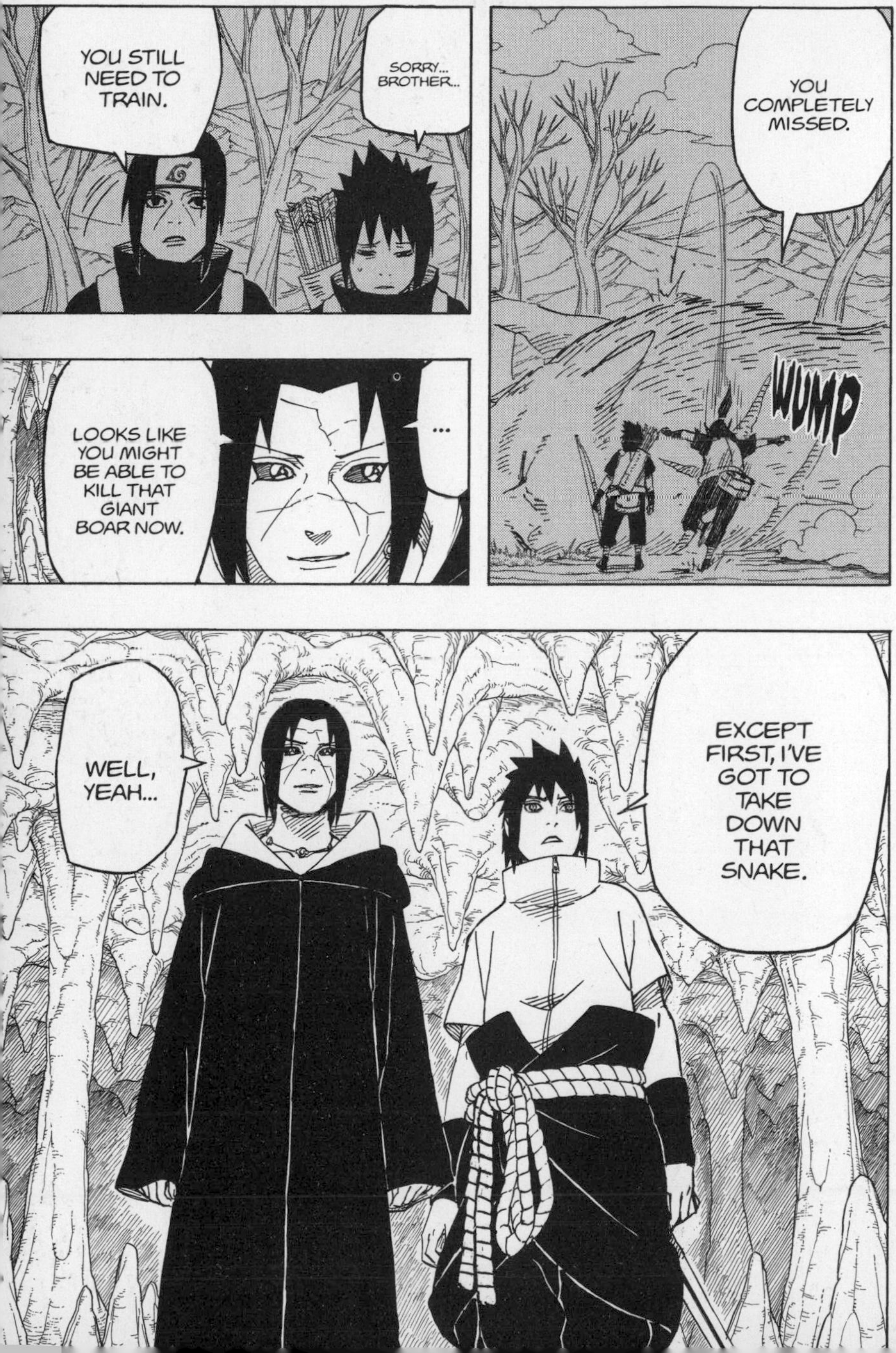
YOU COMPLETELY MISSED.
WUMP
SORRY... BROTHER...
YOU STILL NEED TO TRAIN.
...
LOOKS LIKE YOU MIGHT BE ABLE TO KILL THAT GIANT BOAR NOW.
EXCEPT FIRST, I'VE GOT TO TAKE DOWN THAT SNAKE.
WELL, YEAH...

CLINK

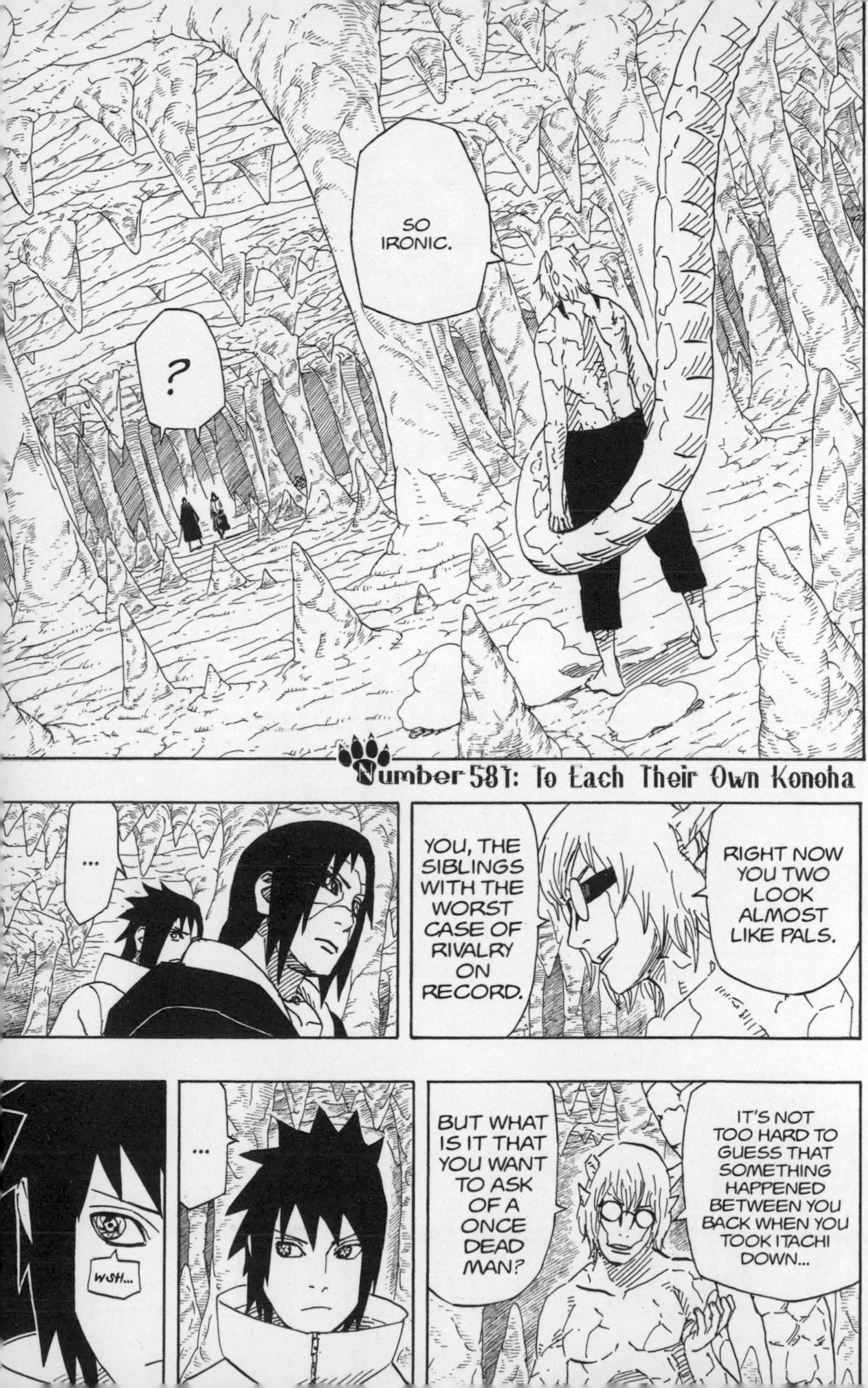
SO IRONIC.
?
Number 581: To Each Their Own Konoha
RIGHT NOW YOU TWO LOOK ALMOST LIKE PALS.
YOU, THE SIBLINGS WITH THE WORST CASE OF RIVALRY ON RECORD.
...
IT'S NOT TOO HARD TO GUESS THAT SOMETHING HAPPENED BETWEEN YOU BACK WHEN YOU TOOK ITACHI DOWN...
BUT WHAT IS IT THAT YOU WANT TO ASK OF A ONCE DEAD MAN?
...
WSH...

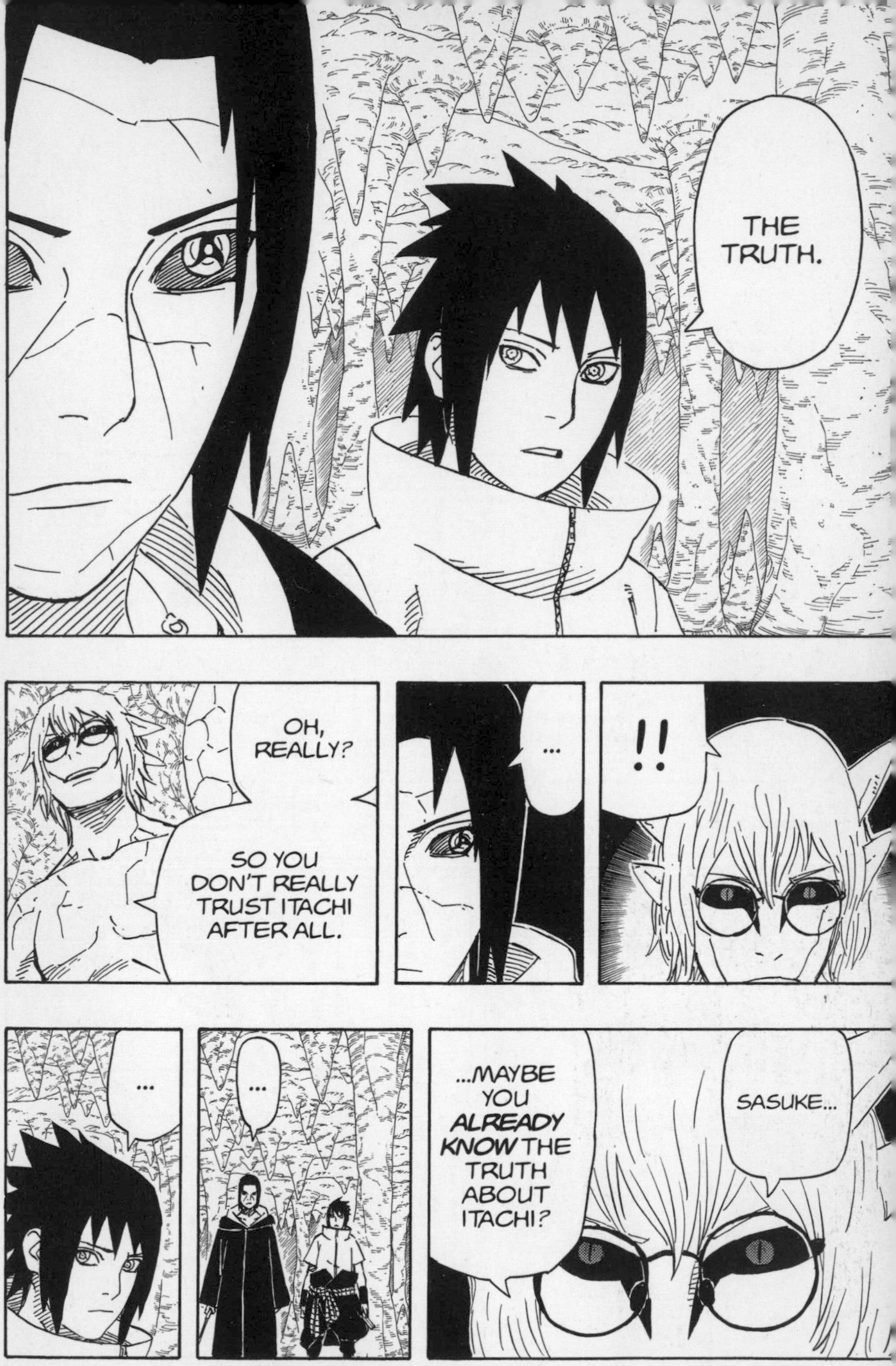
THE TRUTH.
!!
...
OH, REALLY?
SO YOU DON'T REALLY TRUST ITACHI AFTER ALL.
SASUKE...
...MAYBE YOU *ALREADY KNOW* THE TRUTH ABOUT ITACHI?
...
...

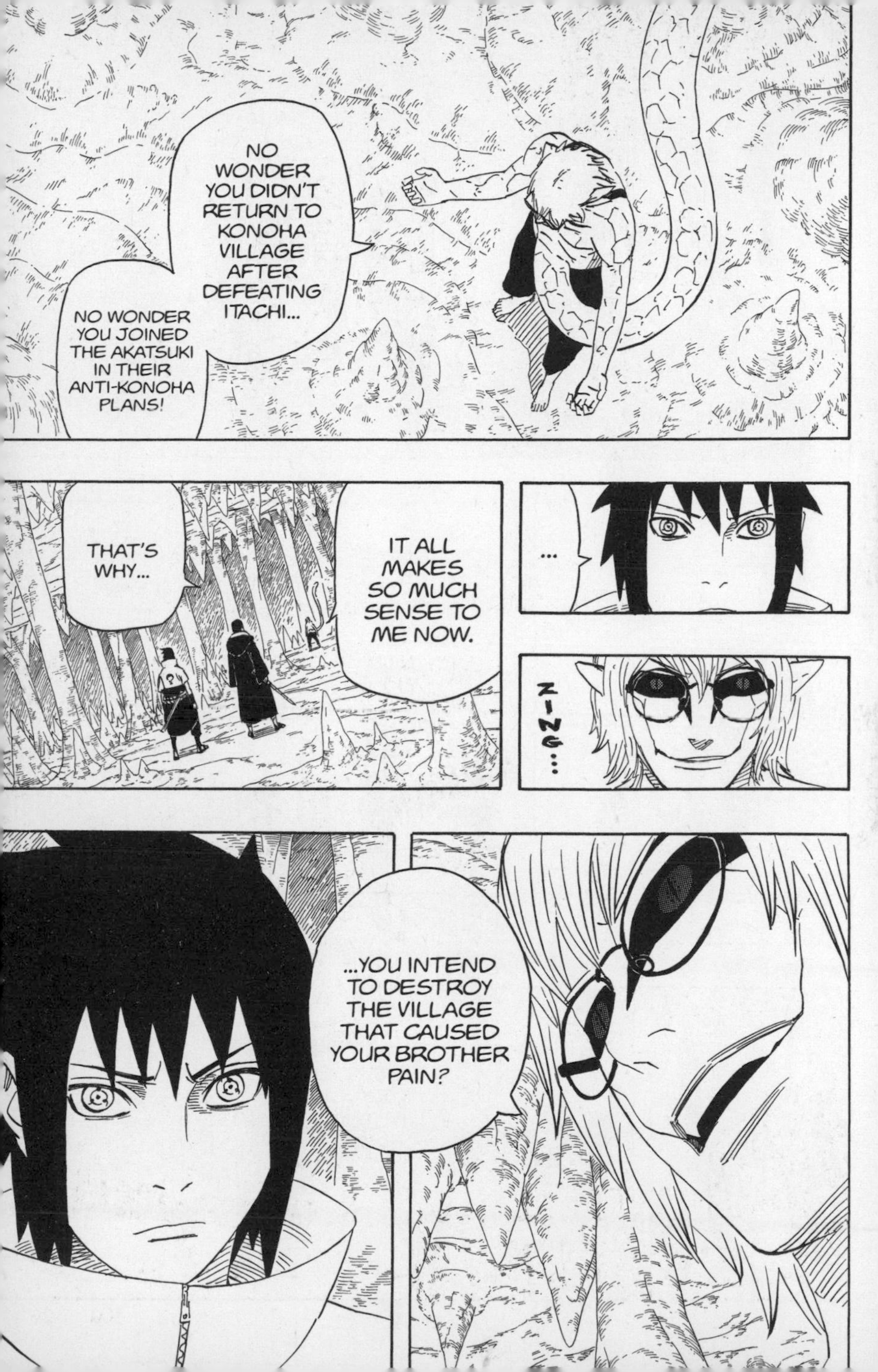
NO WONDER YOU DIDN'T RETURN TO KONOHA VILLAGE AFTER DEFEATING ITACHI...
NO WONDER YOU JOINED THE AKATSUKI IN THEIR ANTI-KONOHA PLANS!
...
ZING...
IT ALL MAKES SO MUCH SENSE TO ME NOW.
THAT'S WHY...
...YOU INTEND TO DESTROY THE VILLAGE THAT CAUSED YOUR BROTHER PAIN?

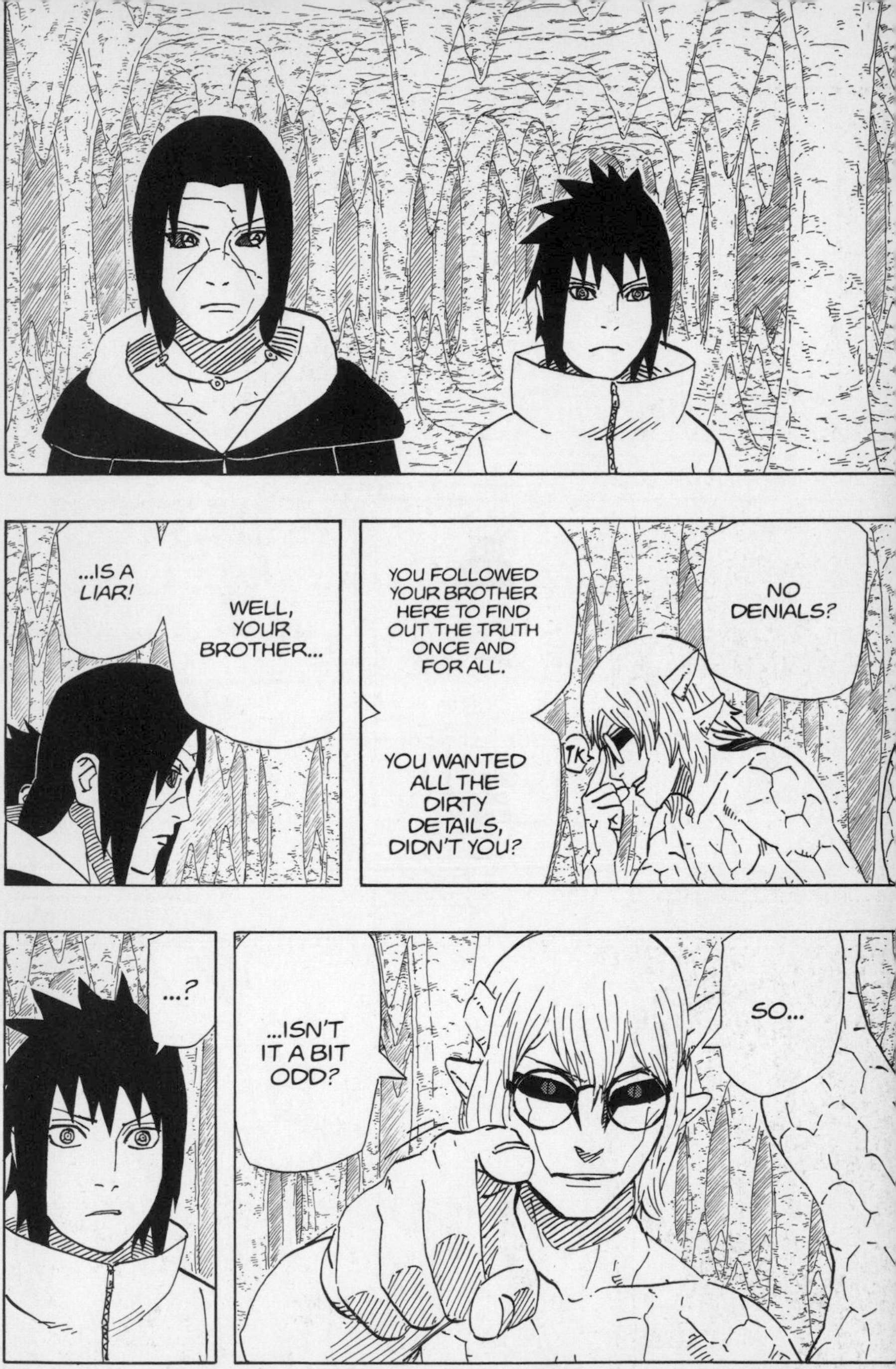
NO DENIALS?
YOU FOLLOWED YOUR BROTHER HERE TO FIND OUT THE TRUTH ONCE AND FOR ALL.
TK
YOU WANTED ALL THE DIRTY DETAILS, DIDN'T YOU?
WELL, YOUR BROTHER...
...IS A LIAR!
SO...
...ISN'T IT A BIT ODD?
...?

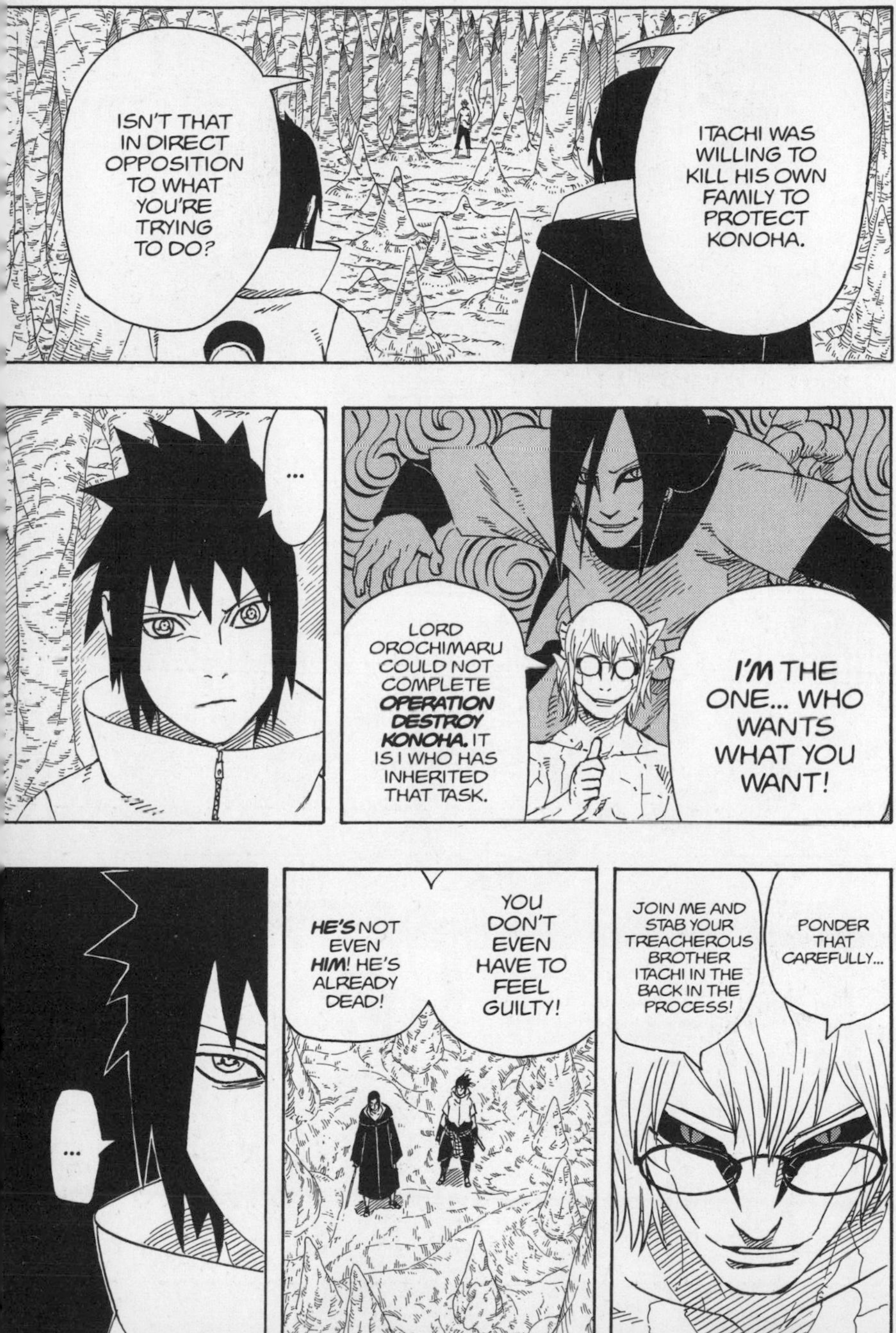
ITACHI WAS WILLING TO KILL HIS OWN FAMILY TO PROTECT KONOHA.
ISN'T THAT IN DIRECT OPPOSITION TO WHAT YOU'RE TRYING TO DO?
I'M THE ONE... WHO WANTS WHAT YOU WANT!
LORD OROCHIMARU COULD NOT COMPLETE OPERATION DESTROY KONOHA. IT IS I WHO HAS INHERITED THAT TASK.
...
PONDER THAT CAREFULLY...
JOIN ME AND STAB YOUR TREACHEROUS BROTHER ITACHI IN THE BACK IN THE PROCESS!
YOU DON'T EVEN HAVE TO FEEL GUILTY!
HE'S NOT EVEN HIM! HE'S ALREADY DEAD!
...

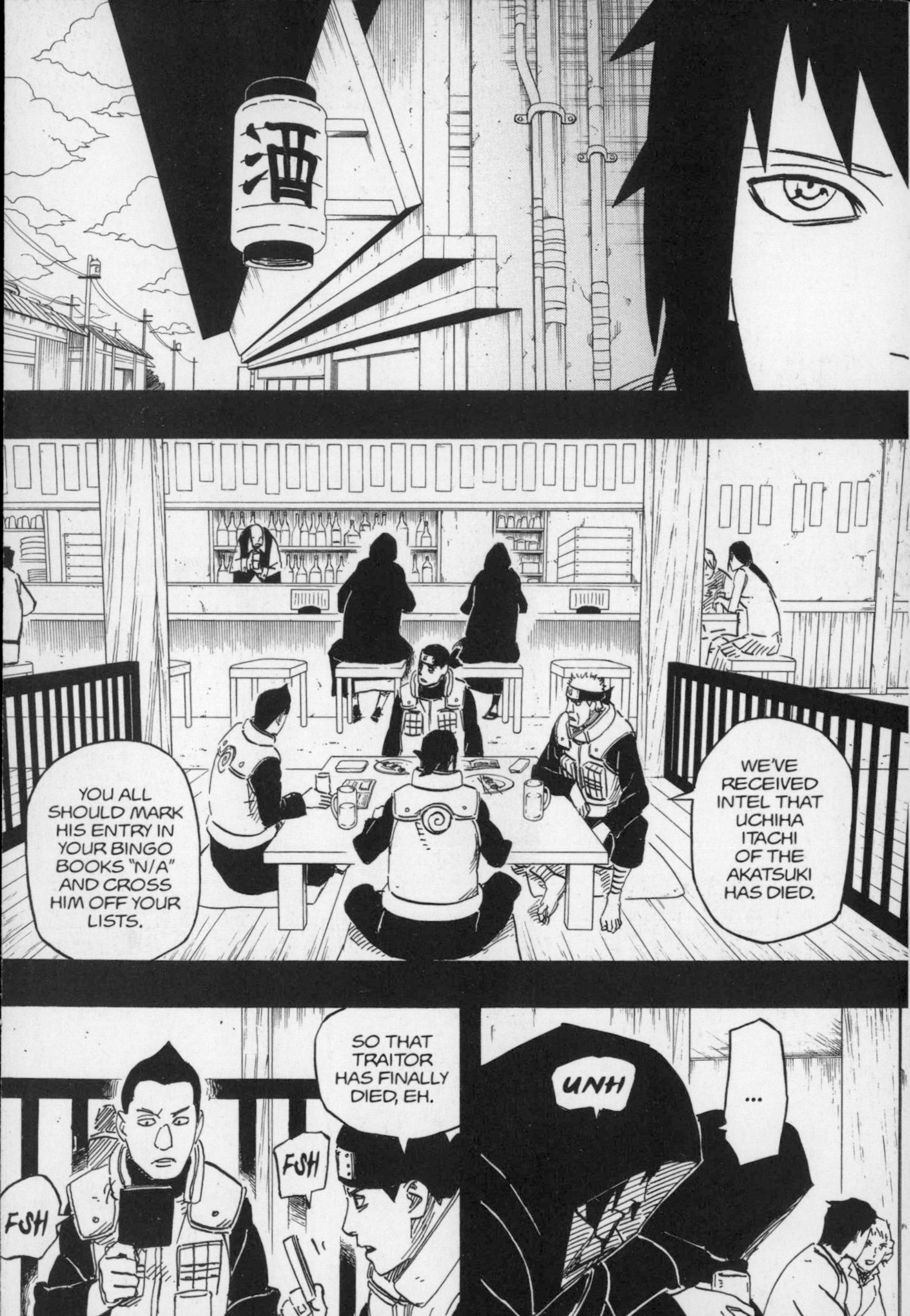
酒
WE'VE RECEIVED INTEL THAT UCHIHA ITACHI OF THE AKATSUKI HAS DIED.
YOU ALL SHOULD MARK HIS ENTRY IN YOUR BINGO BOOKS "N/A" AND CROSS HIM OFF YOUR LISTS.
...
UNH
SO THAT TRAITOR HAS FINALLY DIED, EH.
FSH
FSH

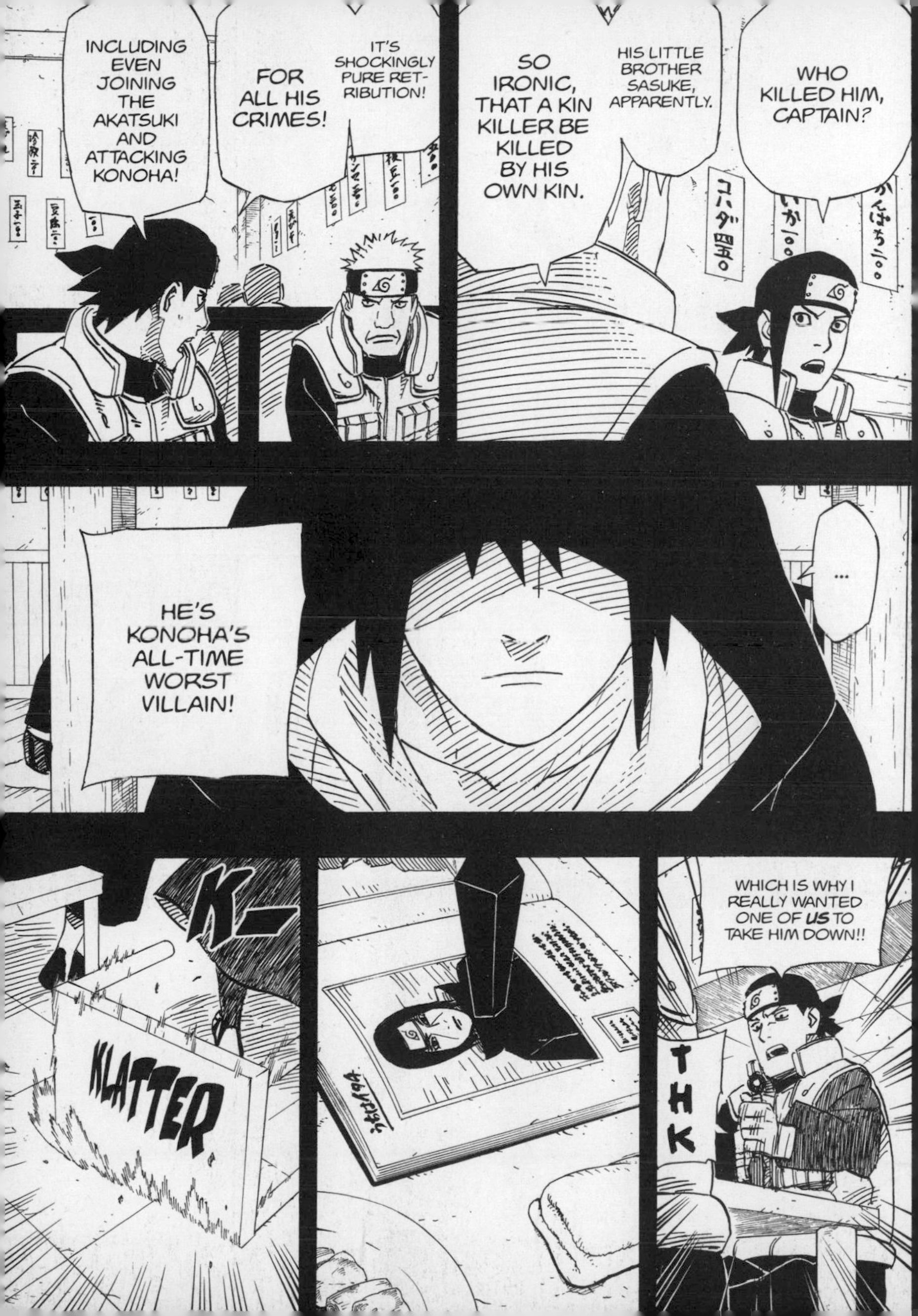
WHO KILLED HIM, CAPTAIN?
かんぱち二〇〇。
いか一〇〇。
コハダ四五〇。
HIS LITTLE BROTHER SASUKE, APPARENTLY.
SO IRONIC, THAT A KIN KILLER BE KILLED BY HIS OWN KIN.
IT'S SHOCKINGLY PURE RETRIBUTION!
FOR ALL HIS CRIMES!
INCLUDING EVEN JOINING THE AKATSUKI AND ATTACKING KONOHA!
...
HE'S KONOHA'S ALL-TIME WORST VILLAIN!
WHICH IS WHY I REALLY WANTED ONE OF US TO TAKE HIM DOWN!!
THK
K-
KLATTER

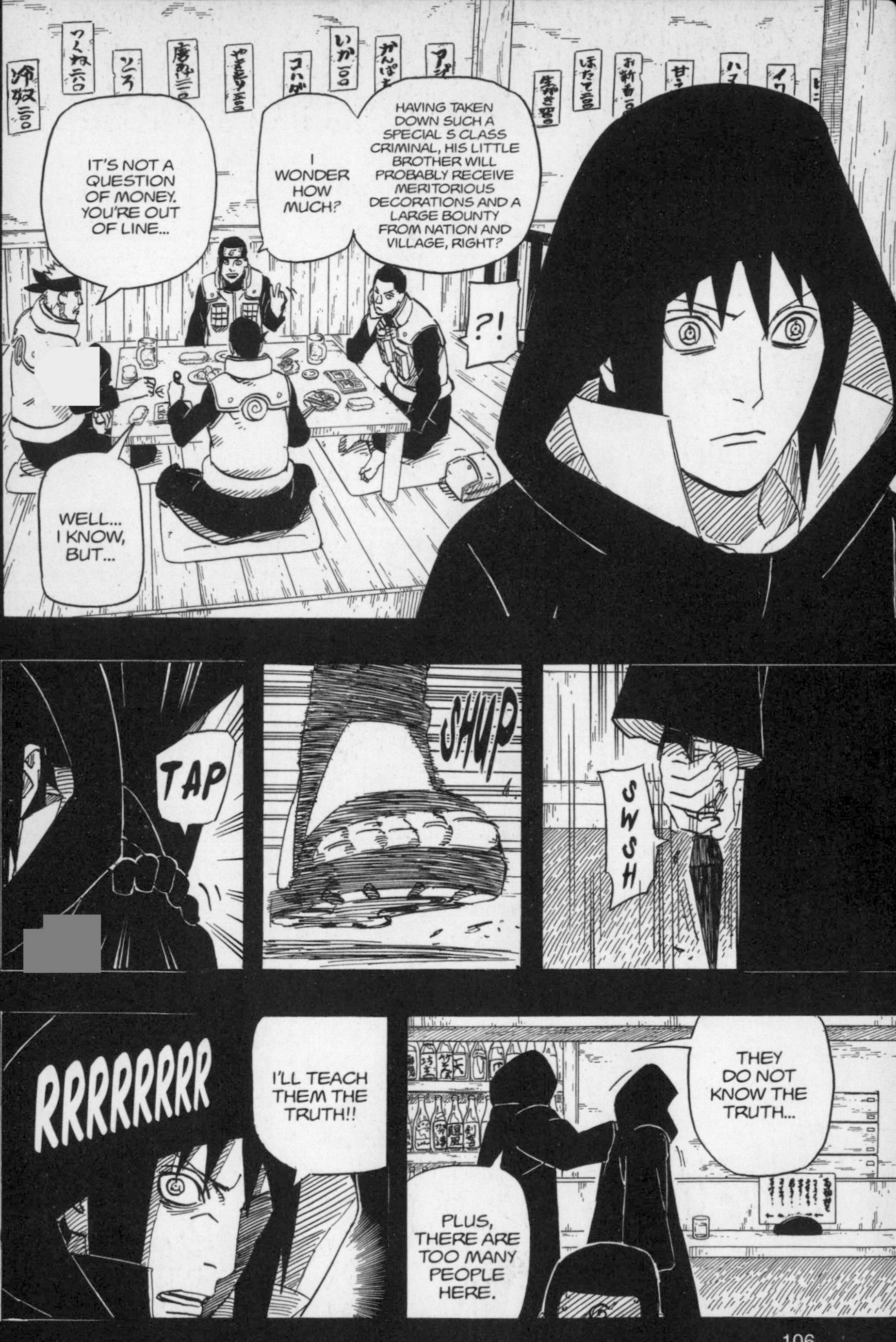
?!
HAVING TAKEN DOWN SUCH A SPECIAL S CLASS CRIMINAL, HIS LITTLE BROTHER WILL PROBABLY RECEIVE MERITORIOUS DECORATIONS AND A LARGE BOUNTY FROM NATION AND VILLAGE, RIGHT?
I WONDER HOW MUCH?
IT'S NOT A QUESTION OF MONEY. YOU'RE OUT OF LINE...
WELL... I KNOW, BUT...
SWSH
SHUP
TAP
THEY DO NOT KNOW THE TRUTH...
PLUS, THERE ARE TOO MANY PEOPLE HERE.
I'LL TEACH THEM THE TRUTH!!
RRRRRRRR

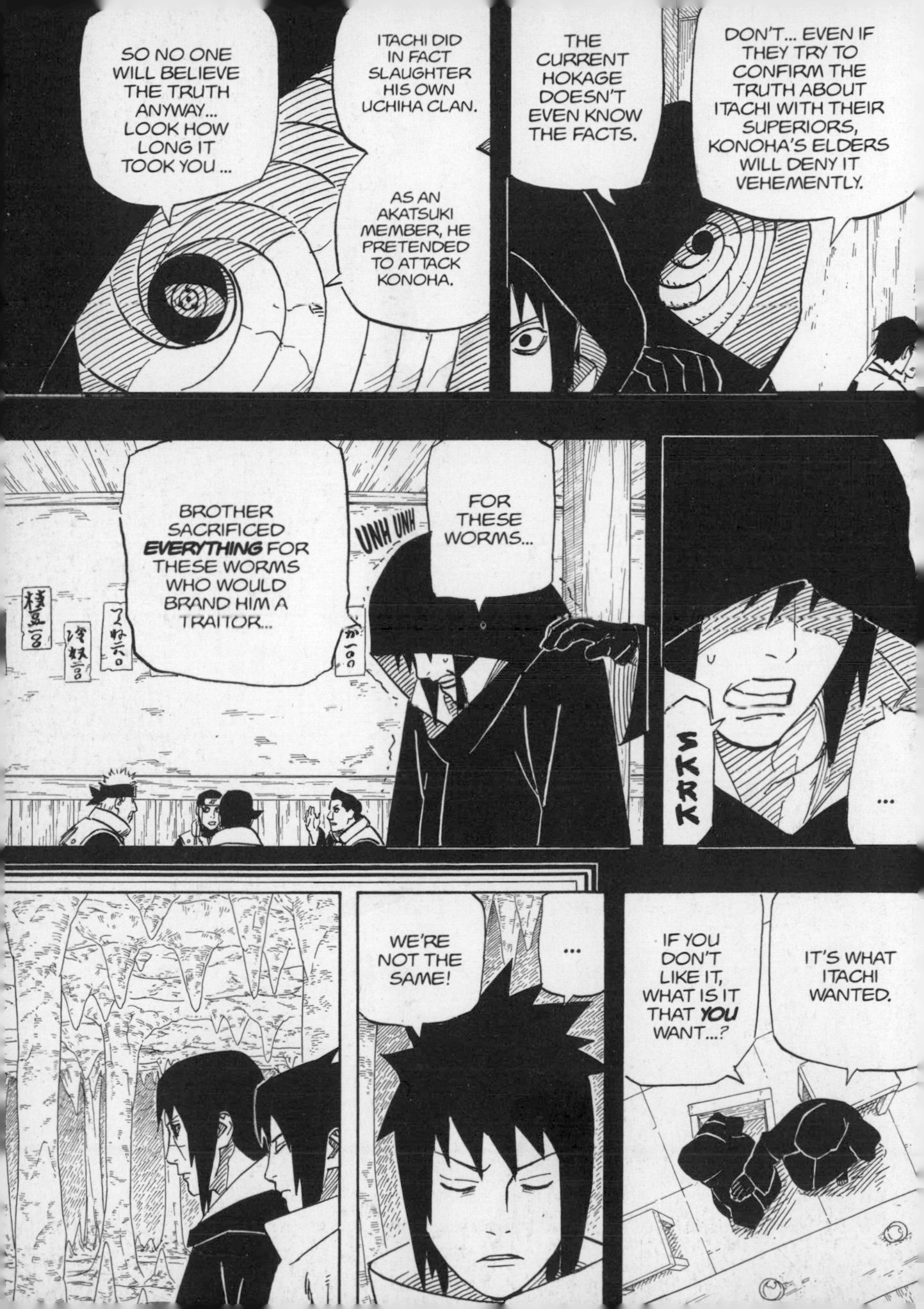
DON'T... EVEN IF THEY TRY TO CONFIRM THE TRUTH ABOUT ITACHI WITH THEIR SUPERIORS, KONOHA'S ELDERS WILL DENY IT VEHEMENTLY.
THE CURRENT HOKAGE DOESN'T EVEN KNOW THE FACTS.
ITACHI DID IN FACT SLAUGHTER HIS OWN UCHIHA CLAN.
AS AN AKATSUKI MEMBER, HE PRETENDED TO ATTACK KONOHA.
SO NO ONE WILL BELIEVE THE TRUTH ANYWAY... LOOK HOW LONG IT TOOK YOU...
...
SKRK
FOR THESE WORMS...
UNH UNH
BROTHER SACRIFICED **EVERYTHING** FOR THESE WORMS WHO WOULD BRAND HIM A TRAITOR...
IT'S WHAT ITACHI WANTED.
IF YOU DON'T LIKE IT, WHAT IS IT THAT **YOU** WANT...?
...
WE'RE NOT THE SAME!

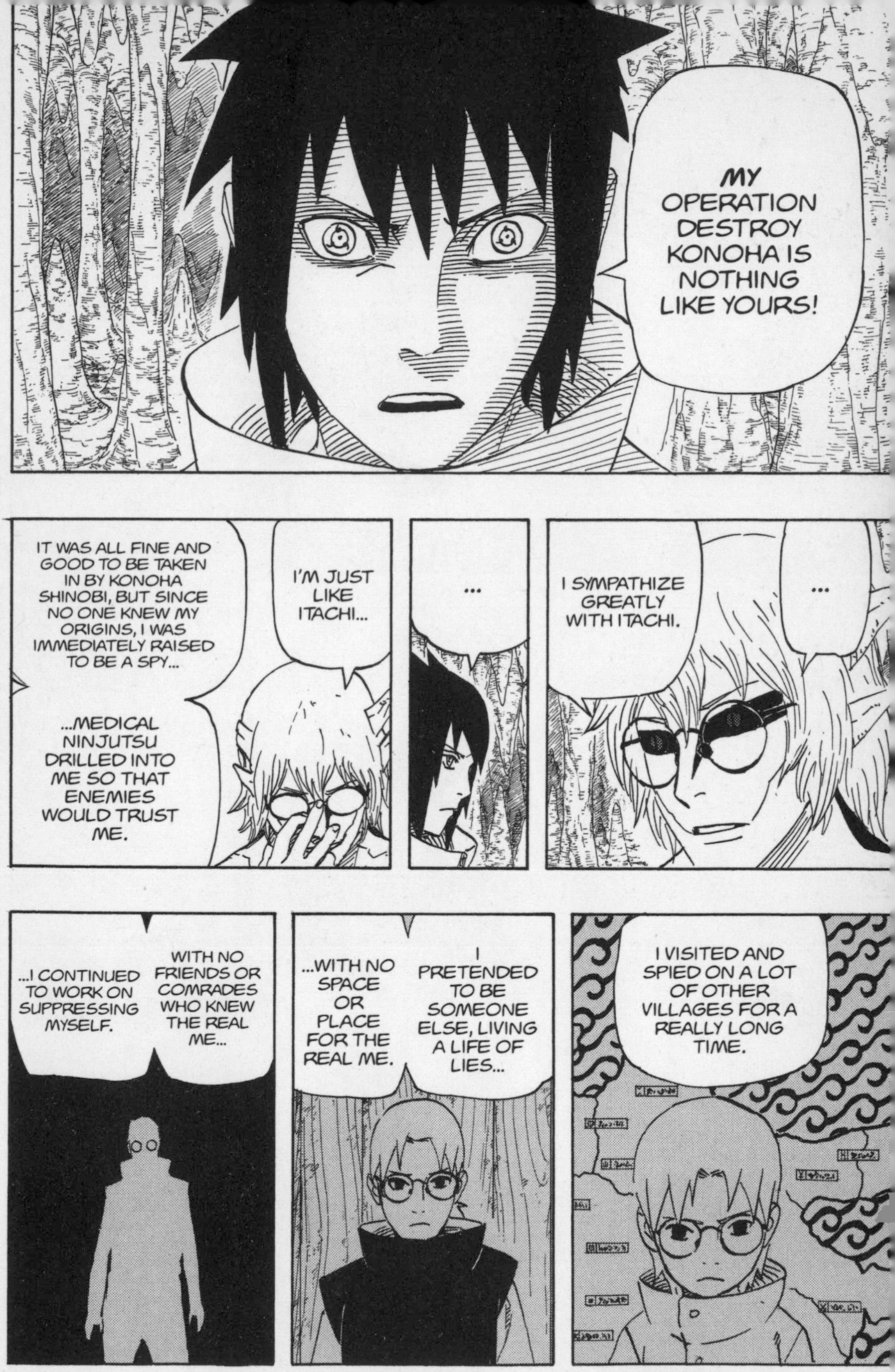
MY OPERATION DESTROY KONOHA IS NOTHING LIKE YOURS!
...
I SYMPATHIZE GREATLY WITH ITACHI.
...
I'M JUST LIKE ITACHI...
IT WAS ALL FINE AND GOOD TO BE TAKEN IN BY KONOHA SHINOBI, BUT SINCE NO ONE KNEW MY ORIGINS, I WAS IMMEDIATELY RAISED TO BE A SPY...
...MEDICAL NINJUTSU DRILLED INTO ME SO THAT ENEMIES WOULD TRUST ME.
I VISITED AND SPIED ON A LOT OF OTHER VILLAGES FOR A REALLY LONG TIME.
I PRETENDED TO BE SOMEONE ELSE, LIVING A LIFE OF LIES...
...WITH NO SPACE OR PLACE FOR THE REAL ME.
WITH NO FRIENDS OR COMRADES WHO KNEW THE REAL ME...
...I CONTINUED TO WORK ON SUPPRESSING MYSELF.

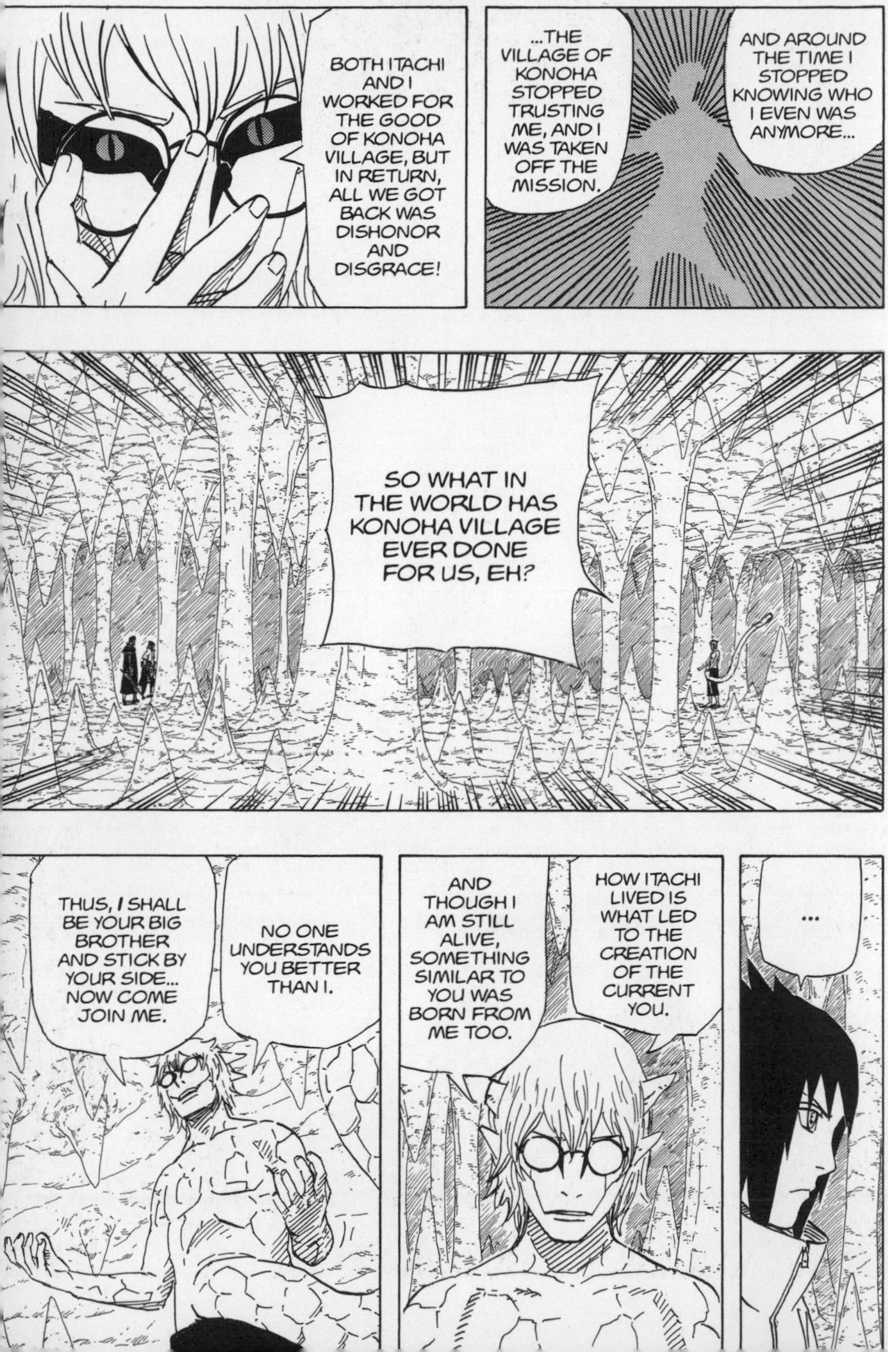
AND AROUND THE TIME I STOPPED KNOWING WHO I EVEN WAS ANYMORE...
...THE VILLAGE OF KONOHA STOPPED TRUSTING ME, AND I WAS TAKEN OFF THE MISSION.
BOTH ITACHI AND I WORKED FOR THE GOOD OF KONOHA VILLAGE, BUT IN RETURN, ALL WE GOT BACK WAS DISHONOR AND DISGRACE!
SO WHAT IN THE WORLD HAS KONOHA VILLAGE EVER DONE FOR US, EH?
...
HOW ITACHI LIVED IS WHAT LED TO THE CREATION OF THE CURRENT YOU.
AND THOUGH I AM STILL ALIVE, SOMETHING SIMILAR TO YOU WAS BORN FROM ME TOO.
NO ONE UNDERSTANDS YOU BETTER THAN I.
THUS, I SHALL BE YOUR BIG BROTHER AND STICK BY YOUR SIDE... NOW COME JOIN ME.

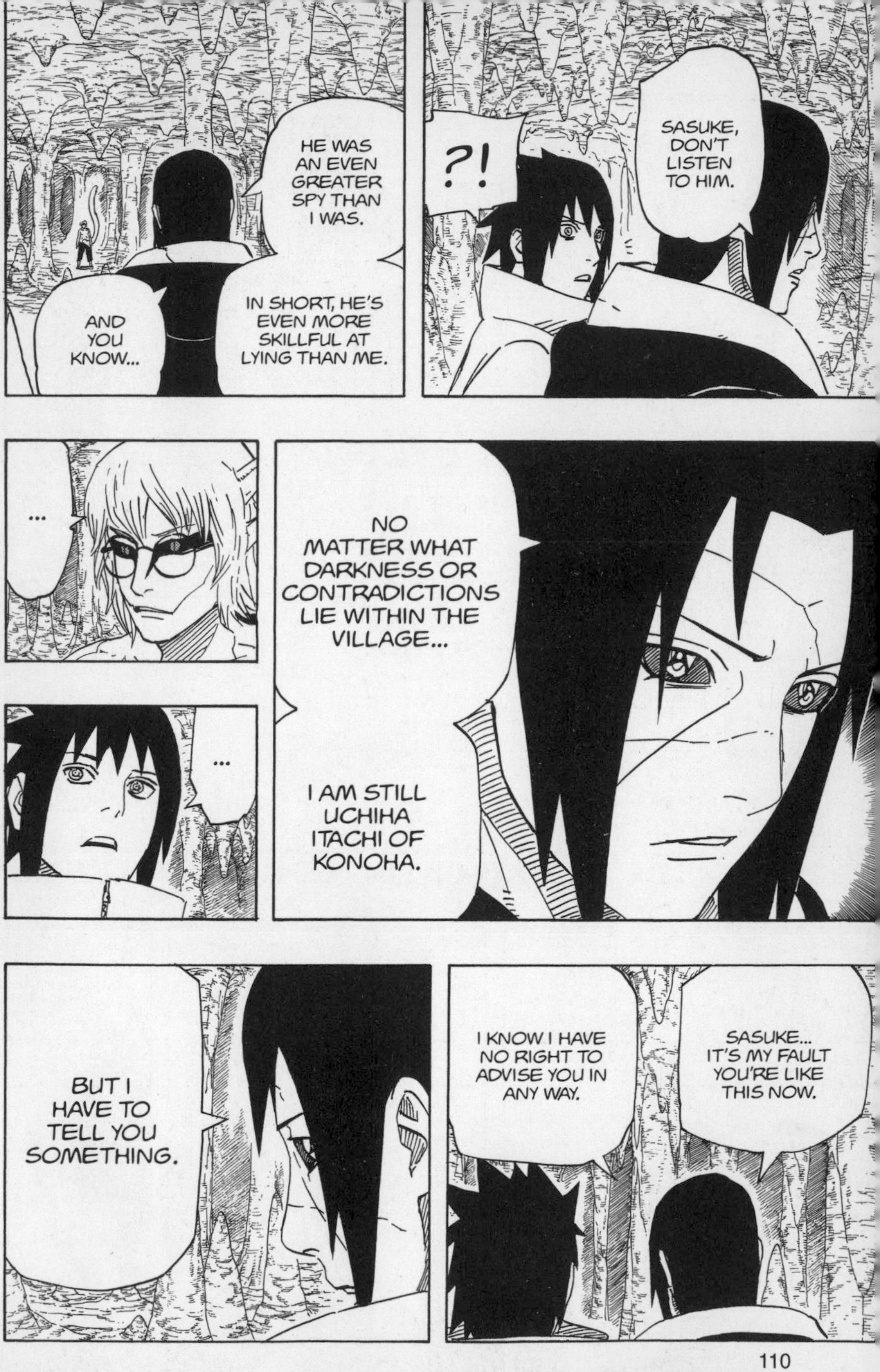
SASUKE, DON'T LISTEN TO HIM.
?!
HE WAS AN EVEN GREATER SPY THAN I WAS.
IN SHORT, HE'S EVEN MORE SKILLFUL AT LYING THAN ME.
AND YOU KNOW...
NO MATTER WHAT DARKNESS OR CONTRADICTIONS LIE WITHIN THE VILLAGE...
I AM STILL UCHIHA ITACHI OF KONOHA.
...
...
SASUKE... IT'S MY FAULT YOU'RE LIKE THIS NOW.
I KNOW I HAVE NO RIGHT TO ADVISE YOU IN ANY WAY.
BUT I HAVE TO TELL YOU SOMETHING.

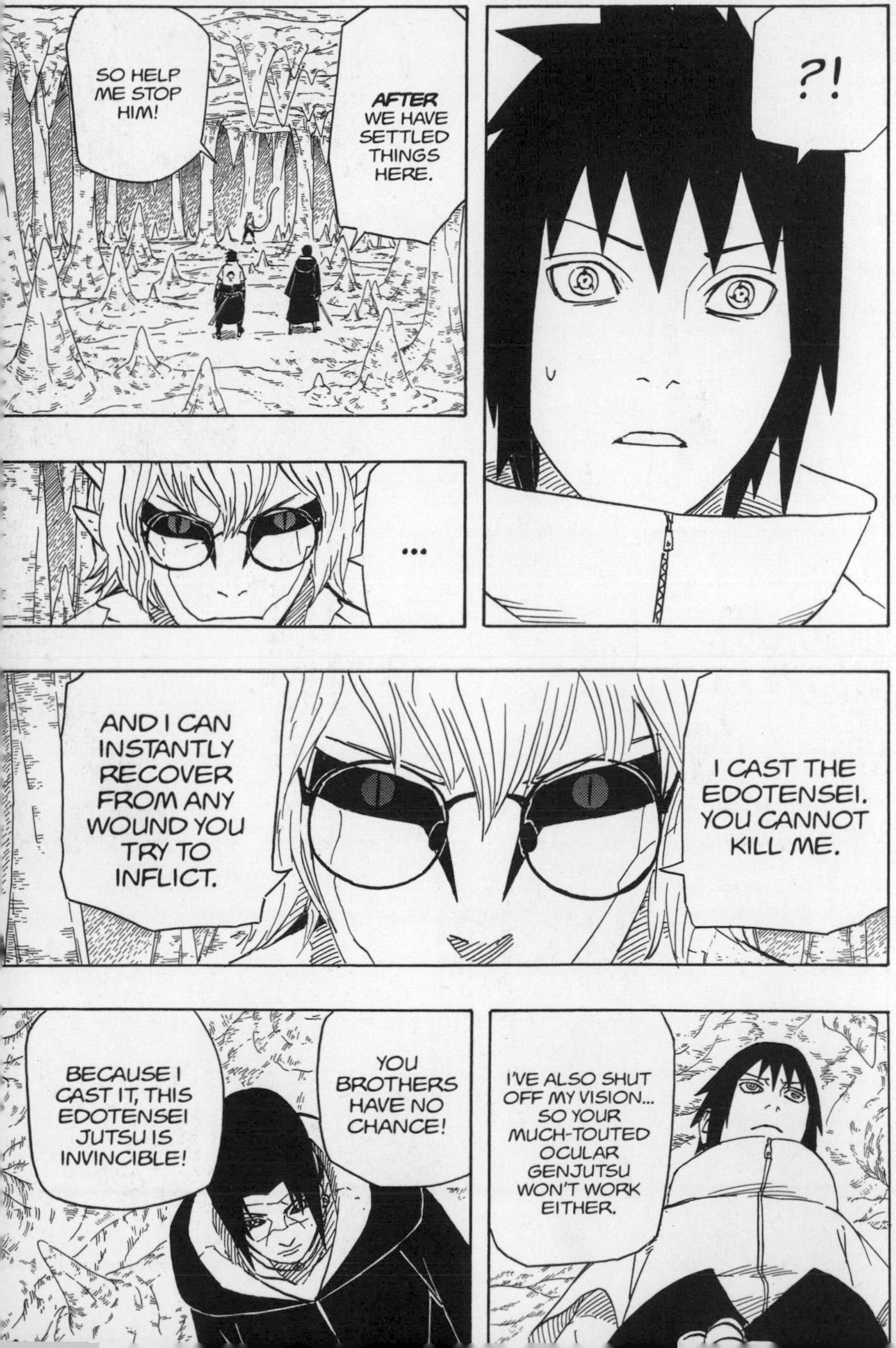
?!
AFTER WE HAVE SETTLED THINGS HERE.
SO HELP ME STOP HIM!
...
I CAST THE EDOTENSEI. YOU CANNOT KILL ME.
AND I CAN INSTANTLY RECOVER FROM ANY WOUND YOU TRY TO INFLICT.
I'VE ALSO SHUT OFF MY VISION... SO YOUR MUCH-TOUTED OCULAR GENJUTSU WON'T WORK EITHER.
YOU BROTHERS HAVE NO CHANCE!
BECAUSE I CAST IT, THIS EDOTENSEI JUTSU IS INVINCIBLE!

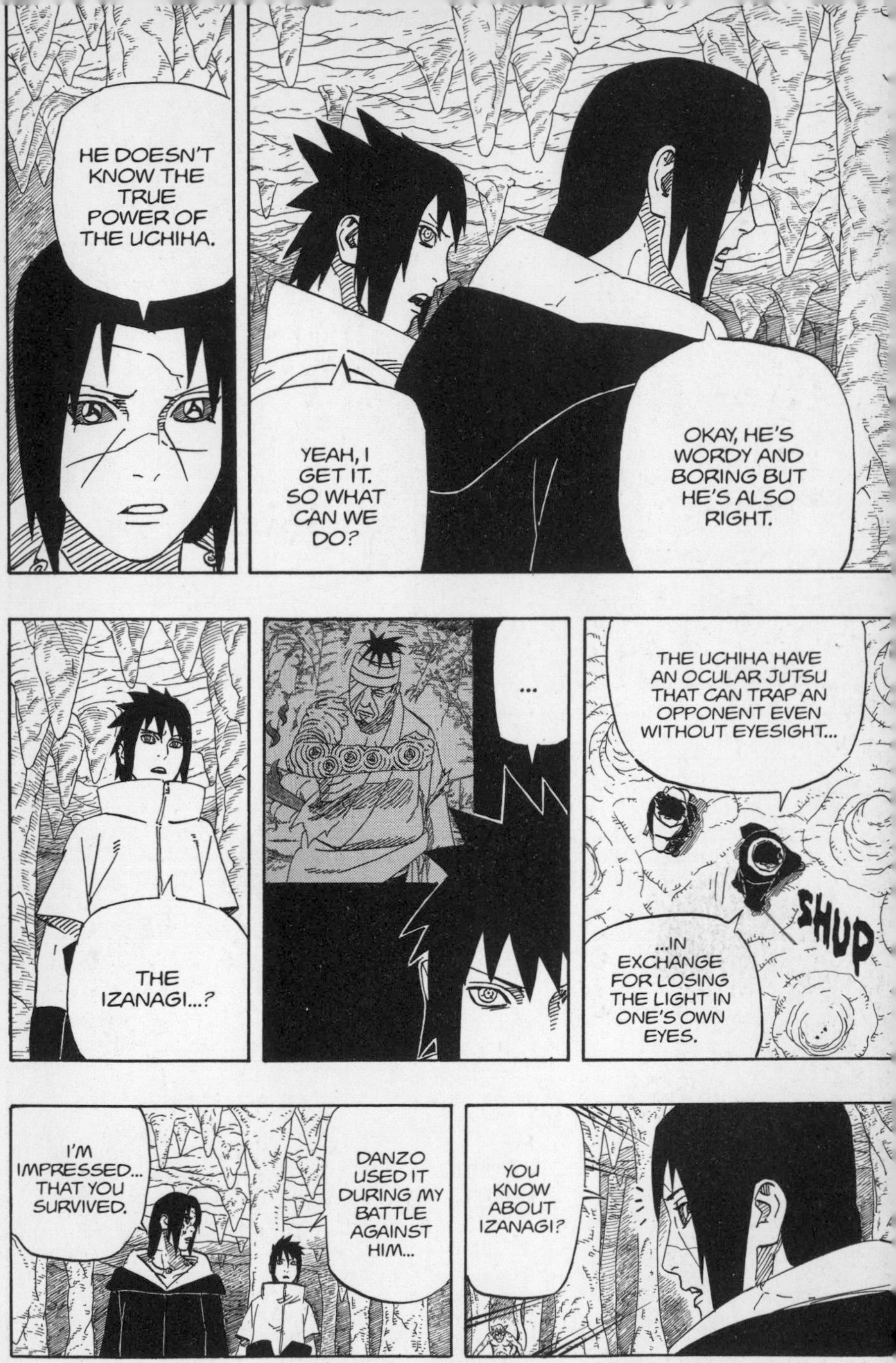
OKAY, HE'S WORDY AND BORING BUT HE'S ALSO RIGHT.
YEAH, I GET IT. SO WHAT CAN WE DO?
HE DOESN'T KNOW THE TRUE POWER OF THE UCHIHA.
THE UCHIHA HAVE AN OCULAR JUTSU THAT CAN TRAP AN OPPONENT EVEN WITHOUT EYESIGHT...
SHUP
...IN EXCHANGE FOR LOSING THE LIGHT IN ONE'S OWN EYES.
...
THE IZANAGI...?
YOU KNOW ABOUT IZANAGI?
DANZO USED IT DURING MY BATTLE AGAINST HIM...
I'M IMPRESSED... THAT YOU SURVIVED.

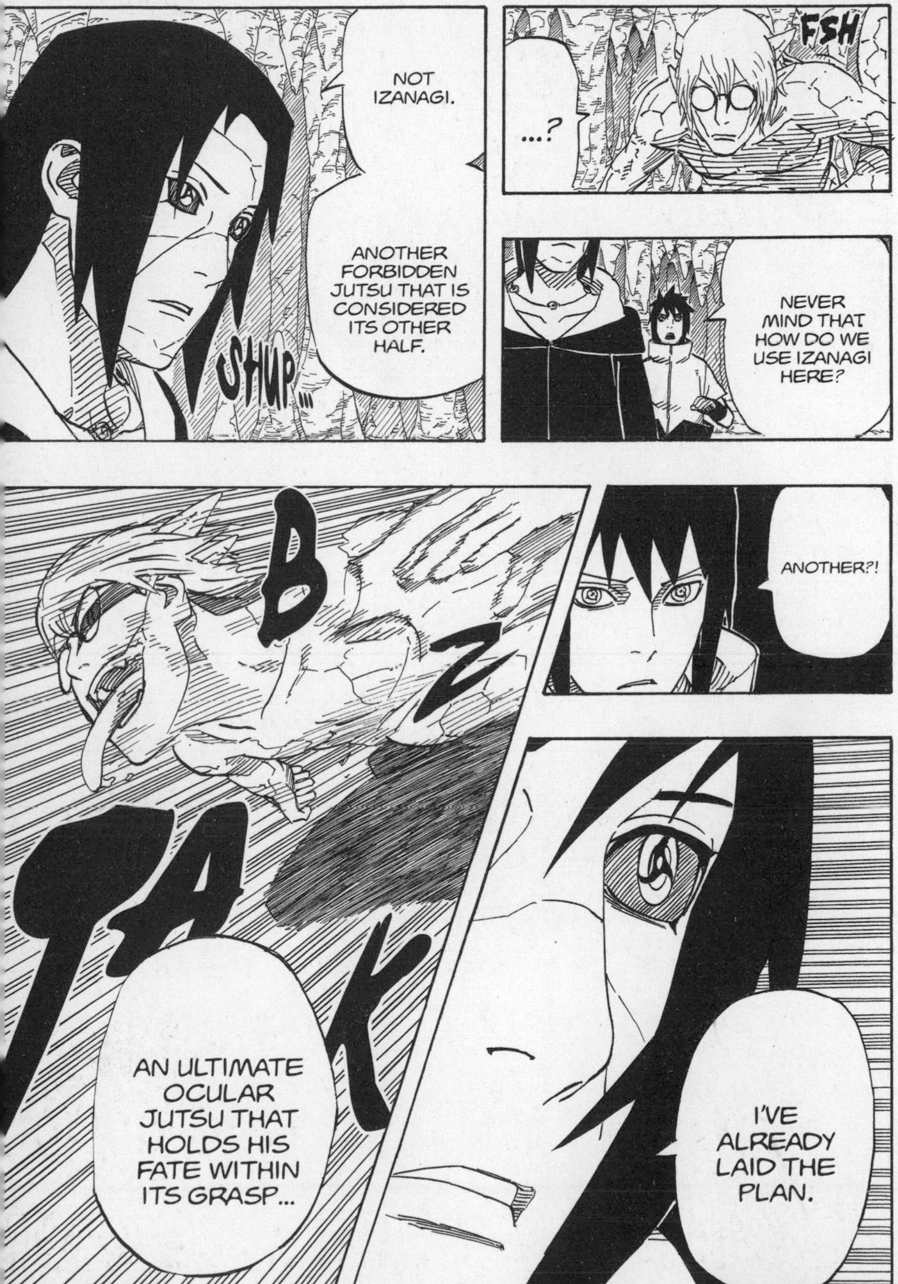
FSH
...?
NEVER MIND THAT. HOW DO WE USE IZANAGI HERE?
NOT IZANAGI.
ANOTHER FORBIDDEN JUTSU THAT IS CONSIDERED ITS OTHER HALF.
SHUP...
ANOTHER?!
I'VE ALREADY LAID THE PLAN.
BZ
TAK
AN ULTIMATE OCULAR JUTSU THAT HOLDS HIS FATE WITHIN ITS GRASP...

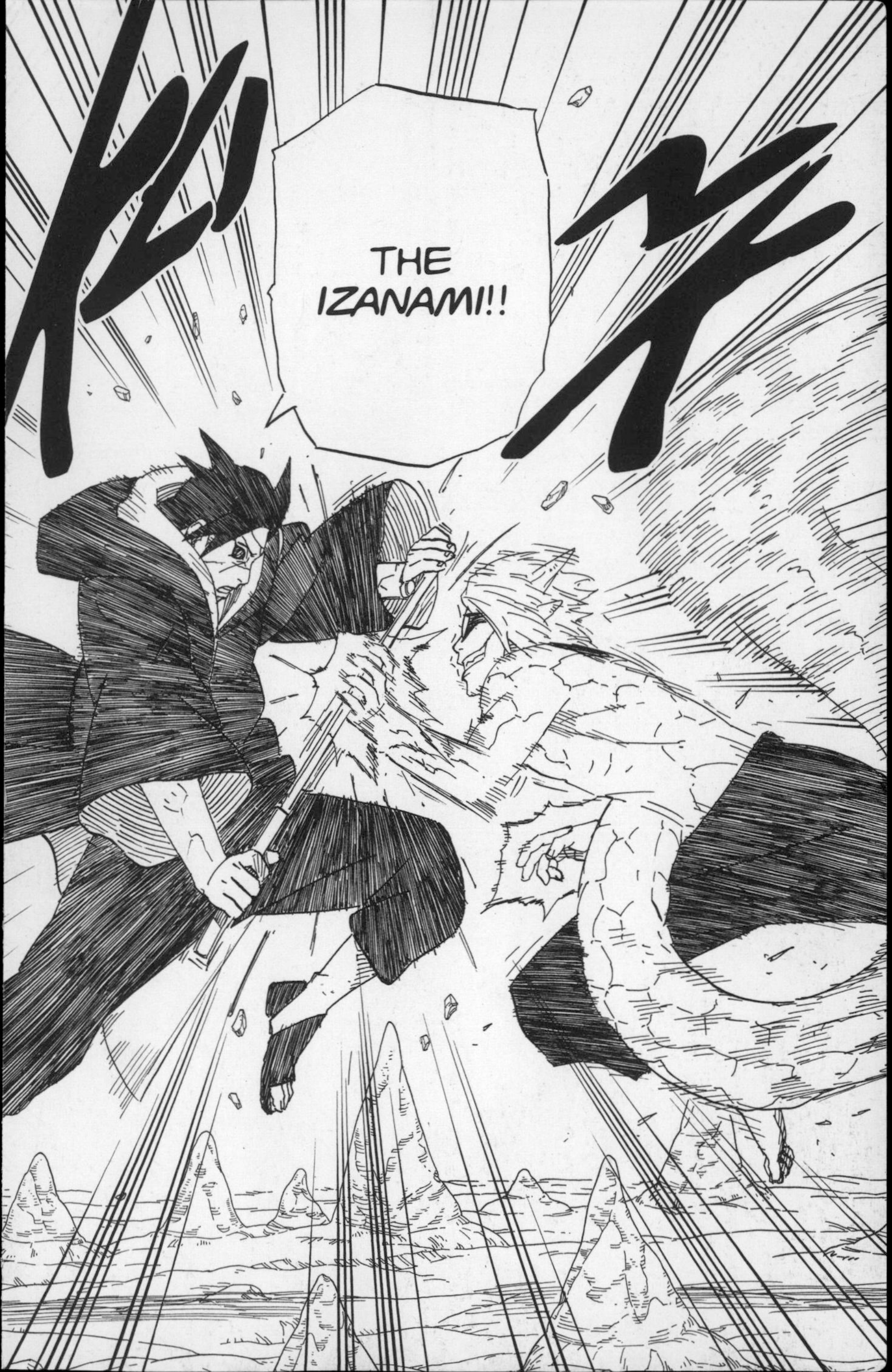
THE IZANAMI!!

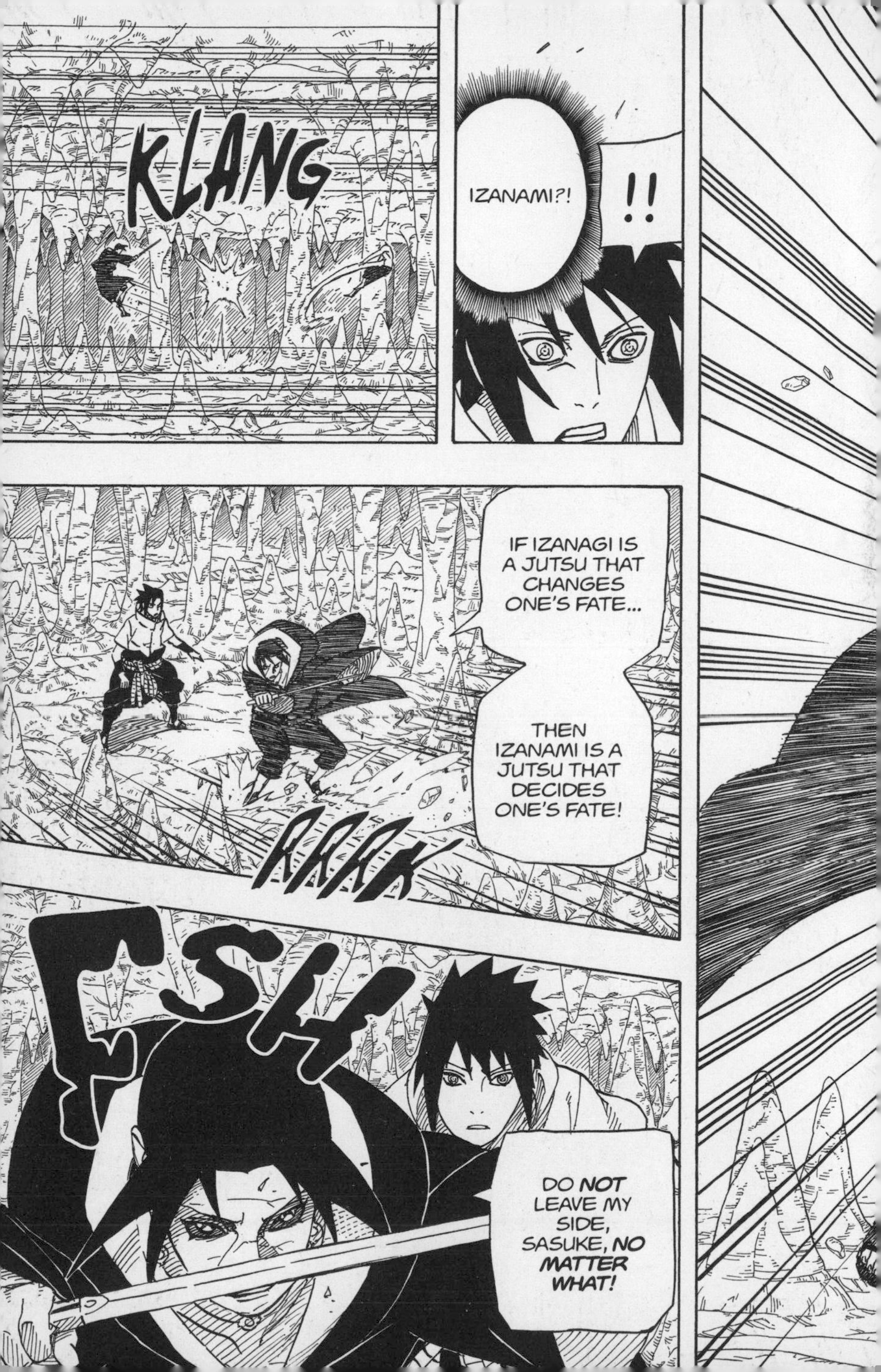
!!
IZANAMI?!
KLANG
IF IZANAGI IS A JUTSU THAT CHANGES ONE'S FATE...
THEN IZANAMI IS A JUTSU THAT DECIDES ONE'S FATE!
RRRK
FSH
DO NOT LEAVE MY SIDE, SASUKE, NO MATTER WHAT!

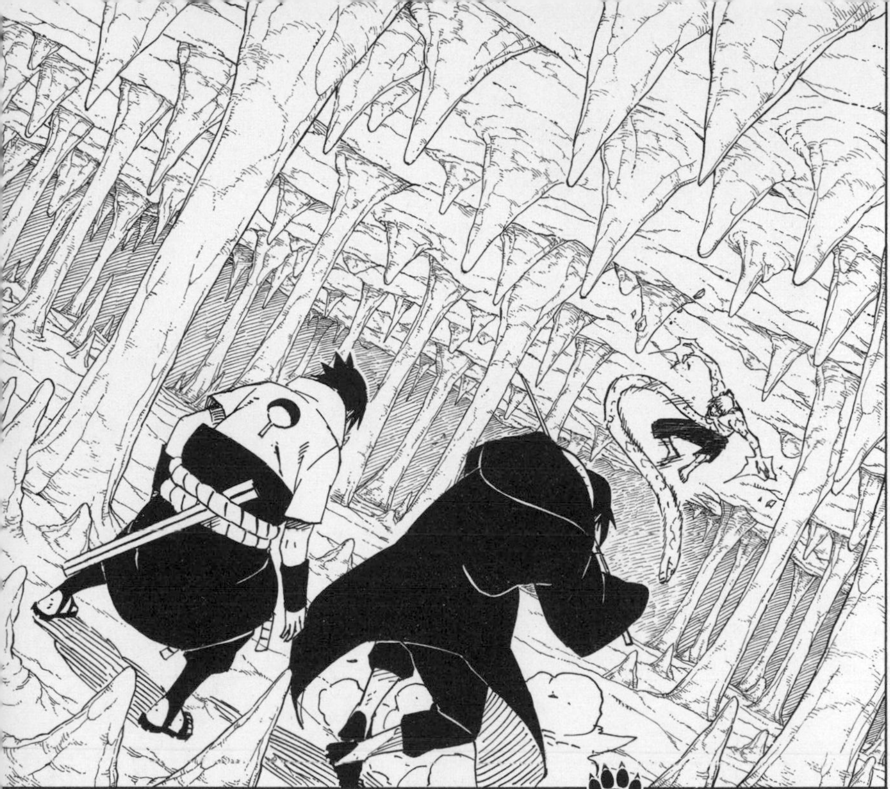

Number 582: Nothing

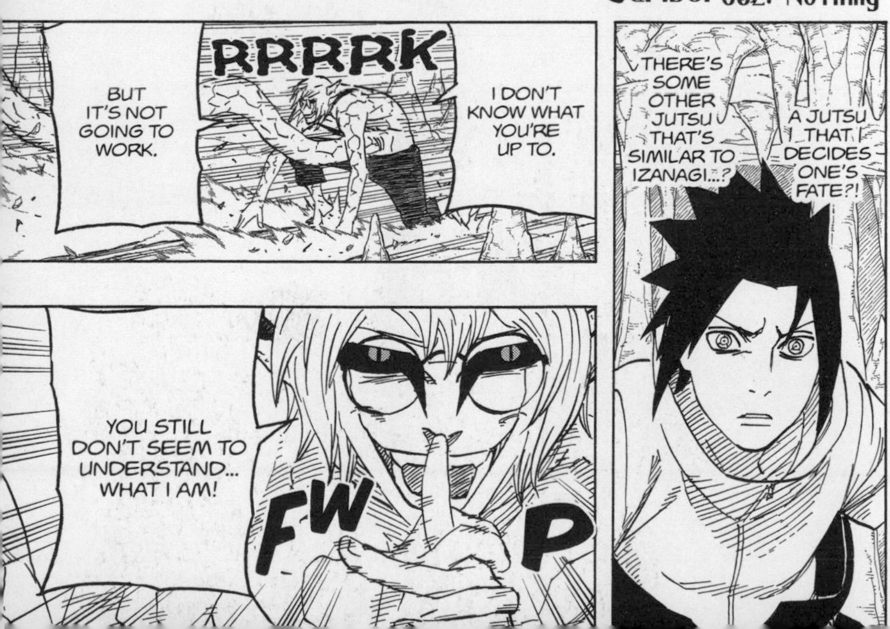
THERE'S SOME OTHER JUTSU THAT'S SIMILAR TO IZANAGI...?
A JUTSU THAT DECIDES ONE'S FATE?!
RRRRK
I DON'T KNOW WHAT YOU'RE UP TO.
BUT IT'S NOT GOING TO WORK.
YOU STILL DON'T SEEM TO UNDERSTAND... WHAT I AM!
FWP

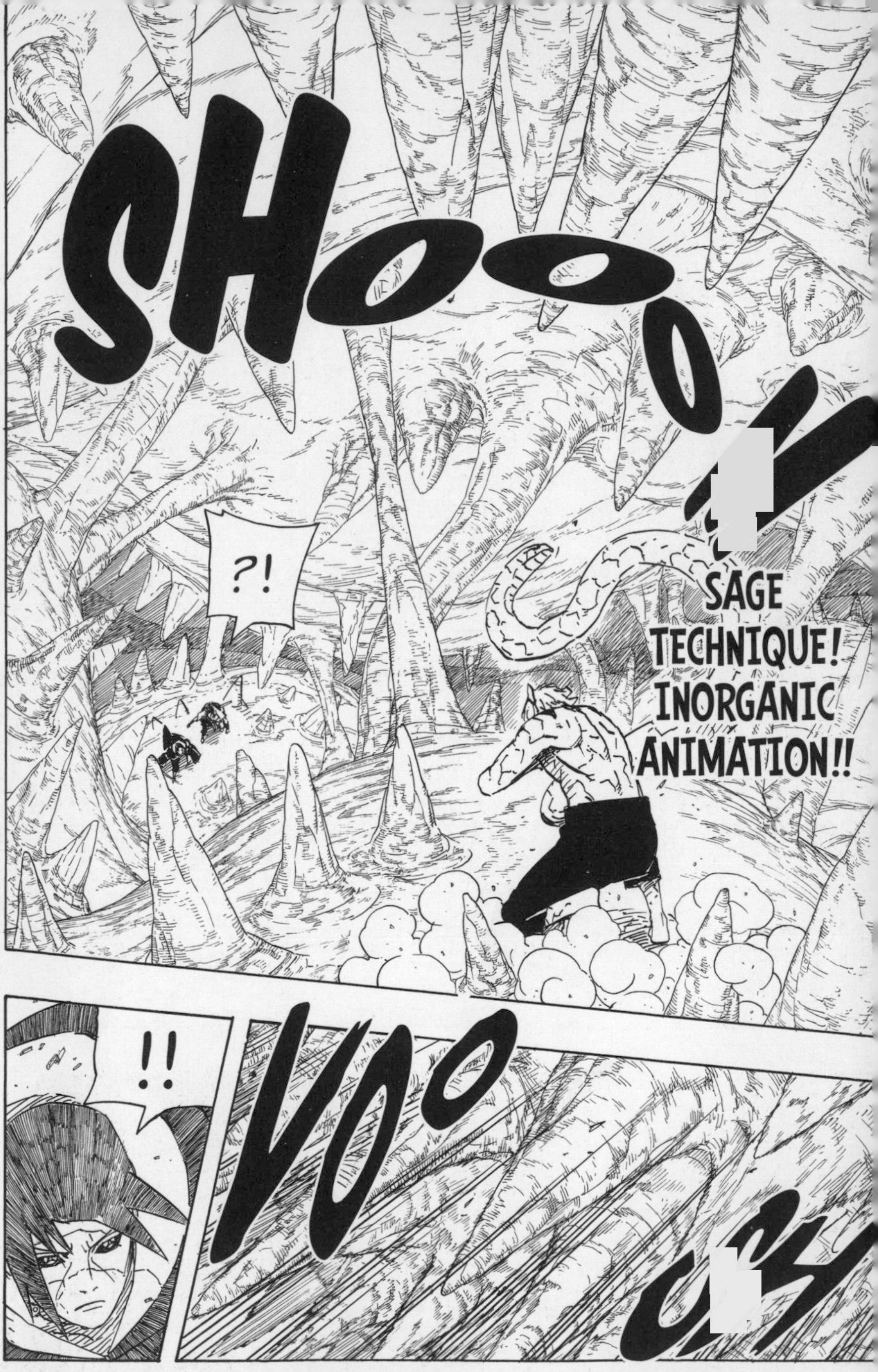
SHOOOO
SAGE TECHNIQUE! INORGANIC ANIMATION!!
?!
!!

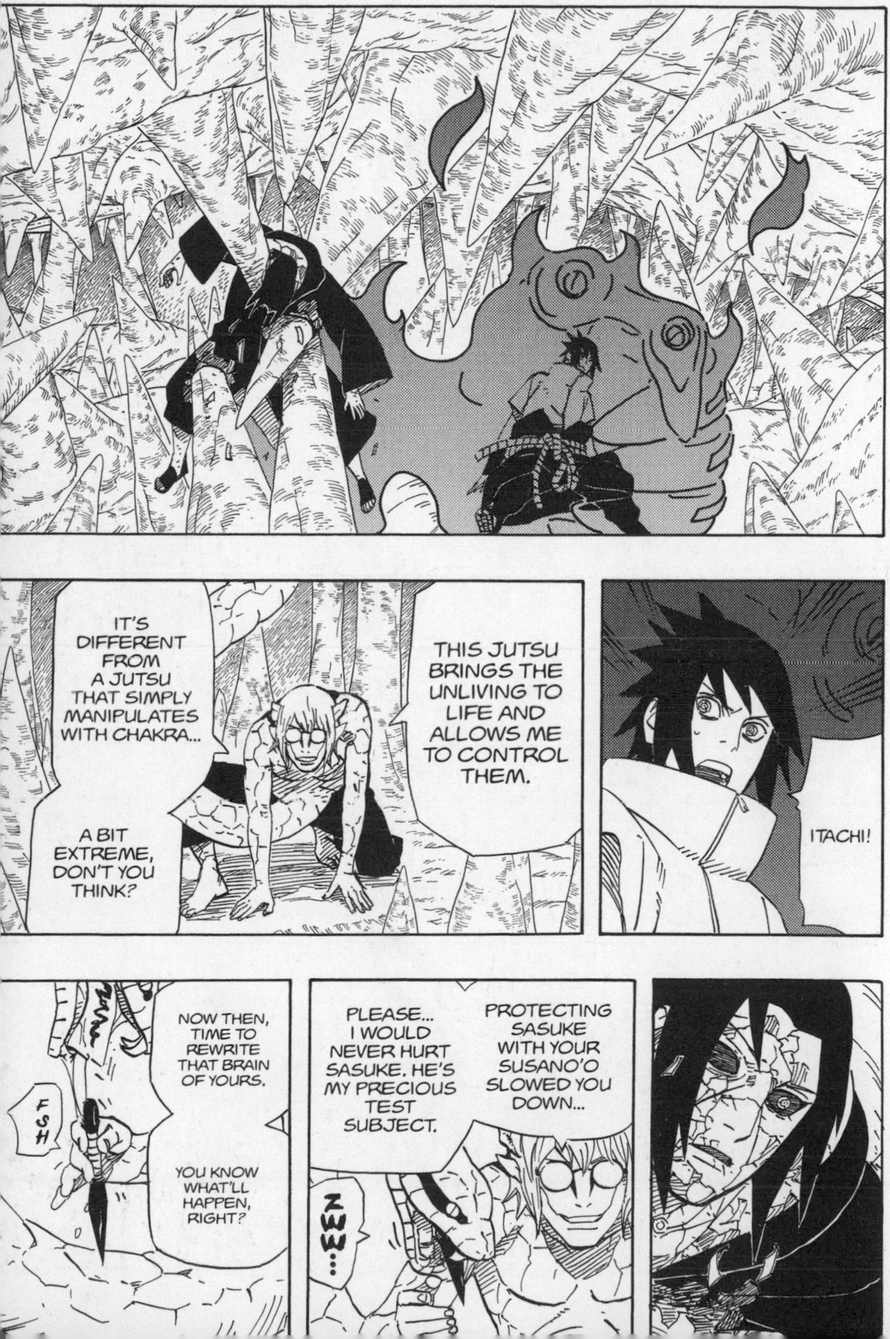
ITACHI!
THIS JUTSU BRINGS THE UNLIVING TO LIFE AND ALLOWS ME TO CONTROL THEM.
IT'S DIFFERENT FROM A JUTSU THAT SIMPLY MANIPULATES WITH CHAKRA...
A BIT EXTREME, DON'T YOU THINK?
PROTECTING SASUKE WITH YOUR SUSANO'O SLOWED YOU DOWN...
PLEASE... I WOULD NEVER HURT SASUKE. HE'S MY PRECIOUS TEST SUBJECT.
ZWW...
NOW THEN, TIME TO REWRITE THAT BRAIN OF YOURS.
FSH
YOU KNOW WHAT'LL HAPPEN, RIGHT?

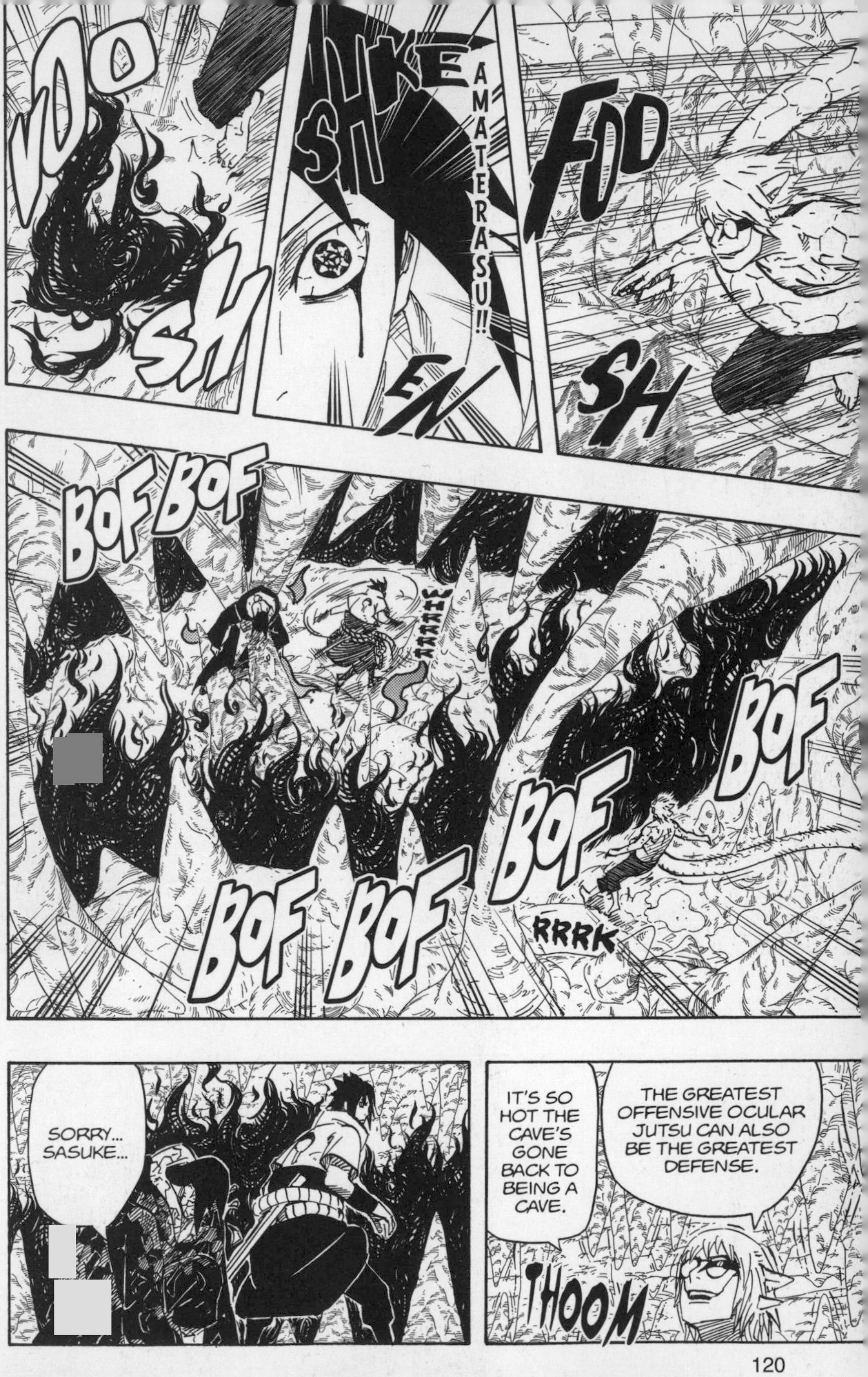
FOD
SH
AMATERASU!!
VOOO
SH
BOF BOF
WHRRRR
BOF
BOF
BOF BOF
RRRK
THE GREATEST OFFENSIVE OCULAR JUTSU CAN ALSO BE THE GREATEST DEFENSE.
IT'S SO HOT THE CAVE'S GONE BACK TO BEING A CAVE.
THOOM
SORRY... SASUKE...

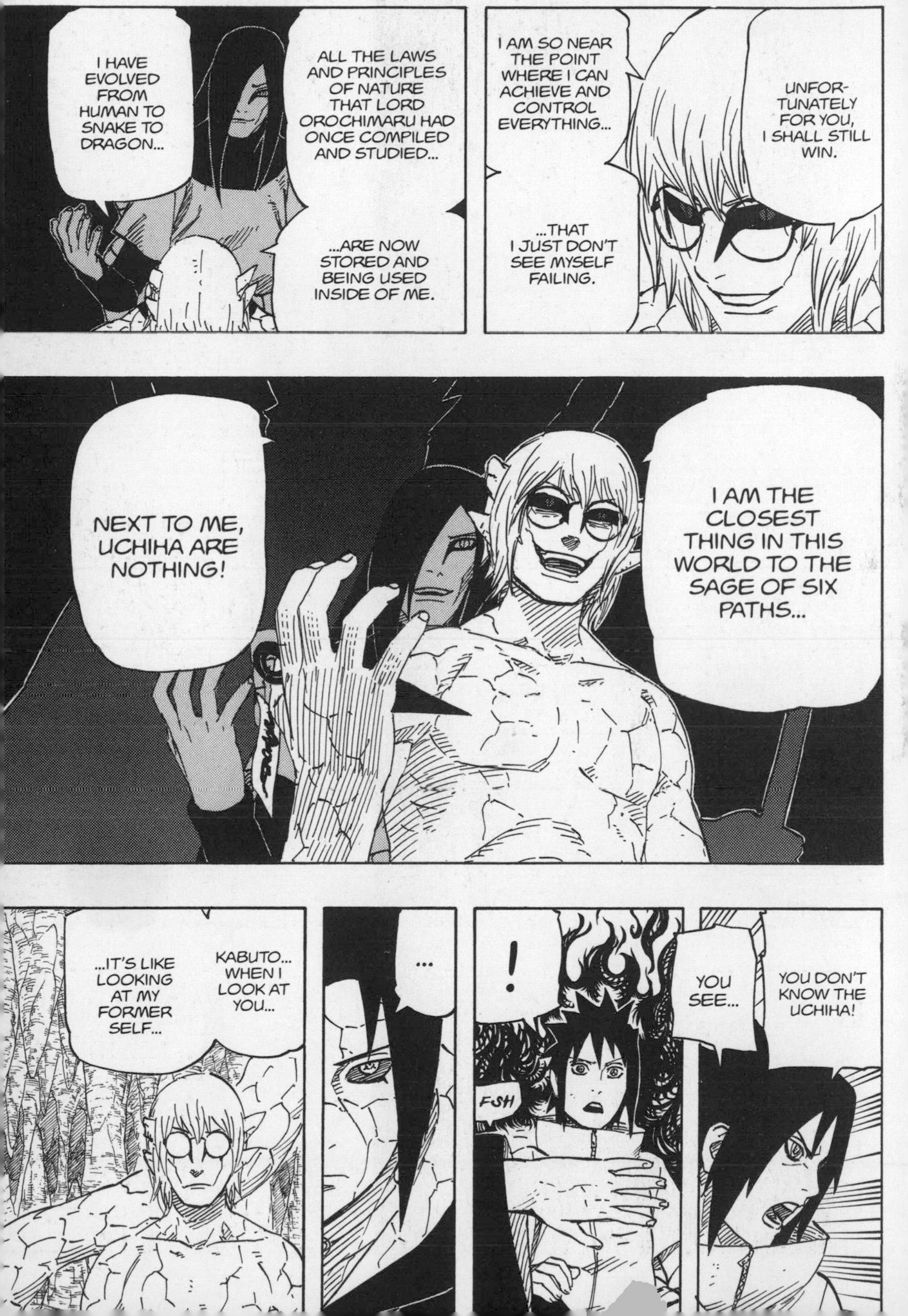
UNFOR-TUNATELY FOR YOU, I SHALL STILL WIN.
I AM SO NEAR THE POINT WHERE I CAN ACHIEVE AND CONTROL EVERYTHING...
...THAT I JUST DON'T SEE MYSELF FAILING.
ALL THE LAWS AND PRINCIPLES OF NATURE THAT LORD OROCHIMARU HAD ONCE COMPILED AND STUDIED...
...ARE NOW STORED AND BEING USED INSIDE OF ME.
I HAVE EVOLVED FROM HUMAN TO SNAKE TO DRAGON...
I AM THE CLOSEST THING IN THIS WORLD TO THE SAGE OF SIX PATHS...
NEXT TO ME, UCHIHA ARE NOTHING!
YOU DON'T KNOW THE UCHIHA!
YOU SEE...
!
FSH
...
KABUTO... WHEN I LOOK AT YOU...
...IT'S LIKE LOOKING AT MY FORMER SELF...

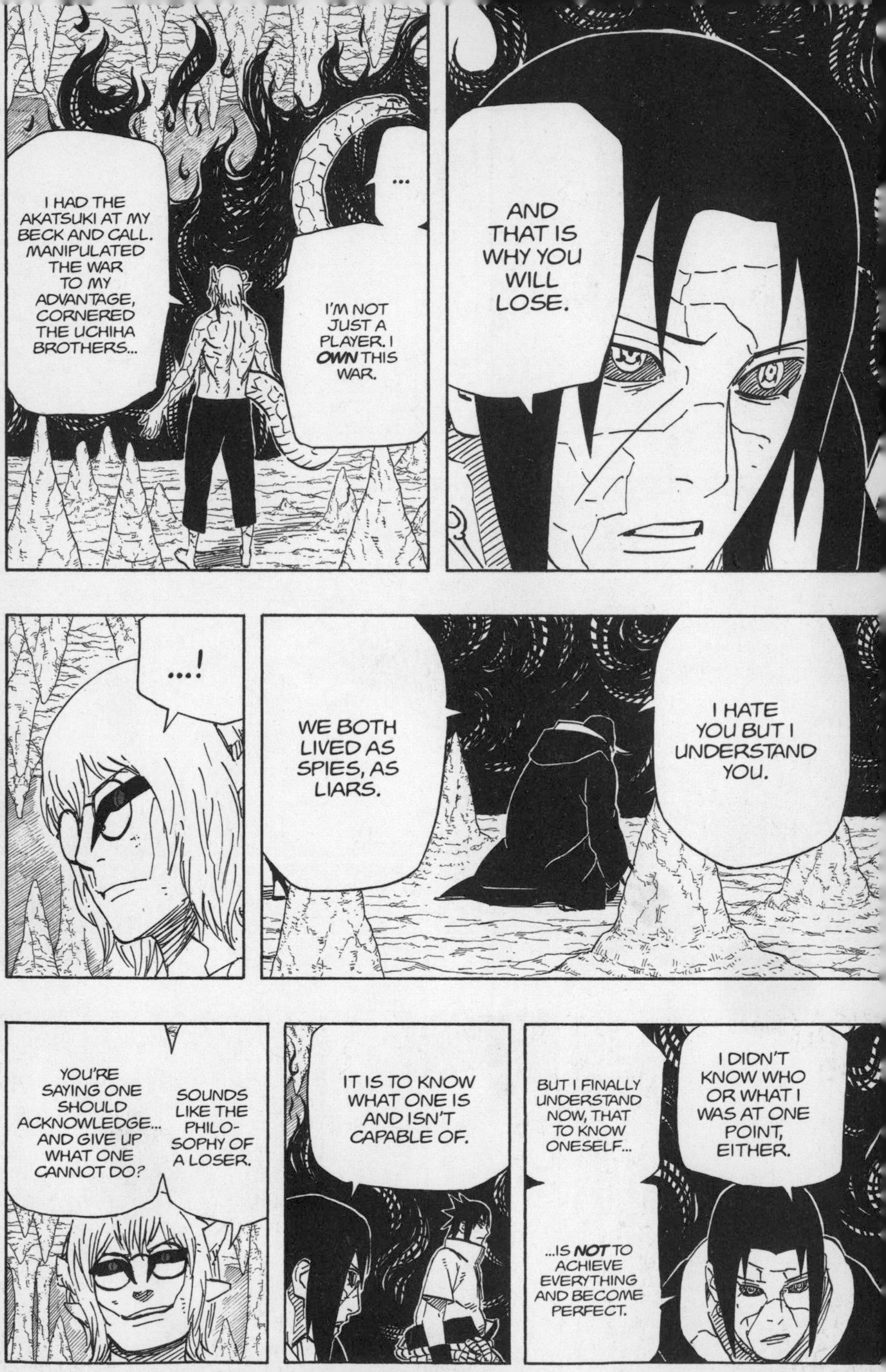
AND THAT IS WHY YOU WILL LOSE.
...
I HAD THE AKATSUKI AT MY BECK AND CALL. MANIPULATED THE WAR TO MY ADVANTAGE, CORNERED THE UCHIHA BROTHERS...
I'M NOT JUST A PLAYER. I **OWN** THIS WAR.
I HATE YOU BUT I UNDERSTAND YOU.
WE BOTH LIVED AS SPIES, AS LIARS.
...!
I DIDN'T KNOW WHO OR WHAT I WAS AT ONE POINT, EITHER.
BUT I FINALLY UNDERSTAND NOW, THAT TO KNOW ONESELF...
...IS **NOT** TO ACHIEVE EVERYTHING AND BECOME PERFECT.
IT IS TO KNOW WHAT ONE IS AND ISN'T CAPABLE OF.
SOUNDS LIKE THE PHILOSOPHY OF A LOSER.
YOU'RE SAYING ONE SHOULD ACKNOWLEDGE... AND GIVE UP WHAT ONE CANNOT DO?

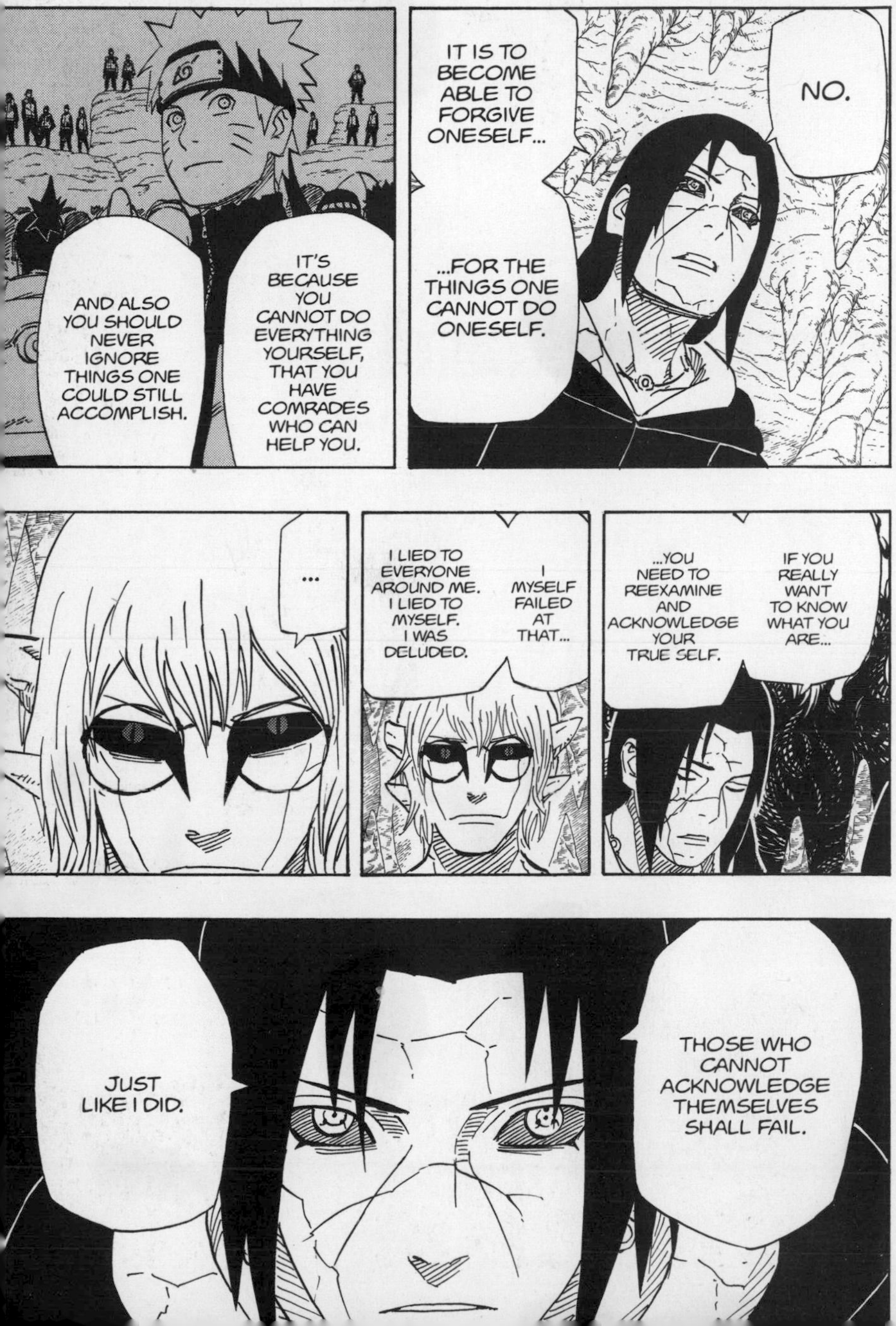
NO.
IT IS TO BECOME ABLE TO FORGIVE ONESELF...
...FOR THE THINGS ONE CANNOT DO ONESELF.
IT'S BECAUSE YOU CANNOT DO EVERYTHING YOURSELF, THAT YOU HAVE COMRADES WHO CAN HELP YOU.
AND ALSO YOU SHOULD NEVER IGNORE THINGS ONE COULD STILL ACCOMPLISH.
IF YOU REALLY WANT TO KNOW WHAT YOU ARE...
...YOU NEED TO REEXAMINE AND ACKNOWLEDGE YOUR TRUE SELF.
I MYSELF FAILED AT THAT...
I LIED TO EVERYONE AROUND ME. I LIED TO MYSELF. I WAS DELUDED.
...
THOSE WHO CANNOT ACKNOWLEDGE THEMSELVES SHALL FAIL.
JUST LIKE I DID.

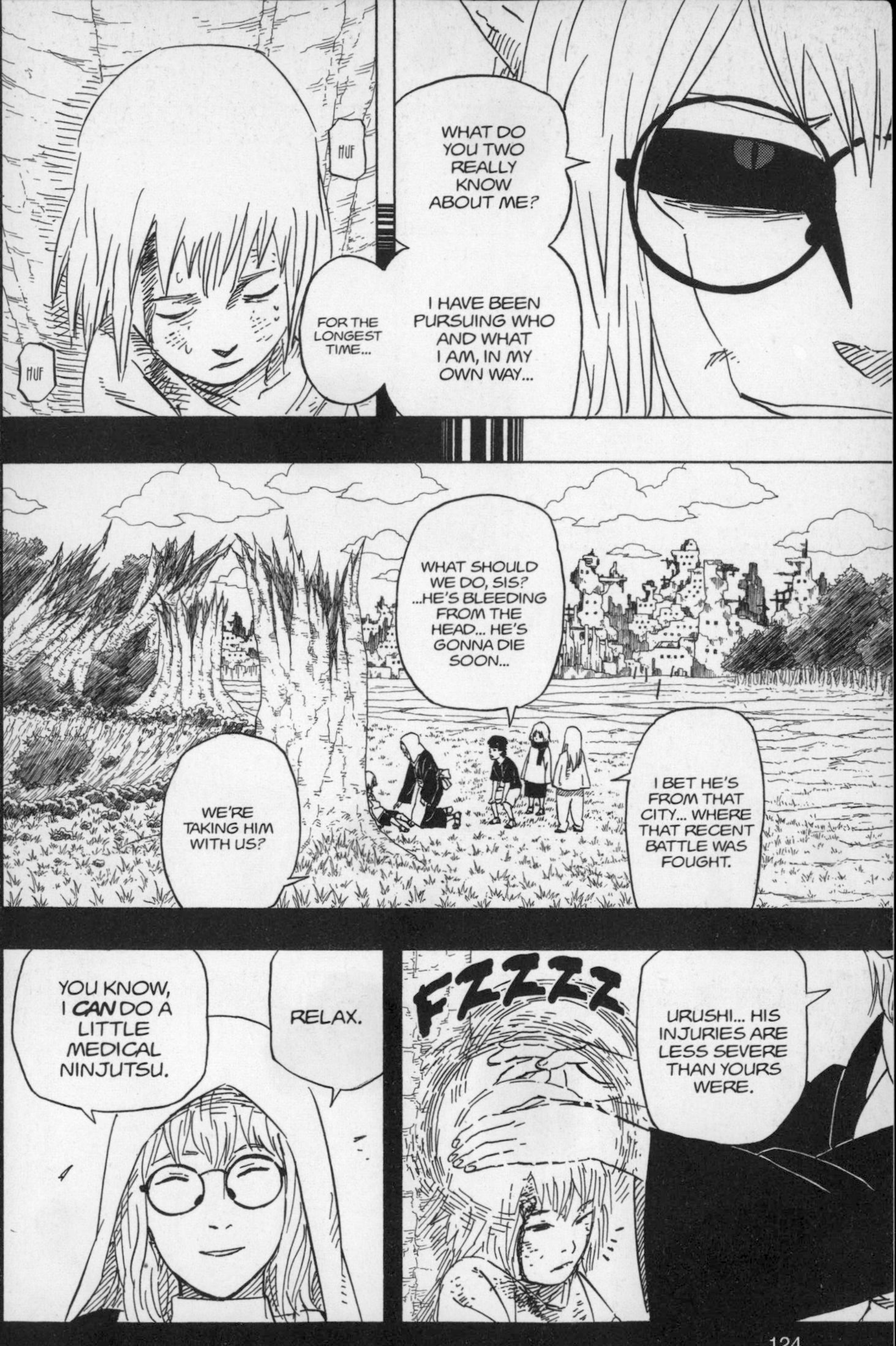
WHAT DO YOU TWO REALLY KNOW ABOUT ME?
I HAVE BEEN PURSUING WHO AND WHAT I AM, IN MY OWN WAY...
FOR THE LONGEST TIME...
HUF
HUF
WHAT SHOULD WE DO, SIS? ...HE'S BLEEDING FROM THE HEAD... HE'S GONNA DIE SOON...
I BET HE'S FROM THAT CITY... WHERE THAT RECENT BATTLE WAS FOUGHT.
WE'RE TAKING HIM WITH US?
FZZZZ
URUSHI... HIS INJURIES ARE LESS SEVERE THAN YOURS WERE.
RELAX.
YOU KNOW, I **CAN** DO A LITTLE MEDICAL NINJUTSU.

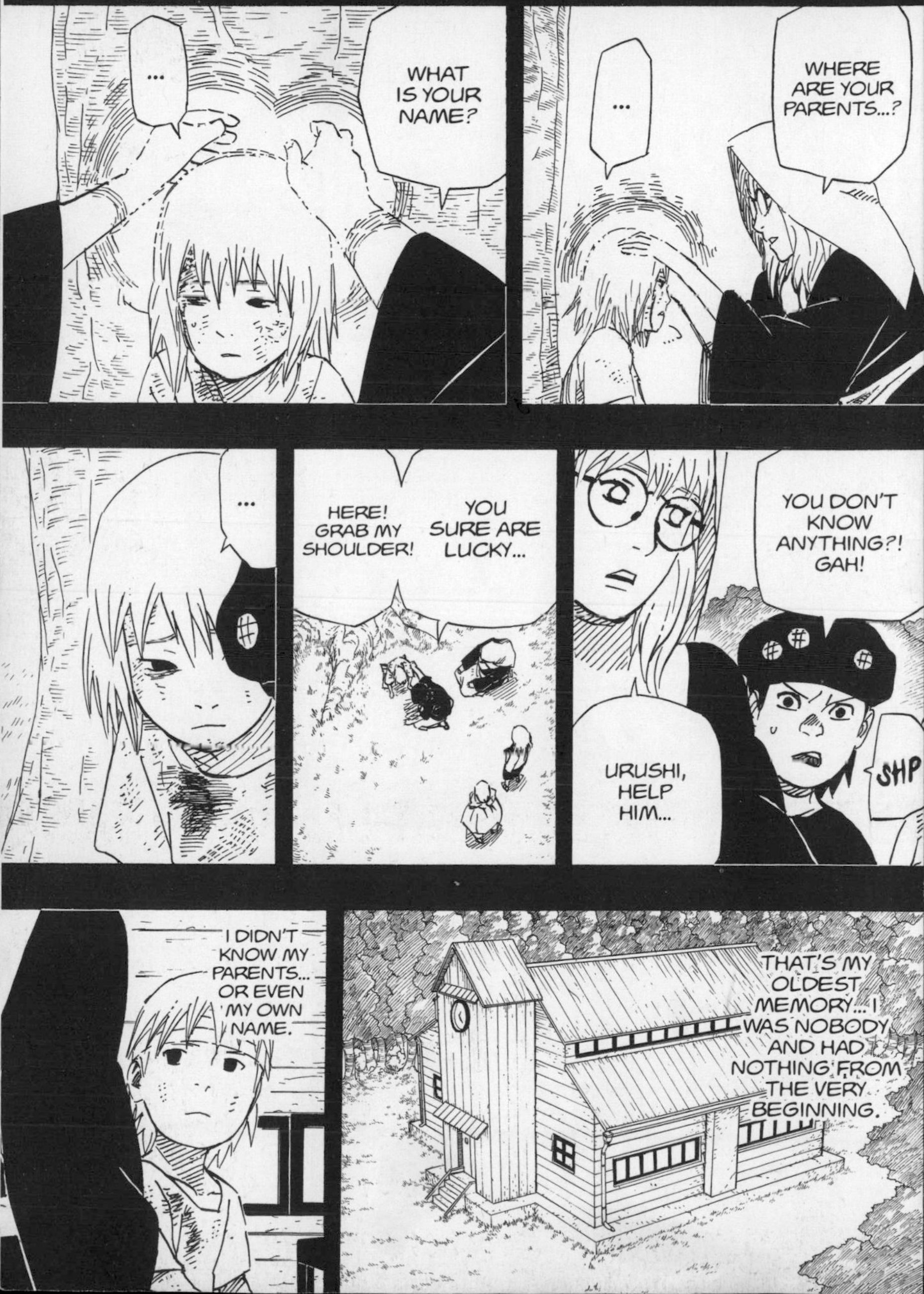
WHERE ARE YOUR PARENTS...?
...
WHAT IS YOUR NAME?
...
YOU DON'T KNOW ANYTHING?! GAH!
SHP
URUSHI, HELP HIM...
YOU SURE ARE LUCKY...
HERE! GRAB MY SHOULDER!
...
THAT'S MY OLDEST MEMORY... I WAS NOBODY AND HAD NOTHING FROM THE VERY BEGINNING.
I DIDN'T KNOW MY PARENTS... OR EVEN MY OWN NAME.

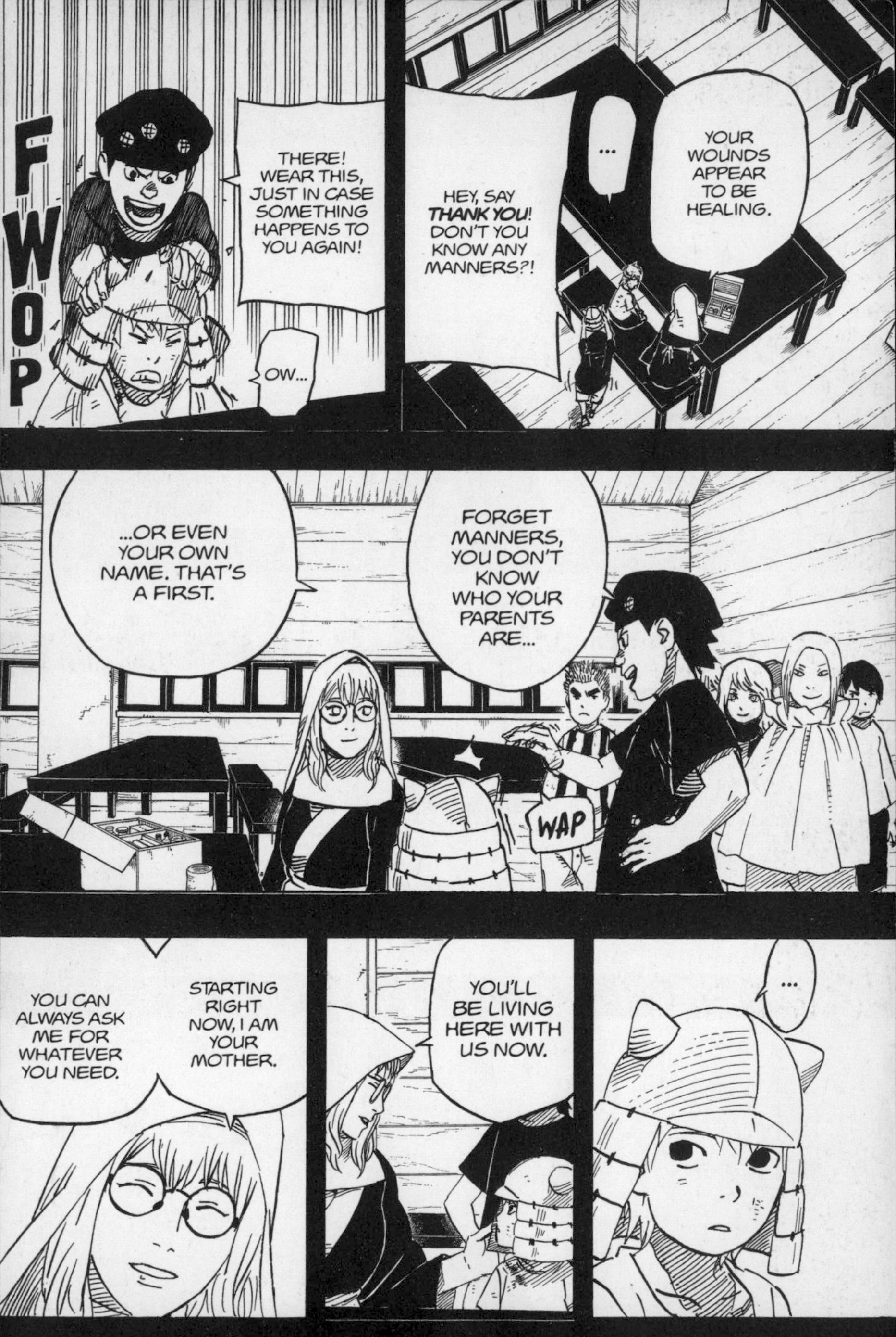
YOUR WOUNDS APPEAR TO BE HEALING.
...
HEY, SAY **THANK YOU**! DON'T YOU KNOW ANY MANNERS?!
FWOP
THERE! WEAR THIS, JUST IN CASE SOMETHING HAPPENS TO YOU AGAIN!
OW...
FORGET MANNERS, YOU DON'T KNOW WHO YOUR PARENTS ARE...
...OR EVEN YOUR OWN NAME. THAT'S A FIRST.
WAP
...
YOU'LL BE LIVING HERE WITH US NOW.
STARTING RIGHT NOW, I AM YOUR MOTHER.
YOU CAN ALWAYS ASK ME FOR WHATEVER YOU NEED.

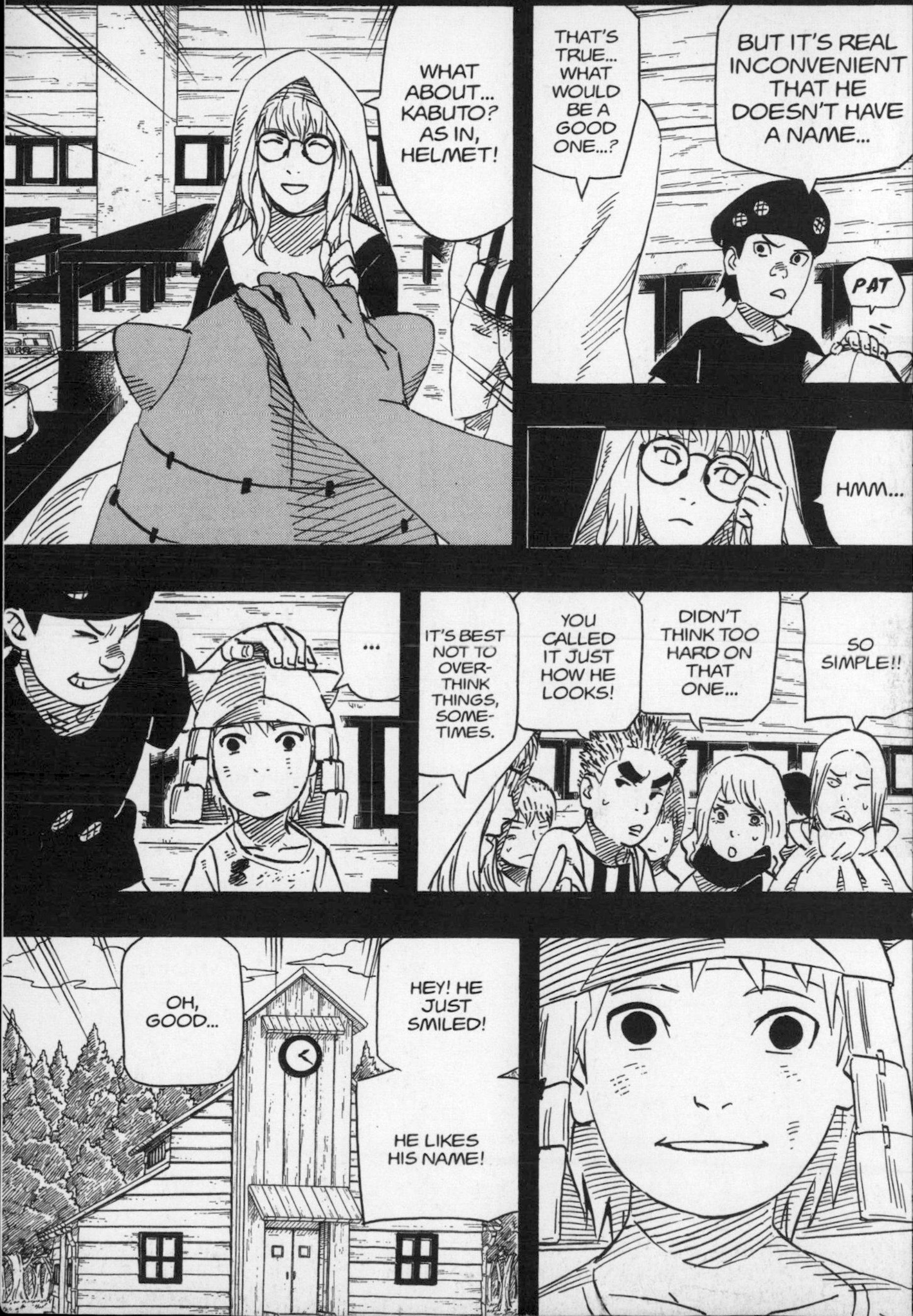
BUT IT'S REAL INCONVENIENT THAT HE DOESN'T HAVE A NAME...
THAT'S TRUE... WHAT WOULD BE A GOOD ONE...?
PAT
HMM...
WHAT ABOUT... KABUTO? AS IN, HELMET!
SO SIMPLE!!
DIDN'T THINK TOO HARD ON THAT ONE...
YOU CALLED IT JUST HOW HE LOOKS!
IT'S BEST NOT TO OVER-THINK THINGS, SOMETIMES.
...
HEY! HE JUST SMILED!
HE LIKES HIS NAME!
OH, GOOD...

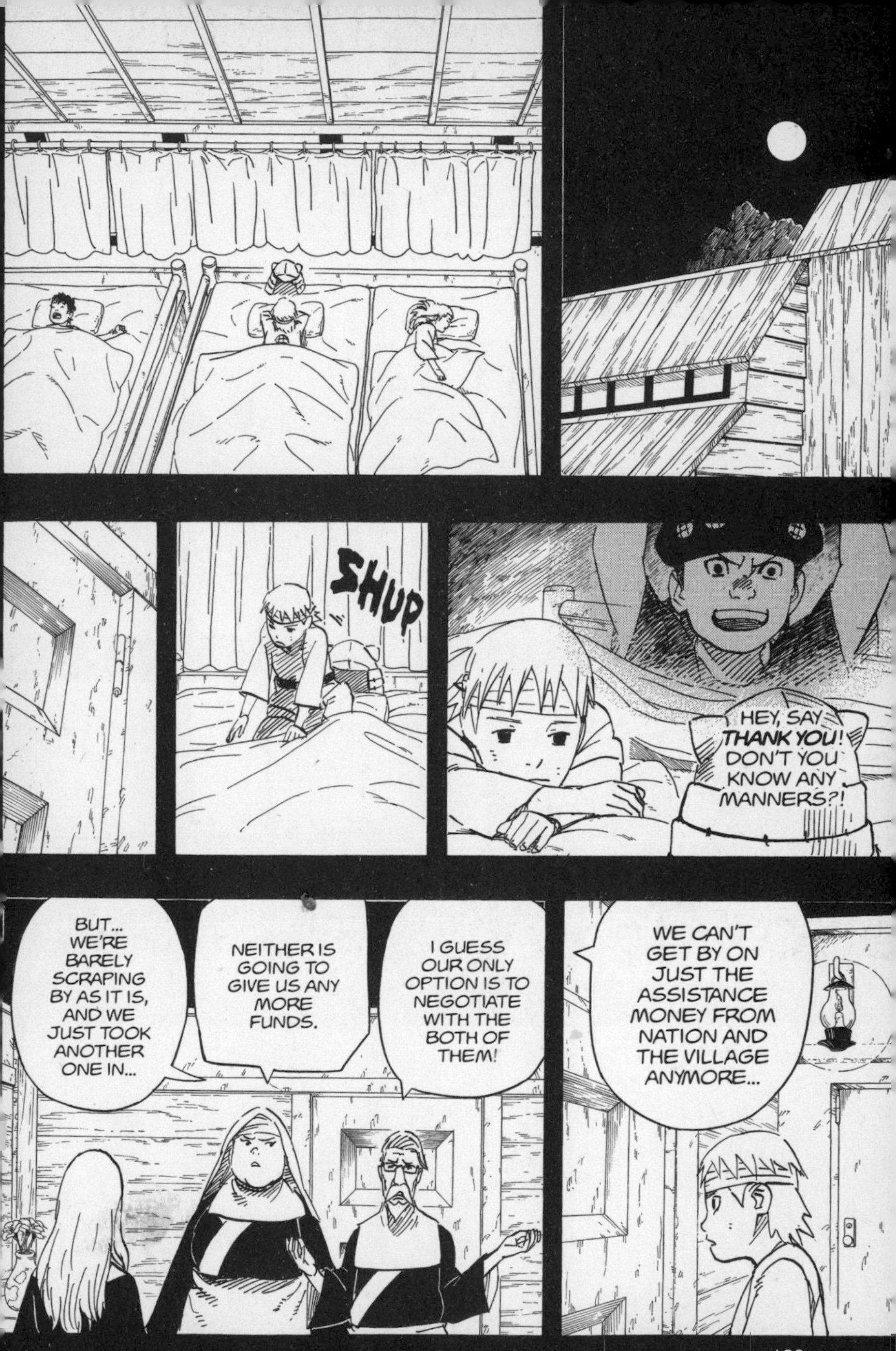
HEY, SAY **THANK YOU**! DON'T YOU KNOW ANY MANNERS?!
SHUP
WE CAN'T GET BY ON JUST THE ASSISTANCE MONEY FROM NATION AND THE VILLAGE ANYMORE...
I GUESS OUR ONLY OPTION IS TO NEGOTIATE WITH THE BOTH OF THEM!
NEITHER IS GOING TO GIVE US ANY MORE FUNDS.
BUT... WE'RE BARELY SCRAPING BY AS IT IS, AND WE JUST TOOK ANOTHER ONE IN...

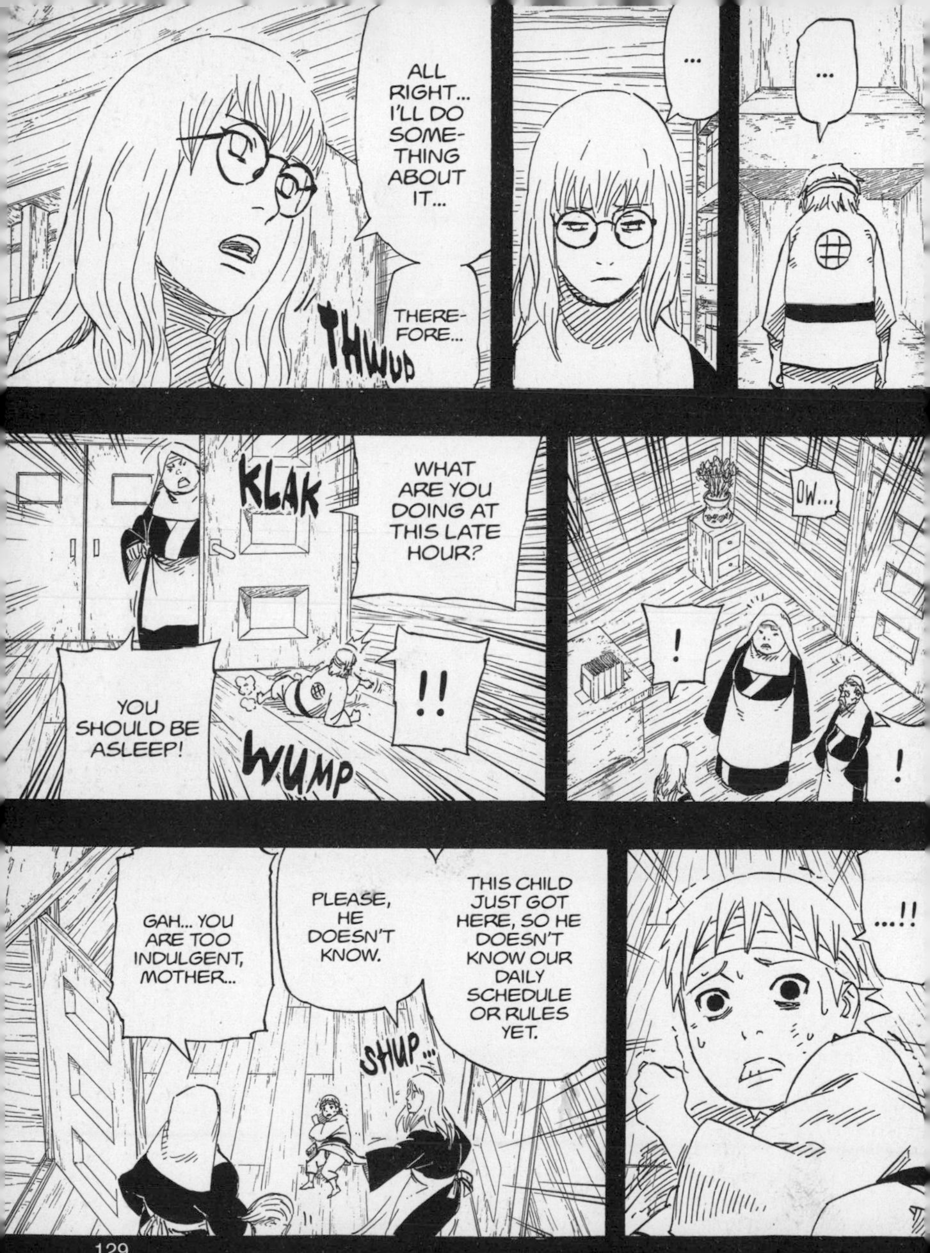
...
...
ALL RIGHT... I'LL DO SOME-THING ABOUT IT...
THERE-FORE...
THWUD
OW...
!
!
WHAT ARE YOU DOING AT THIS LATE HOUR?
KLAK
!!
YOU SHOULD BE ASLEEP!
WUMP
...!!
THIS CHILD JUST GOT HERE, SO HE DOESN'T KNOW OUR DAILY SCHEDULE OR RULES YET.
PLEASE, HE DOESN'T KNOW.
GAH... YOU ARE TOO INDULGENT, MOTHER...
SHUP...

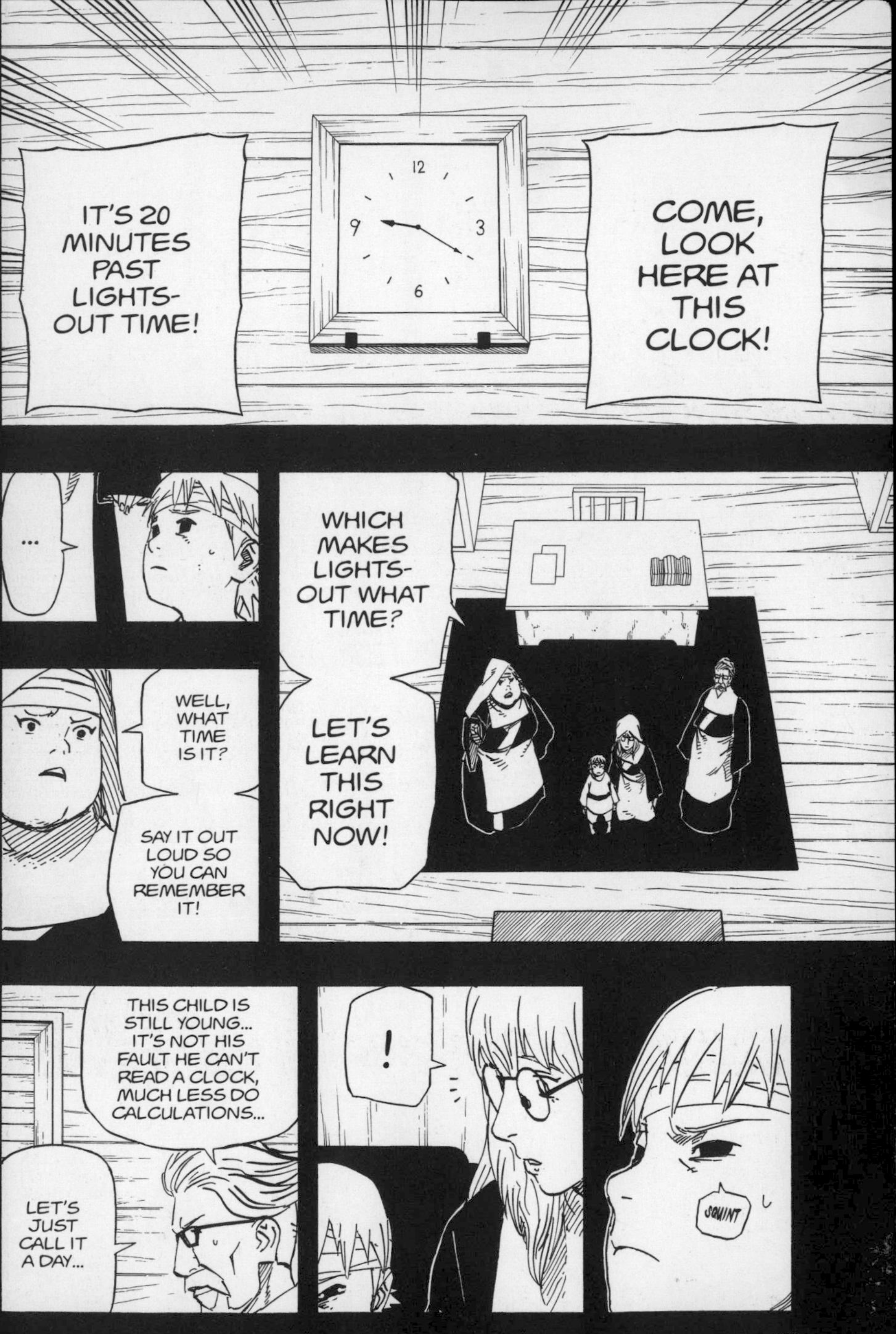
COME, LOOK HERE AT THIS CLOCK!
IT'S 20 MINUTES PAST LIGHTS-OUT TIME!
12
9
3
6
WHICH MAKES LIGHTS-OUT WHAT TIME?
LET'S LEARN THIS RIGHT NOW!
...
WELL, WHAT TIME IS IT?
SAY IT OUT LOUD SO YOU CAN REMEMBER IT!
!
SQUINT
THIS CHILD IS STILL YOUNG... IT'S NOT HIS FAULT HE CAN'T READ A CLOCK, MUCH LESS DO CALCULATIONS...
LET'S JUST CALL IT A DAY...

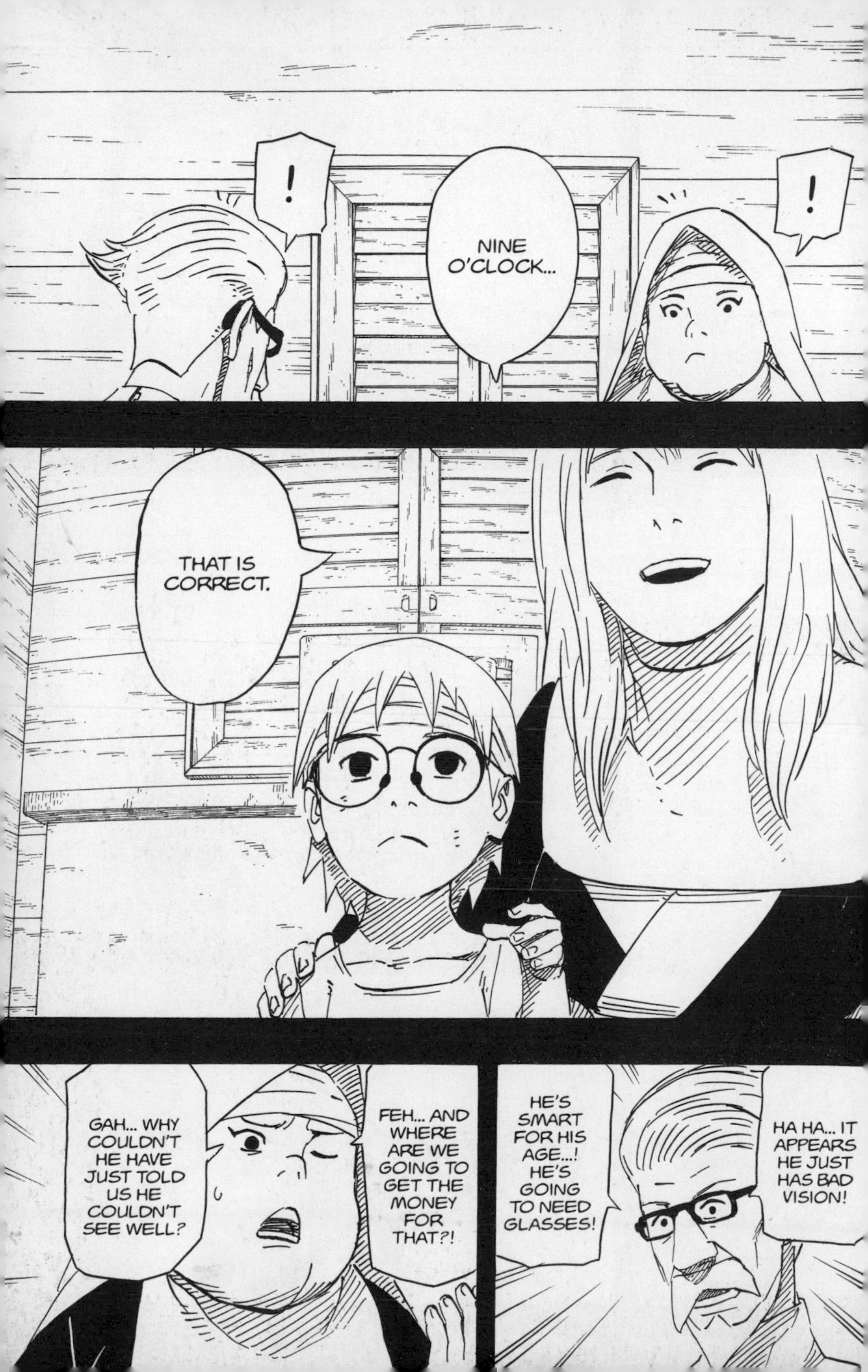
NINE O'CLOCK...
!
!
THAT IS CORRECT.
HA HA... IT APPEARS HE JUST HAS BAD VISION!
HE'S SMART FOR HIS AGE...! HE'S GOING TO NEED GLASSES!
FEH... AND WHERE ARE WE GOING TO GET THE MONEY FOR THAT?!
GAH... WHY COULDN'T HE HAVE JUST TOLD US HE COULDN'T SEE WELL?

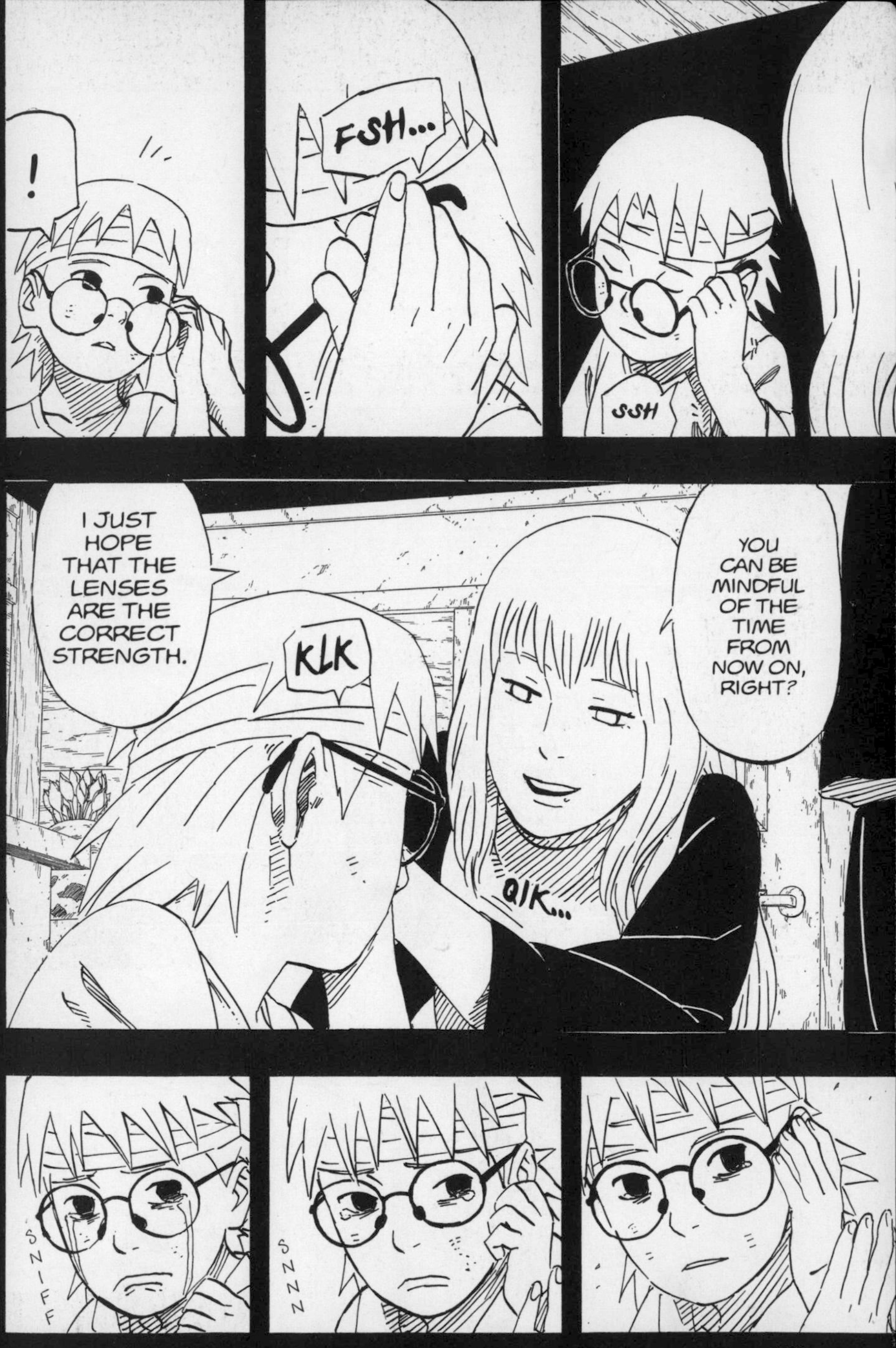
SSH
FSH...
!
YOU CAN BE MINDFUL OF THE TIME FROM NOW ON, RIGHT?
I JUST HOPE THAT THE LENSES ARE THE CORRECT STRENGTH.
KLK
QIK...
SNNN
SNIFF

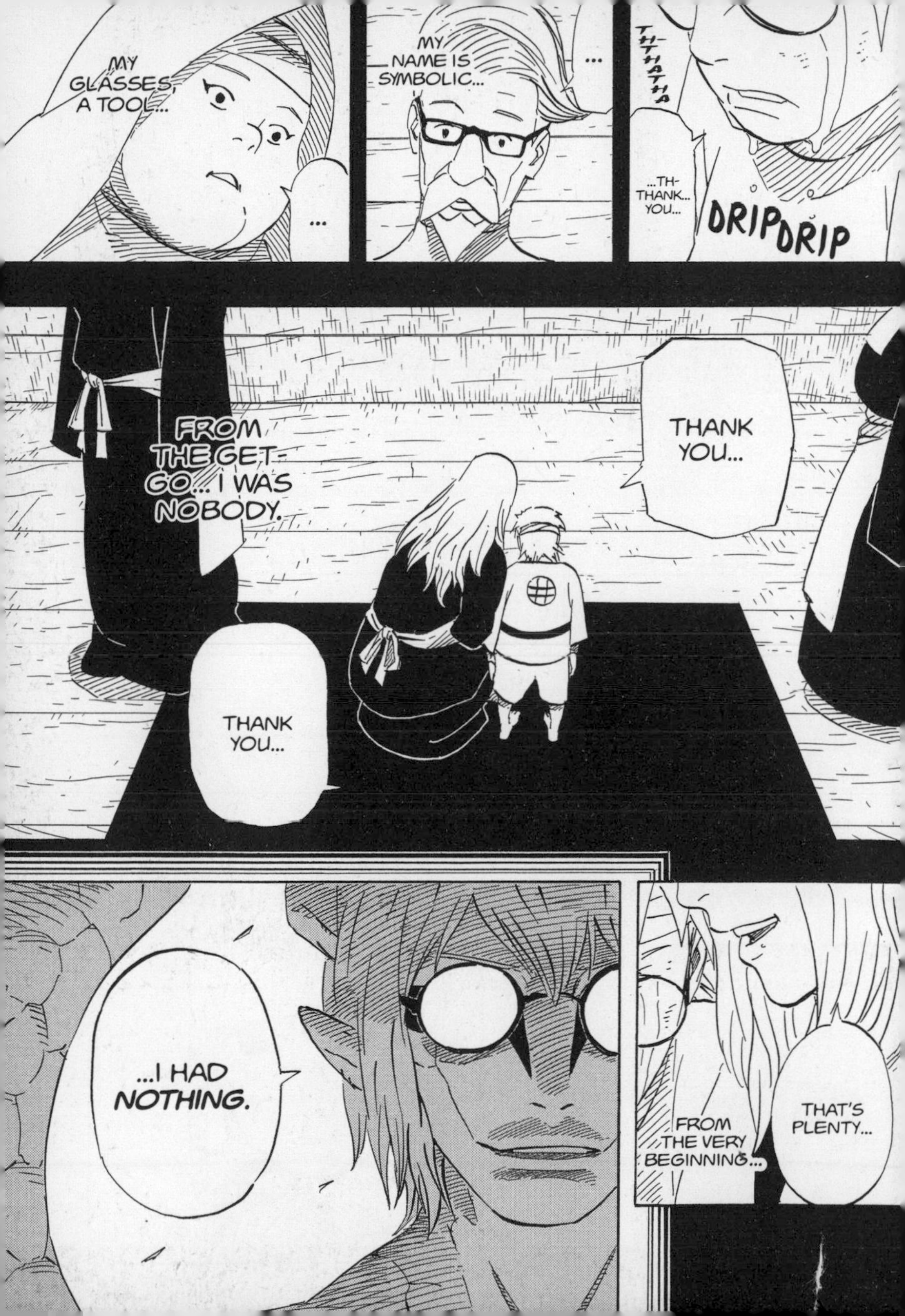
THTHATHA
...TH-THANK... YOU...
DRIP DRIP
MY NAME IS SYMBOLIC...
...
MY GLASSES, A TOOL...
...
THANK YOU...
FROM THE GET-GO... I WAS NOBODY.
THANK YOU...
THAT'S PLENTY...
FROM THE VERY BEGINNING...
...I HAD NOTHING.

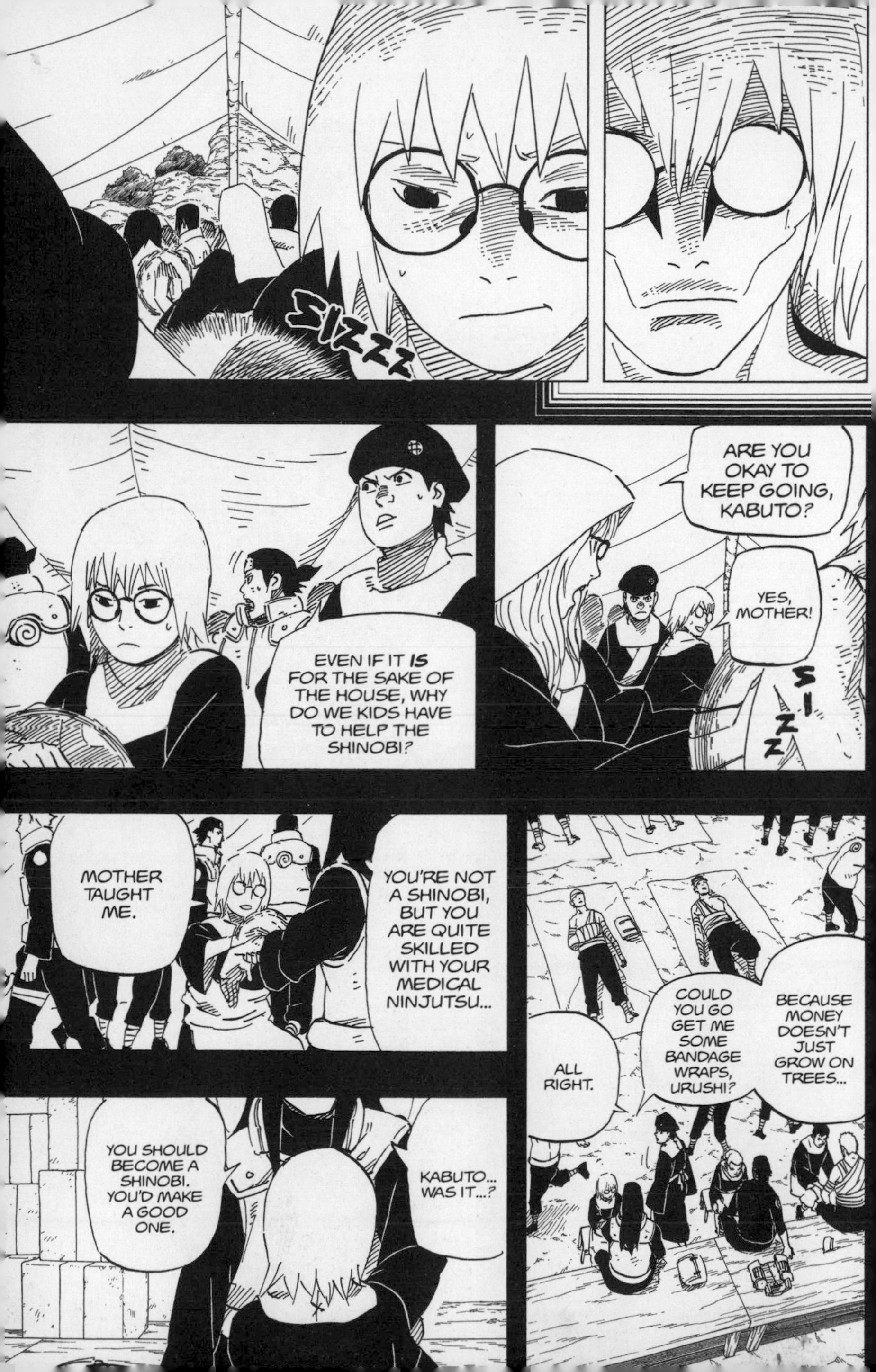
SIZZZ
ARE YOU OKAY TO KEEP GOING, KABUTO?
YES, MOTHER!
SIZZZ
EVEN IF IT IS FOR THE SAKE OF THE HOUSE, WHY DO WE KIDS HAVE TO HELP THE SHINOBI?
BECAUSE MONEY DOESN'T JUST GROW ON TREES...
COULD YOU GO GET ME SOME BANDAGE WRAPS, URUSHI?
ALL RIGHT.
YOU'RE NOT A SHINOBI, BUT YOU ARE QUITE SKILLED WITH YOUR MEDICAL NINJUTSU...
MOTHER TAUGHT ME.
KABUTO... WAS IT...?
YOU SHOULD BECOME A SHINOBI. YOU'D MAKE A GOOD ONE.

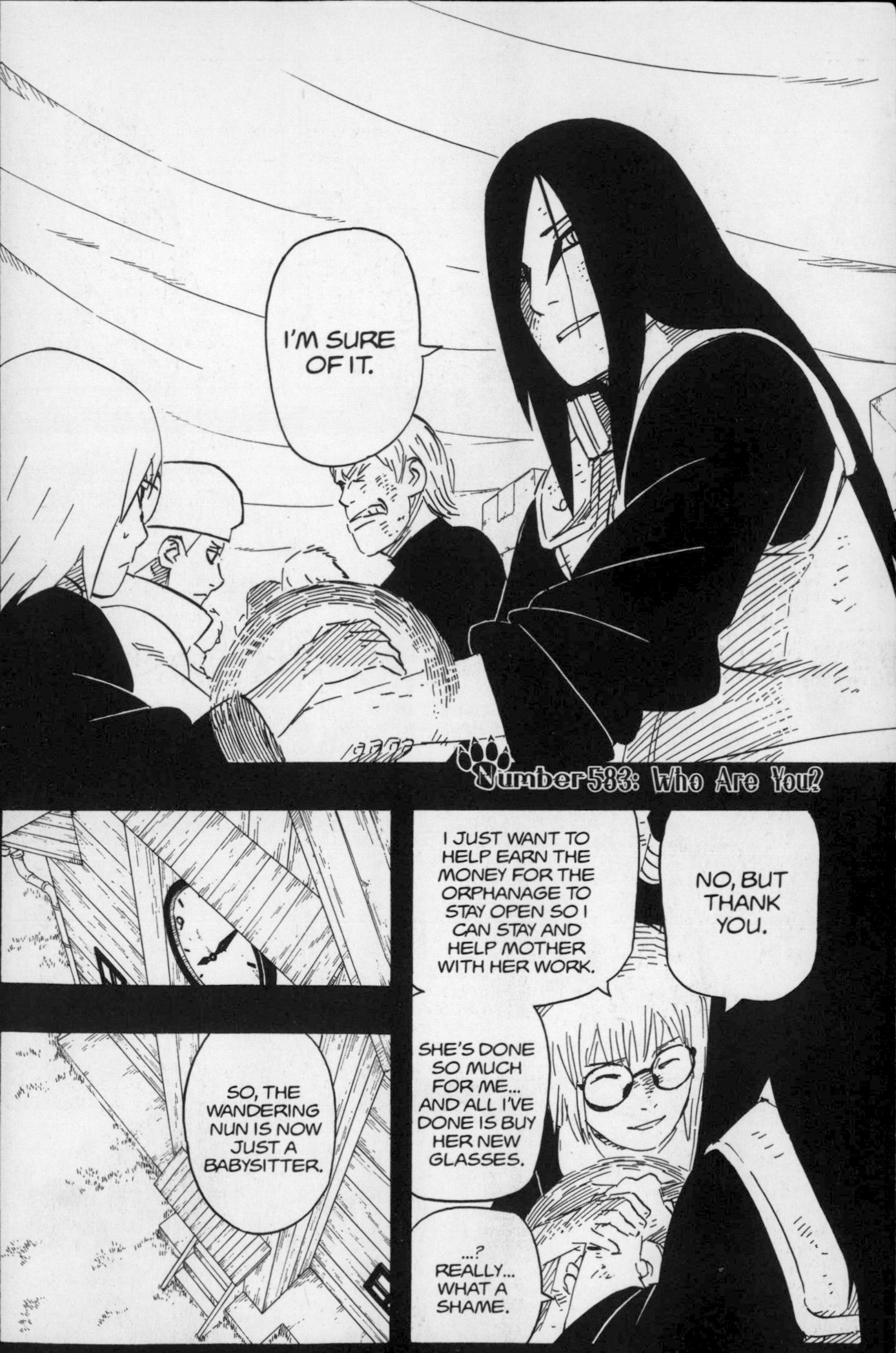
I'M SURE OF IT.
Number 583: Who Are You?
NO, BUT THANK YOU.
I JUST WANT TO HELP EARN THE MONEY FOR THE ORPHANAGE TO STAY OPEN SO I CAN STAY AND HELP MOTHER WITH HER WORK.
SHE'S DONE SO MUCH FOR ME... AND ALL I'VE DONE IS BUY HER NEW GLASSES.
...? REALLY... WHAT A SHAME.
SO, THE WANDERING NUN IS NOW JUST A BABYSITTER.

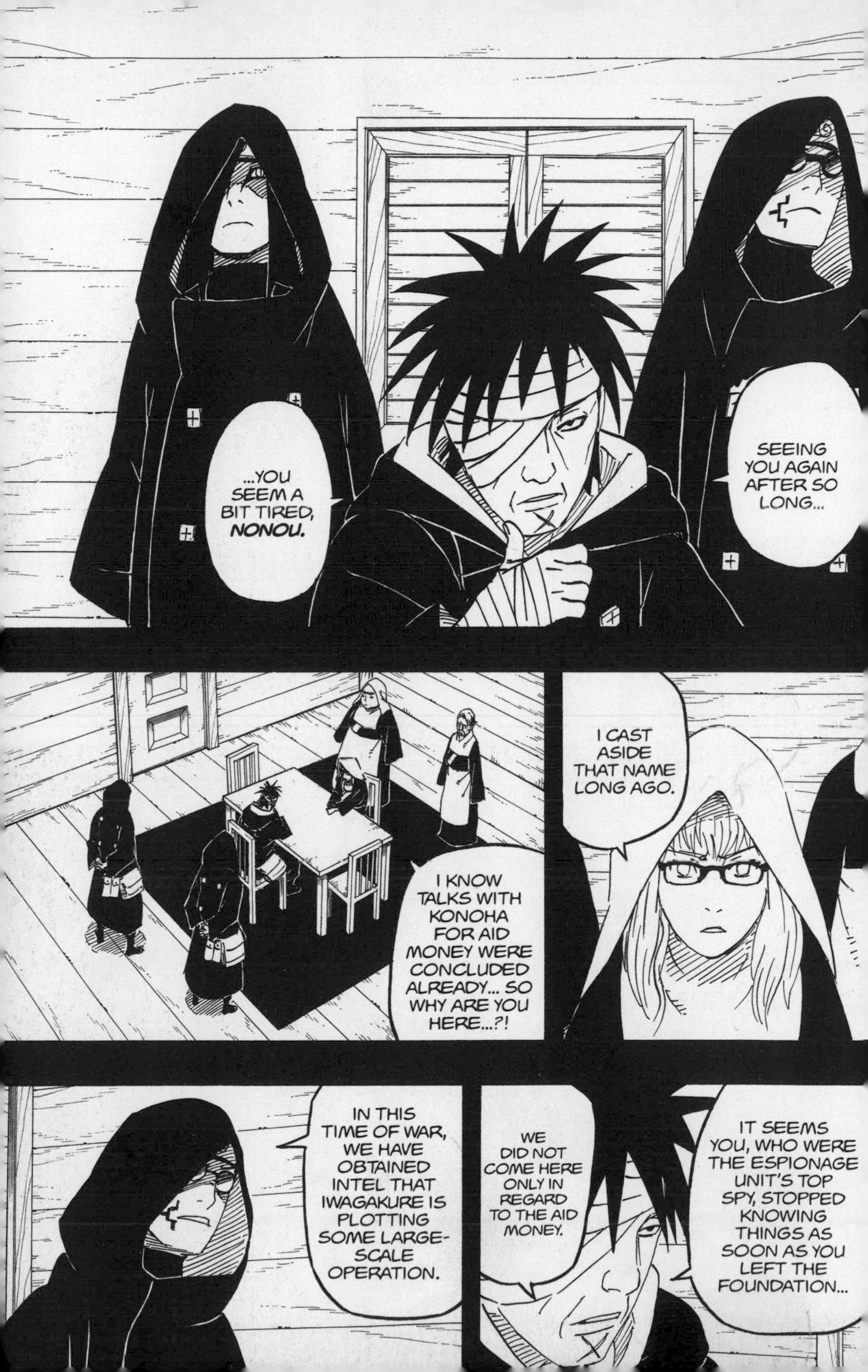
SEEING YOU AGAIN AFTER SO LONG...
...YOU SEEM A BIT TIRED, **NONOU.**
I CAST ASIDE THAT NAME LONG AGO.
I KNOW TALKS WITH KONOHA FOR AID MONEY WERE CONCLUDED ALREADY... SO WHY ARE YOU HERE...?!
IT SEEMS YOU, WHO WERE THE ESPIONAGE UNIT'S TOP SPY, STOPPED KNOWING THINGS AS SOON AS YOU LEFT THE FOUNDATION...
WE DID NOT COME HERE ONLY IN REGARD TO THE AID MONEY.
IN THIS TIME OF WAR, WE HAVE OBTAINED INTEL THAT IWAGAKURE IS PLOTTING SOME LARGE-SCALE OPERATION.

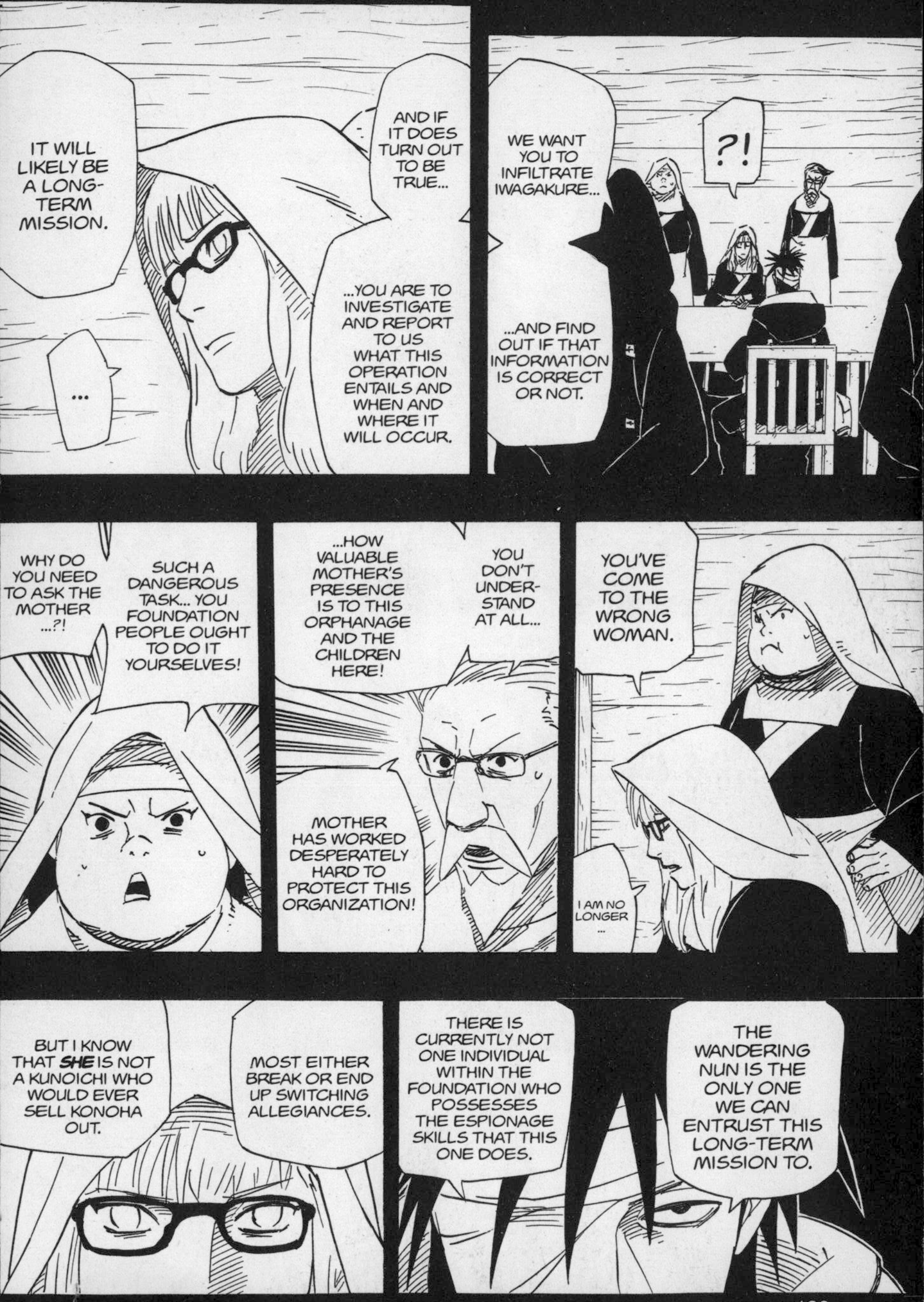
?!
WE WANT YOU TO INFILTRATE IWAGAKURE...
...AND FIND OUT IF THAT INFORMATION IS CORRECT OR NOT.
AND IF IT DOES TURN OUT TO BE TRUE...
...YOU ARE TO INVESTIGATE AND REPORT TO US WHAT THIS OPERATION ENTAILS AND WHEN AND WHERE IT WILL OCCUR.
IT WILL LIKELY BE A LONG-TERM MISSION.
...
YOU'VE COME TO THE WRONG WOMAN.
I AM NO LONGER ...
YOU DON'T UNDER-STAND AT ALL...
...HOW VALUABLE MOTHER'S PRESENCE IS TO THIS ORPHANAGE AND THE CHILDREN HERE!
MOTHER HAS WORKED DESPERATELY HARD TO PROTECT THIS ORGANIZATION!
SUCH A DANGEROUS TASK... YOU FOUNDATION PEOPLE OUGHT TO DO IT YOURSELVES!
WHY DO YOU NEED TO ASK THE MOTHER ...?!
THE WANDERING NUN IS THE ONLY ONE WE CAN ENTRUST THIS LONG-TERM MISSION TO.
THERE IS CURRENTLY NOT ONE INDIVIDUAL WITHIN THE FOUNDATION WHO POSSESSES THE ESPIONAGE SKILLS THAT THIS ONE DOES.
MOST EITHER BREAK OR END UP SWITCHING ALLEGIANCES.
BUT I KNOW THAT ***SHE*** IS NOT A KUNOICHI WHO WOULD EVER SELL KONOHA OUT.

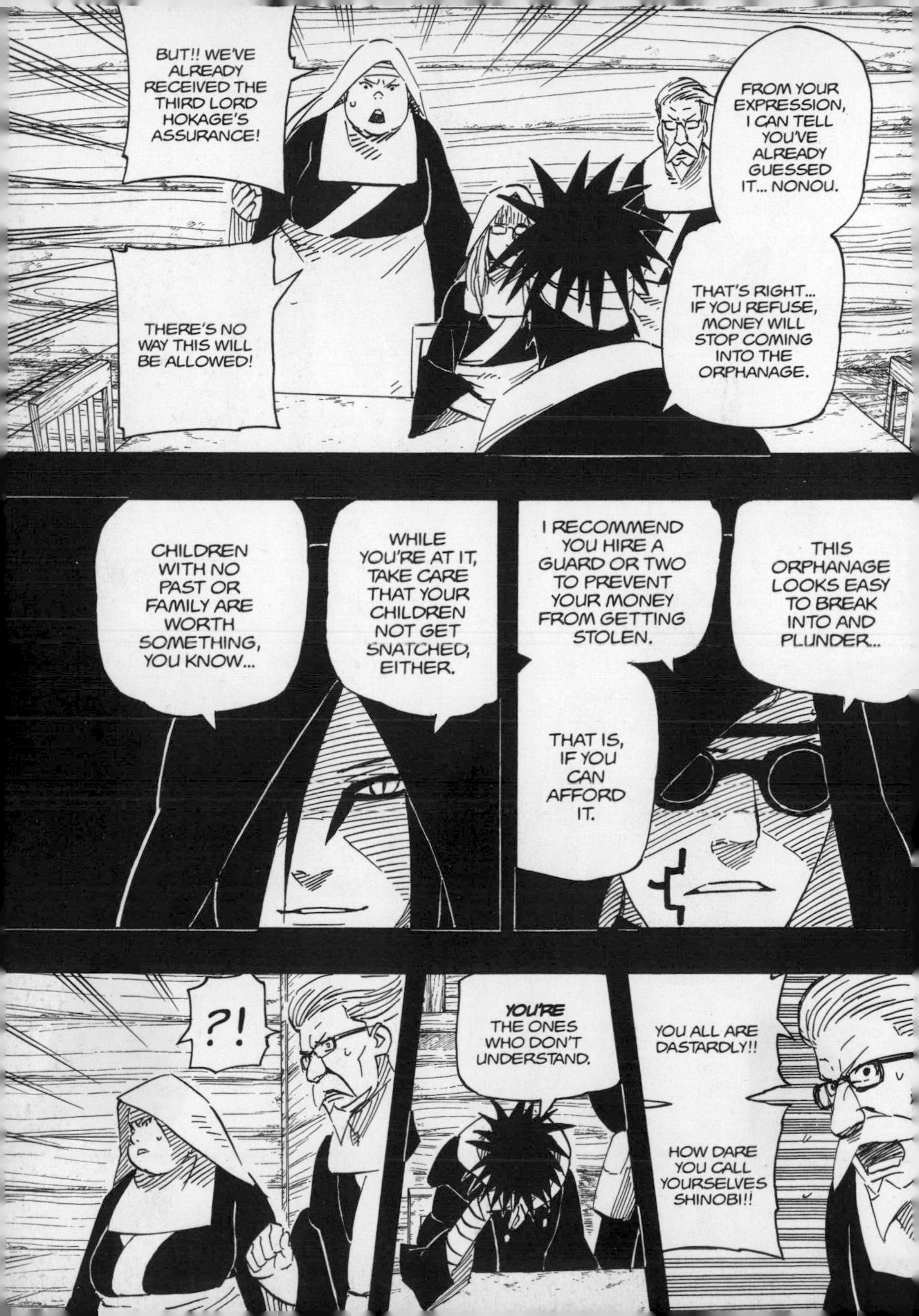
FROM YOUR EXPRESSION, I CAN TELL YOU'VE ALREADY GUESSED IT... NONOU.
THAT'S RIGHT... IF YOU REFUSE, MONEY WILL STOP COMING INTO THE ORPHANAGE.
BUT!! WE'VE ALREADY RECEIVED THE THIRD LORD HOKAGE'S ASSURANCE!
THERE'S NO WAY THIS WILL BE ALLOWED!
THIS ORPHANAGE LOOKS EASY TO BREAK INTO AND PLUNDER...
I RECOMMEND YOU HIRE A GUARD OR TWO TO PREVENT YOUR MONEY FROM GETTING STOLEN.
THAT IS, IF YOU CAN AFFORD IT.
WHILE YOU'RE AT IT, TAKE CARE THAT YOUR CHILDREN NOT GET SNATCHED, EITHER.
CHILDREN WITH NO PAST OR FAMILY ARE WORTH SOMETHING, YOU KNOW...
YOU ALL ARE DASTARDLY!!
HOW DARE YOU CALL YOURSELVES SHINOBI!!
YOU'RE THE ONES WHO DON'T UNDERSTAND.
?!

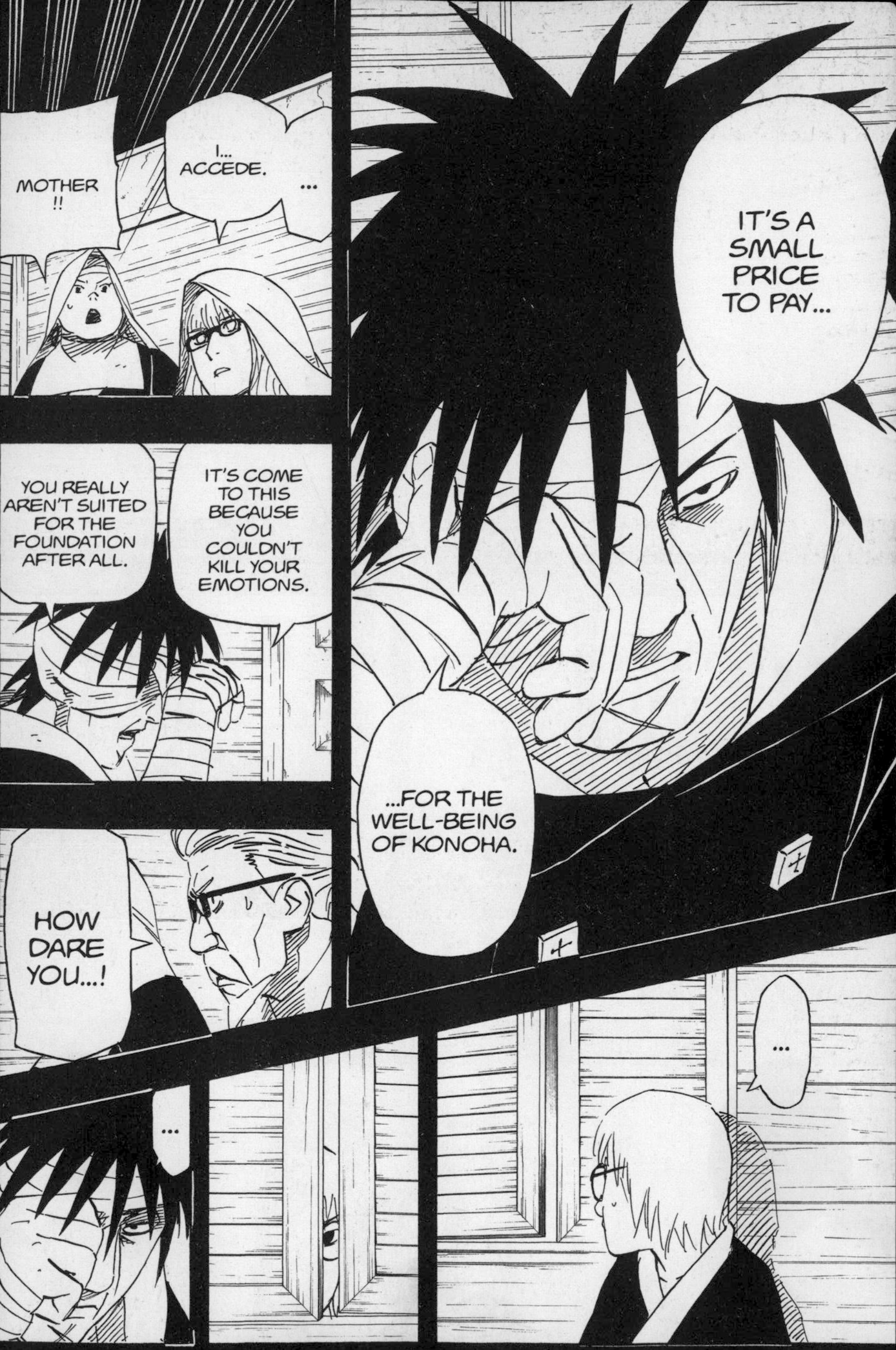
IT'S A SMALL PRICE TO PAY...
...FOR THE WELL-BEING OF KONOHA.
I... ACCEDE.
...
MOTHER !!
IT'S COME TO THIS BECAUSE YOU COULDN'T KILL YOUR EMOTIONS.
YOU REALLY AREN'T SUITED FOR THE FOUNDATION AFTER ALL.
HOW DARE YOU...!
...
...

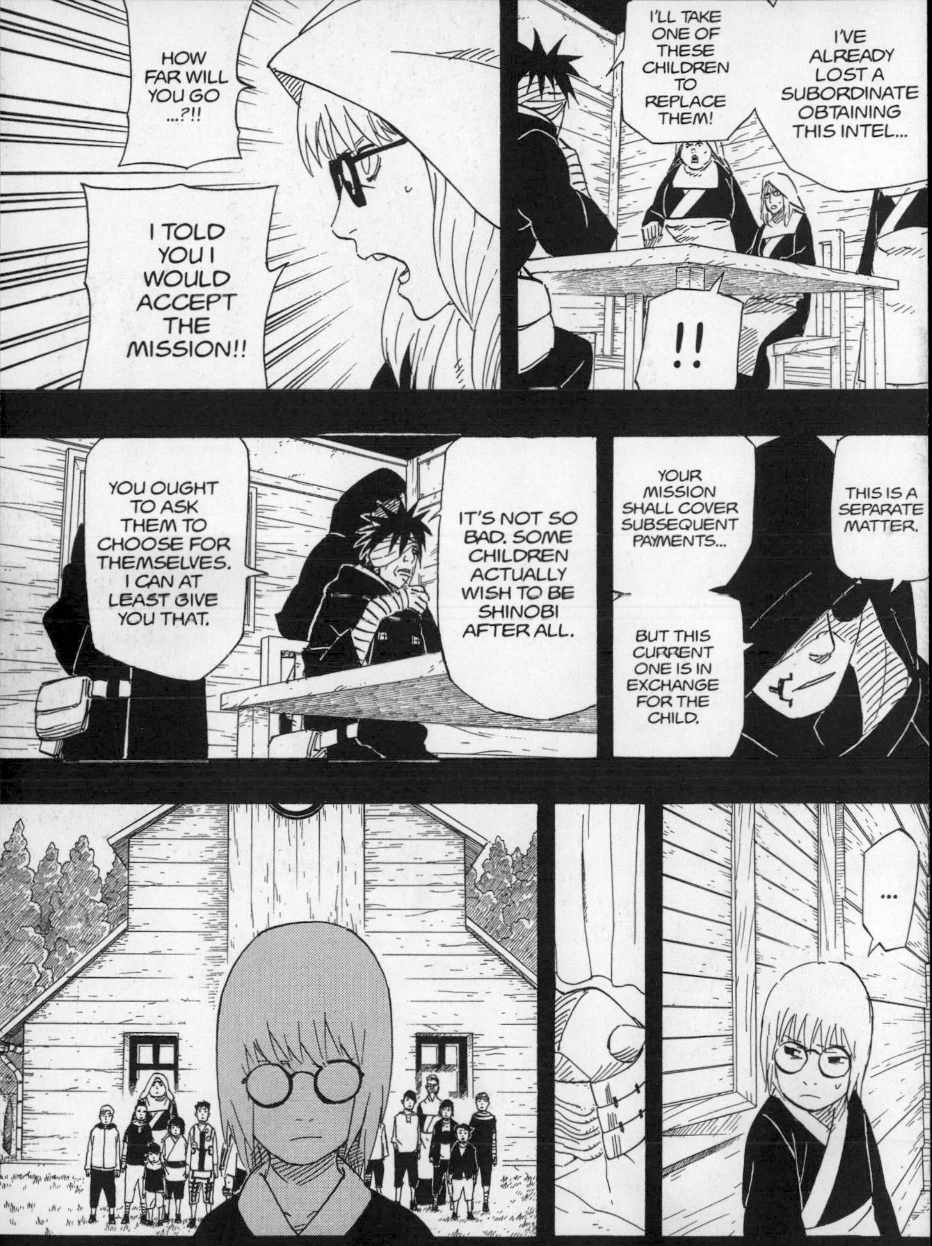
I'VE ALREADY LOST A SUBORDINATE OBTAINING THIS INTEL...
I'LL TAKE ONE OF THESE CHILDREN TO REPLACE THEM!
!!
HOW FAR WILL YOU GO ...?!!
I TOLD YOU I WOULD ACCEPT THE MISSION!!
THIS IS A SEPARATE MATTER.
YOUR MISSION SHALL COVER SUBSEQUENT PAYMENTS...
BUT THIS CURRENT ONE IS IN EXCHANGE FOR THE CHILD.
IT'S NOT SO BAD. SOME CHILDREN ACTUALLY WISH TO BE SHINOBI AFTER ALL.
YOU OUGHT TO ASK THEM TO CHOOSE FOR THEMSELVES. I CAN AT LEAST GIVE YOU THAT.
...

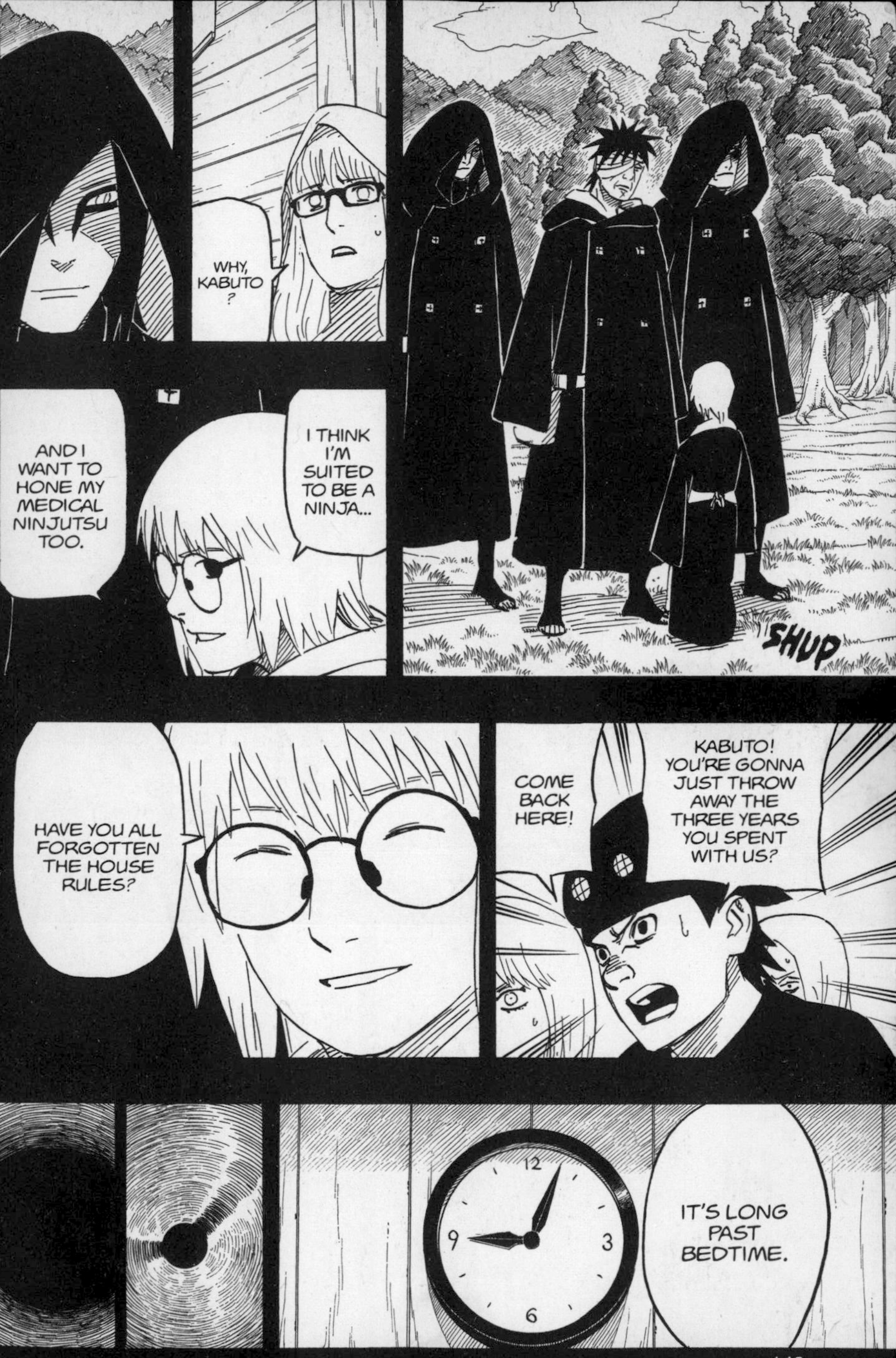
SHUP
WHY, KABUTO?
I THINK I'M SUITED TO BE A NINJA...
AND I WANT TO HONE MY MEDICAL NINJUTSU TOO.
KABUTO! YOU'RE GONNA JUST THROW AWAY THE THREE YEARS YOU SPENT WITH US?
COME BACK HERE!
HAVE YOU ALL FORGOTTEN THE HOUSE RULES?
IT'S LONG PAST BEDTIME.

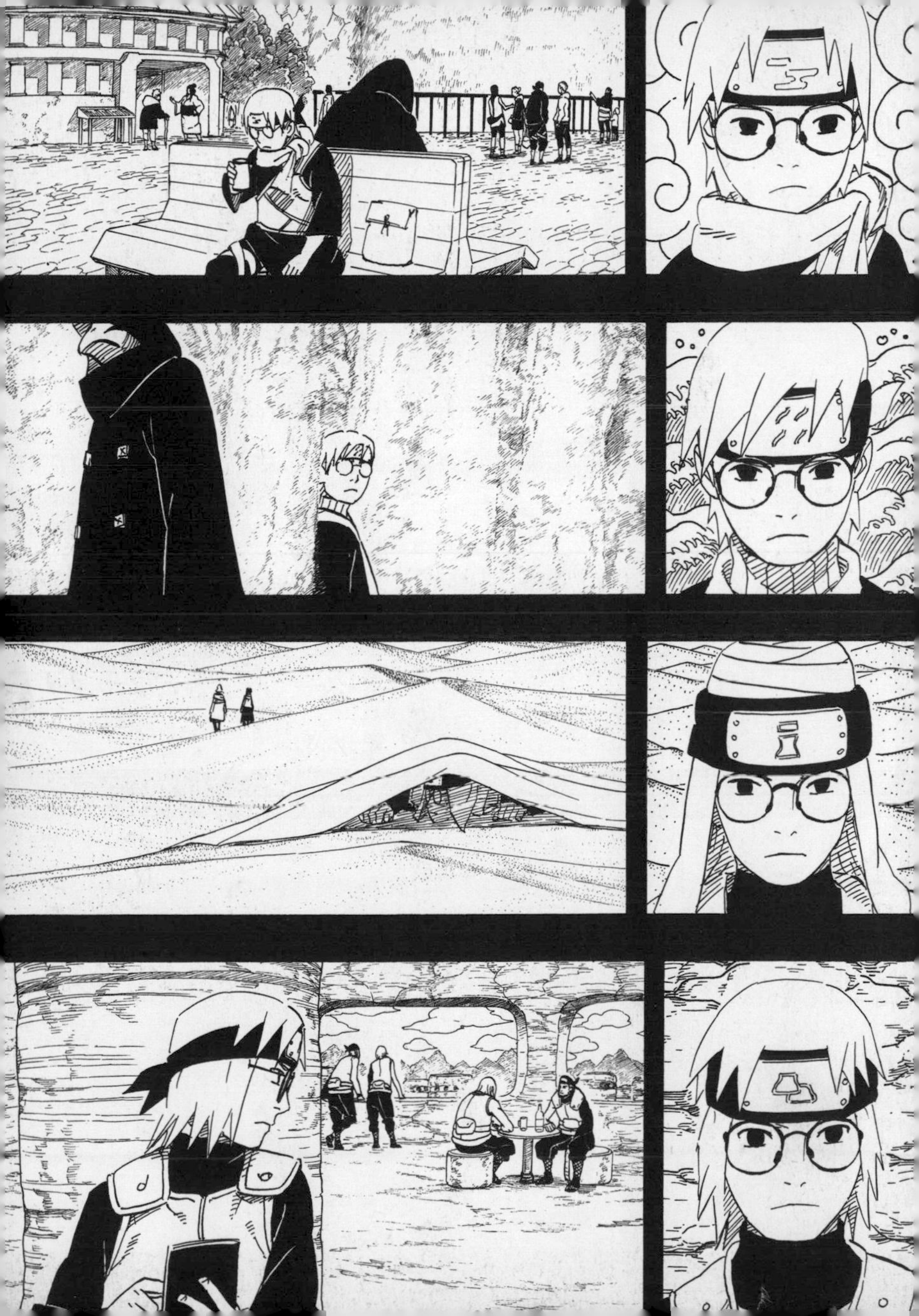

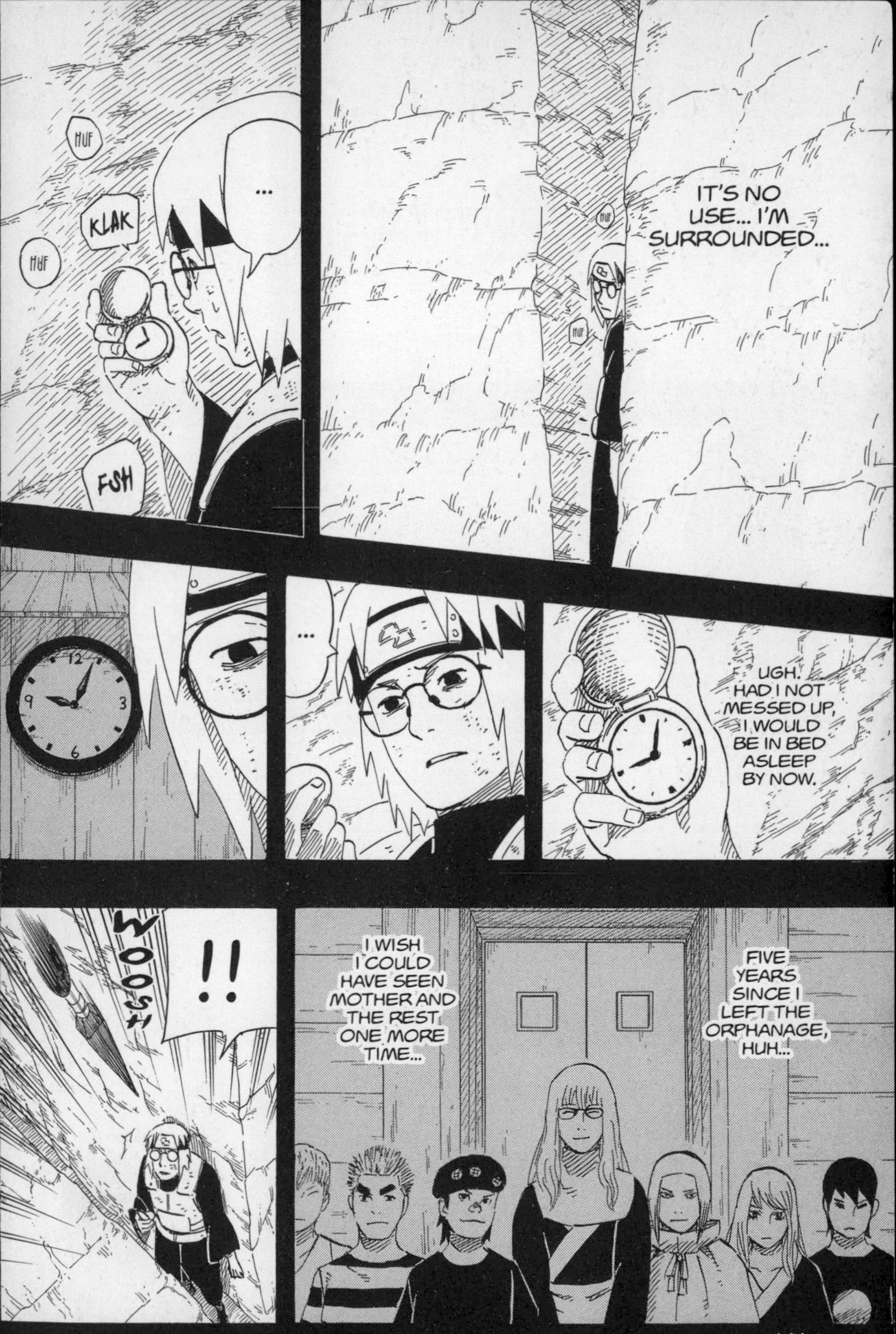
IT'S NO USE... I'M SURROUNDED...
HUF
HUF
...
HUF
KLAK
HUF
FSH
UGH. HAD I NOT MESSED UP, I WOULD BE IN BED ASLEEP BY NOW.
...
FIVE YEARS SINCE I LEFT THE ORPHANAGE, HUH...
I WISH I COULD HAVE SEEN MOTHER AND THE REST ONE MORE TIME...
!!
WOOSH

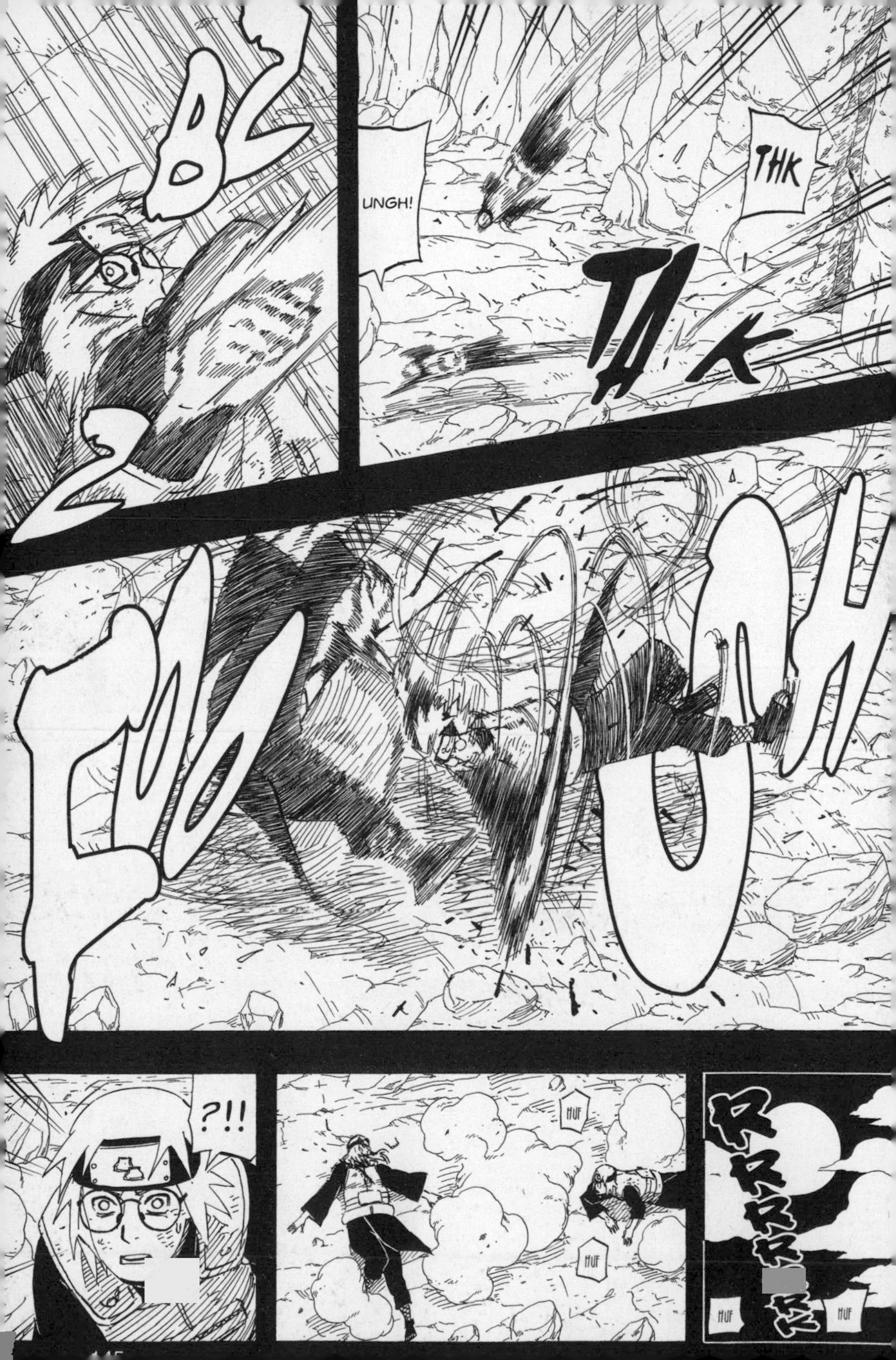
THK
UNGH!
HUF
HUF
HUF
HUF
?!!

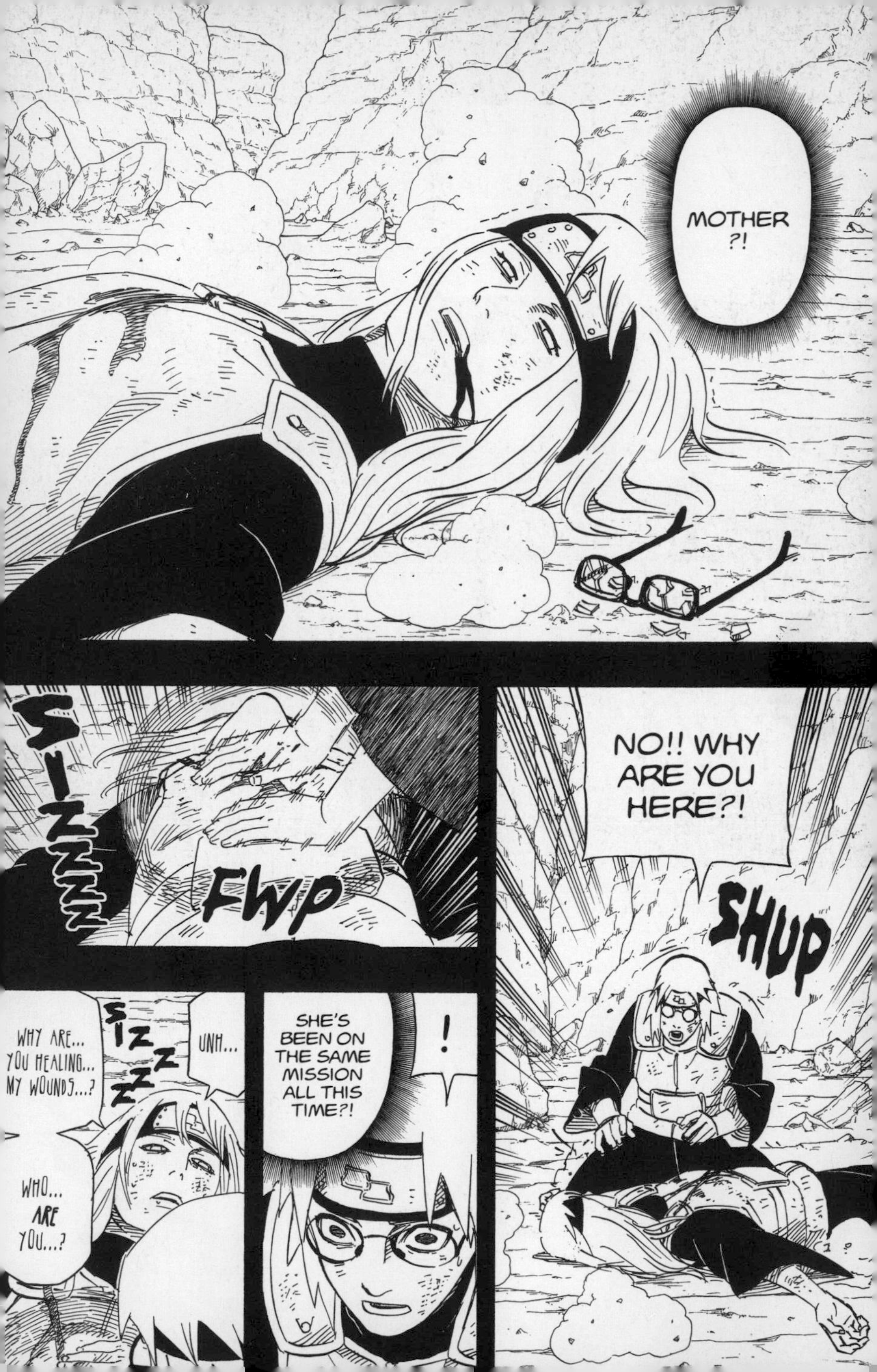
MOTHER ?!
NO!! WHY ARE YOU HERE?!
SHUP
SIZZZZ
FWP
!
SHE'S BEEN ON THE SAME MISSION ALL THIS TIME?!
UNH...
SIZZZ
WHY ARE... YOU HEALING... MY WOUNDS...?
WHO... ARE YOU...?

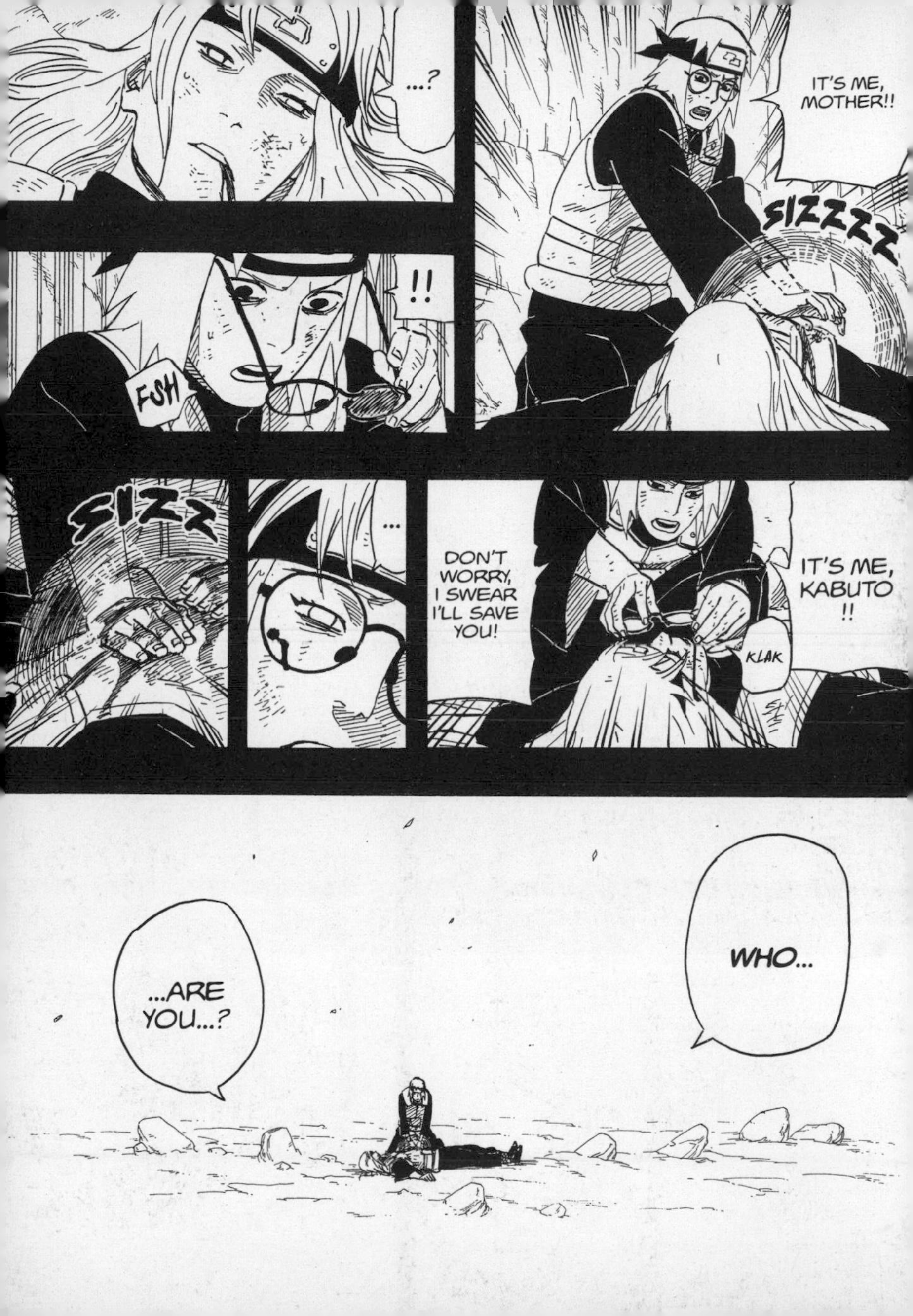
IT'S ME, MOTHER!!
SIZZZZZ
...?
!!
FSH
IT'S ME, KABUTO!!
KLAK
DON'T WORRY, I SWEAR I'LL SAVE YOU!
...
SIZZZ
WHO...
...ARE YOU...?

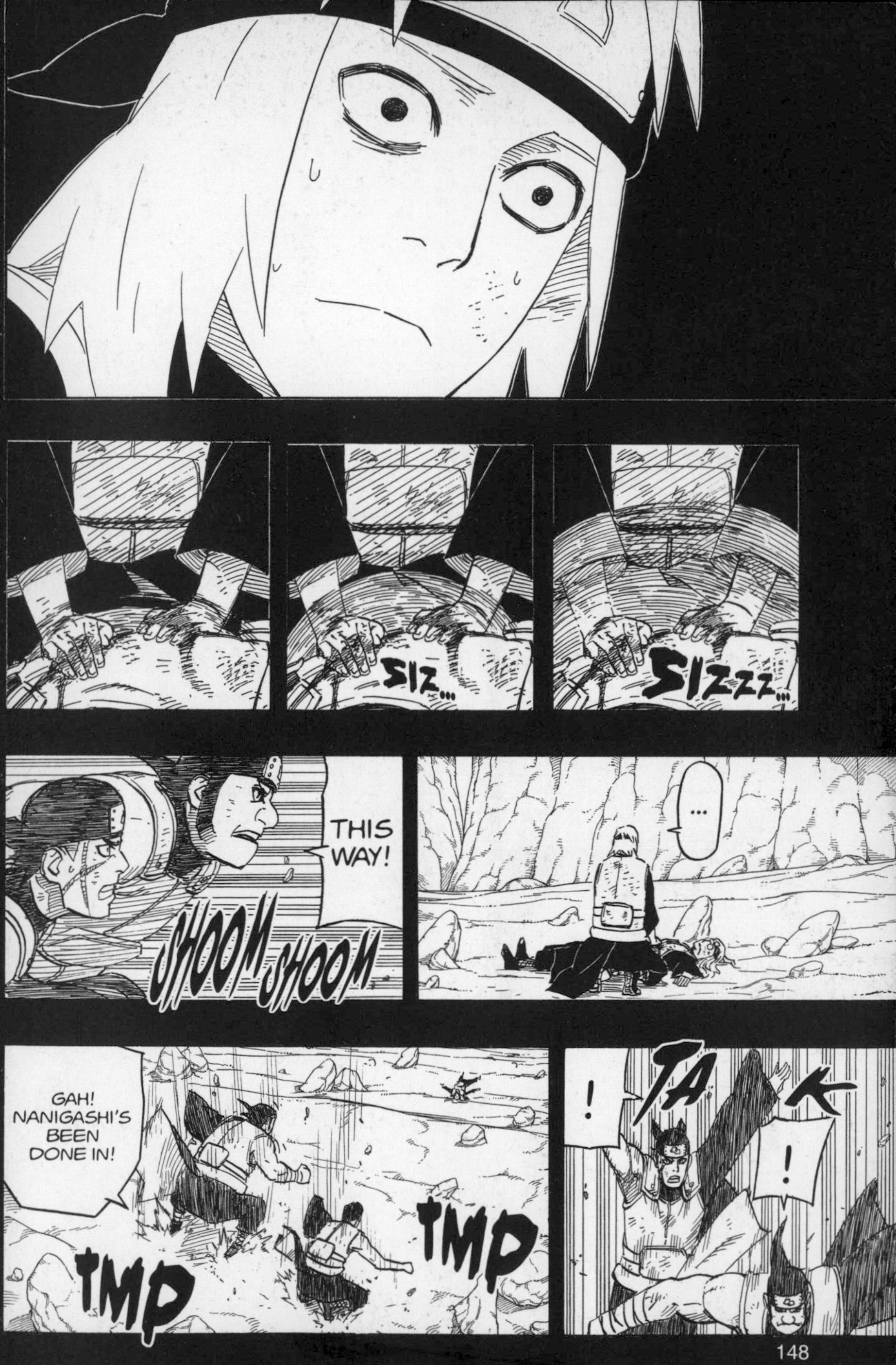
SIZZZZ...
SIZ...
...
THIS WAY!
SHOOM SHOOM
TAK
!
!
GAH! NANIGASHI'S BEEN DONE IN!
TMP
TMP

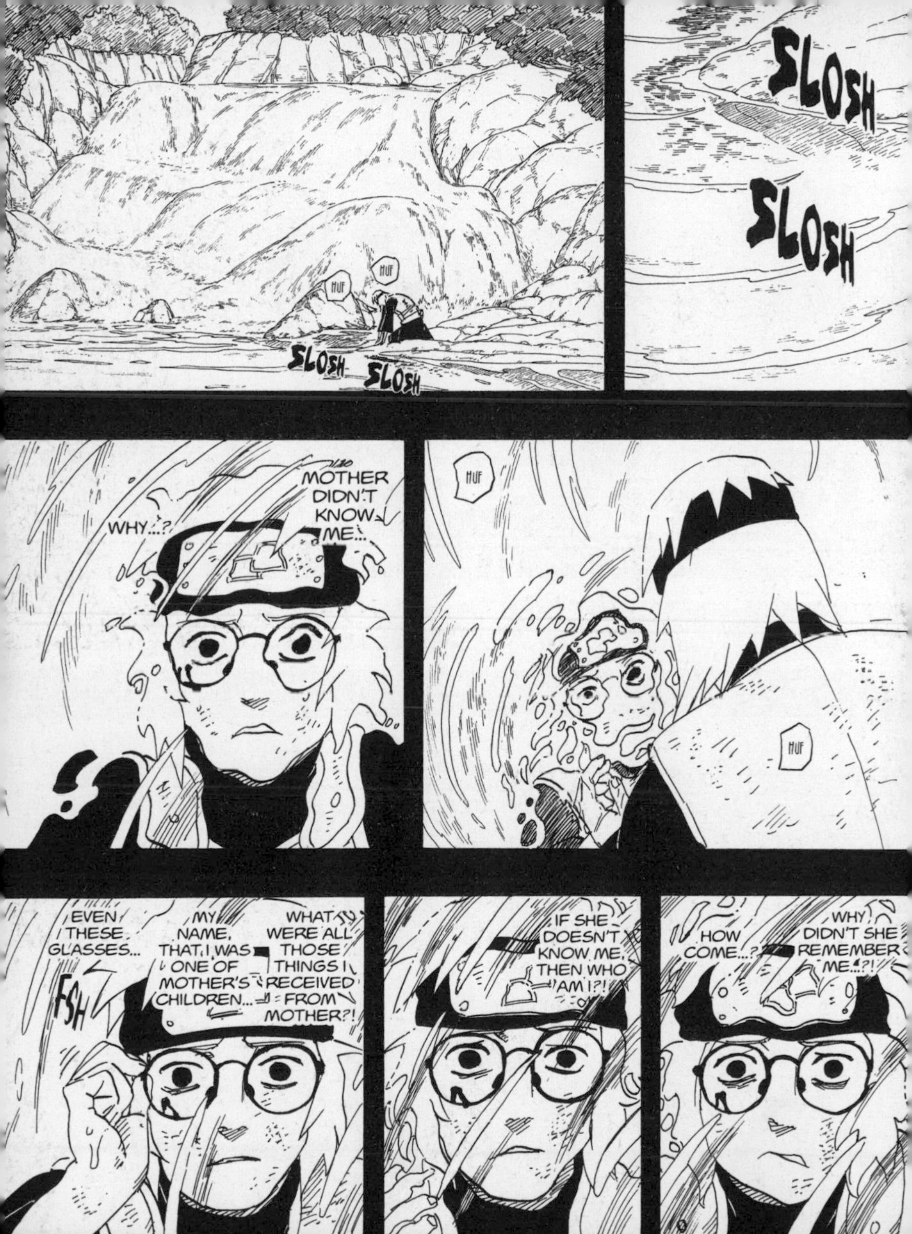
SLOSH
SLOSH
HUF
HUF
SLOSH
SLOSH
HUF
HUF
MOTHER DIDN'T KNOW ME...
WHY...?
WHY DIDN'T SHE REMEMBER ME...?!
HOW COME...?
IF SHE DOESN'T KNOW ME, THEN WHO AM I?!
WHAT WERE ALL THOSE THINGS I RECEIVED FROM MOTHER?!
MY NAME, THAT I WAS ONE OF MOTHER'S CHILDREN...
EVEN THESE GLASSES...
FSH

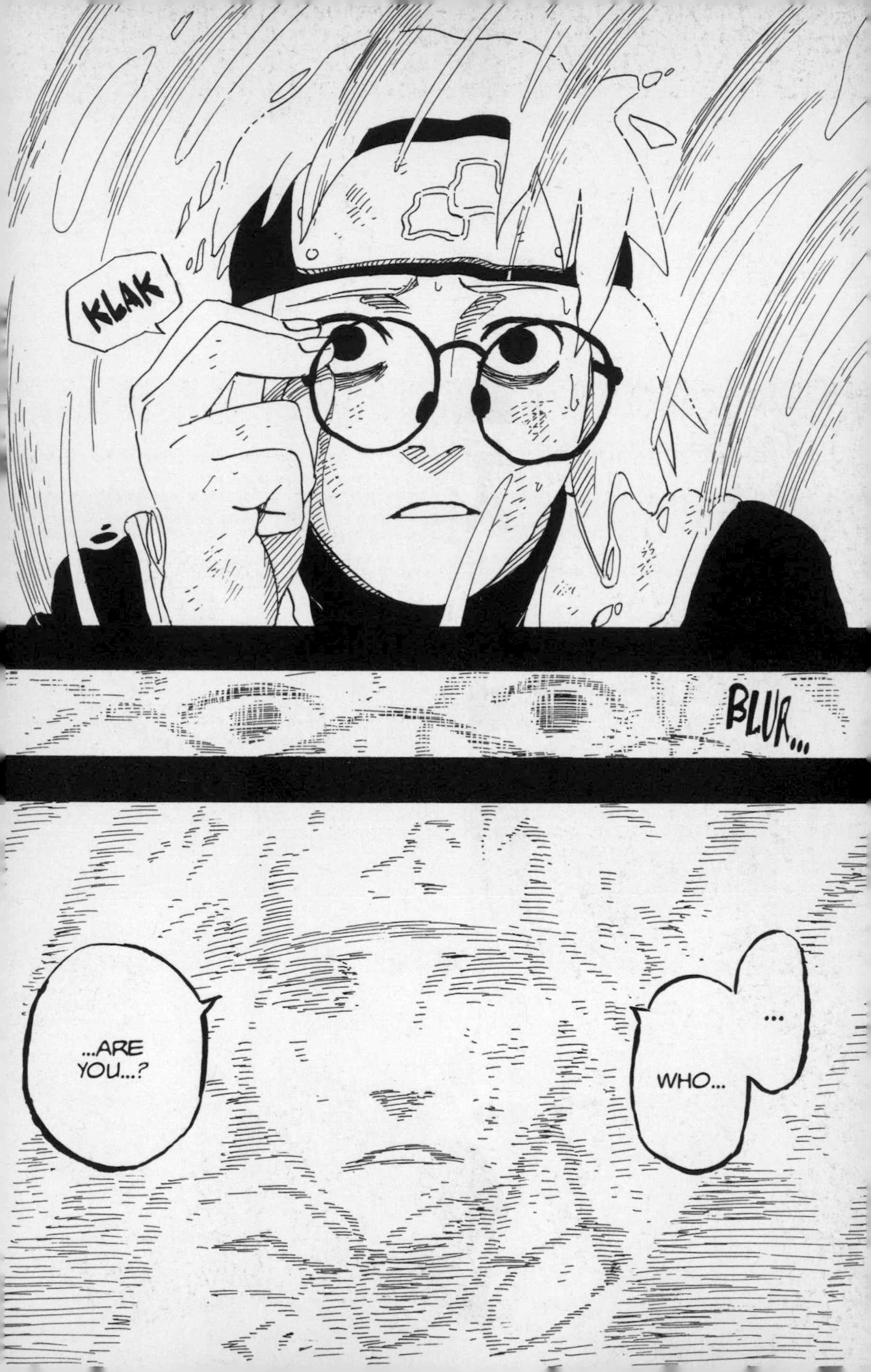
KLAK
BLUR...
... WHO...
...ARE YOU...?

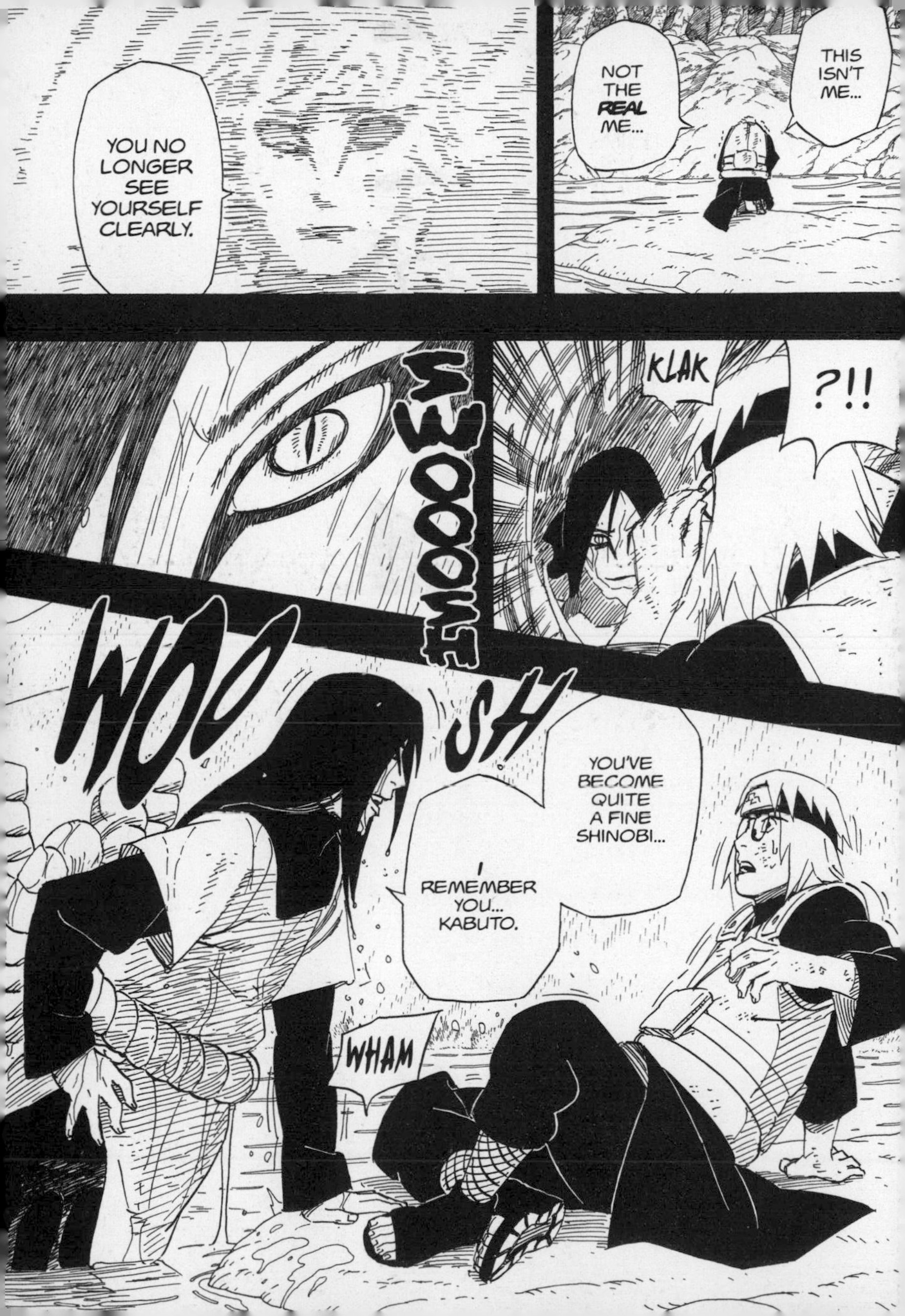
THIS ISN'T ME...
NOT THE REAL ME...
YOU NO LONGER SEE YOURSELF CLEARLY.
KLAK
?!!
WOOSH
YOU'VE BECOME QUITE A FINE SHINOBI...
I REMEMBER YOU... KABUTO.
WHAM

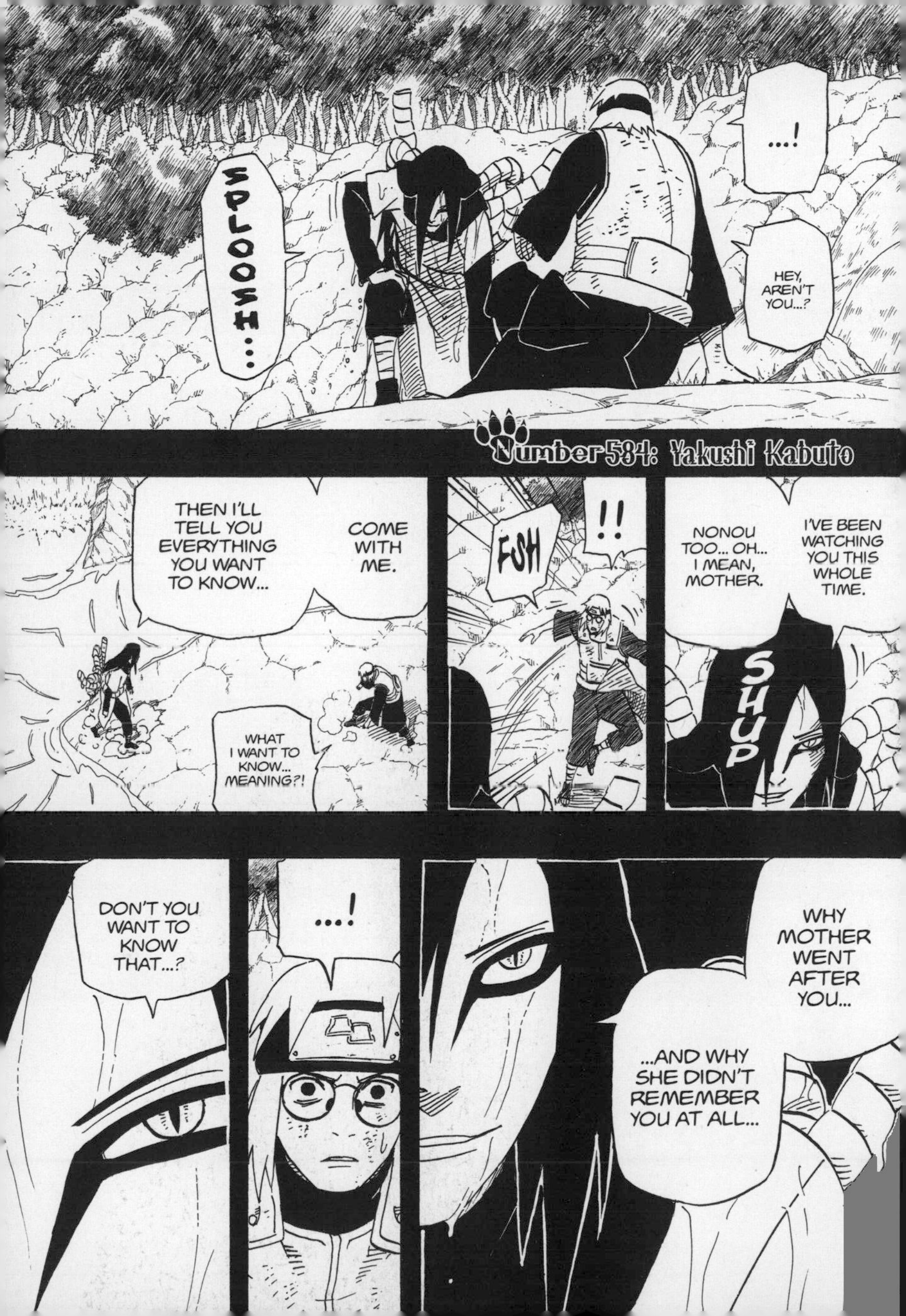
...!
HEY, AREN'T YOU...?
SPLOOSH...
Number 584: Yakushi Kabuto
I'VE BEEN WATCHING YOU THIS WHOLE TIME.
NONOU TOO... OH... I MEAN, MOTHER.
SHUP
!!
FSH
COME WITH ME.
THEN I'LL TELL YOU EVERYTHING YOU WANT TO KNOW...
WHAT I WANT TO KNOW... MEANING?!
WHY MOTHER WENT AFTER YOU...
...AND WHY SHE DIDN'T REMEMBER YOU AT ALL...
...!
DON'T YOU WANT TO KNOW THAT...?

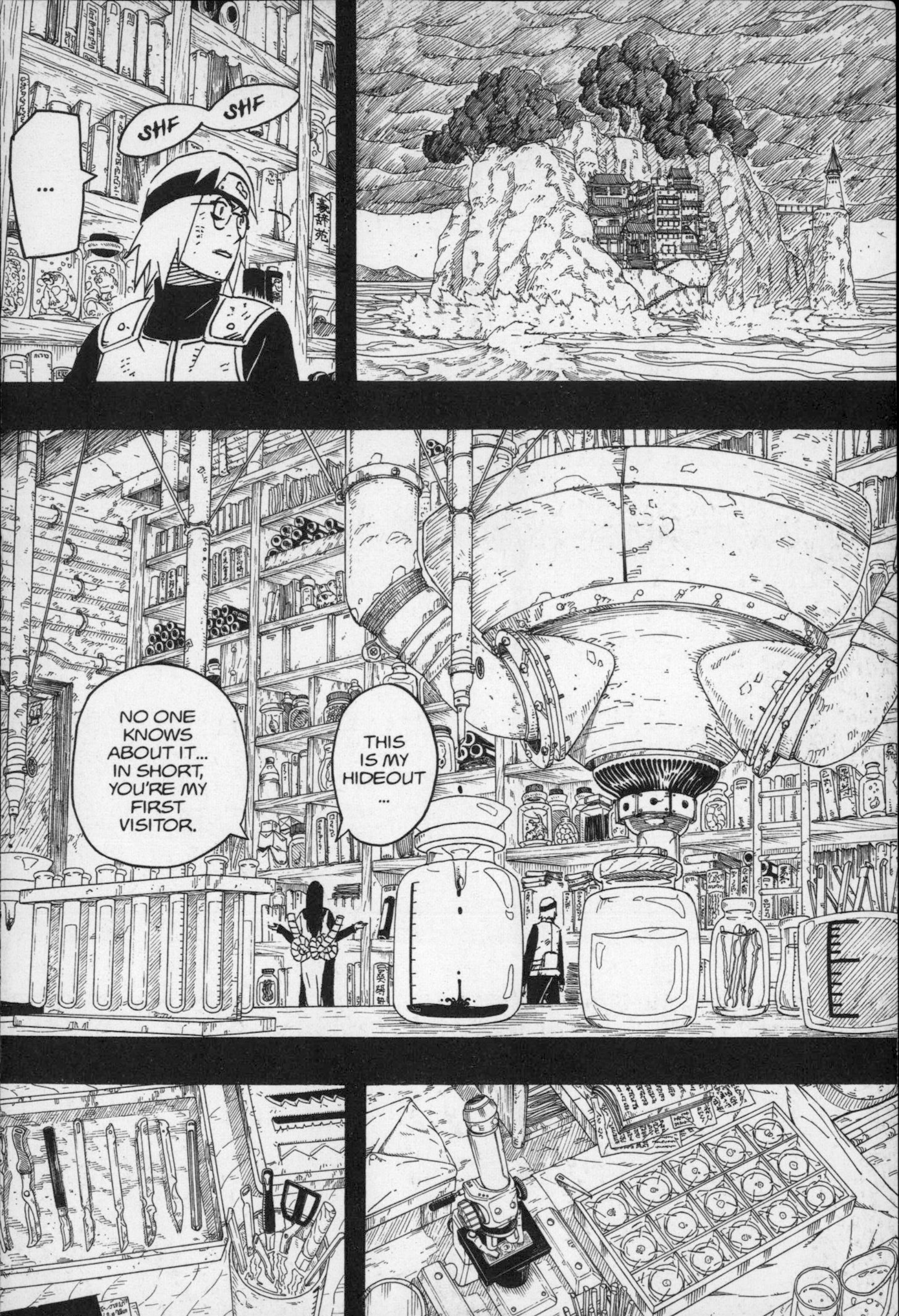
SHF SHF
...
THIS IS MY HIDEOUT ...
NO ONE KNOWS ABOUT IT... IN SHORT, YOU'RE MY FIRST VISITOR.

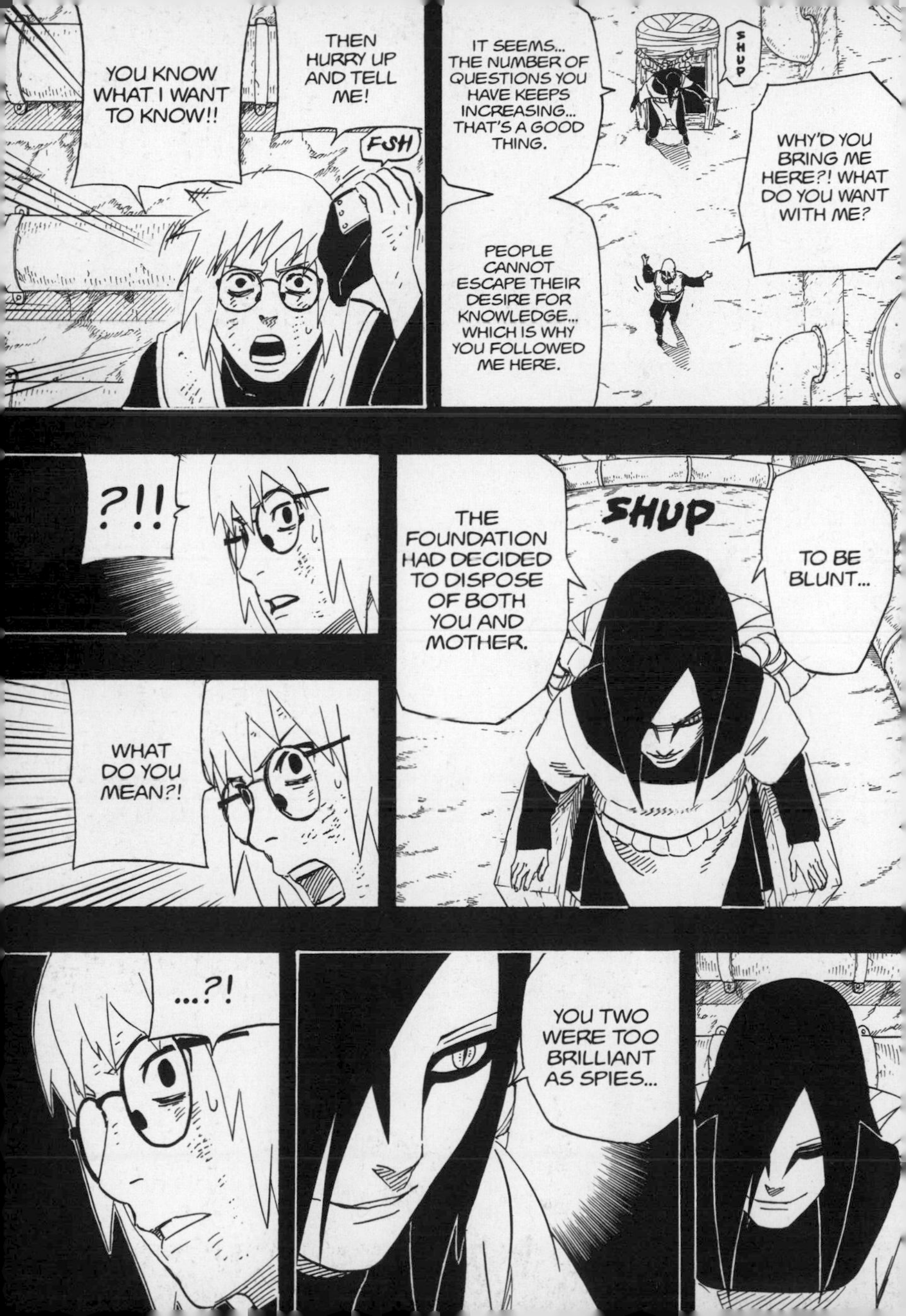
SHUP
WHY'D YOU BRING ME HERE?! WHAT DO YOU WANT WITH ME?
IT SEEMS... THE NUMBER OF QUESTIONS YOU HAVE KEEPS INCREASING... THAT'S A GOOD THING.
PEOPLE CANNOT ESCAPE THEIR DESIRE FOR KNOWLEDGE... WHICH IS WHY YOU FOLLOWED ME HERE.
THEN HURRY UP AND TELL ME!
FSH
YOU KNOW WHAT I WANT TO KNOW!!
TO BE BLUNT...
SHUP
THE FOUNDATION HAD DECIDED TO DISPOSE OF BOTH YOU AND MOTHER.
?!!
WHAT DO YOU MEAN?!
YOU TWO WERE TOO BRILLIANT AS SPIES...
...?!

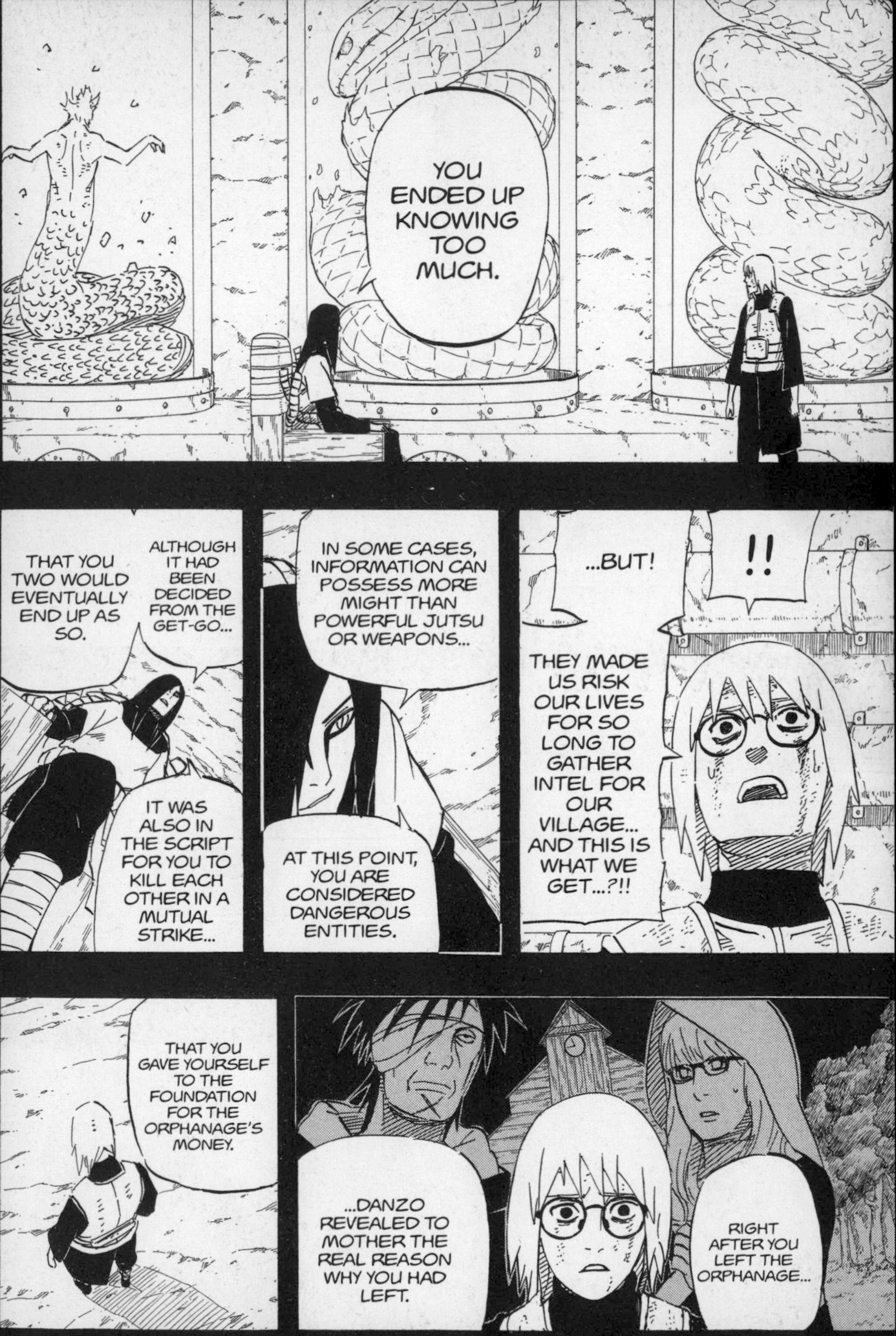
YOU ENDED UP KNOWING TOO MUCH.
!!
...BUT!
THEY MADE US RISK OUR LIVES FOR SO LONG TO GATHER INTEL FOR OUR VILLAGE... AND THIS IS WHAT WE GET...?!!
IN SOME CASES, INFORMATION CAN POSSESS MORE MIGHT THAN POWERFUL JUTSU OR WEAPONS...
AT THIS POINT, YOU ARE CONSIDERED DANGEROUS ENTITIES.
ALTHOUGH IT HAD BEEN DECIDED FROM THE GET-GO...
THAT YOU TWO WOULD EVENTUALLY END UP AS SO.
IT WAS ALSO IN THE SCRIPT FOR YOU TO KILL EACH OTHER IN A MUTUAL STRIKE...
RIGHT AFTER YOU LEFT THE ORPHANAGE...
...DANZO REVEALED TO MOTHER THE REAL REASON WHY YOU HAD LEFT.
THAT YOU GAVE YOURSELF TO THE FOUNDATION FOR THE ORPHANAGE'S MONEY.

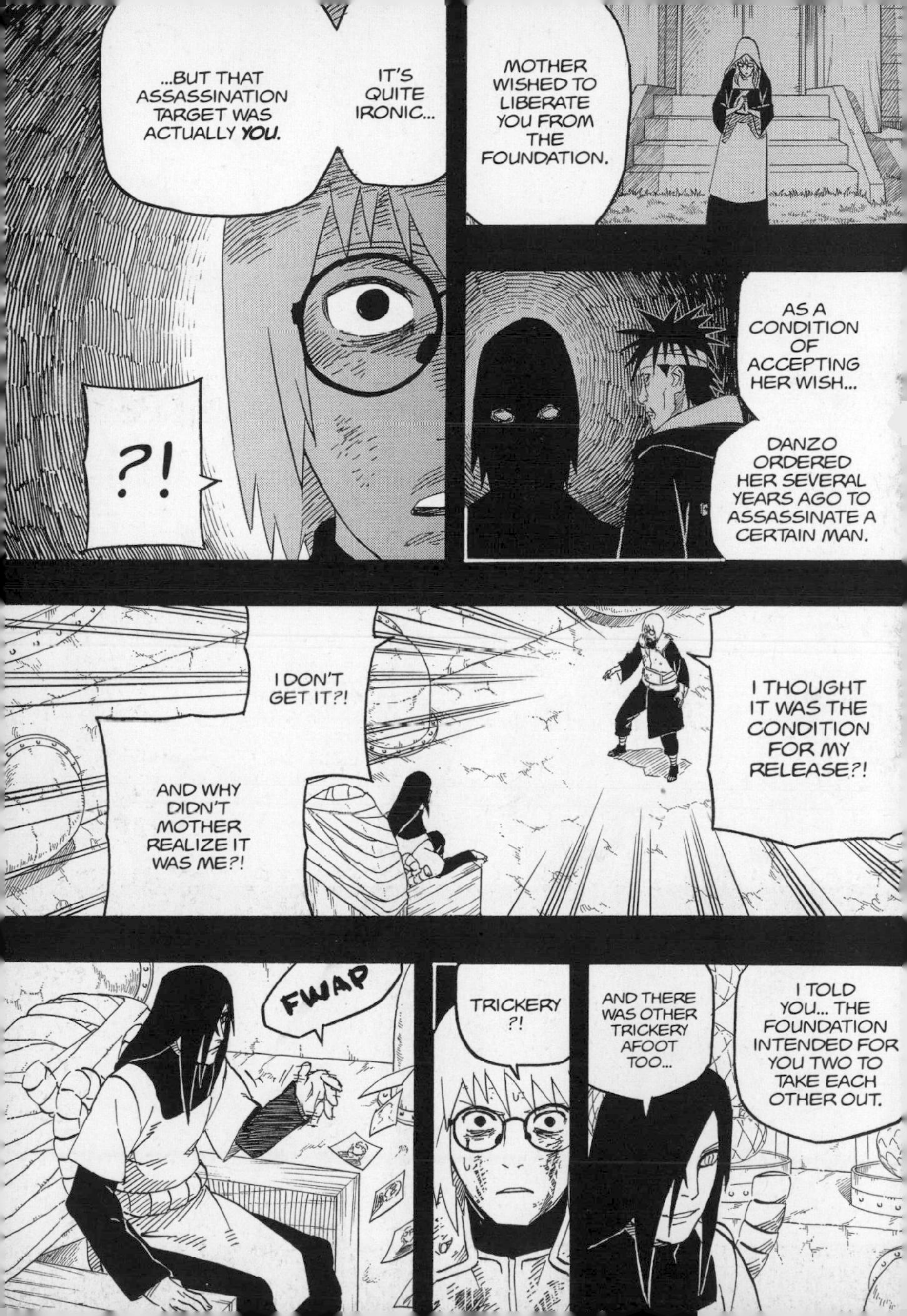
MOTHER WISHED TO LIBERATE YOU FROM THE FOUNDATION.
AS A CONDITION OF ACCEPTING HER WISH...
DANZO ORDERED HER SEVERAL YEARS AGO TO ASSASSINATE A CERTAIN MAN.
IT'S QUITE IRONIC...
...BUT THAT ASSASSINATION TARGET WAS ACTUALLY **YOU**.
?!
I THOUGHT IT WAS THE CONDITION FOR MY RELEASE?!
I DON'T GET IT?!
AND WHY DIDN'T MOTHER REALIZE IT WAS ME?!
I TOLD YOU... THE FOUNDATION INTENDED FOR YOU TWO TO TAKE EACH OTHER OUT.
AND THERE WAS OTHER TRICKERY AFOOT TOO...
TRICKERY?!
FWAP

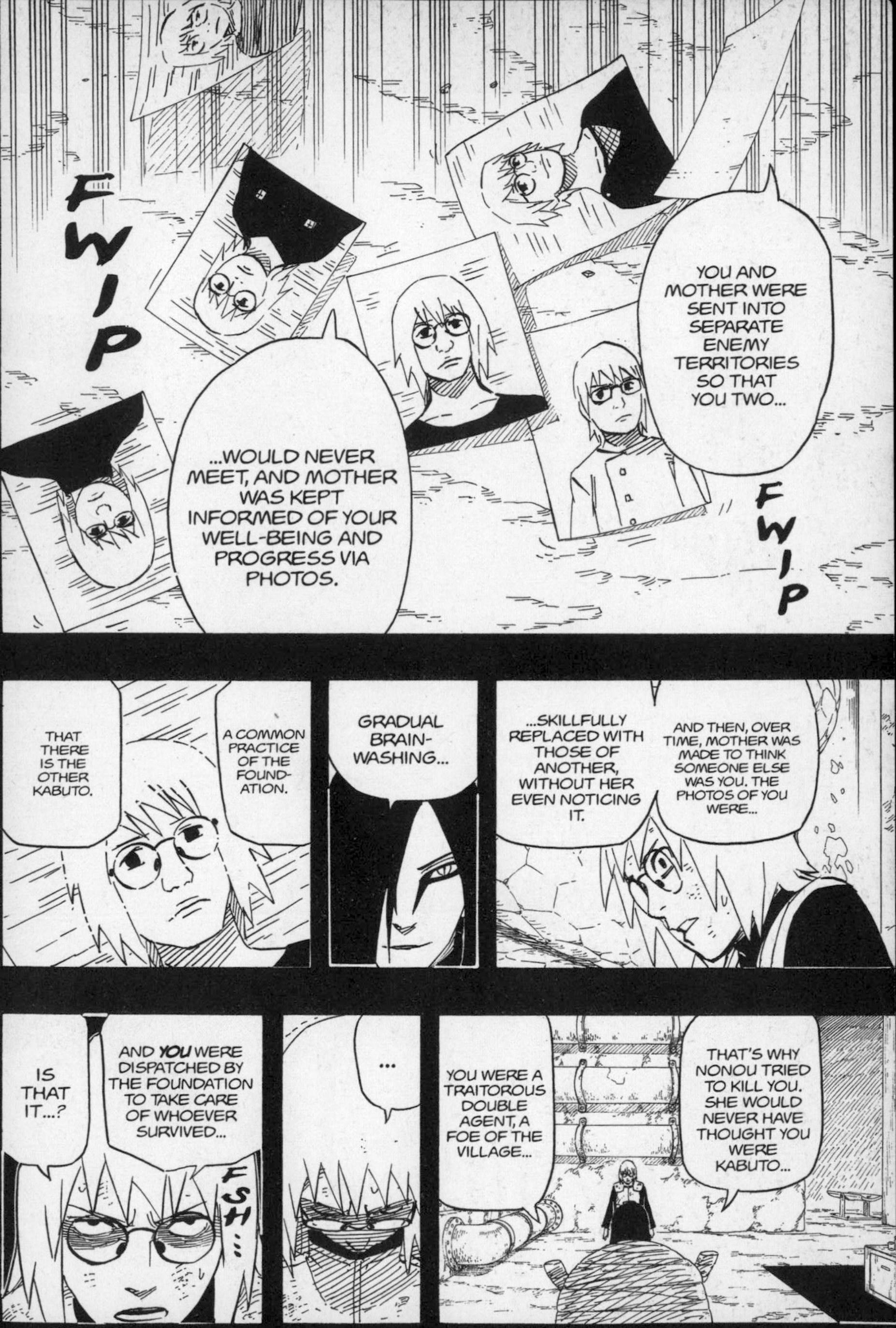
YOU AND MOTHER WERE SENT INTO SEPARATE ENEMY TERRITORIES SO THAT YOU TWO...
...WOULD NEVER MEET, AND MOTHER WAS KEPT INFORMED OF YOUR WELL-BEING AND PROGRESS VIA PHOTOS.
FWIP
FWIP
AND THEN, OVER TIME, MOTHER WAS MADE TO THINK SOMEONE ELSE WAS YOU. THE PHOTOS OF YOU WERE...
...SKILLFULLY REPLACED WITH THOSE OF ANOTHER, WITHOUT HER EVEN NOTICING IT.
GRADUAL BRAIN-WASHING...
A COMMON PRACTICE OF THE FOUND-ATION.
THAT THERE IS THE OTHER KABUTO.
THAT'S WHY NONOU TRIED TO KILL YOU. SHE WOULD NEVER HAVE THOUGHT YOU WERE KABUTO...
YOU WERE A TRAITOROUS DOUBLE AGENT, A FOE OF THE VILLAGE...
...
AND YOU WERE DISPATCHED BY THE FOUNDATION TO TAKE CARE OF WHOEVER SURVIVED...
IS THAT IT...?
FSH...

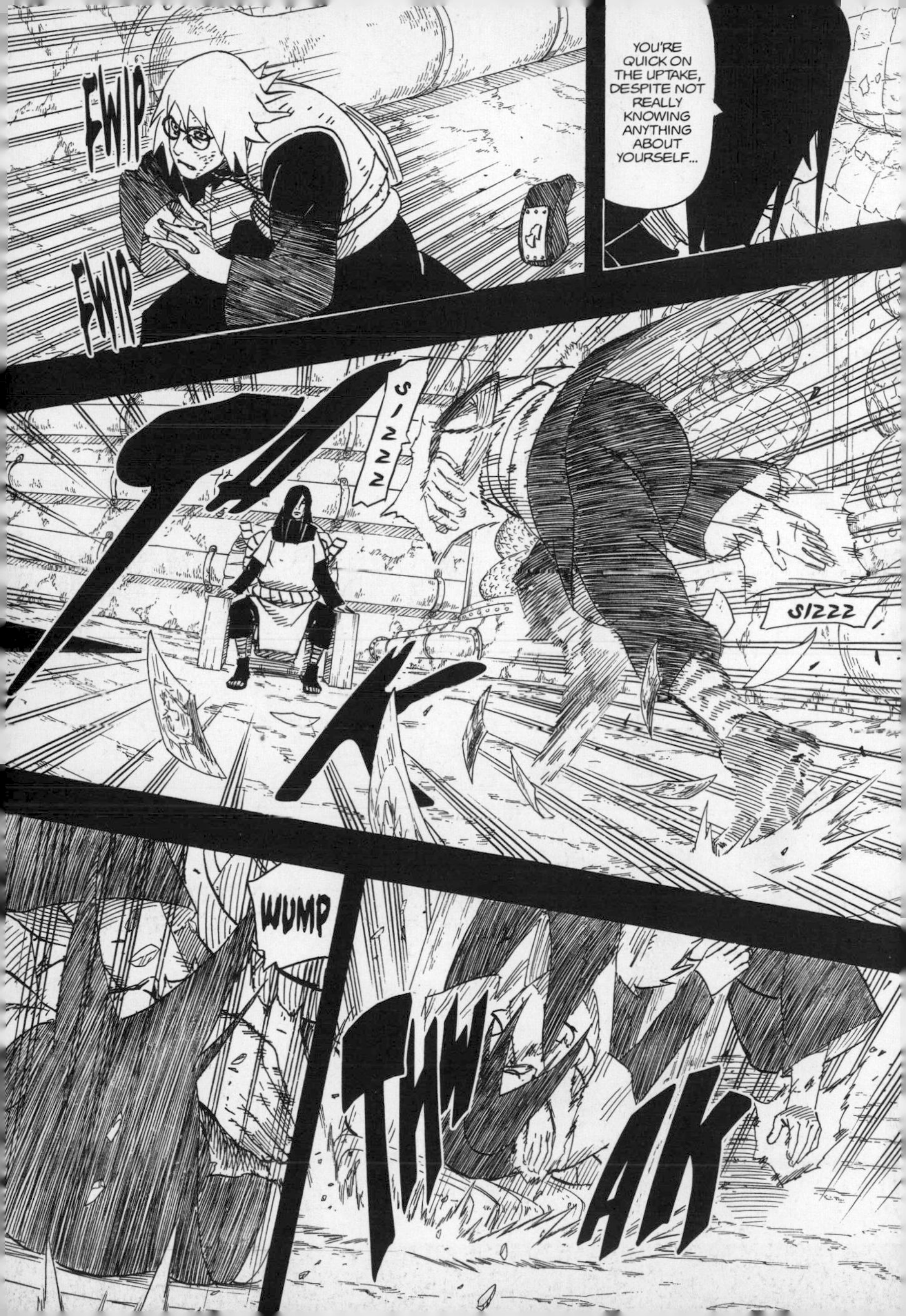
YOU'RE QUICK ON THE UPTAKE, DESPITE NOT REALLY KNOWING ANYTHING ABOUT YOURSELF...
FWIP
FWIP
SIZZZ
TAK
SIZZZ
WUMP
THWAK

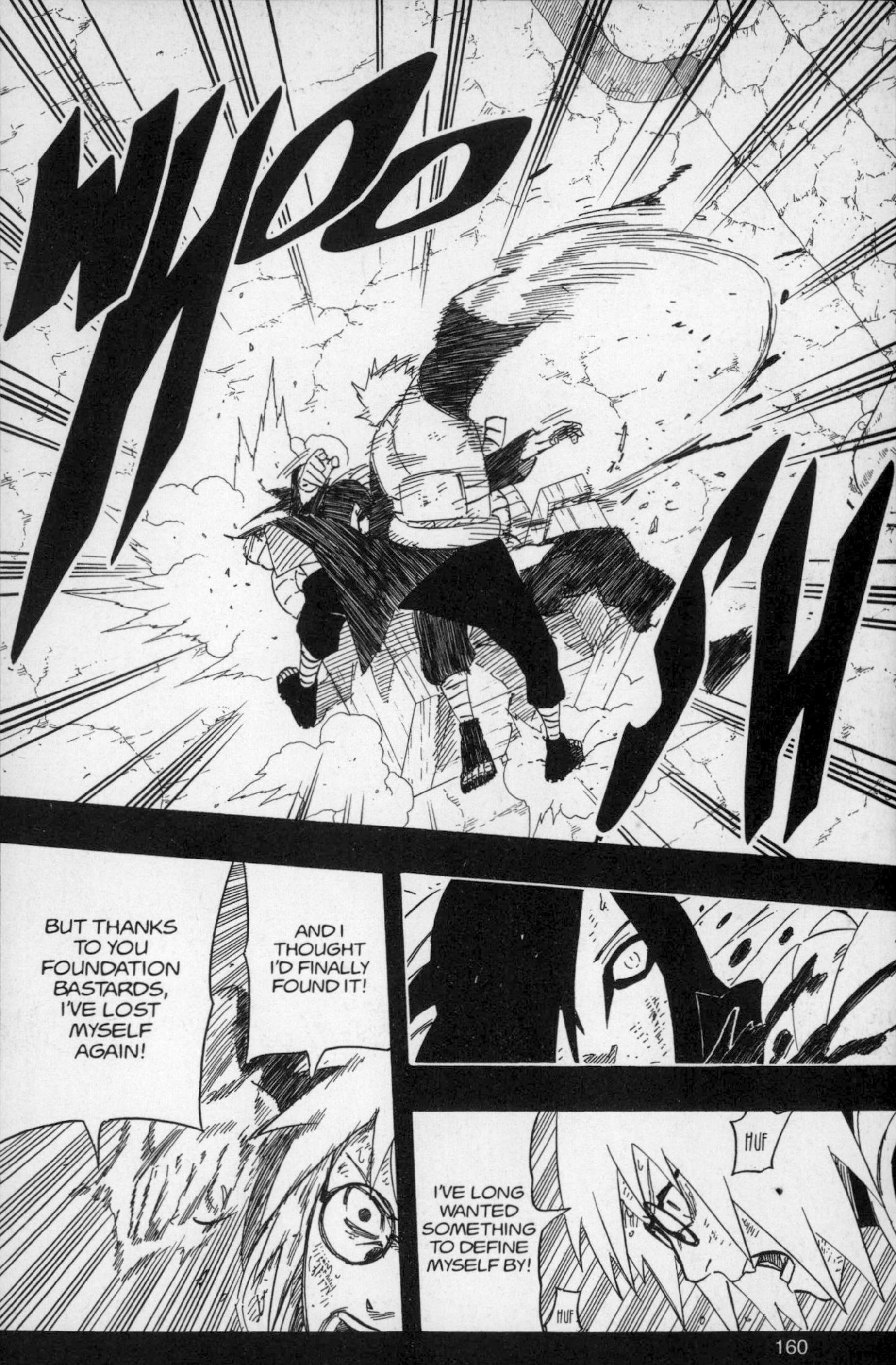
WHOOSH
HUF
I'VE LONG WANTED SOMETHING TO DEFINE MYSELF BY!
HUF
AND I THOUGHT I'D FINALLY FOUND IT!
BUT THANKS TO YOU FOUNDATION BASTARDS, I'VE LOST MYSELF AGAIN!

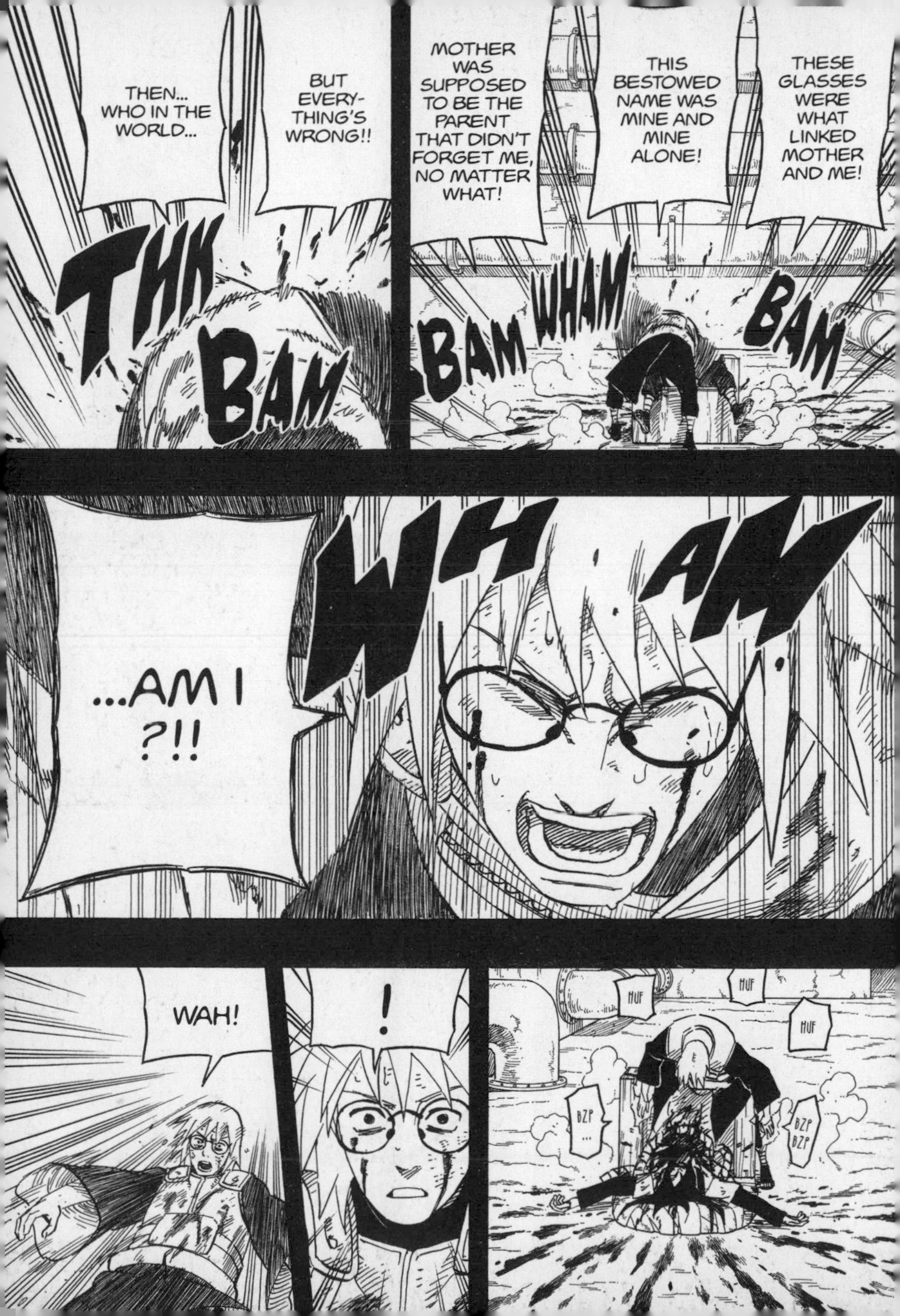
THESE GLASSES WERE WHAT LINKED MOTHER AND ME!
THIS BESTOWED NAME WAS MINE AND MINE ALONE!
MOTHER WAS SUPPOSED TO BE THE PARENT THAT DIDN'T FORGET ME, NO MATTER WHAT!
BAM
WHAM
BAM
BUT EVERY-THING'S WRONG!!
THEN... WHO IN THE WORLD...
THK
BAM
WHAM
...AM I ?!!
HUF
HUF
HUF
BZP BZP
BZP ...
!
WAH!

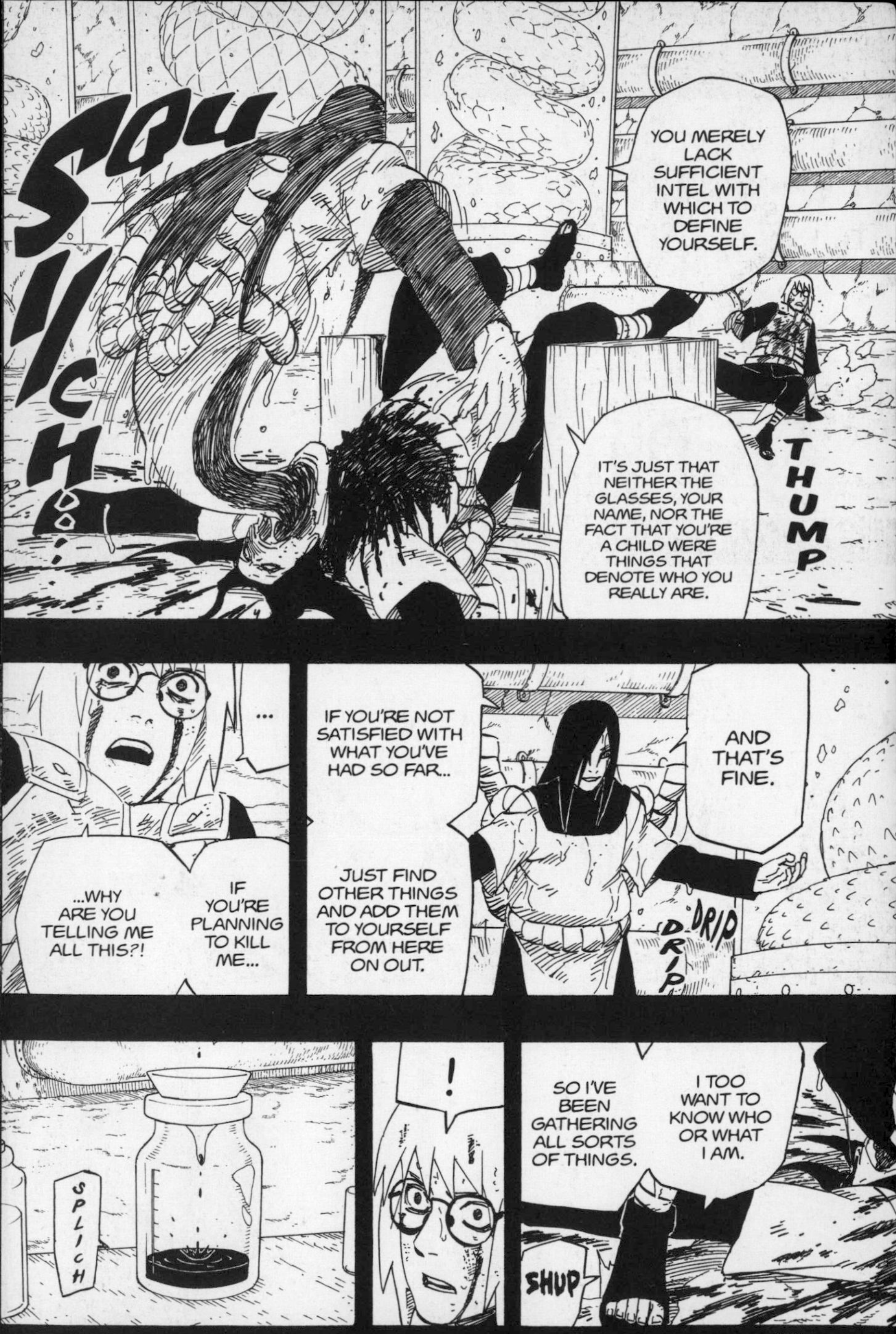
YOU MERELY LACK SUFFICIENT INTEL WITH WHICH TO DEFINE YOURSELF.
THUMP
IT'S JUST THAT NEITHER THE GLASSES, YOUR NAME, NOR THE FACT THAT YOU'RE A CHILD WERE THINGS THAT DENOTE WHO YOU REALLY ARE.
AND THAT'S FINE.
IF YOU'RE NOT SATISFIED WITH WHAT YOU'VE HAD SO FAR...
JUST FIND OTHER THINGS AND ADD THEM TO YOURSELF FROM HERE ON OUT.
DRIP
DRIP
...
IF YOU'RE PLANNING TO KILL ME...
...WHY ARE YOU TELLING ME ALL THIS?!
I TOO WANT TO KNOW WHO OR WHAT I AM.
SO I'VE BEEN GATHERING ALL SORTS OF THINGS.
SHUP
!
SPLICH

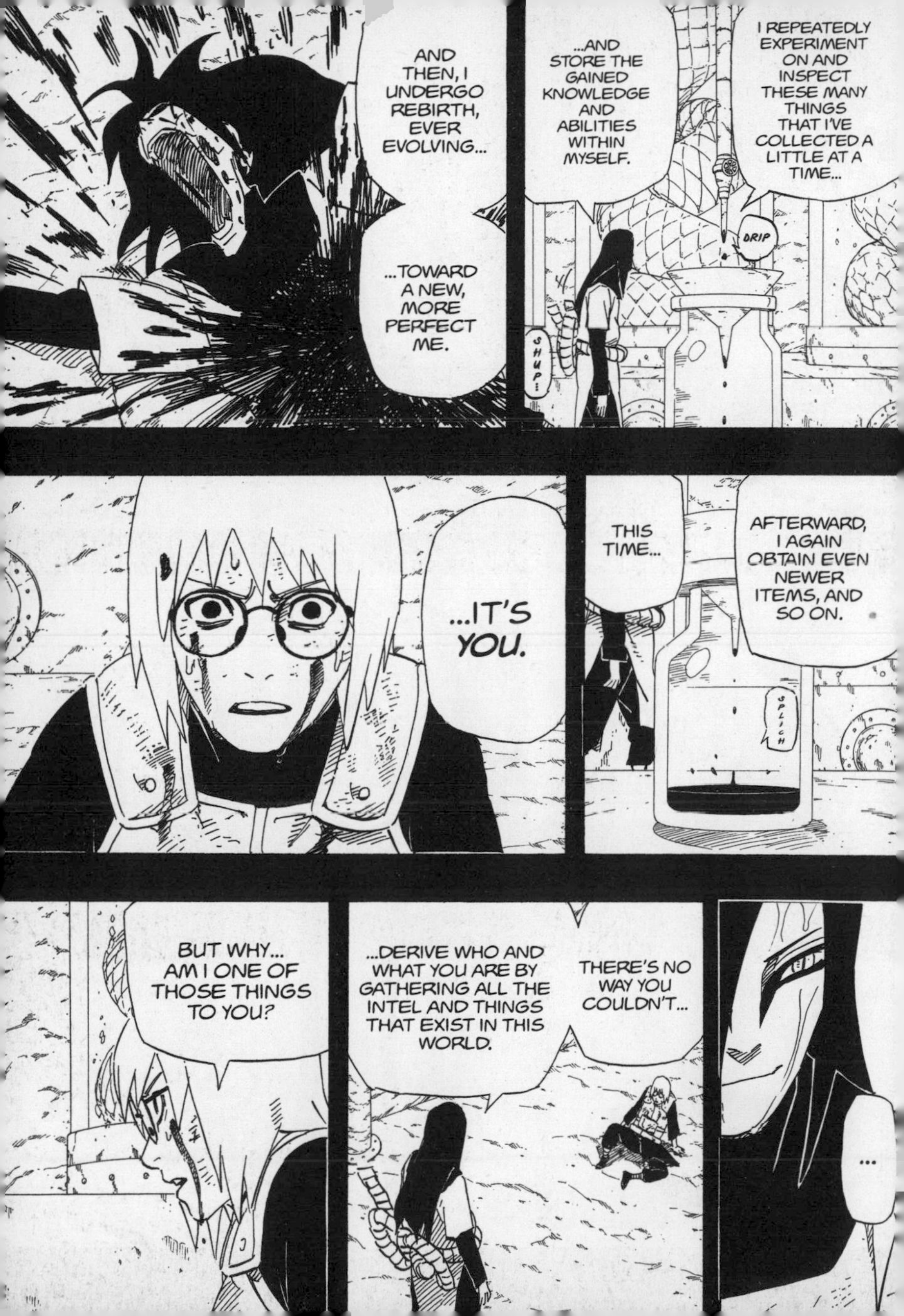
I REPEATEDLY EXPERIMENT ON AND INSPECT THESE MANY THINGS THAT I'VE COLLECTED A LITTLE AT A TIME...
...AND STORE THE GAINED KNOWLEDGE AND ABILITIES WITHIN MYSELF.
DRIP
SHUP...
AND THEN, I UNDERGO REBIRTH, EVER EVOLVING...
...TOWARD A NEW, MORE PERFECT ME.
AFTERWARD, I AGAIN OBTAIN EVEN NEWER ITEMS, AND SO ON.
THIS TIME...
SPLICH
...IT'S YOU.
...
THERE'S NO WAY YOU COULDN'T...
...DERIVE WHO AND WHAT YOU ARE BY GATHERING ALL THE INTEL AND THINGS THAT EXIST IN THIS WORLD.
BUT WHY... AM I ONE OF THOSE THINGS TO YOU?

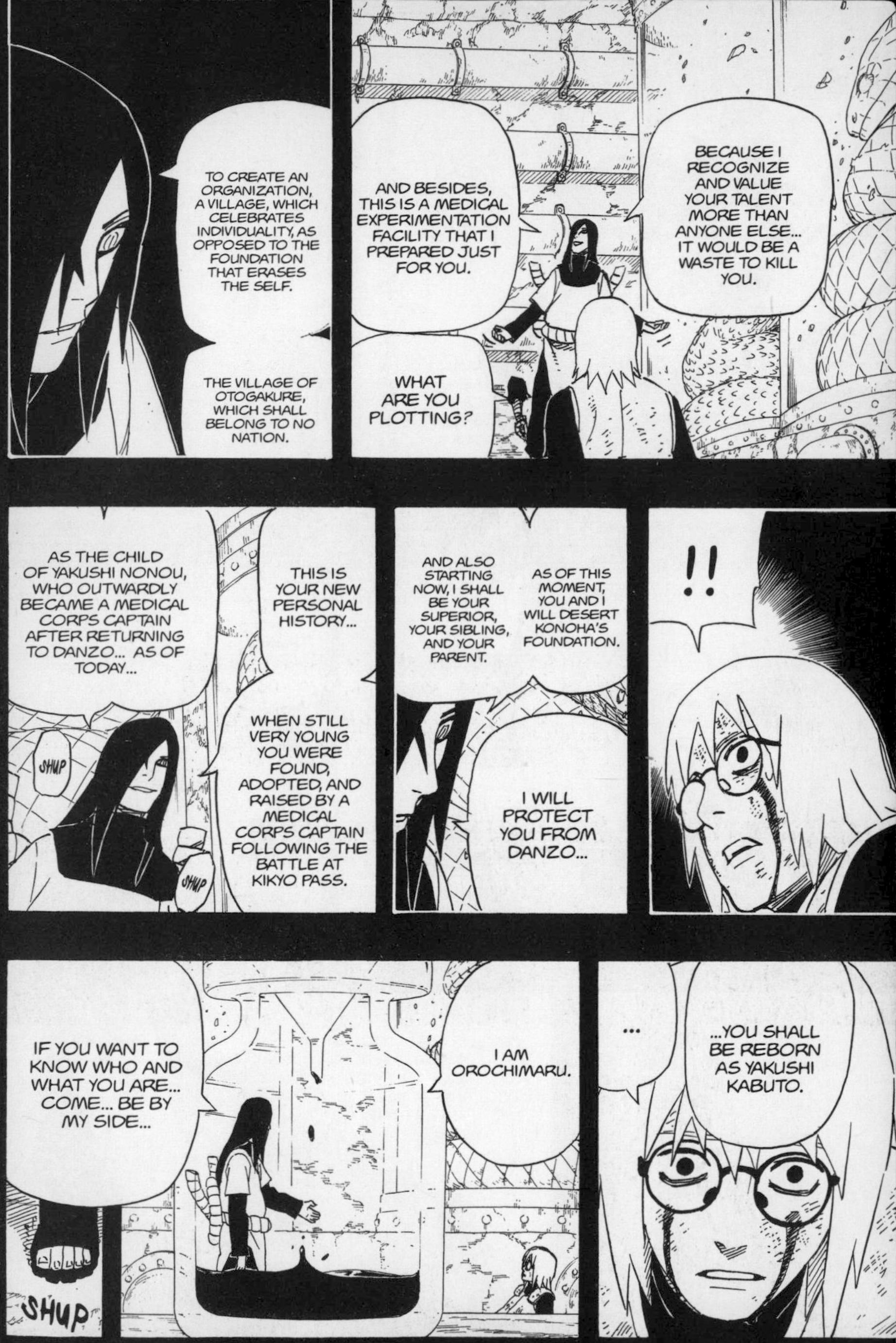
BECAUSE I RECOGNIZE AND VALUE YOUR TALENT MORE THAN ANYONE ELSE... IT WOULD BE A WASTE TO KILL YOU.
AND BESIDES, THIS IS A MEDICAL EXPERIMENTATION FACILITY THAT I PREPARED JUST FOR YOU.
WHAT ARE YOU PLOTTING?
TO CREATE AN ORGANIZATION, A VILLAGE, WHICH CELEBRATES INDIVIDUALITY, AS OPPOSED TO THE FOUNDATION THAT ERASES THE SELF.
THE VILLAGE OF OTOGAKURE, WHICH SHALL BELONG TO NO NATION.
!!
AS OF THIS MOMENT, YOU AND I WILL DESERT KONOHA'S FOUNDATION.
AND ALSO STARTING NOW, I SHALL BE YOUR SUPERIOR, YOUR SIBLING, AND YOUR PARENT.
I WILL PROTECT YOU FROM DANZO...
THIS IS YOUR NEW PERSONAL HISTORY...
AS THE CHILD OF YAKUSHI NONOU, WHO OUTWARDLY BECAME A MEDICAL CORPS CAPTAIN AFTER RETURNING TO DANZO... AS OF TODAY...
WHEN STILL VERY YOUNG YOU WERE FOUND, ADOPTED, AND RAISED BY A MEDICAL CORPS CAPTAIN FOLLOWING THE BATTLE AT KIKYO PASS.
SHUP
SHUP
...YOU SHALL BE REBORN AS YAKUSHI KABUTO.
...
I AM OROCHIMARU.
IF YOU WANT TO KNOW WHO AND WHAT YOU ARE... COME... BE BY MY SIDE...
SHUP

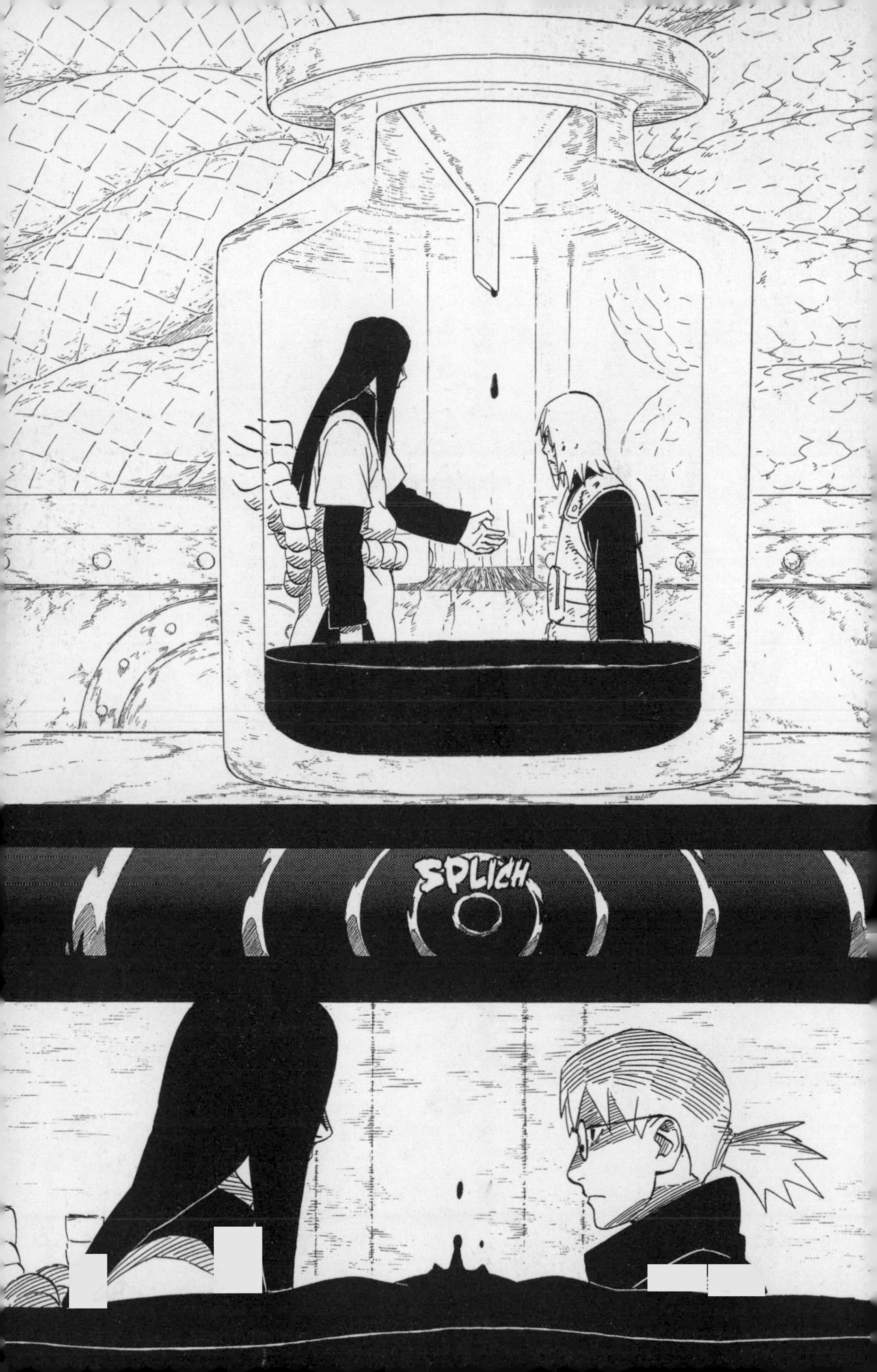
SPLICH

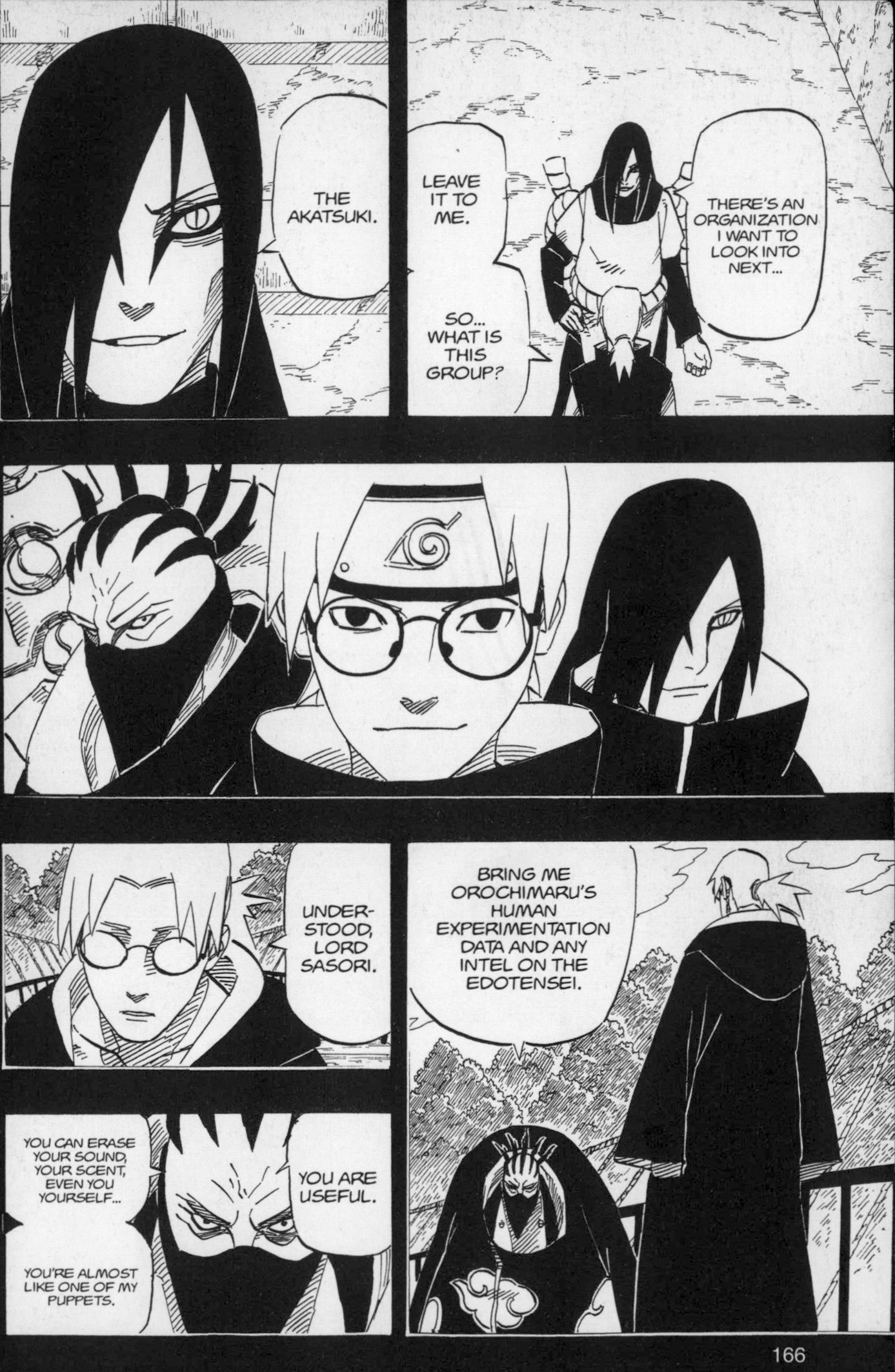
THERE'S AN ORGANIZATION I WANT TO LOOK INTO NEXT...
LEAVE IT TO ME.
SO... WHAT IS THIS GROUP?
THE AKATSUKI.
BRING ME OROCHIMARU'S HUMAN EXPERIMENTATION DATA AND ANY INTEL ON THE EDOTENSEI.
UNDER-STOOD, LORD SASORI.
YOU ARE USEFUL.
YOU CAN ERASE YOUR SOUND, YOUR SCENT, EVEN YOU YOURSELF...
YOU'RE ALMOST LIKE ONE OF MY PUPPETS.

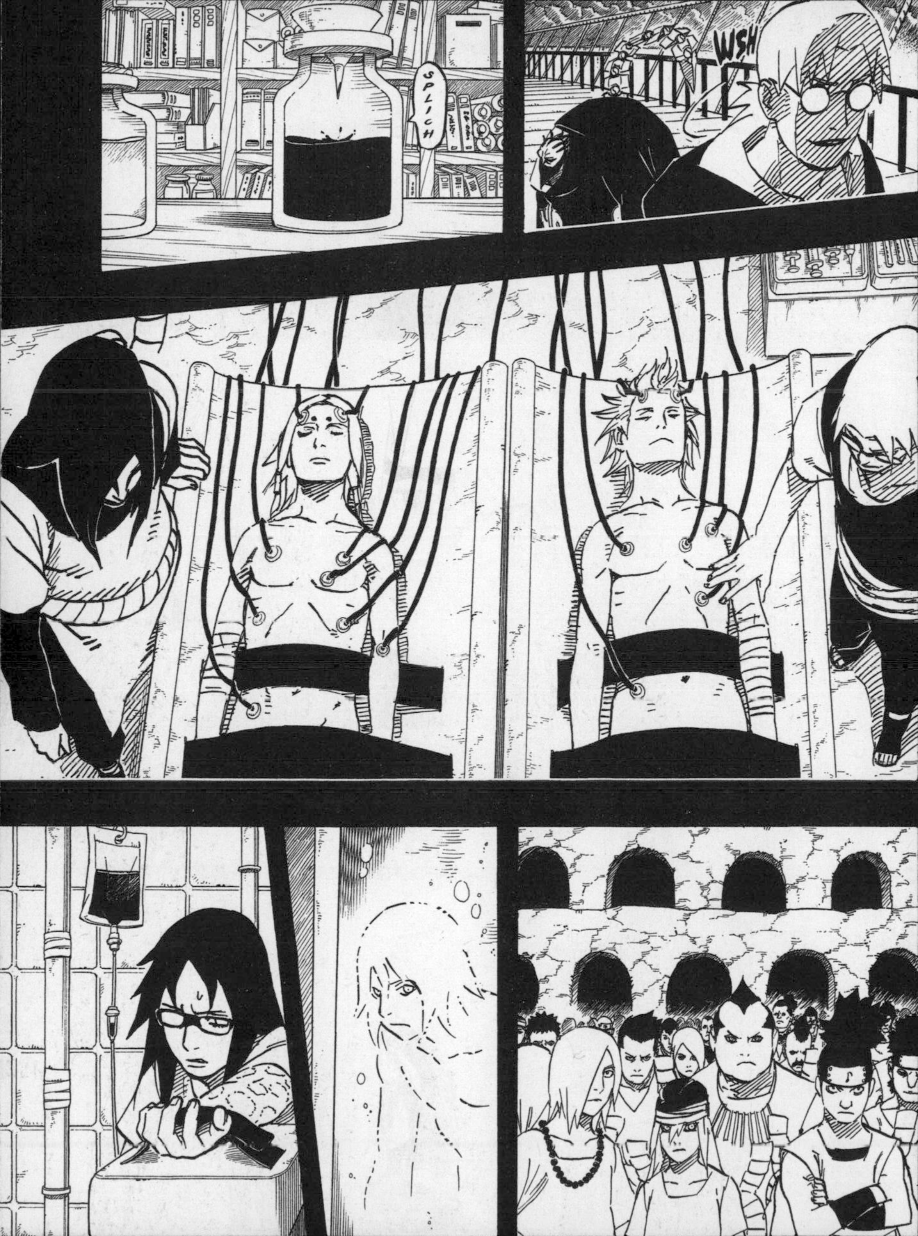
WSH
SPLICH

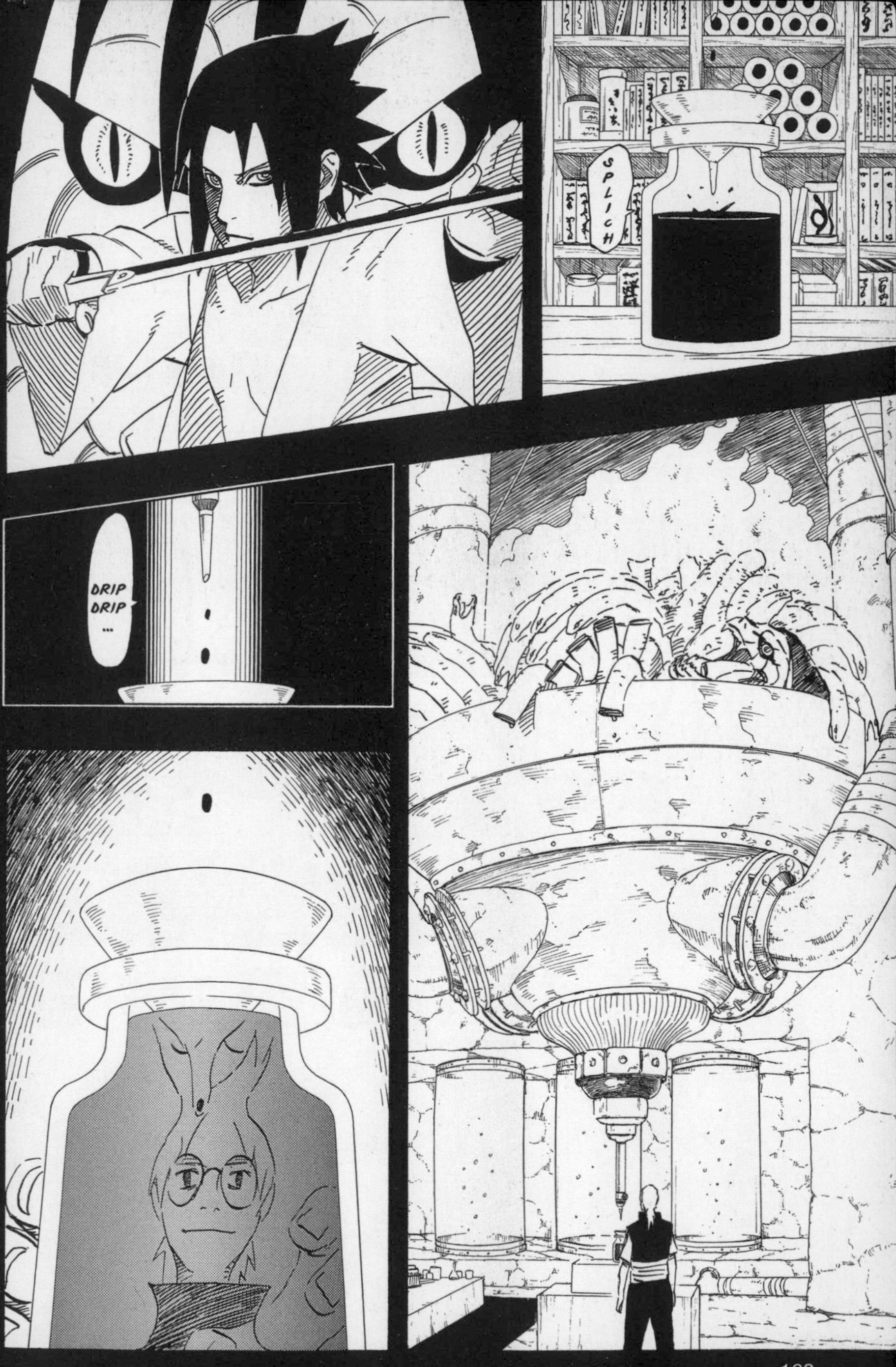
SPLICH
DRIP DRIP ...

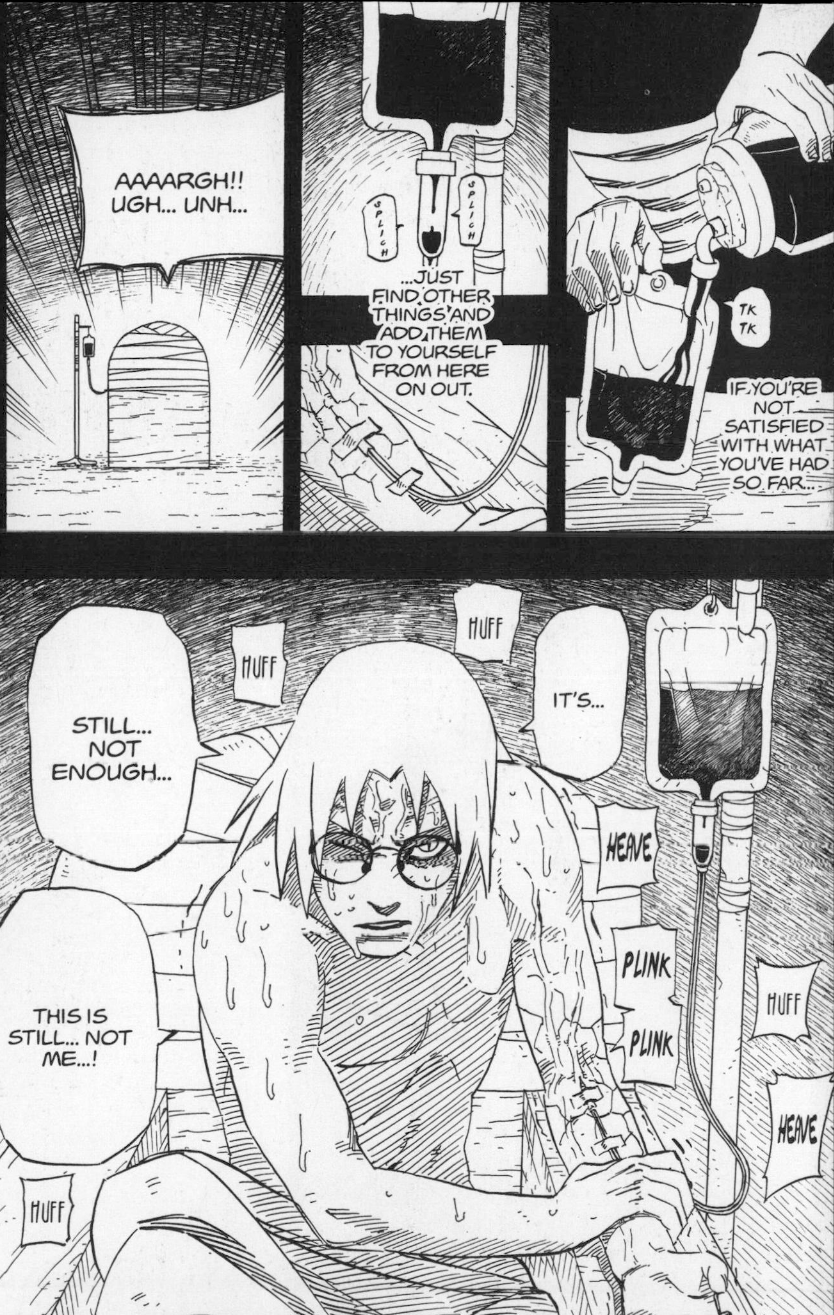
IF YOU'RE NOT SATISFIED WITH WHAT YOU'VE HAD SO FAR...
TK TK
SPLICH
SPLICH
...JUST FIND OTHER THINGS AND ADD THEM TO YOURSELF FROM HERE ON OUT.
AAAARGH!! UGH... UNH...
HUFF
IT'S...
HUFF
STILL... NOT ENOUGH...
HEAVE
PLINK
PLINK
HUFF
HEAVE
THIS IS STILL... NOT ME...!
HUFF

NARUTO

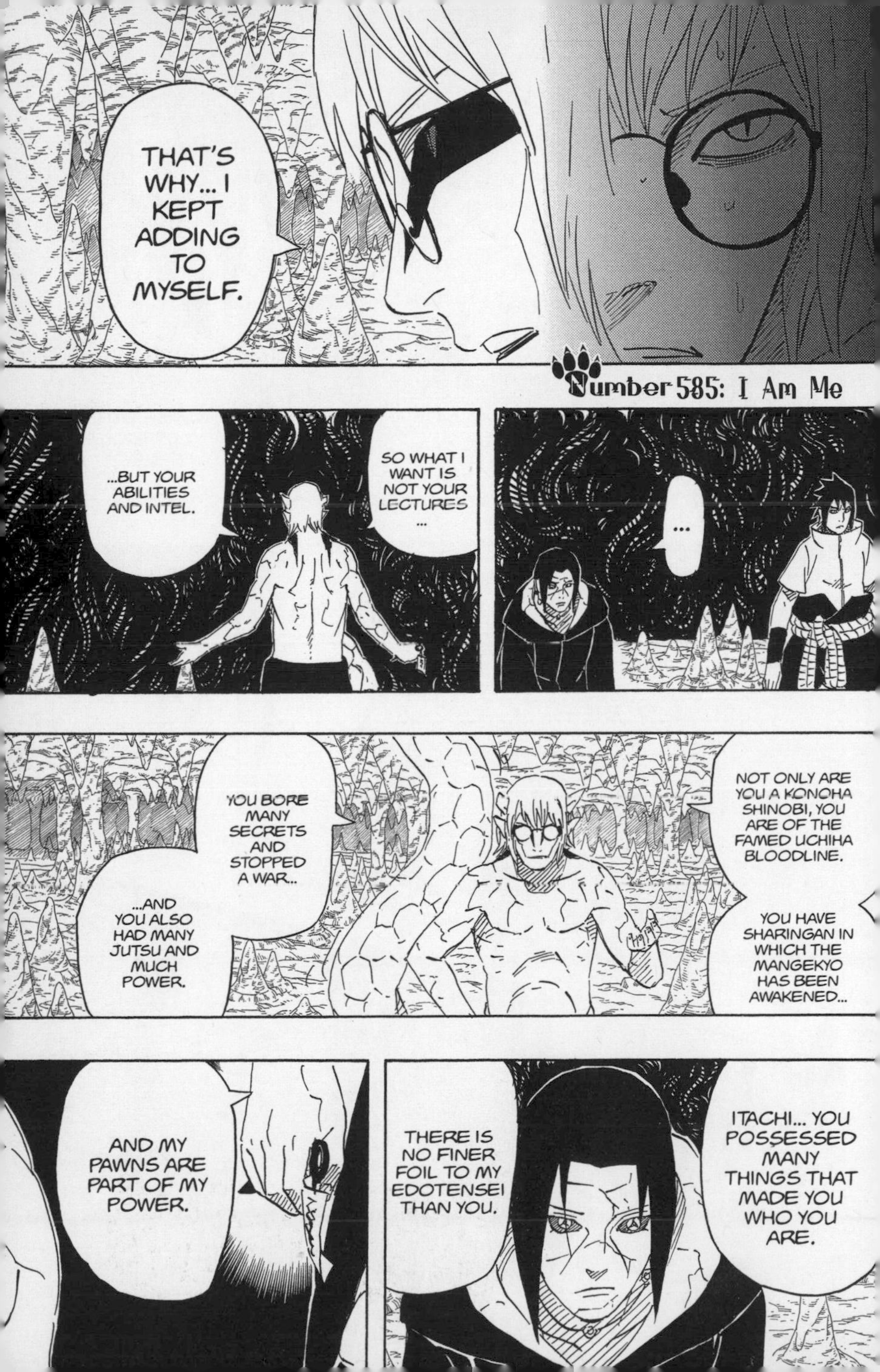
THAT'S WHY... I KEPT ADDING TO MYSELF.
Number 585: I Am Me
...
SO WHAT I WANT IS NOT YOUR LECTURES ...
...BUT YOUR ABILITIES AND INTEL.
NOT ONLY ARE YOU A KONOHA SHINOBI, YOU ARE OF THE FAMED UCHIHA BLOODLINE.
YOU HAVE SHARINGAN IN WHICH THE MANGEKYO HAS BEEN AWAKENED...
YOU BORE MANY SECRETS AND STOPPED A WAR...
...AND YOU ALSO HAD MANY JUTSU AND MUCH POWER.
ITACHI... YOU POSSESSED MANY THINGS THAT MADE YOU WHO YOU ARE.
THERE IS NO FINER FOIL TO MY EDOTENSEI THAN YOU.
AND MY PAWNS ARE PART OF MY POWER.

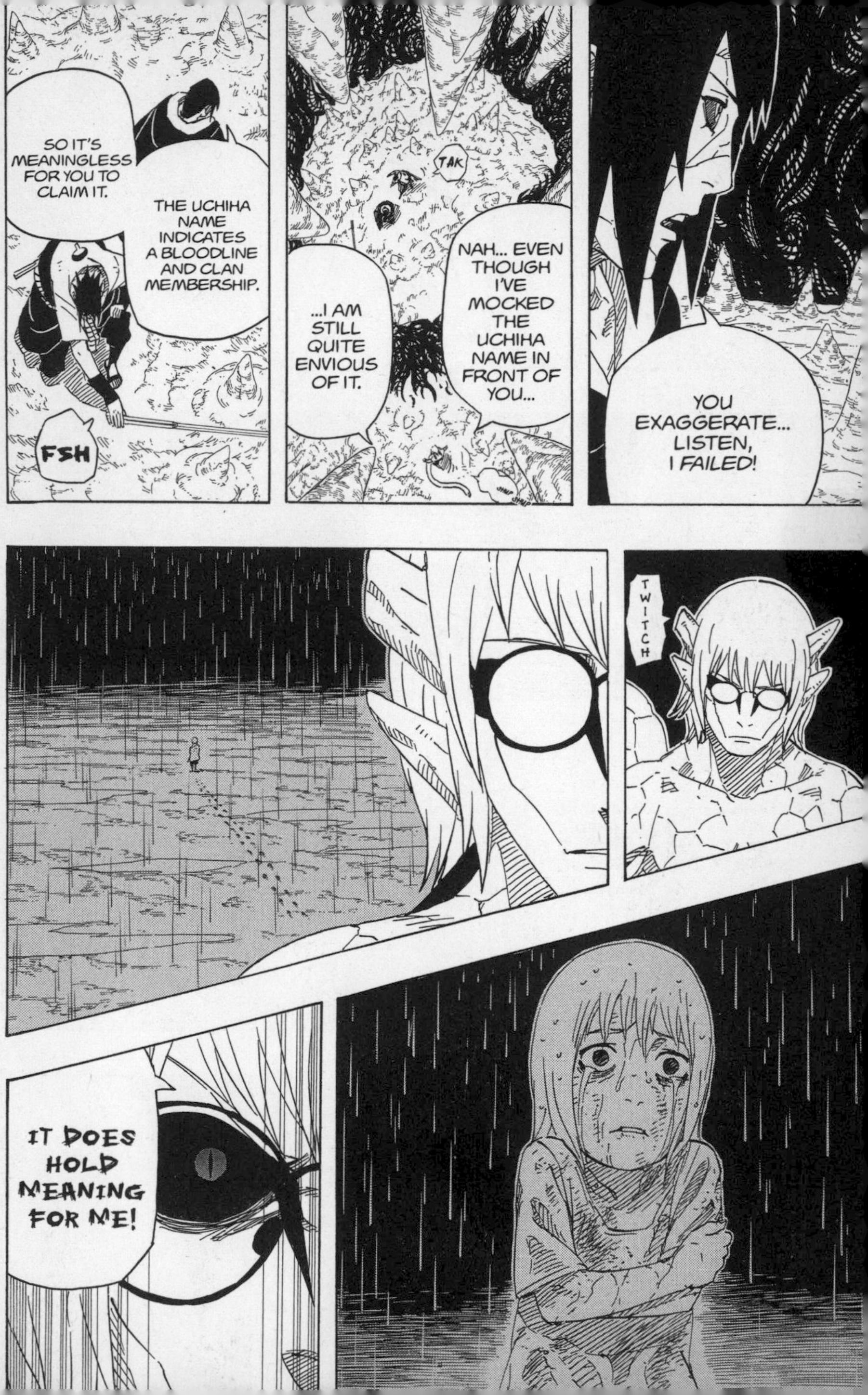
YOU EXAGGERATE... LISTEN, I FAILED!
TAK
NAH... EVEN THOUGH I'VE MOCKED THE UCHIHA NAME IN FRONT OF YOU...
...I AM STILL QUITE ENVIOUS OF IT.
THE UCHIHA NAME INDICATES A BLOODLINE AND CLAN MEMBERSHIP.
SO IT'S MEANINGLESS FOR YOU TO CLAIM IT.
FSH
TWITCH
IT DOES HOLD MEANING FOR ME!

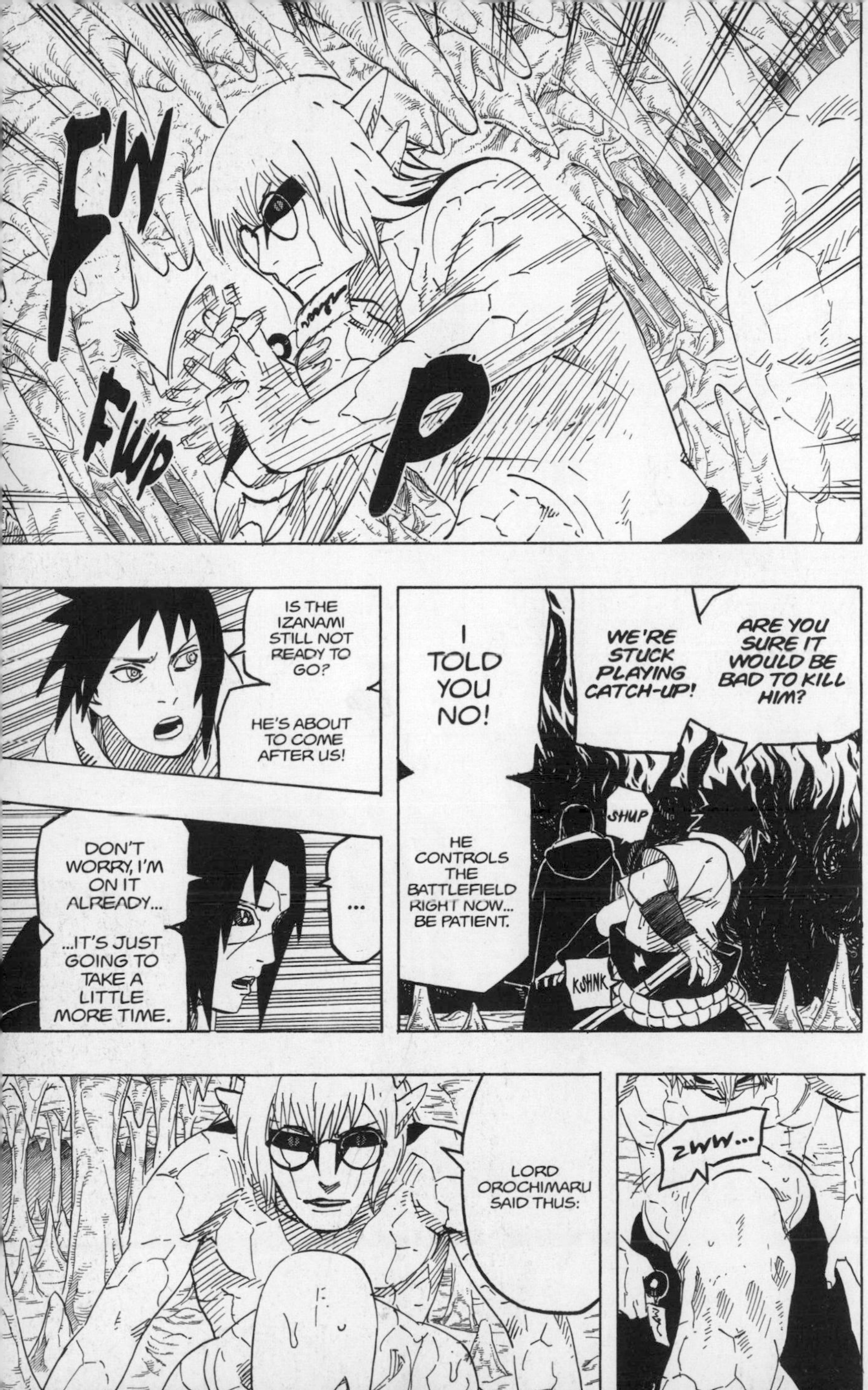
P
FW
FWP
ARE YOU SURE IT WOULD BE BAD TO KILL HIM?
WE'RE STUCK PLAYING CATCH-UP!
I TOLD YOU NO!
HE CONTROLS THE BATTLEFIELD RIGHT NOW... BE PATIENT.
SHUP
KSHNK
IS THE IZANAMI STILL NOT READY TO GO?
HE'S ABOUT TO COME AFTER US!
...
DON'T WORRY, I'M ON IT ALREADY...
...IT'S JUST GOING TO TAKE A LITTLE MORE TIME.
ZWW...
LORD OROCHIMARU SAID THUS:

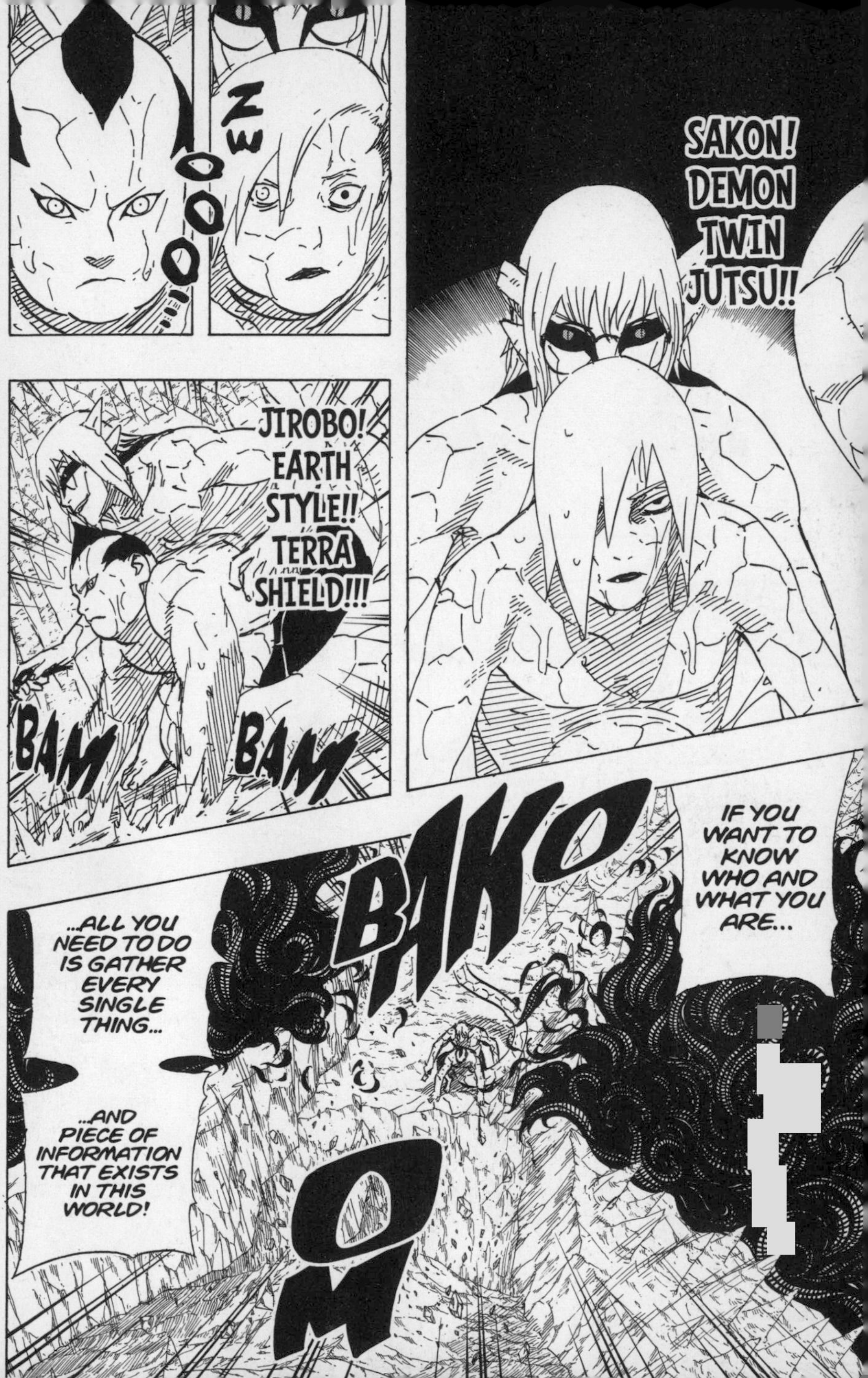
SAKON! DEMON TWIN JUTSU!!
ZWOOOO...!!
JIROBO! EARTH STYLE!! TERRA SHIELD!!!
BAM
BAM
IF YOU WANT TO KNOW WHO AND WHAT YOU ARE...
BAKO
...ALL YOU NEED TO DO IS GATHER EVERY SINGLE THING...
...AND PIECE OF INFORMATION THAT EXISTS IN THIS WORLD!
OM

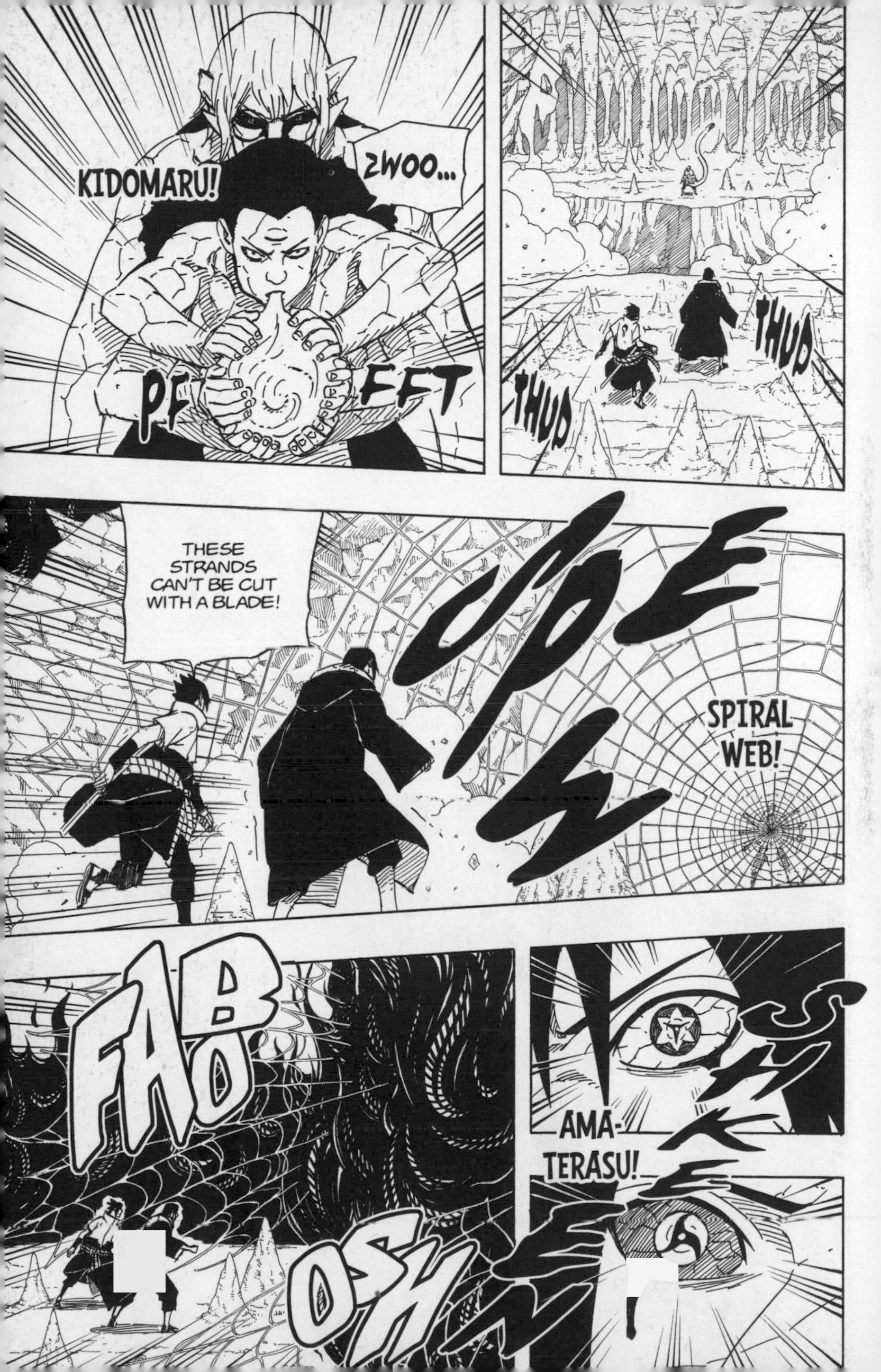
THUD
THUD
KIDOMARU!
ZWOO...
PF EFT
SPIRAL WEB!
THESE STRANDS CAN'T BE CUT WITH A BLADE!
AMA-TERASU!

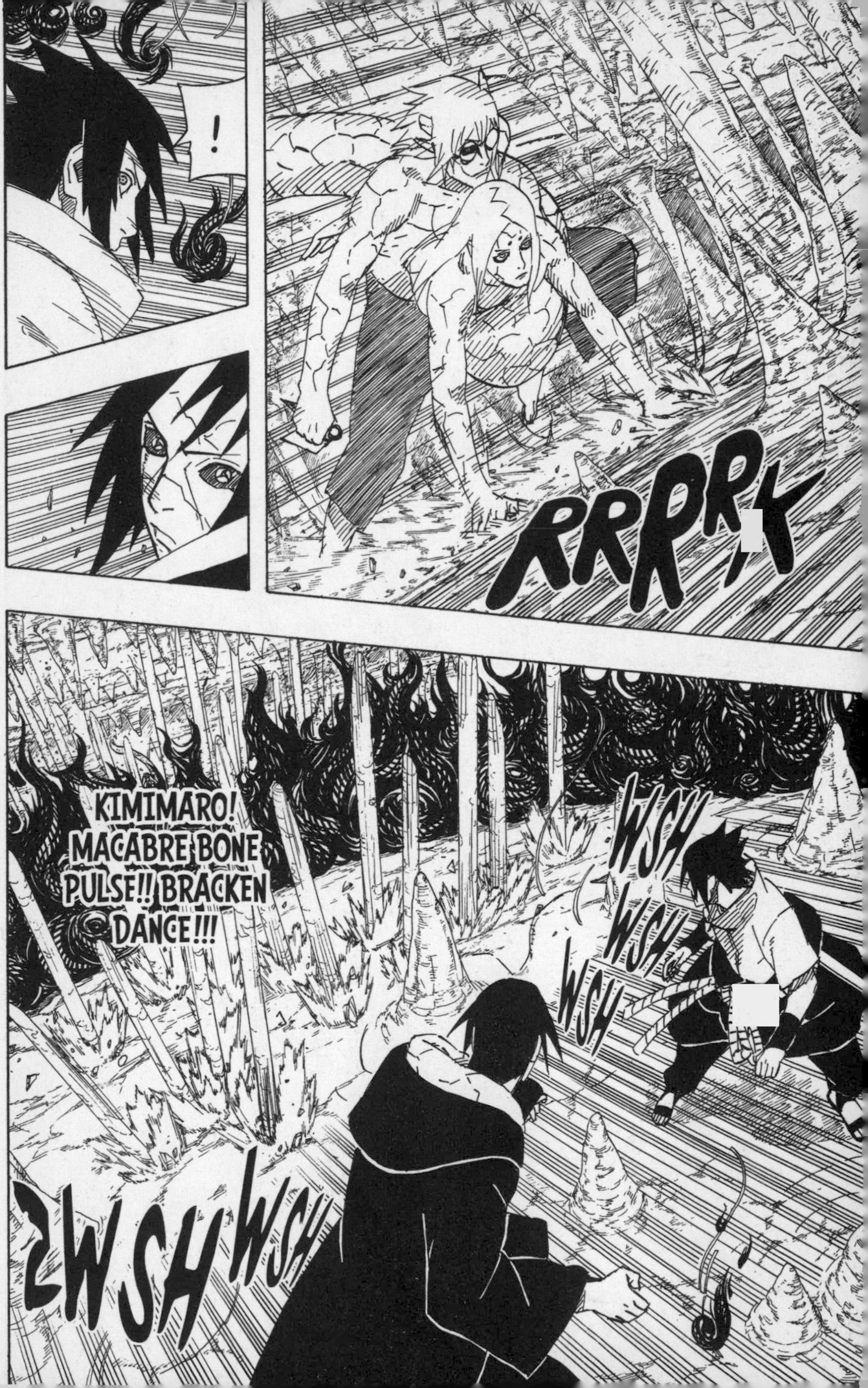
RRRRK
!
KIMIMARO! MACABRE BONE PULSE!! BRACKEN DANCE!!!
WSH
WSH
WSH
WSH
WSH

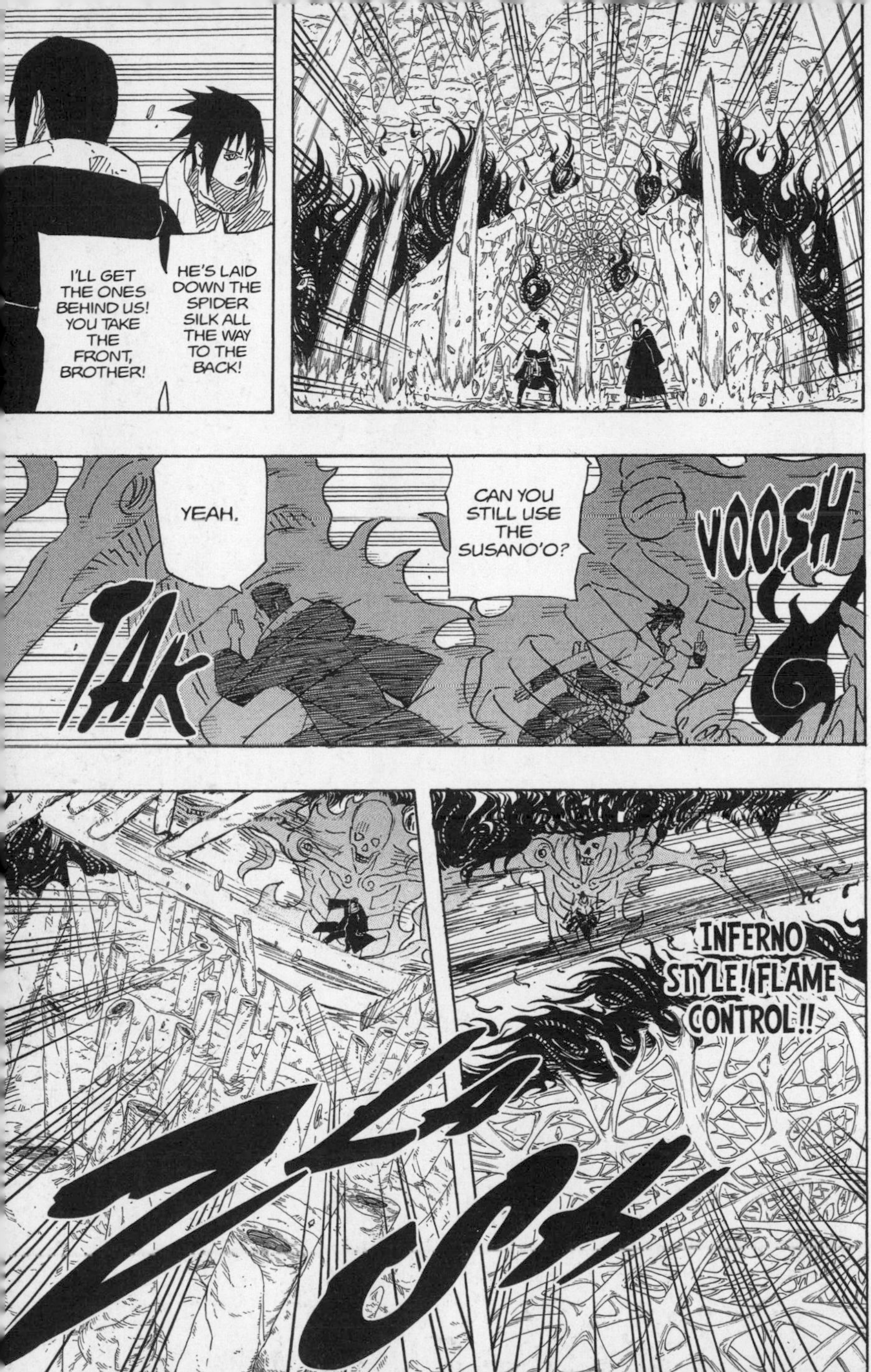
HE'S LAID DOWN THE SPIDER SILK ALL THE WAY TO THE BACK!
I'LL GET THE ONES BEHIND US! YOU TAKE THE FRONT, BROTHER!
VOOSH
CAN YOU STILL USE THE SUSANO'O?
YEAH.
TAK
INFERNO STYLE! FLAME CONTROL!!

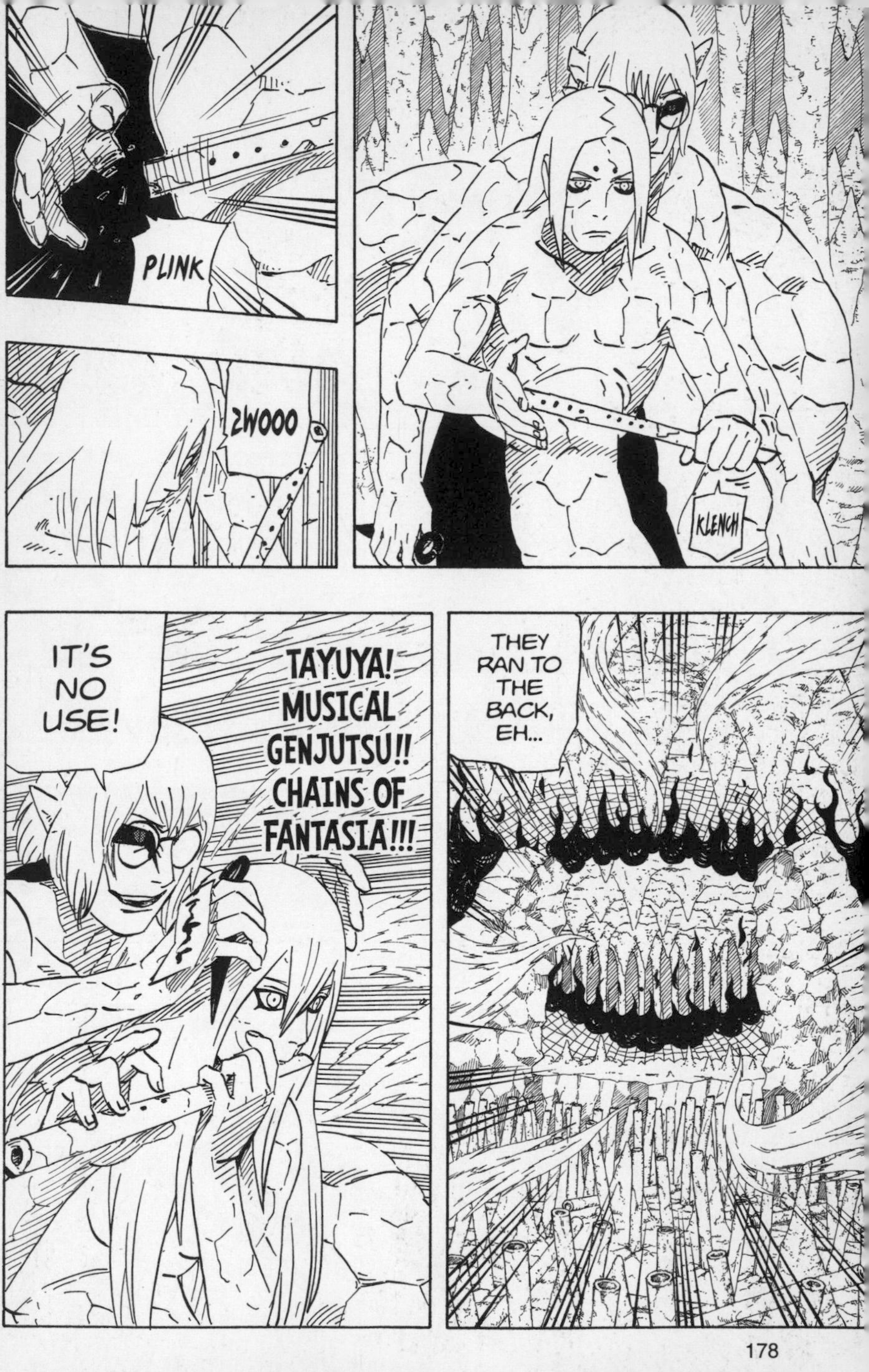
KLENCH
PLINK
ZWOOO
THEY RAN TO THE BACK, EH...
IT'S NO USE!
TAYUYA! MUSICAL GENJUTSU!! CHAINS OF FANTASIA!!!

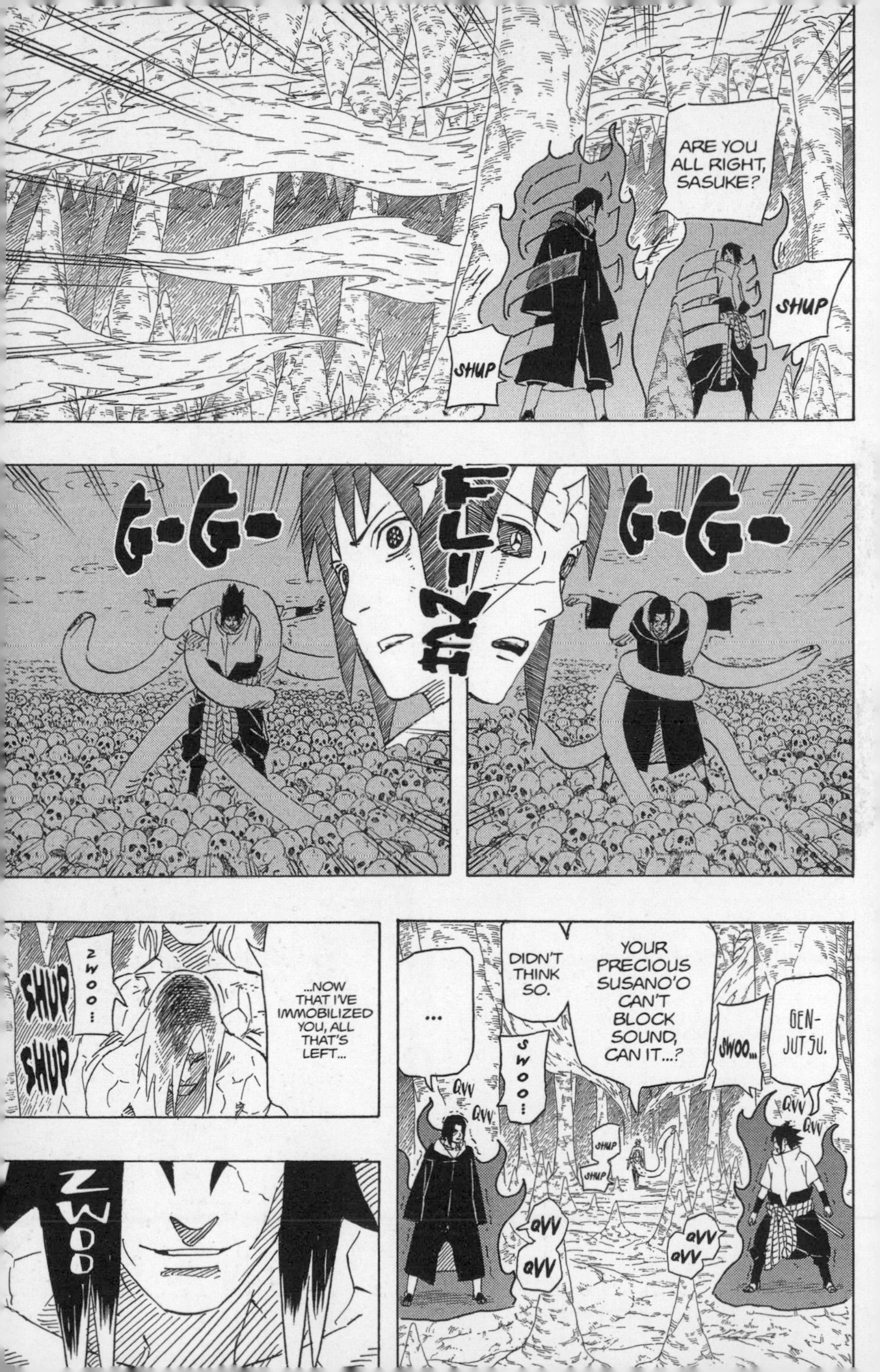
ARE YOU ALL RIGHT, SASUKE?
SHUP
SHUP
G-G-
FLINCH
G-G-
GEN-JUTSU.
SWOO...
QVV
QVV
YOUR PRECIOUS SUSANO'O CAN'T BLOCK SOUND, CAN IT...?
DIDN'T THINK SO.
SWOO...
...
QVV
QVV
SHUP
SHUP
QVV
QVV
QVV
QVV
ZWOO...
SHUP
SHUP
...NOW THAT I'VE IMMOBILIZED YOU, ALL THAT'S LEFT...
ZWOO

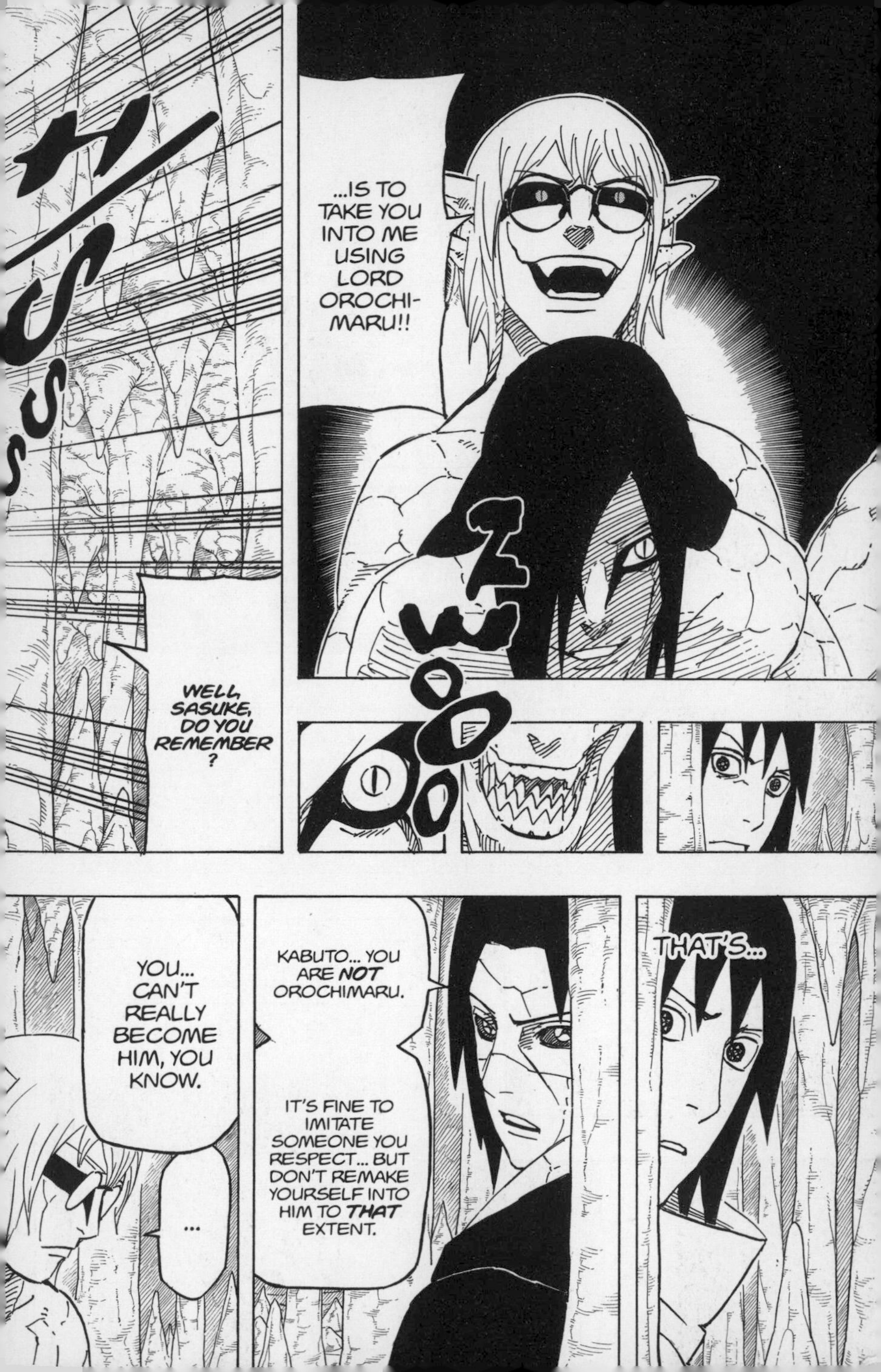
...IS TO TAKE YOU INTO ME USING LORD OROCHI-MARU!!
WELL, SASUKE, DO YOU REMEMBER?
THAT'S...
KABUTO... YOU ARE **NOT** OROCHIMARU.
IT'S FINE TO IMITATE SOMEONE YOU RESPECT... BUT DON'T REMAKE YOURSELF INTO HIM TO **THAT** EXTENT.
YOU... CAN'T REALLY BECOME HIM, YOU KNOW.
...

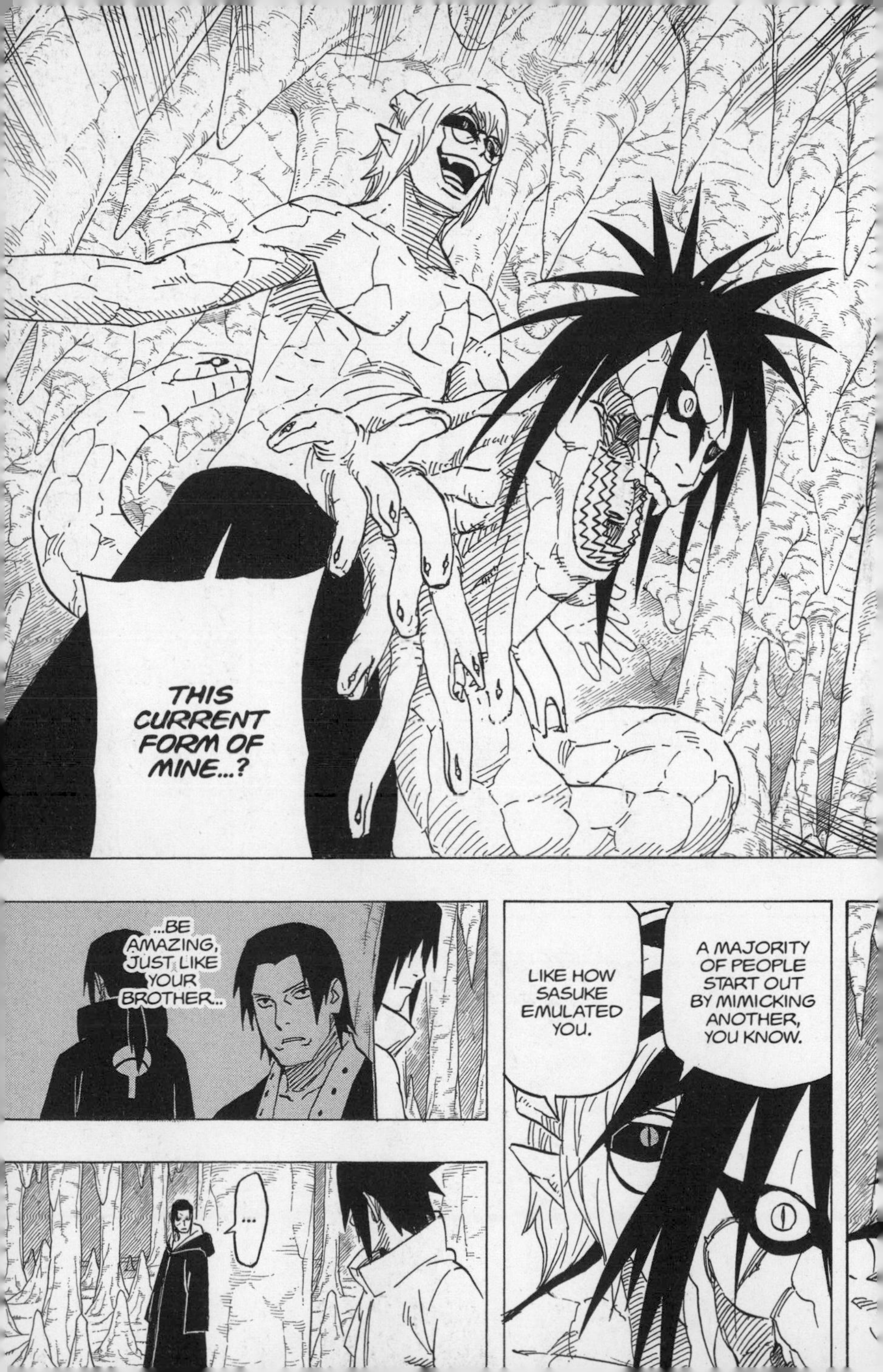
THIS CURRENT FORM OF MINE...?
A MAJORITY OF PEOPLE START OUT BY MIMICKING ANOTHER, YOU KNOW.
LIKE HOW SASUKE EMULATED YOU.
...BE AMAZING, JUST LIKE YOUR BROTHER...
...

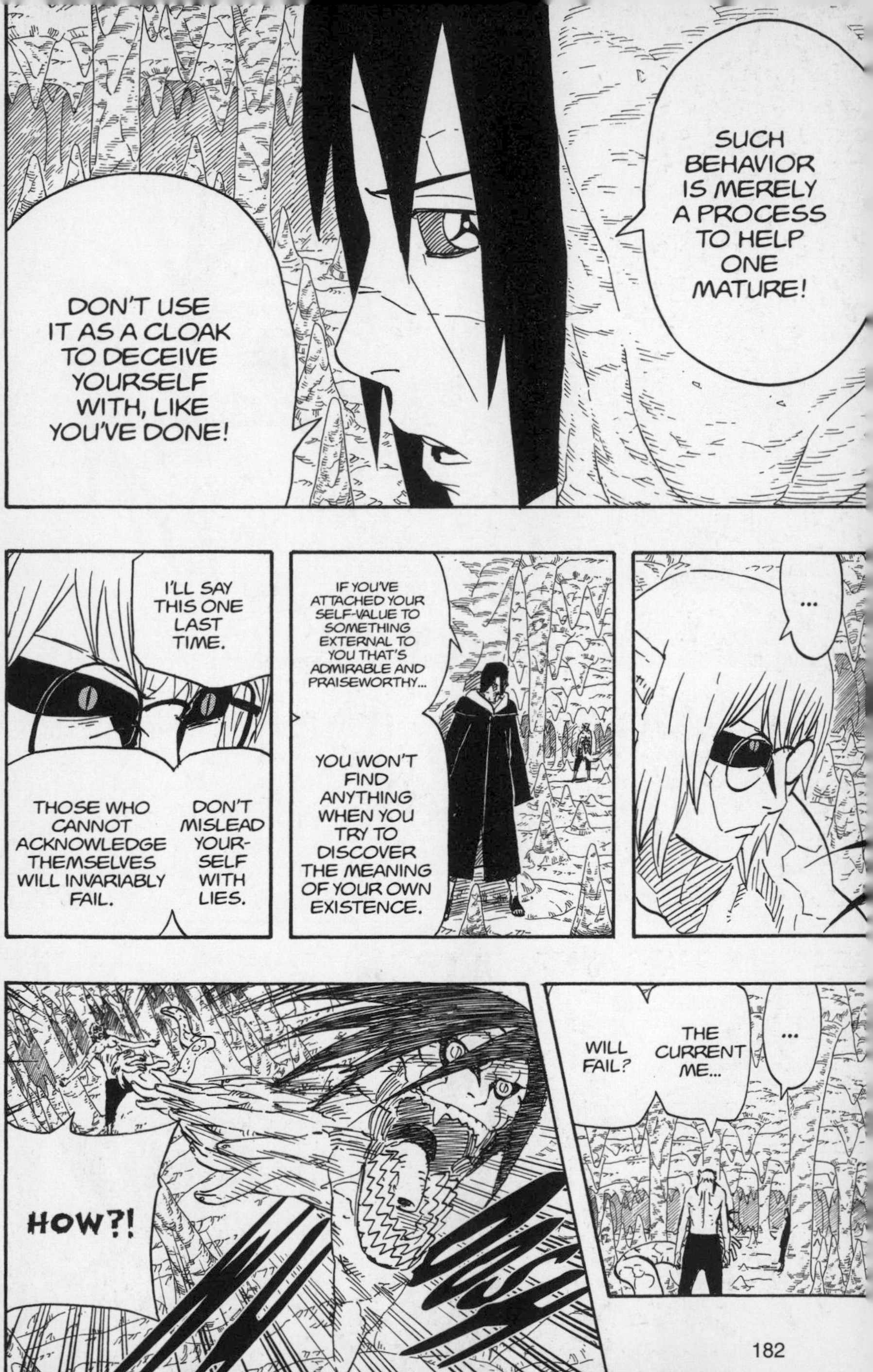
SUCH BEHAVIOR IS MERELY A PROCESS TO HELP ONE MATURE!
DON'T USE IT AS A CLOAK TO DECEIVE YOURSELF WITH, LIKE YOU'VE DONE!
...
IF YOU'VE ATTACHED YOUR SELF-VALUE TO SOMETHING EXTERNAL TO YOU THAT'S ADMIRABLE AND PRAISEWORTHY...
YOU WON'T FIND ANYTHING WHEN YOU TRY TO DISCOVER THE MEANING OF YOUR OWN EXISTENCE.
I'LL SAY THIS ONE LAST TIME.
DON'T MISLEAD YOURSELF WITH LIES.
THOSE WHO CANNOT ACKNOWLEDGE THEMSELVES WILL INVARIABLY FAIL.
...
THE CURRENT ME...
WILL FAIL?
HOW?!

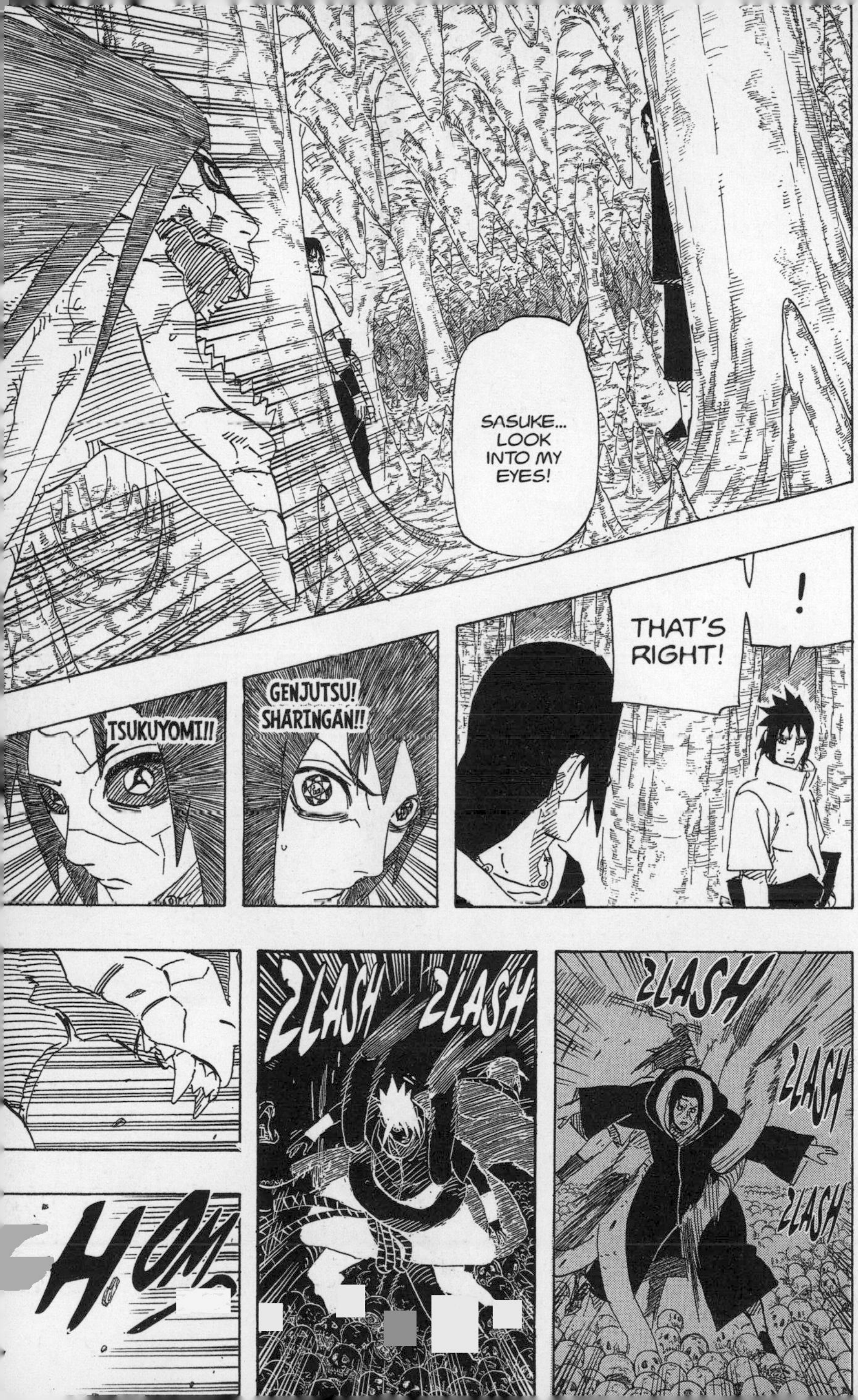
SASUKE... LOOK INTO MY EYES!
!
THAT'S RIGHT!
GENJUTSU! SHARINGAN!!
TSUKUYOMI!!
ZLASH
ZLASH
ZLASH
ZLASH
ZLASH

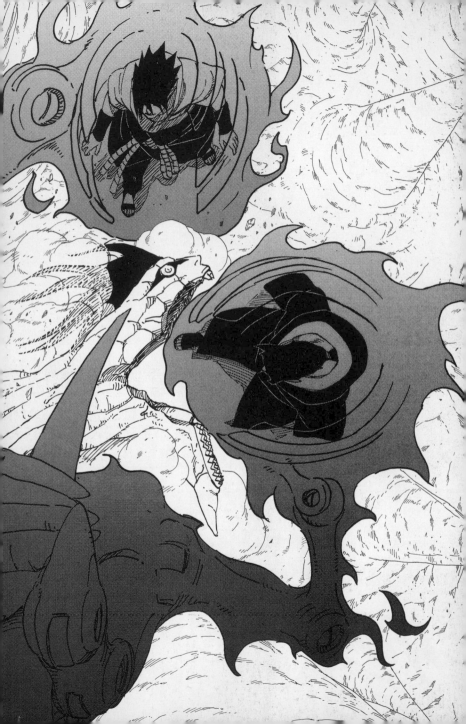

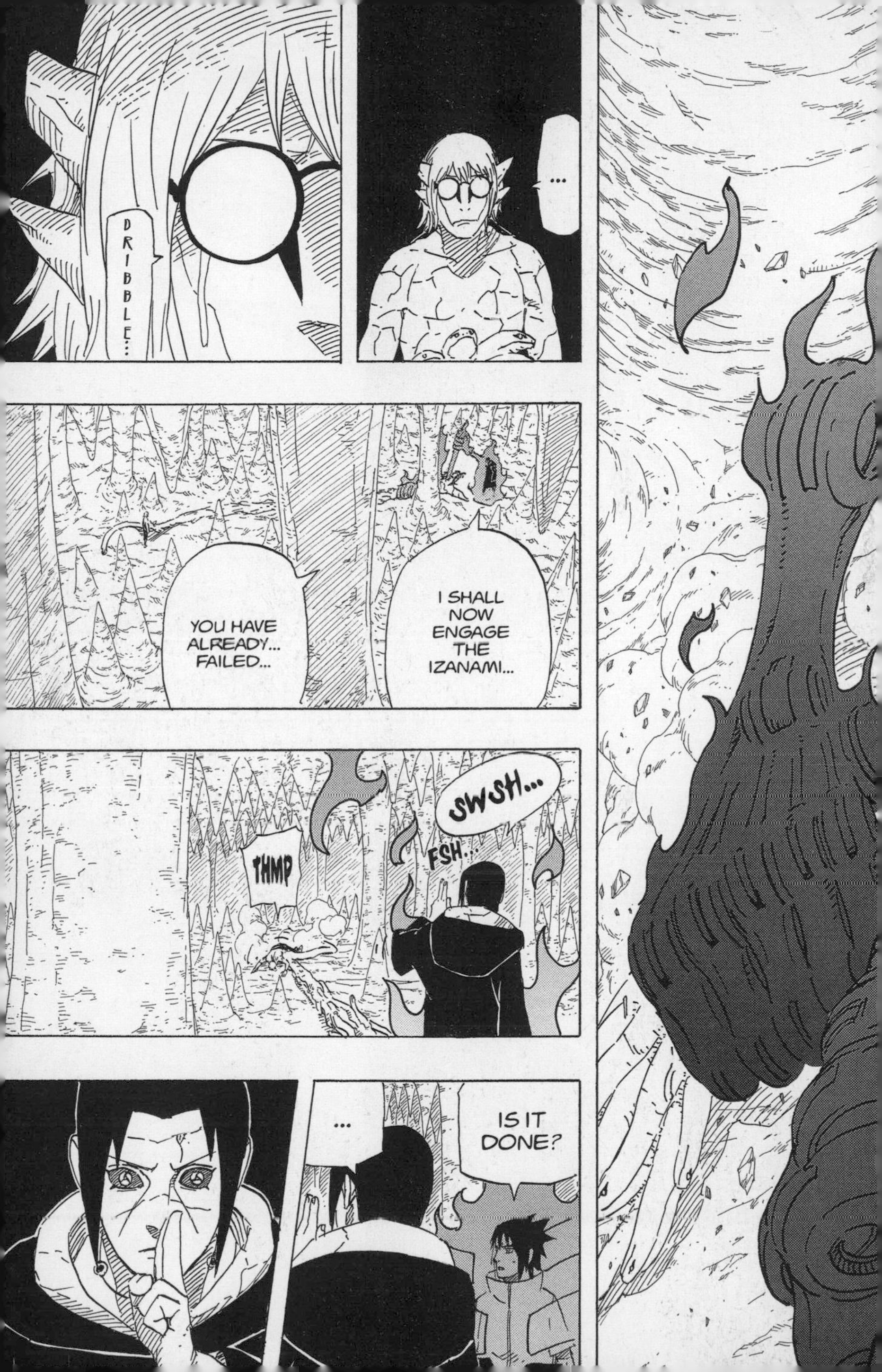
...
DRIBBLE...
I SHALL NOW ENGAGE THE IZANAMI...
YOU HAVE ALREADY... FAILED...
SWSH...
FSH...
THMP
IS IT DONE?
...

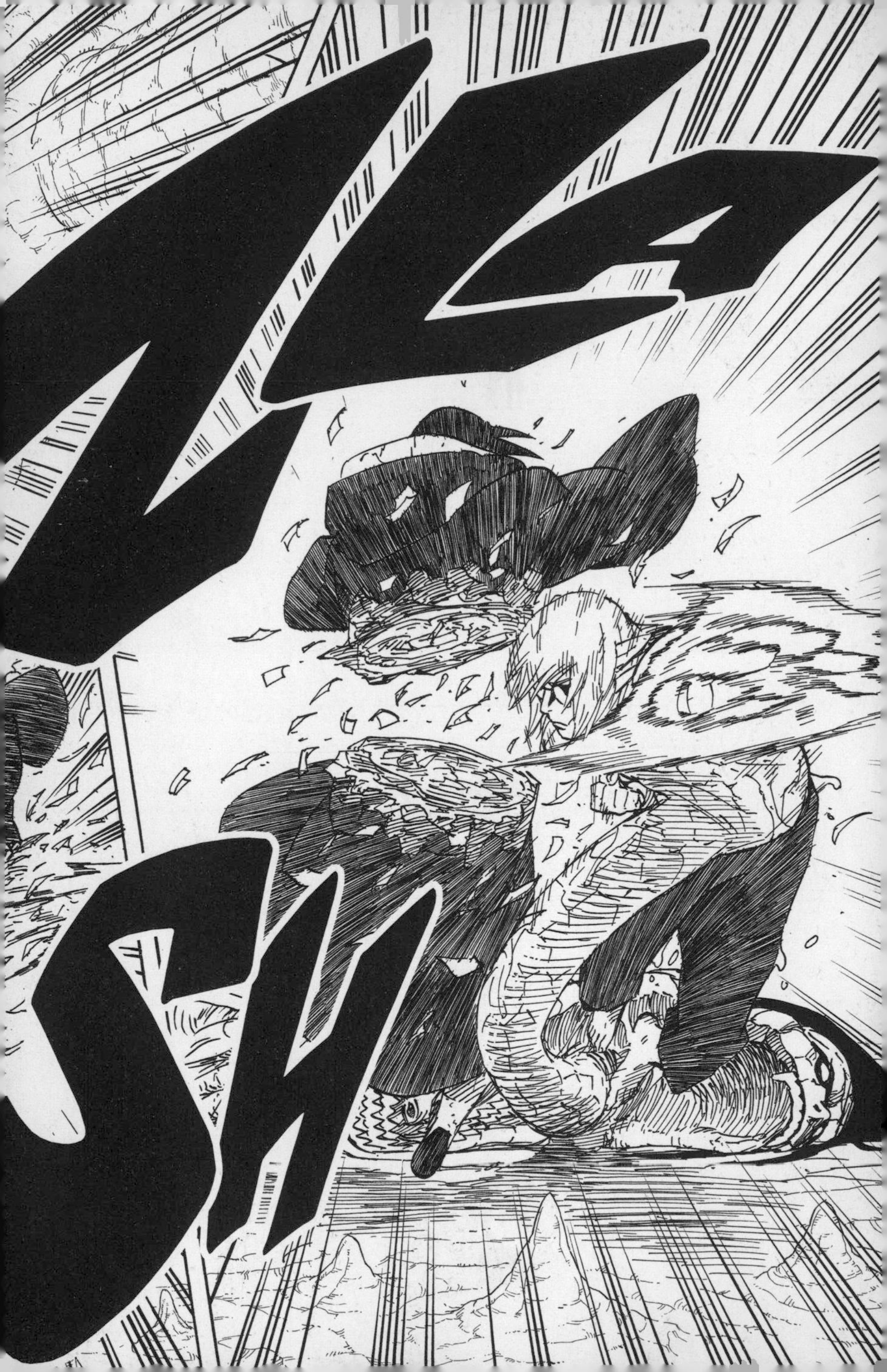

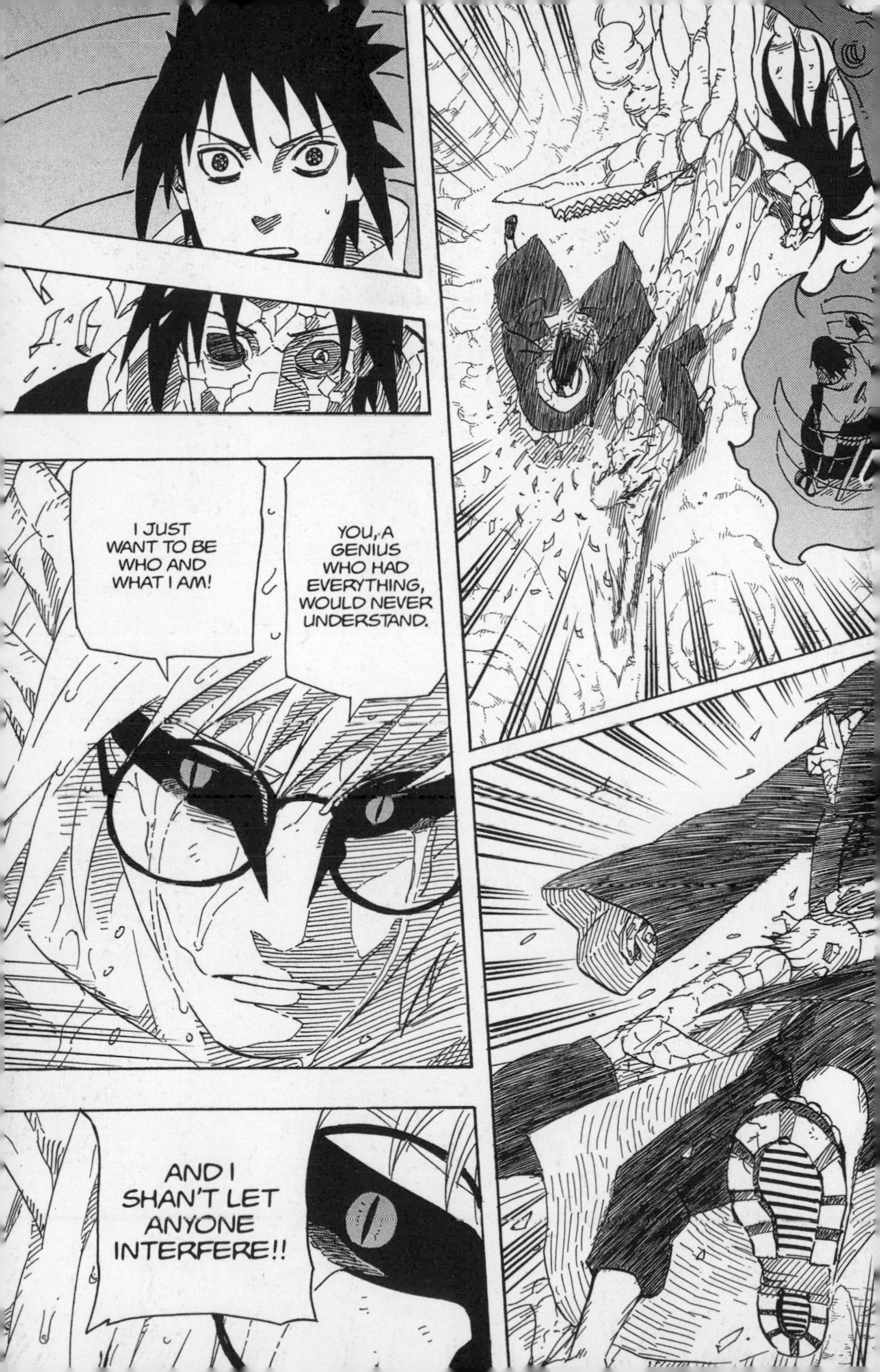
YOU, A GENIUS WHO HAD EVERYTHING, WOULD NEVER UNDERSTAND.
I JUST WANT TO BE WHO AND WHAT I AM!
AND I SHAN'T LET ANYONE INTERFERE!!

NARUTO

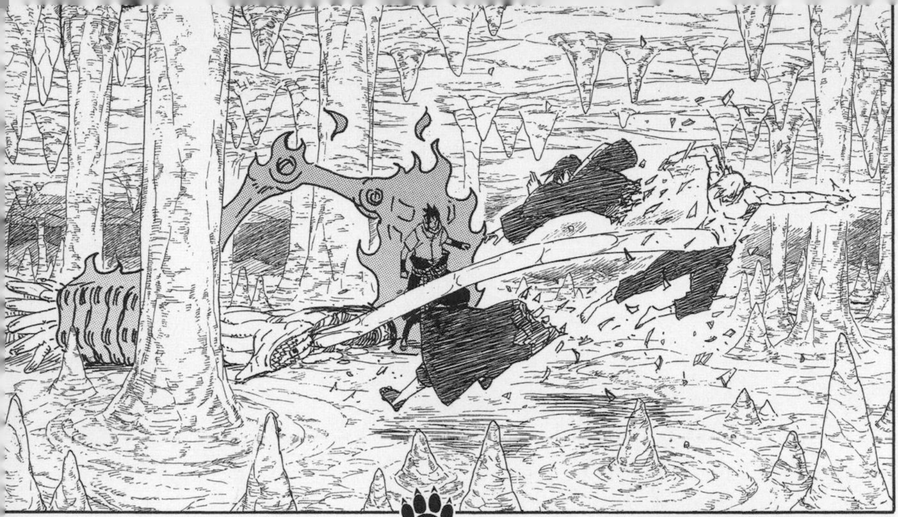

Number 586: The Izanami Activated

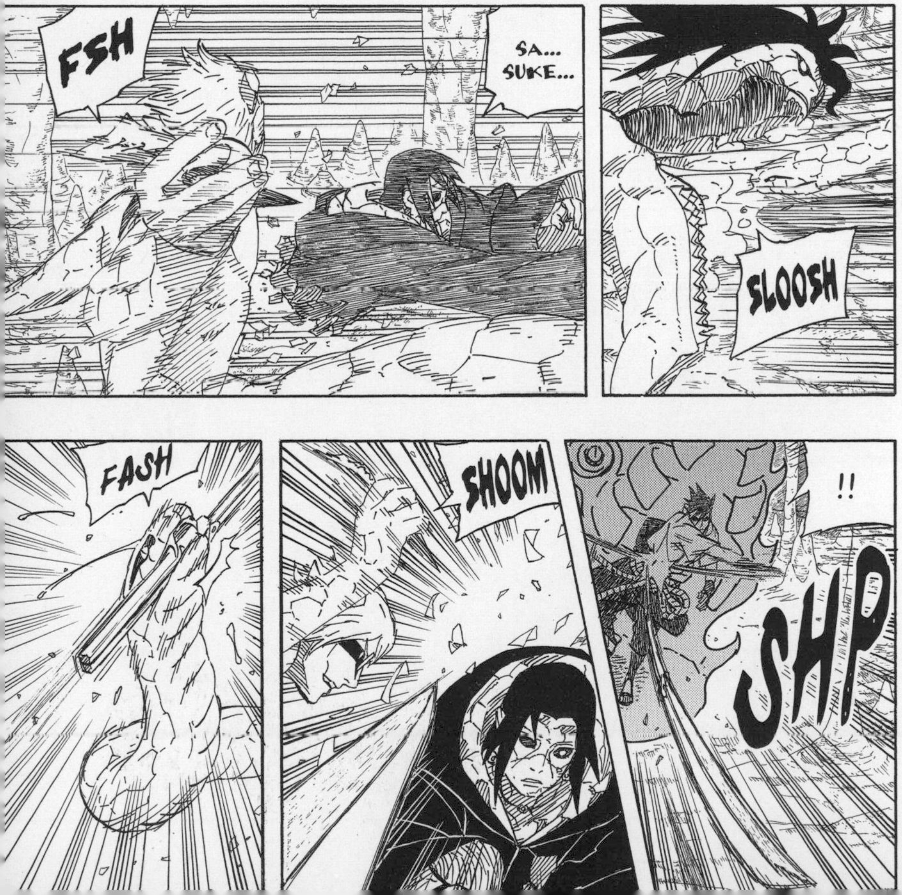
SLOOSH
SA... SUKE...
FSH
!!
SHP
SHOOM
FASH

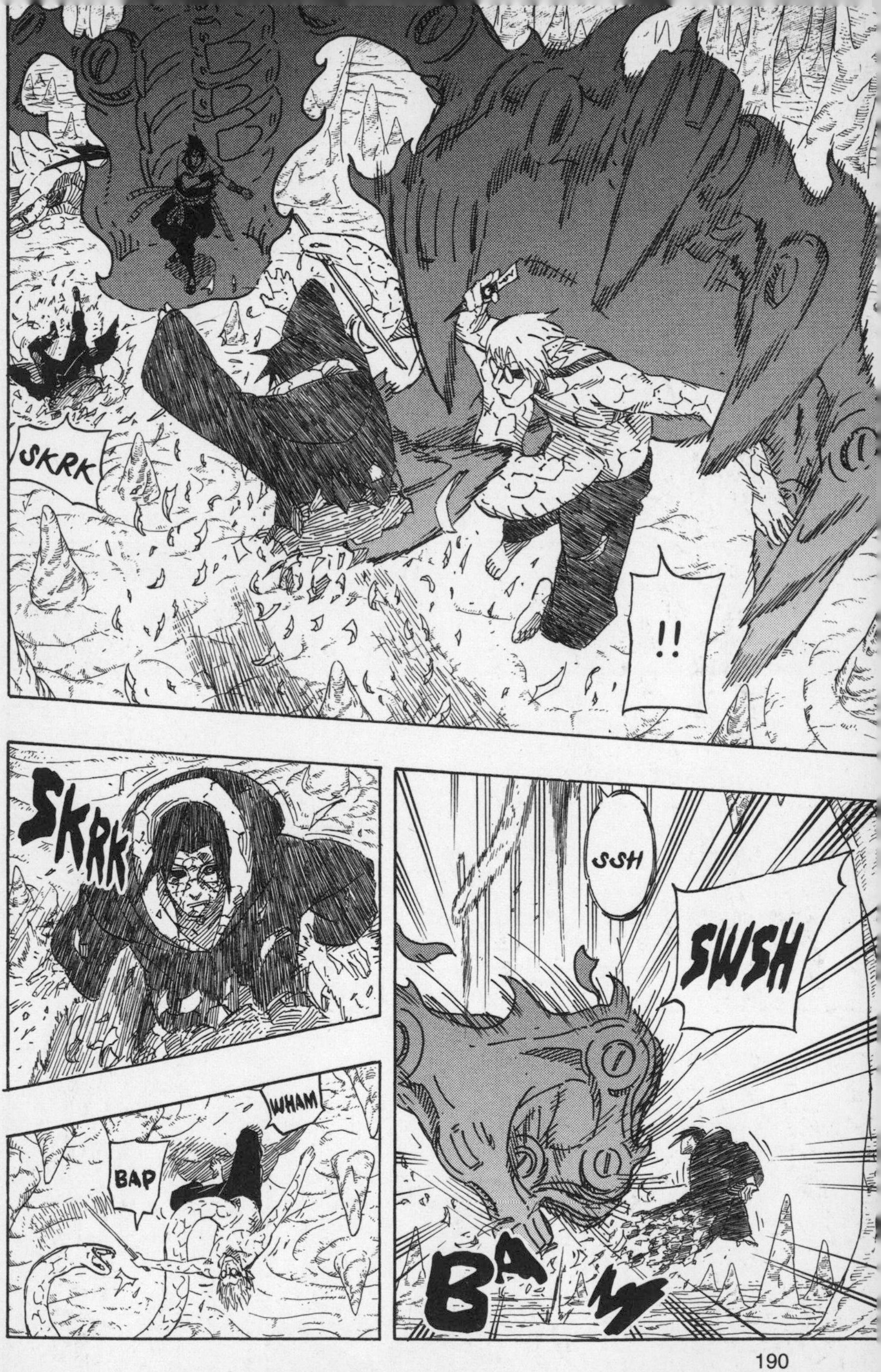
!!
SKRK
SSH
SWSH
BAM
SKRK
WHAM
BAP

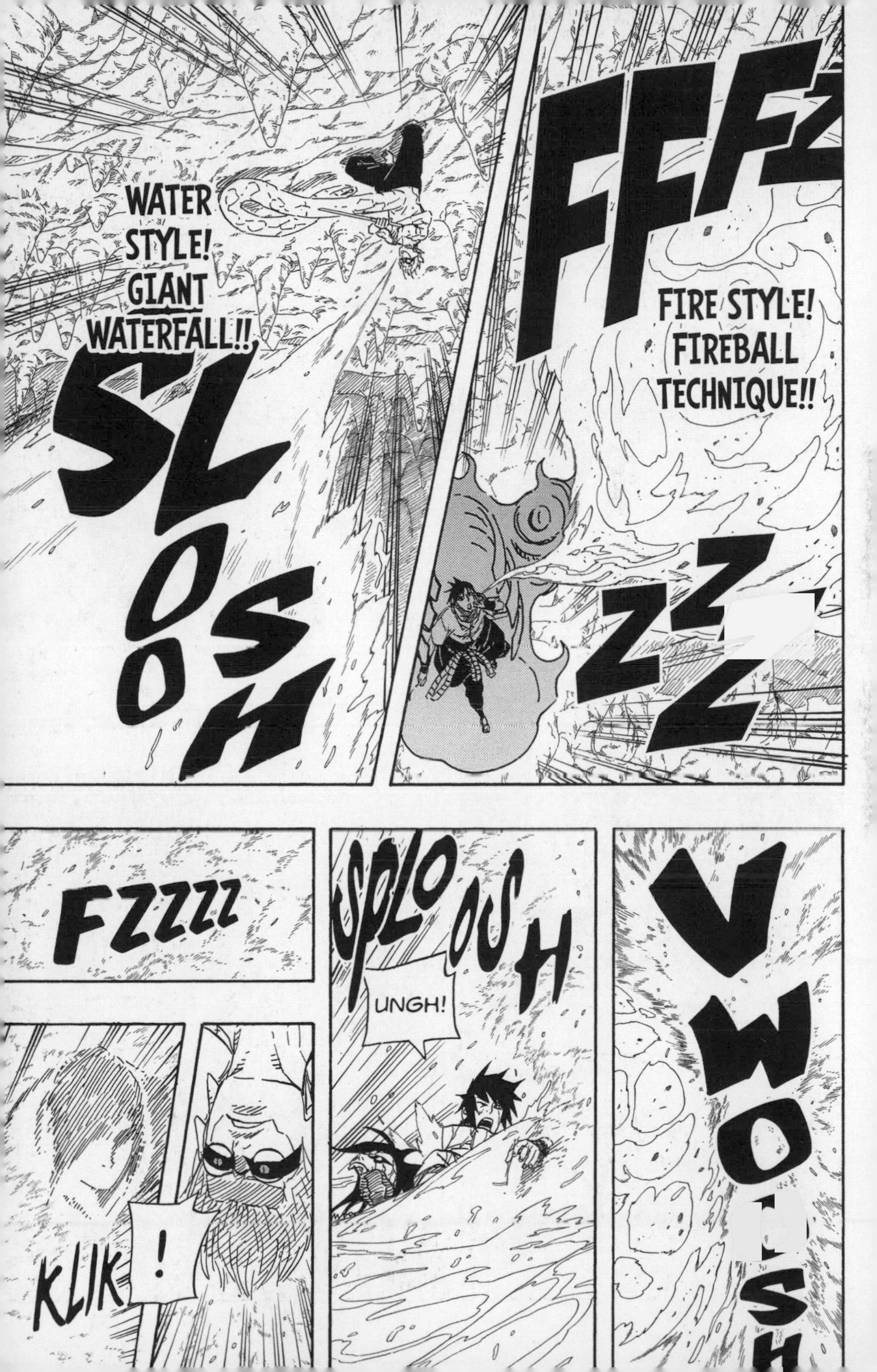
FFFZ
ZZZ
FIRE STYLE! FIREBALL TECHNIQUE!!
WATER STYLE! GIANT WATERFALL!!
SLOSH
VWO
SH
SPLOOSH
UNGH!
FZZZZ
!
KLIK

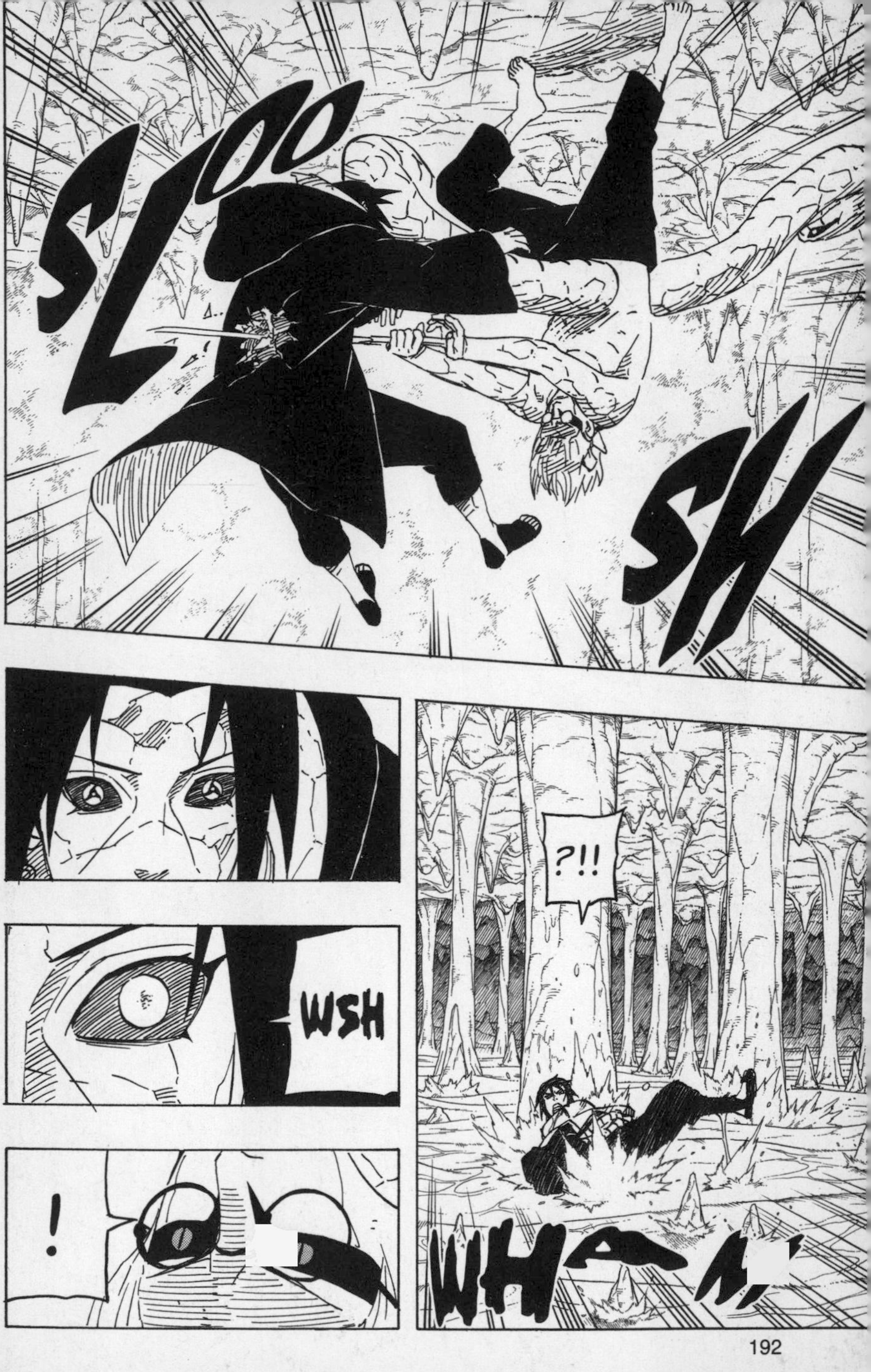
SLOO
SH
?!!
WHAM
WSH
!

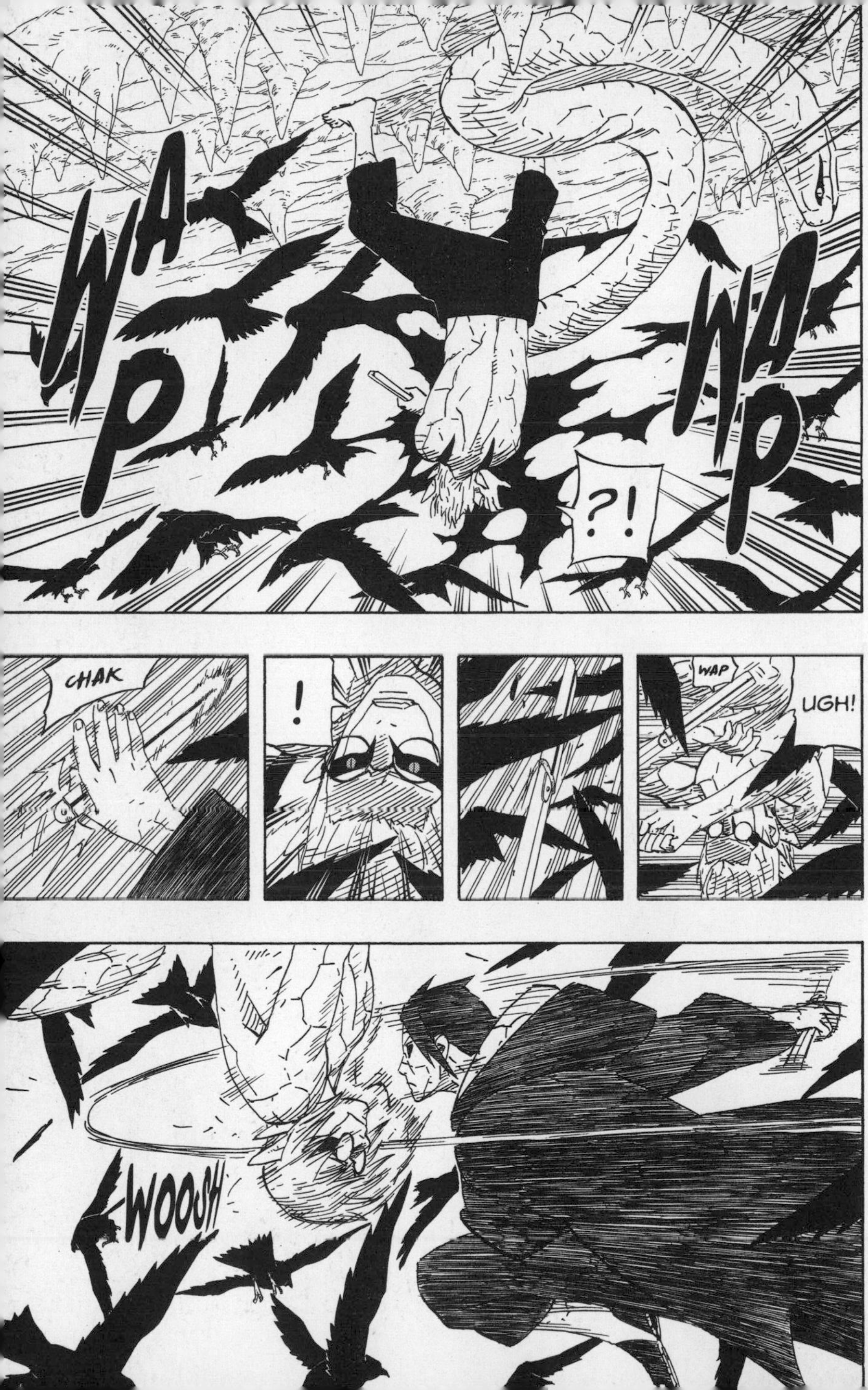
WAP
?!
WAP
WAP
UGH!
!
CHAK
WOOSH

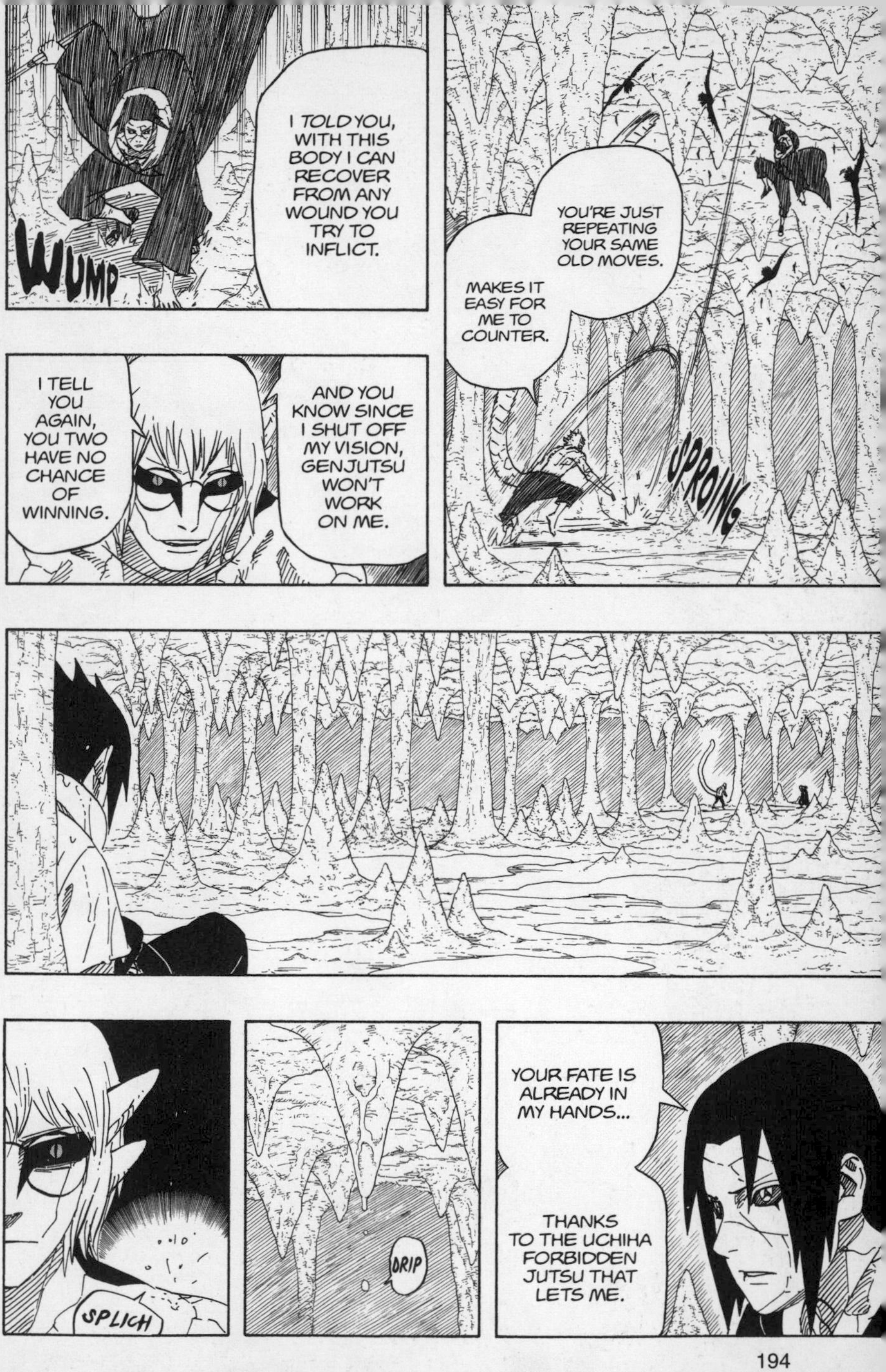
YOU'RE JUST REPEATING YOUR SAME OLD MOVES.
MAKES IT EASY FOR ME TO COUNTER.
SPROING
I *TOLD* YOU, WITH THIS BODY I CAN RECOVER FROM ANY WOUND YOU TRY TO INFLICT.
WUMP
AND YOU KNOW SINCE I SHUT OFF MY VISION, GENJUTSU WON'T WORK ON ME.
I TELL YOU AGAIN, YOU TWO HAVE NO CHANCE OF WINNING.
YOUR FATE IS ALREADY IN MY HANDS...
THANKS TO THE UCHIHA FORBIDDEN JUTSU THAT LETS ME.
DRIP
SPLICH

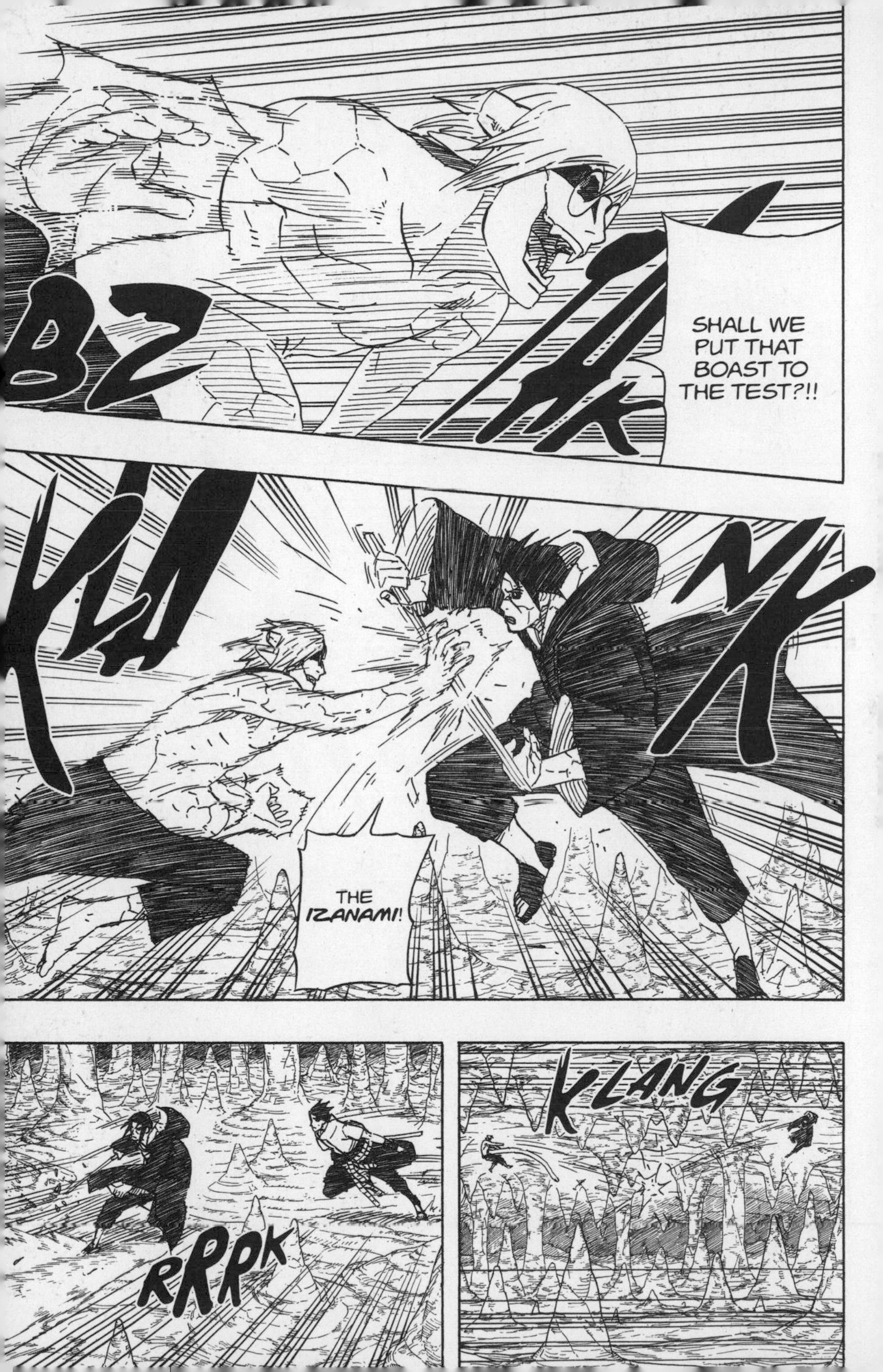
SHALL WE PUT THAT BOAST TO THE TEST?!!
THE IZANAMI!
KLANG
RRRK

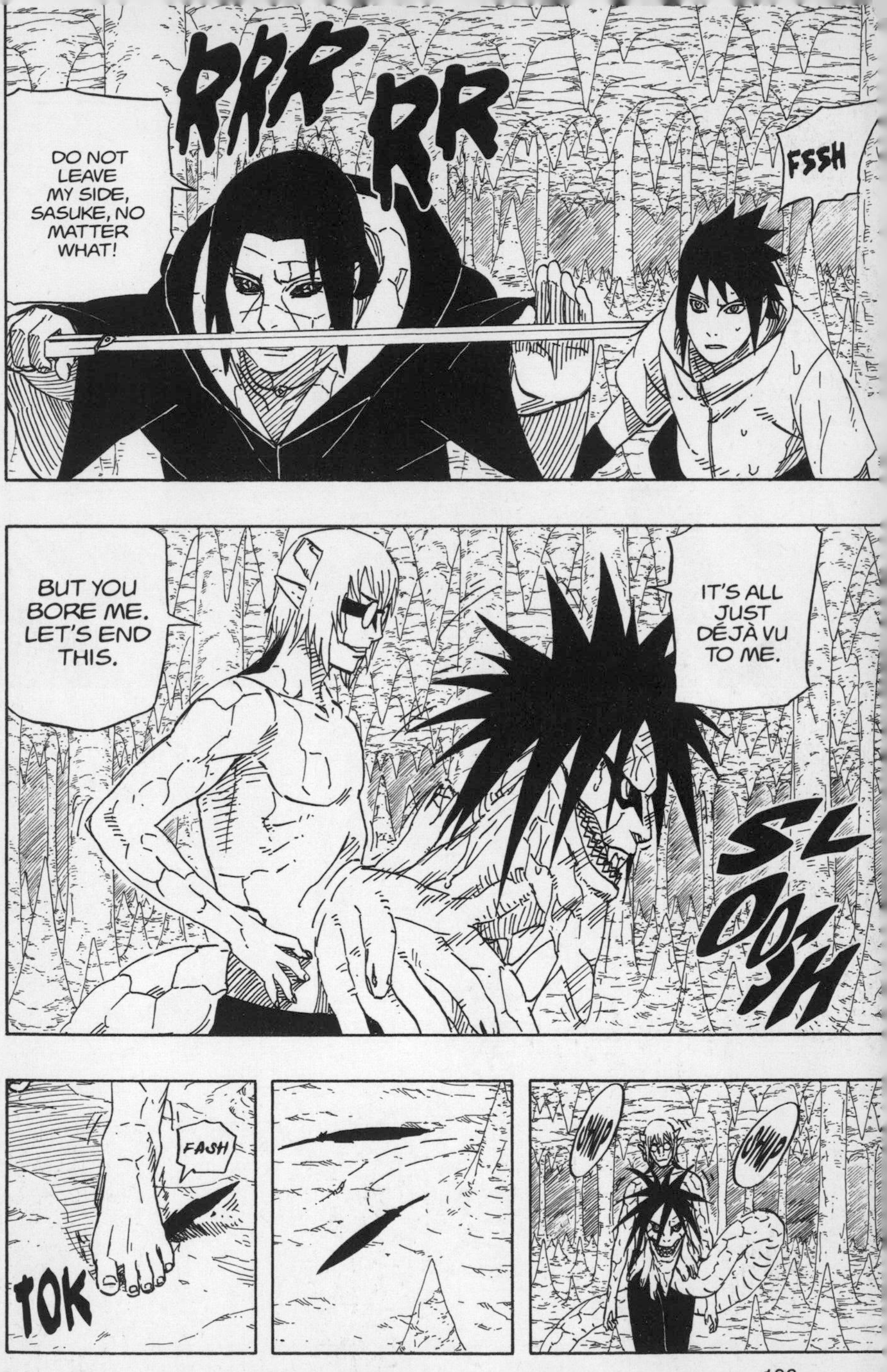
RRR RR
FSSH
DO NOT LEAVE MY SIDE, SASUKE, NO MATTER WHAT!
IT'S ALL JUST DÉJÀ VU TO ME.
BUT YOU BORE ME. LET'S END THIS.
SLOOSH
CHP
CHP
FASH
TOK

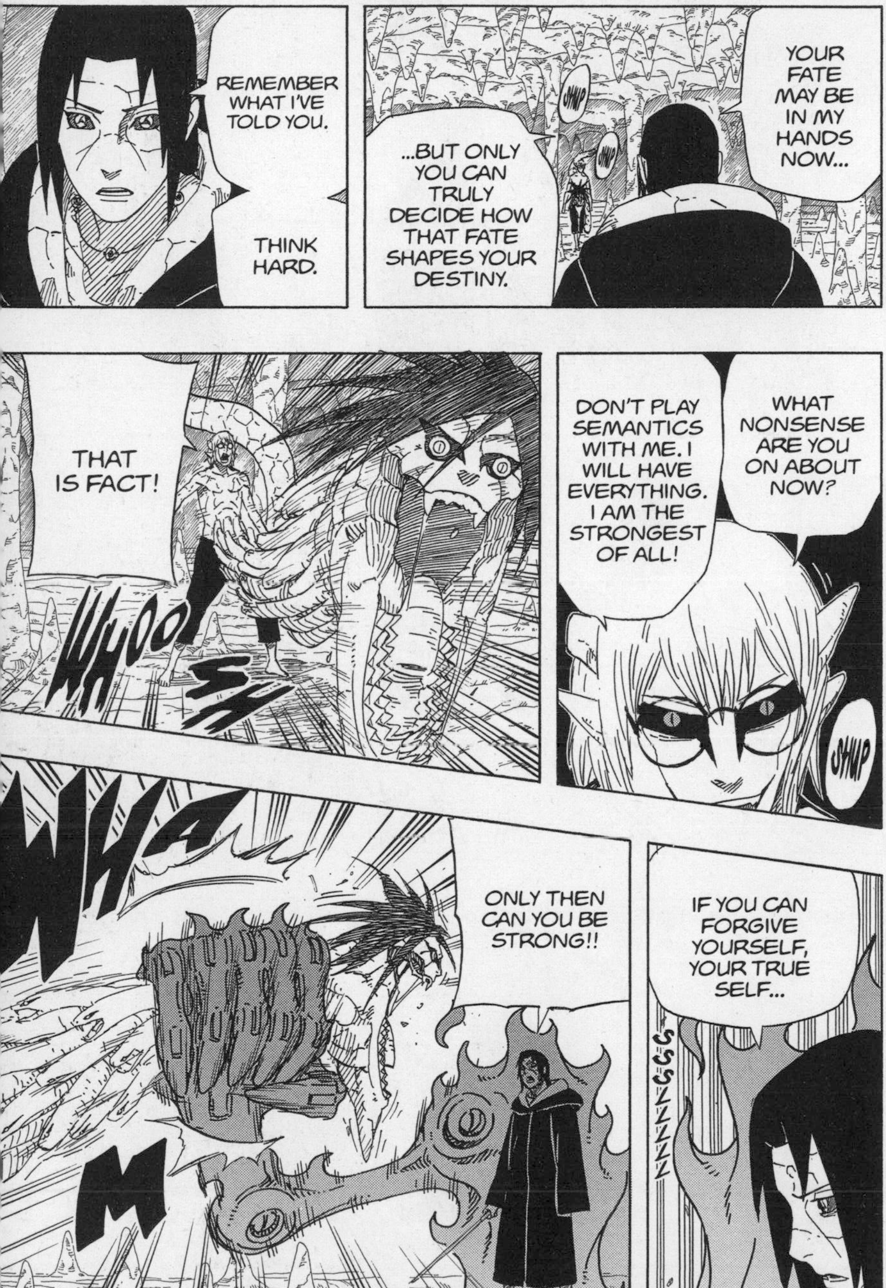
YOUR FATE MAY BE IN MY HANDS NOW...
SHUP
SHUP
...BUT ONLY YOU CAN TRULY DECIDE HOW THAT FATE SHAPES YOUR DESTINY.
REMEMBER WHAT I'VE TOLD YOU.
THINK HARD.
WHAT NONSENSE ARE YOU ON ABOUT NOW?
DON'T PLAY SEMANTICS WITH ME. I WILL HAVE EVERYTHING. I AM THE STRONGEST OF ALL!
SHUP
THAT IS FACT!
WHOOOSH
IF YOU CAN FORGIVE YOURSELF, YOUR TRUE SELF...
ONLY THEN CAN YOU BE STRONG!!
WHAM

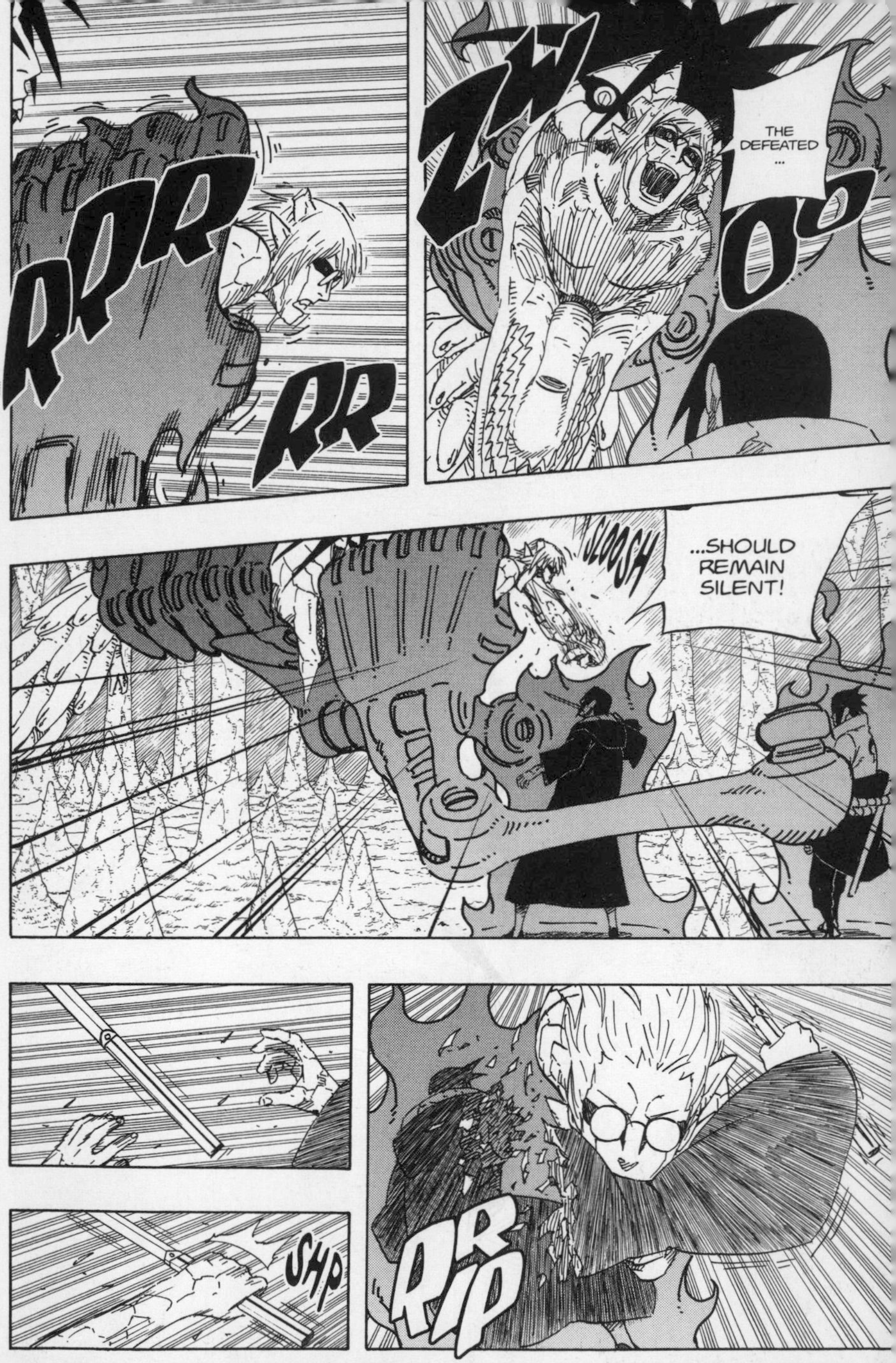
ZWOO
THE DEFEATED...
RRR
RR
SLOOSH
...SHOULD REMAIN SILENT!
RRIP
SHP

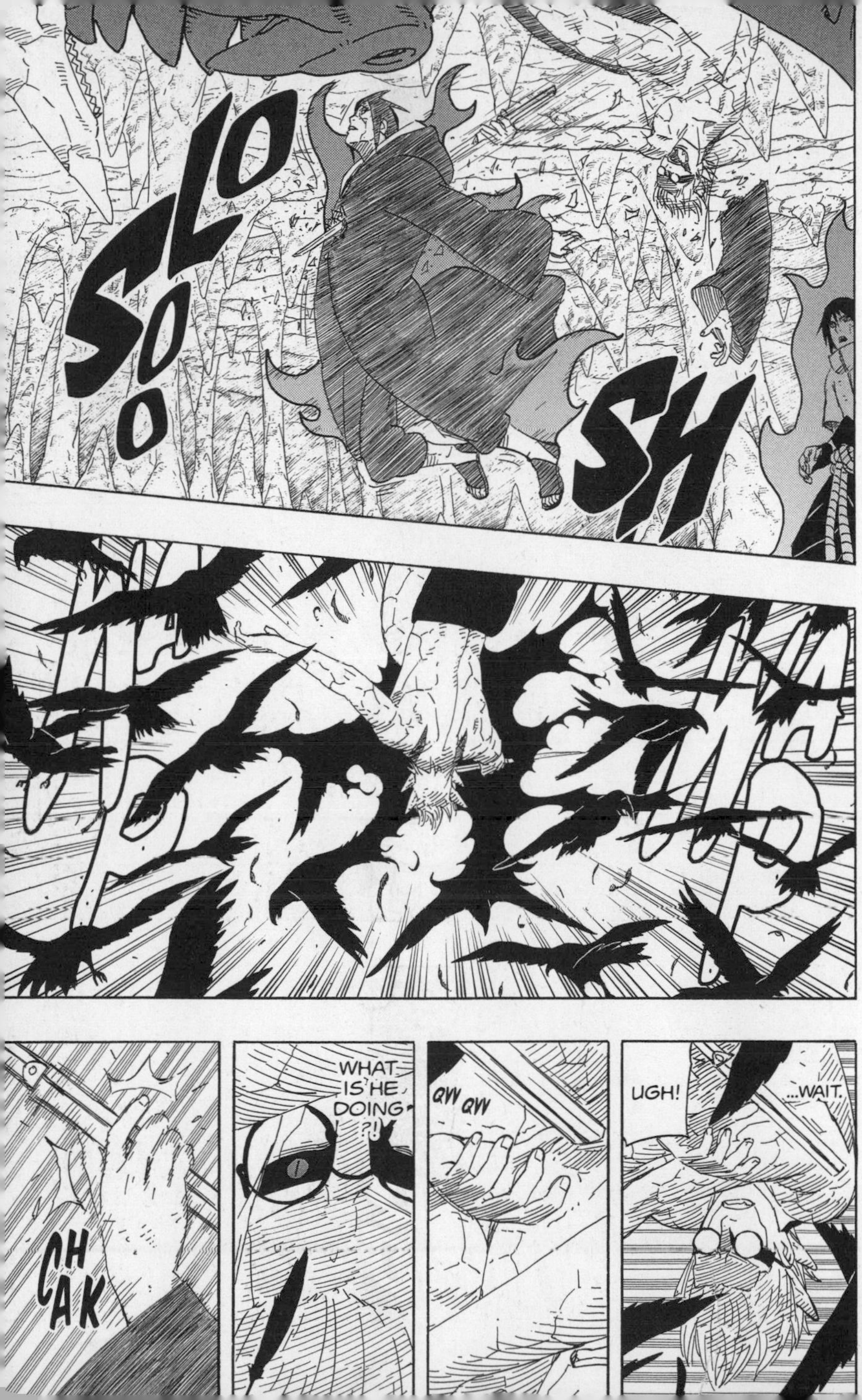
SH
...WAIT.
UGH!
WHAT IS HE DOING?!
CHAK

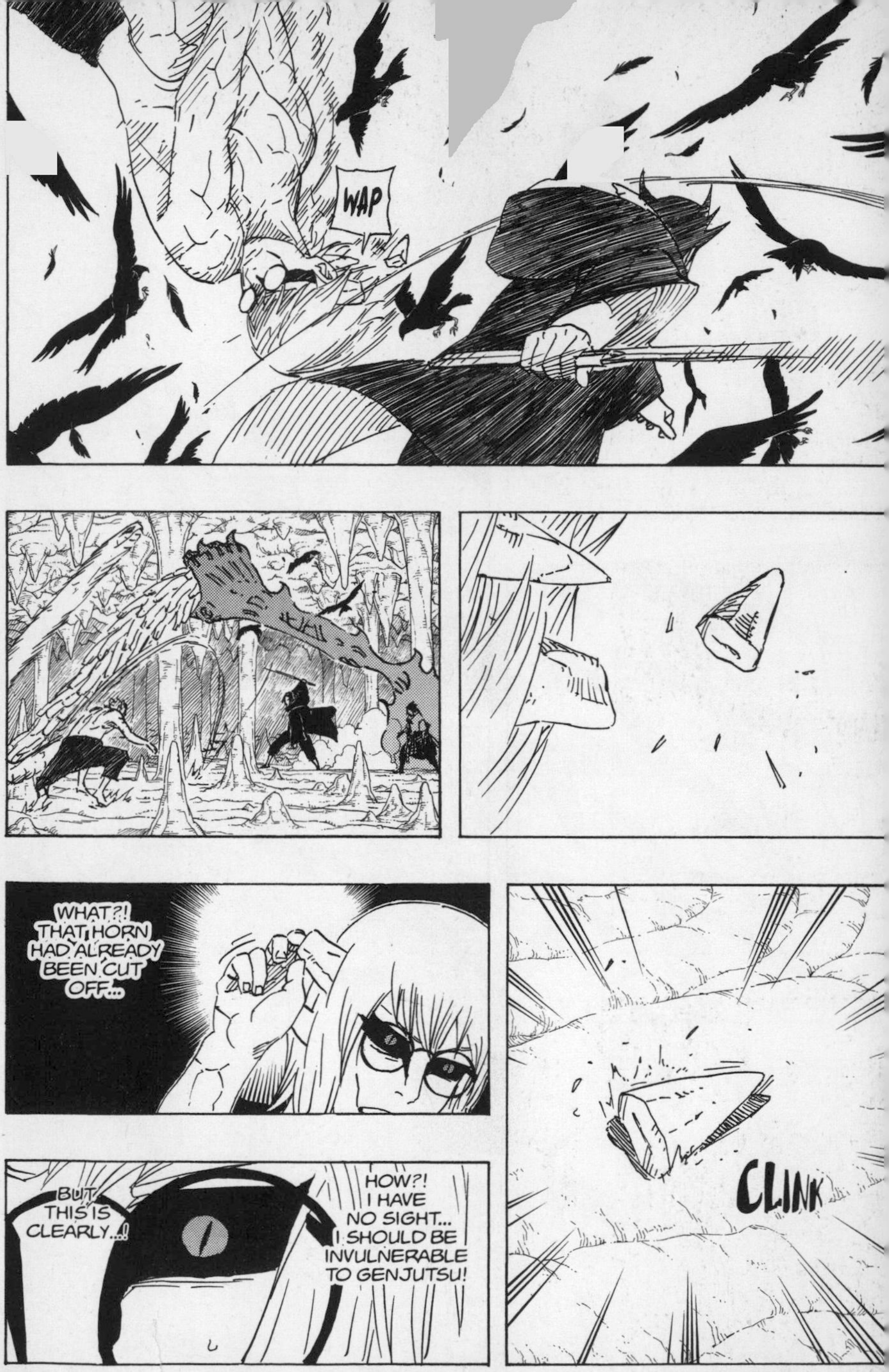
WAP
CLINK
WHAT?! THAT HORN HAD ALREADY BEEN CUT OFF...
HOW?! I HAVE NO SIGHT... I SHOULD BE INVULNERABLE TO GENJUTSU!
BUT THIS IS CLEARLY...!

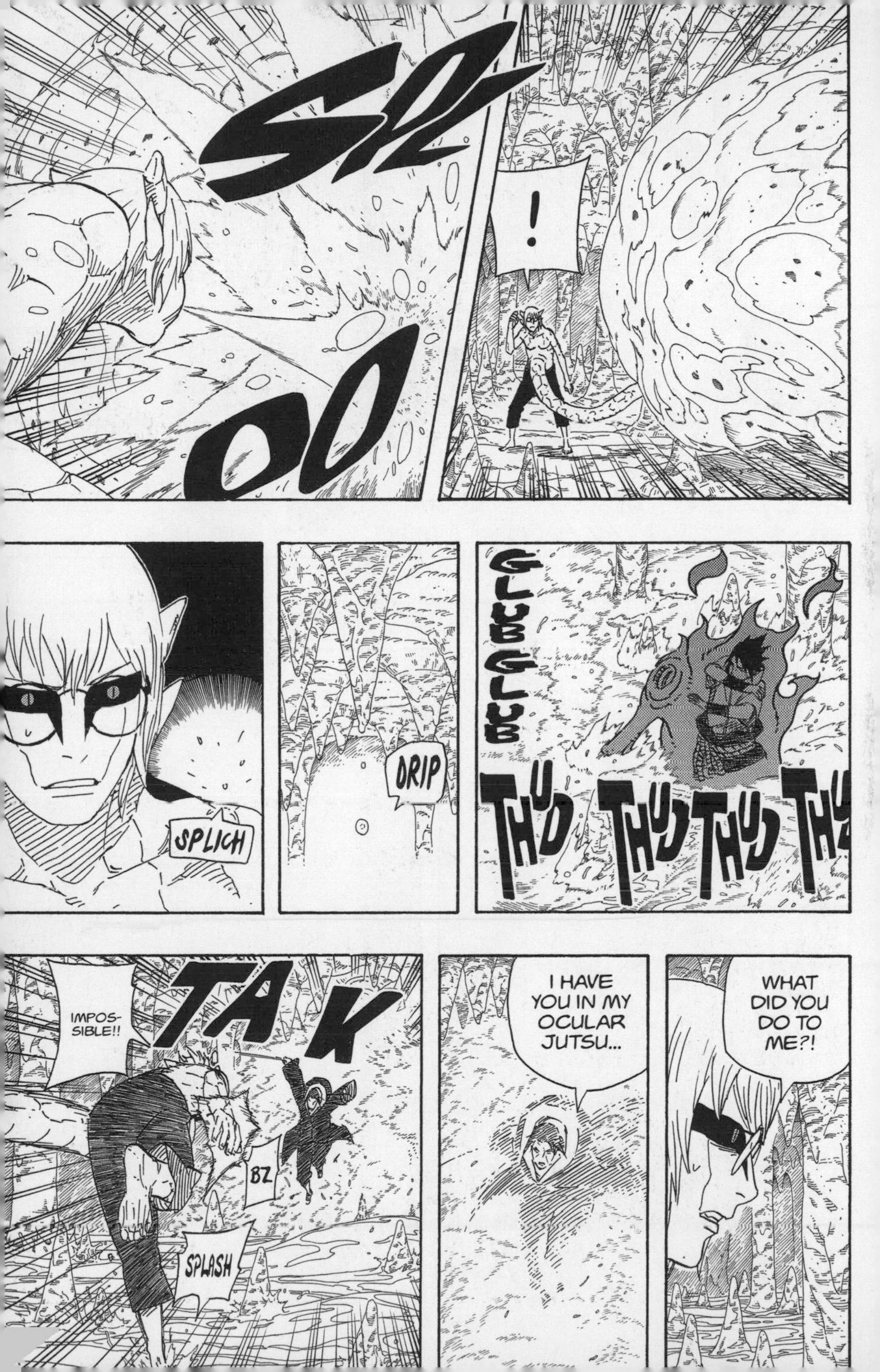
!
SPLOO
GLUB GLUB
THUD THUD THUD THU
DRIP
SPLICH
WHAT DID YOU DO TO ME?!
I HAVE YOU IN MY OCULAR JUTSU...
IMPOSSIBLE!!
TAK
BZ
SPLASH

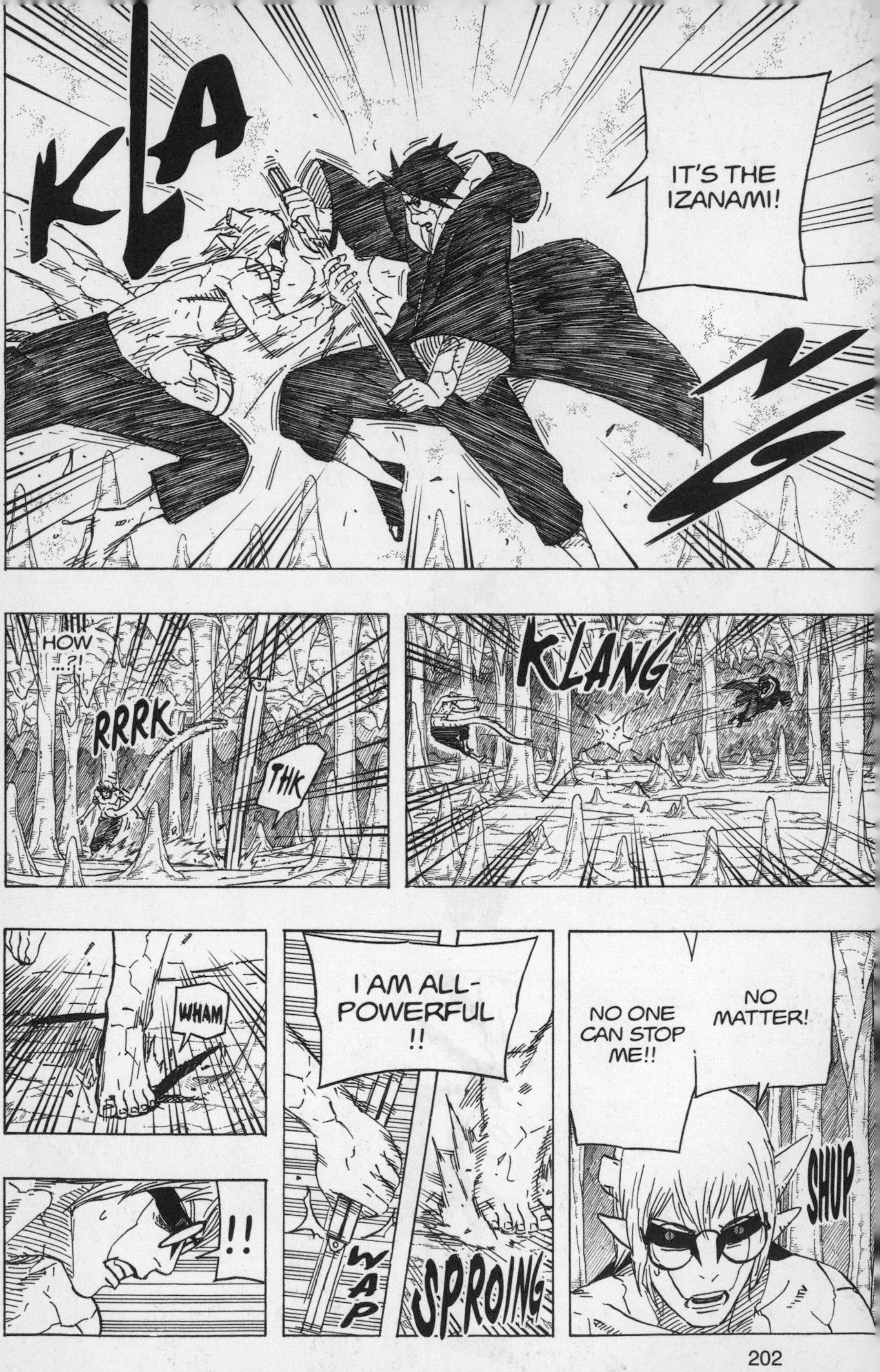
IT'S THE IZANAMI!
KLA
NG
KLANG
HOW ...?!
RRRK
THK
NO MATTER!
NO ONE CAN STOP ME!!
SHUP
I AM ALL-POWERFUL !!
WAP
SPROING
WHAM
!!

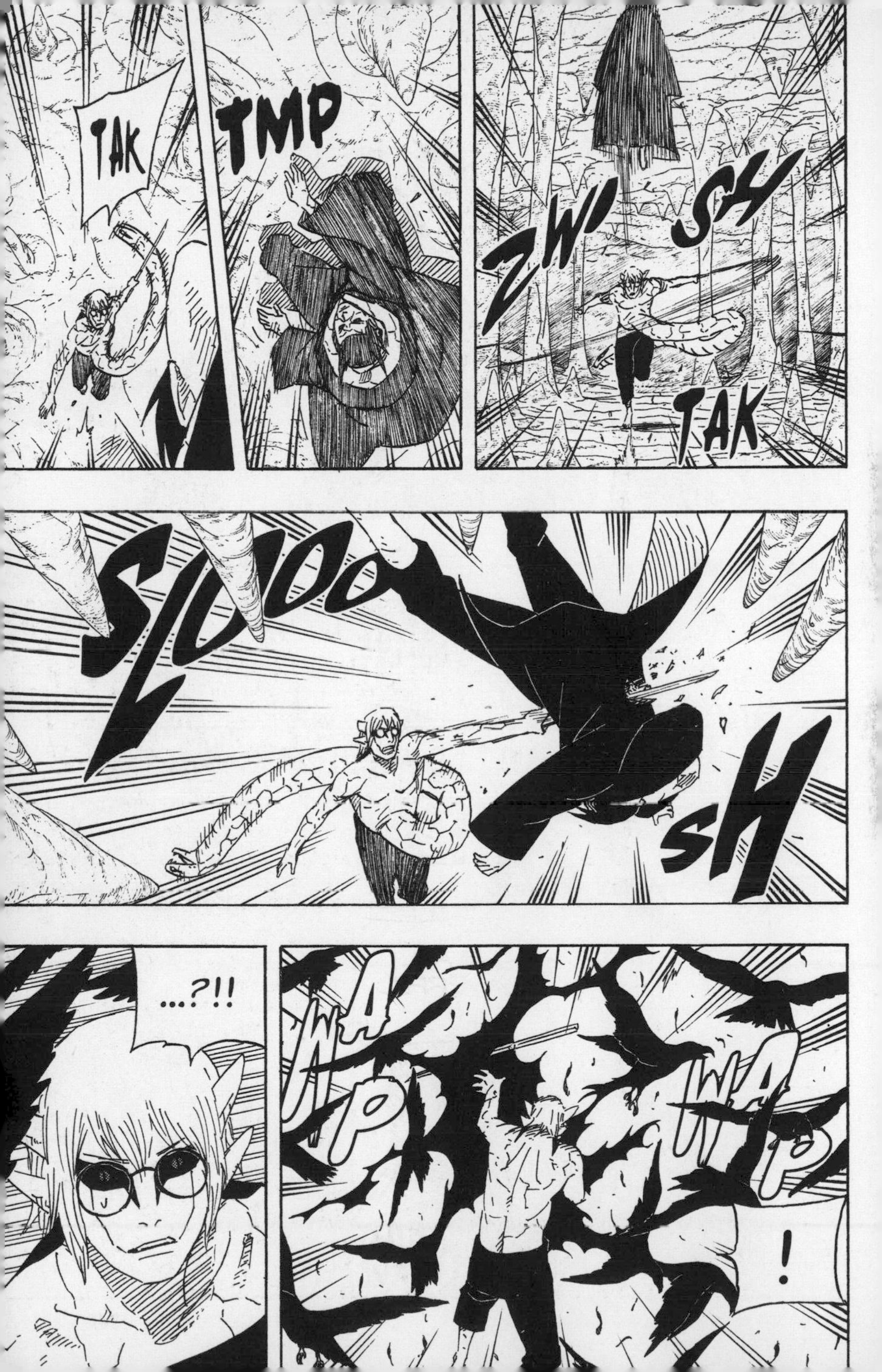
ZWI SH
TAK
TMP
TAK
SWOO
SH
WAP
WAP
!
...?!!

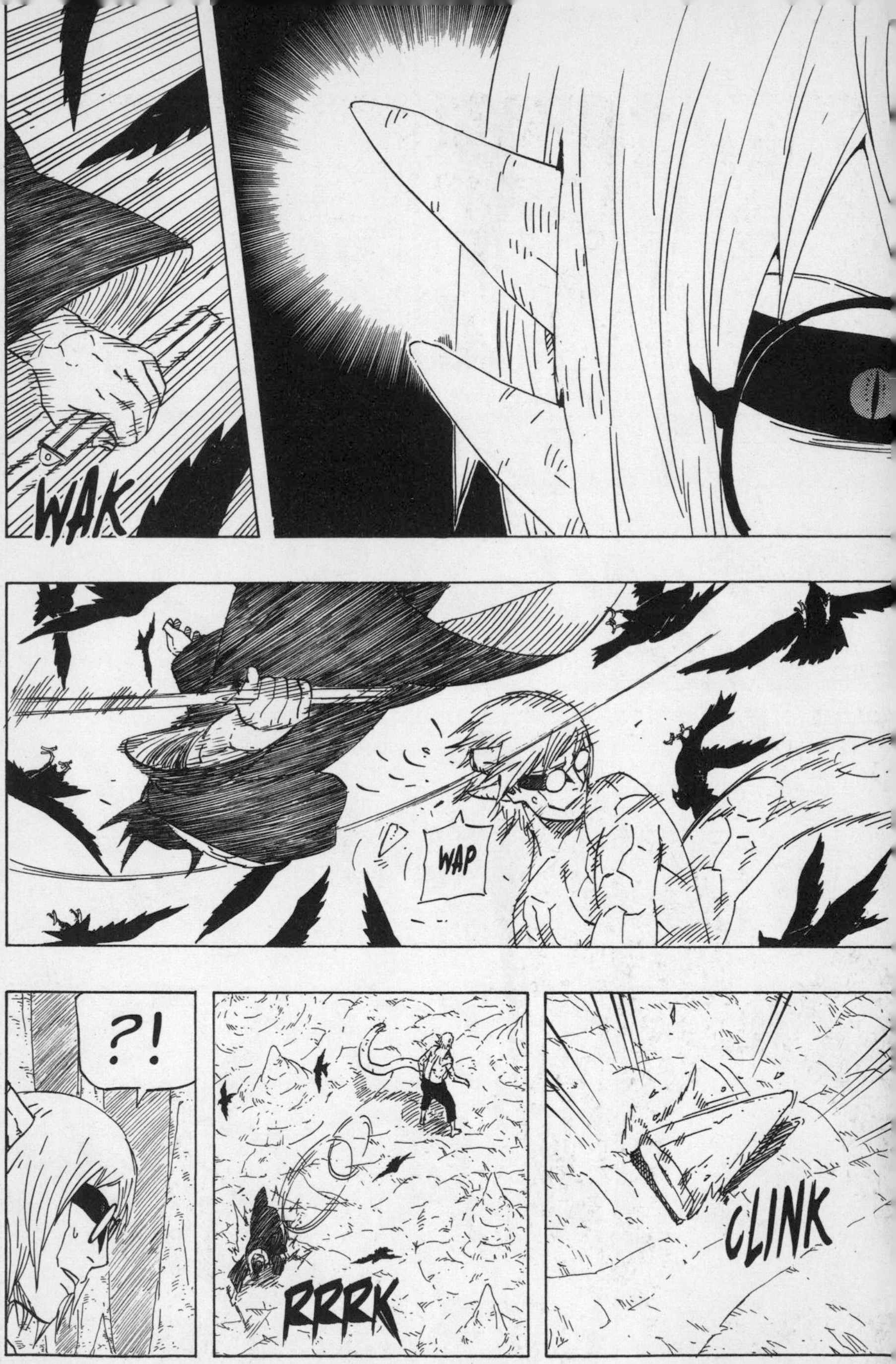
WAK
WAP
CLINK
RRRK
?!

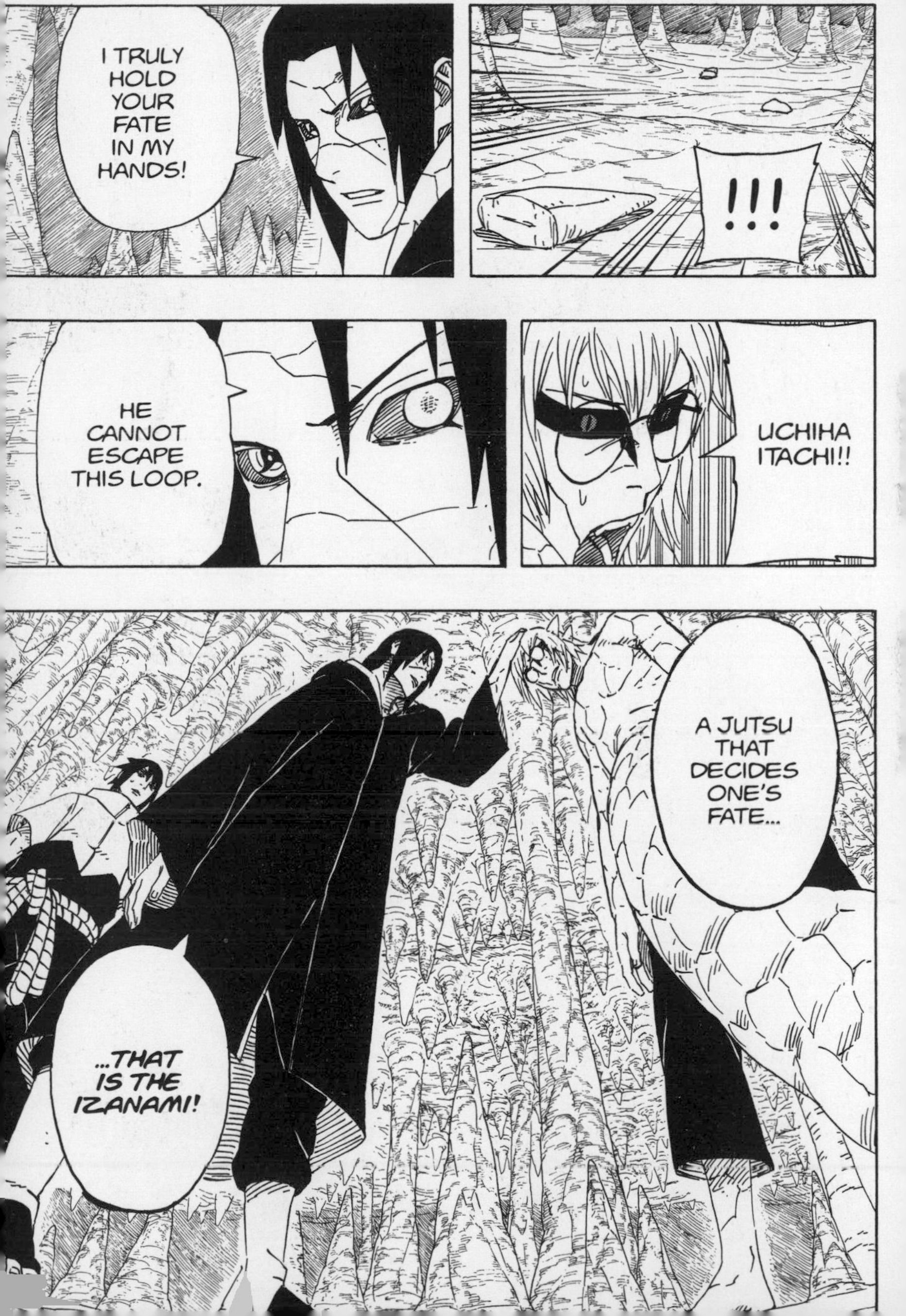
!!!
I TRULY HOLD YOUR FATE IN MY HANDS!
UCHIHA ITACHI!!
HE CANNOT ESCAPE THIS LOOP.
A JUTSU THAT DECIDES ONE'S FATE...
...THAT IS THE IZANAMI!

NARUTO

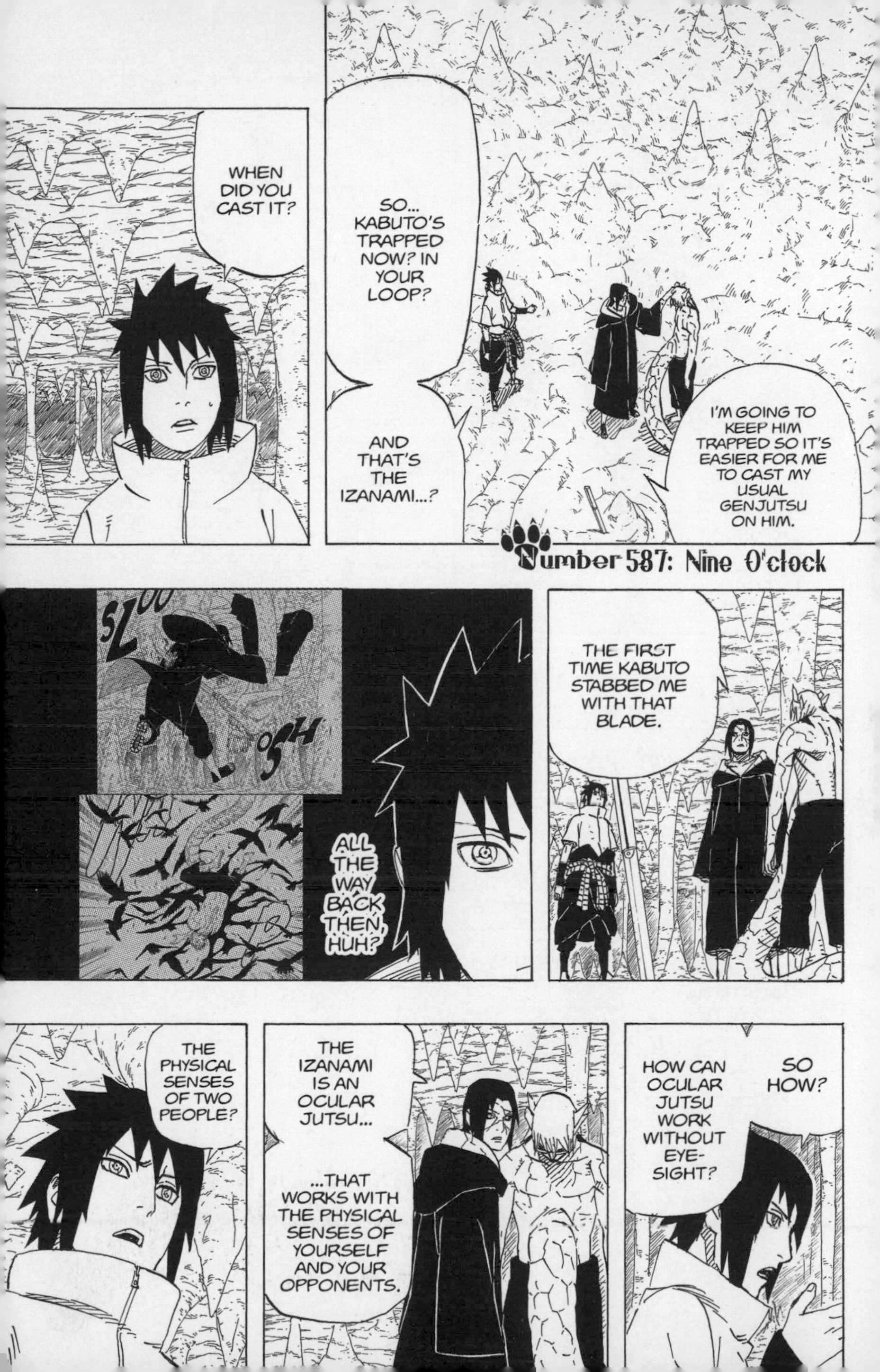
SO... KABUTO'S TRAPPED NOW? IN YOUR LOOP?
AND THAT'S THE IZANAMI...?
I'M GOING TO KEEP HIM TRAPPED SO IT'S EASIER FOR ME TO CAST MY USUAL GENJUTSU ON HIM.
WHEN DID YOU CAST IT?
Number 587: Nine O'clock
THE FIRST TIME KABUTO STABBED ME WITH THAT BLADE.
ALL THE WAY BACK THEN, HUH?
SLOOSH
SO HOW?
HOW CAN OCULAR JUTSU WORK WITHOUT EYE-SIGHT?
THE IZANAMI IS AN OCULAR JUTSU...
...THAT WORKS WITH THE PHYSICAL SENSES OF YOURSELF AND YOUR OPPONENTS.
THE PHYSICAL SENSES OF TWO PEOPLE?

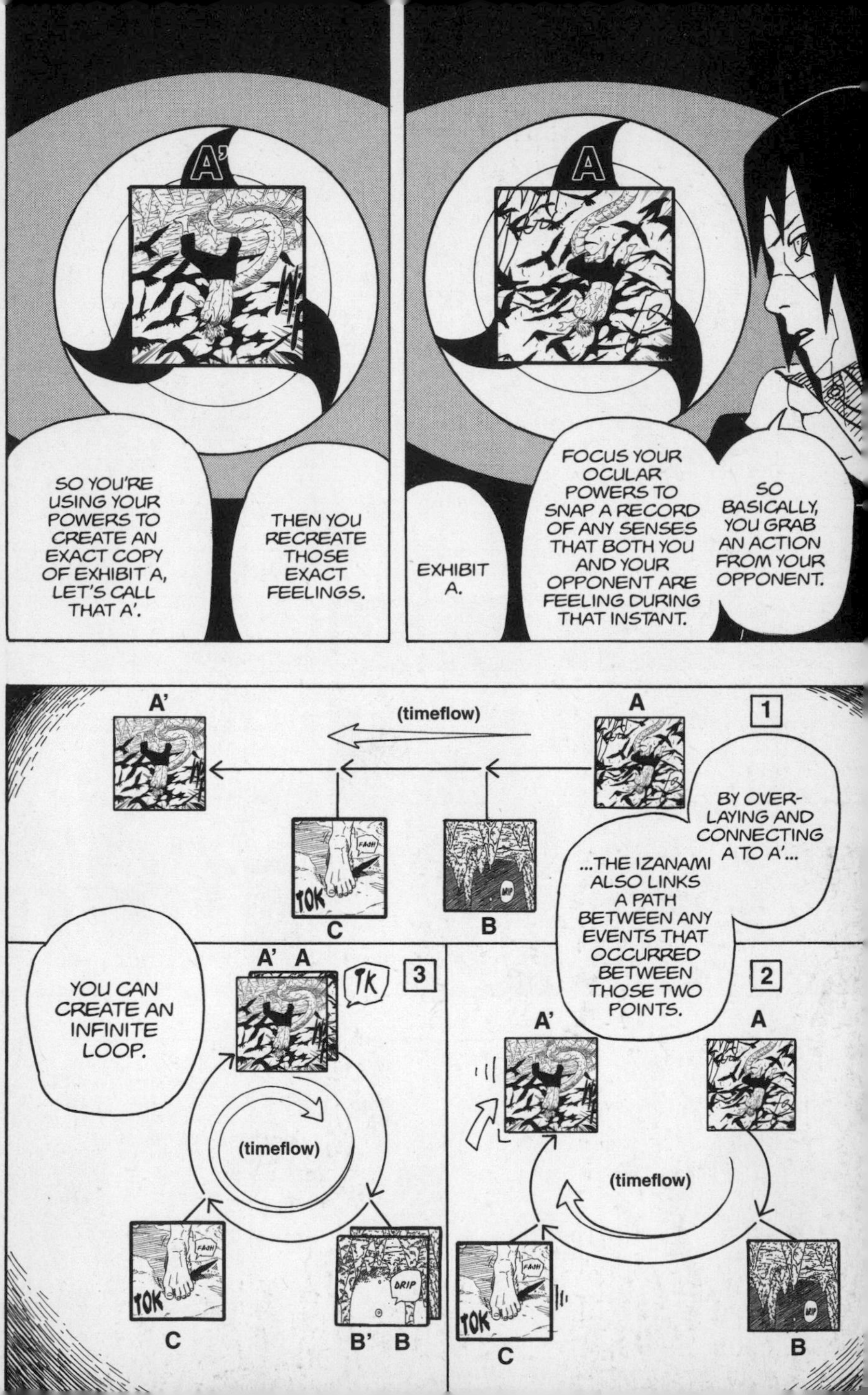
A
SO BASICALLY, YOU GRAB AN ACTION FROM YOUR OPPONENT.
FOCUS YOUR OCULAR POWERS TO SNAP A RECORD OF ANY SENSES THAT BOTH YOU AND YOUR OPPONENT ARE FEELING DURING THAT INSTANT.
EXHIBIT A.
A'
THEN YOU RECREATE THOSE EXACT FEELINGS.
SO YOU'RE USING YOUR POWERS TO CREATE AN EXACT COPY OF EXHIBIT A, LET'S CALL THAT A'.
1
A
(timeflow)
A'
BY OVER-LAYING AND CONNECTING A TO A'...
B
DRIP
C
FASH
TOK
...THE IZANAMI ALSO LINKS A PATH BETWEEN ANY EVENTS THAT OCCURRED BETWEEN THOSE TWO POINTS.
2
A
A'
(timeflow)
B
C
FASH
TOK
3
A' A
TK
YOU CAN CREATE AN INFINITE LOOP.
(timeflow)
FASH
TOK
C
DRIP
B' B

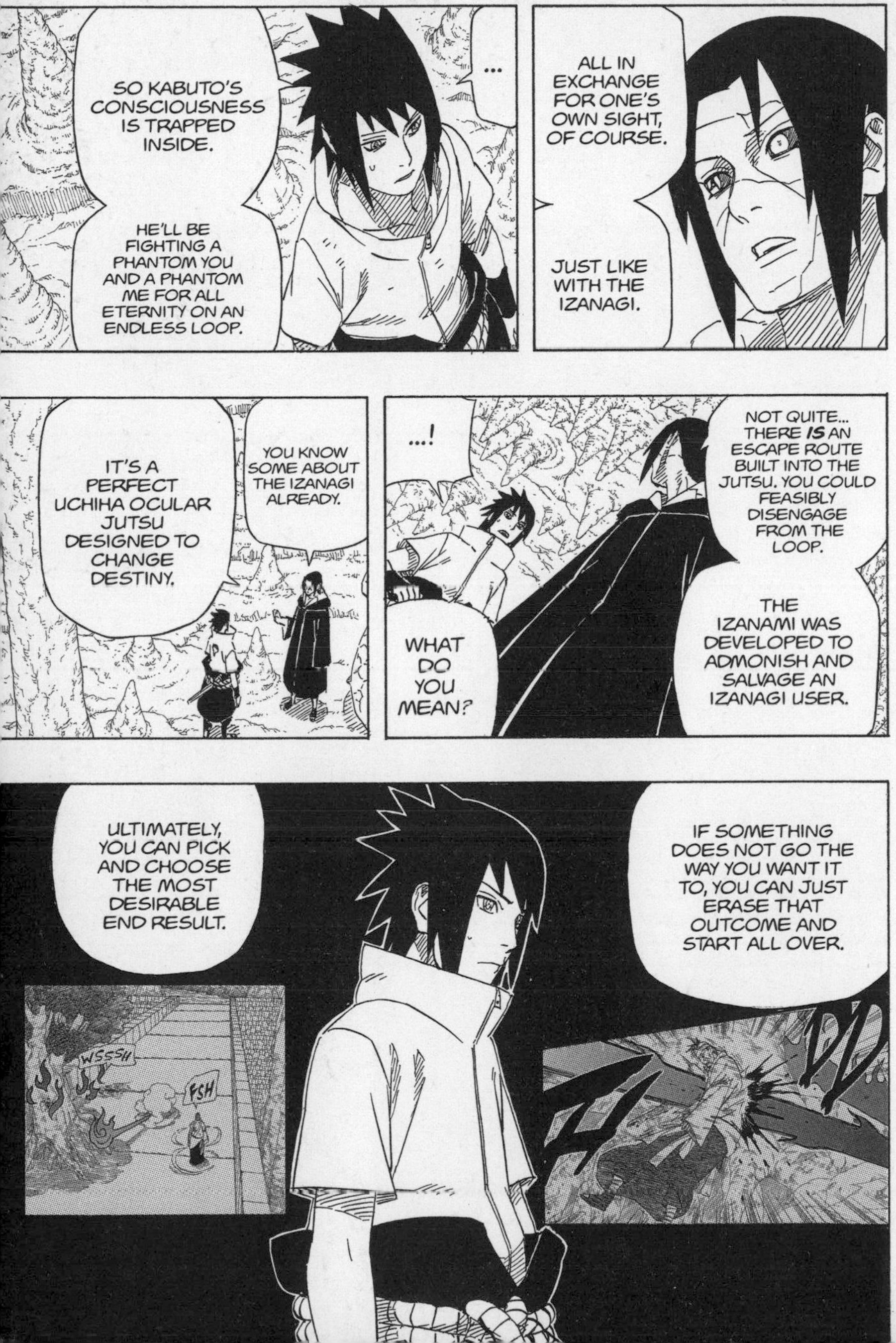
ALL IN EXCHANGE FOR ONE'S OWN SIGHT, OF COURSE.
JUST LIKE WITH THE IZANAGI.
...
SO KABUTO'S CONSCIOUSNESS IS TRAPPED INSIDE.
HE'LL BE FIGHTING A PHANTOM YOU AND A PHANTOM ME FOR ALL ETERNITY ON AN ENDLESS LOOP.
NOT QUITE... THERE ***IS*** AN ESCAPE ROUTE BUILT INTO THE JUTSU. YOU COULD FEASIBLY DISENGAGE FROM THE LOOP.
...!
WHAT DO YOU MEAN?
THE IZANAMI WAS DEVELOPED TO ADMONISH AND SALVAGE AN IZANAGI USER.
YOU KNOW SOME ABOUT THE IZANAGI ALREADY.
IT'S A PERFECT UCHIHA OCULAR JUTSU DESIGNED TO CHANGE DESTINY.
IF SOMETHING DOES NOT GO THE WAY YOU WANT IT TO, YOU CAN JUST ERASE THAT OUTCOME AND START ALL OVER.
ULTIMATELY, YOU CAN PICK AND CHOOSE THE MOST DESIRABLE END RESULT.
WSSSH
FSH

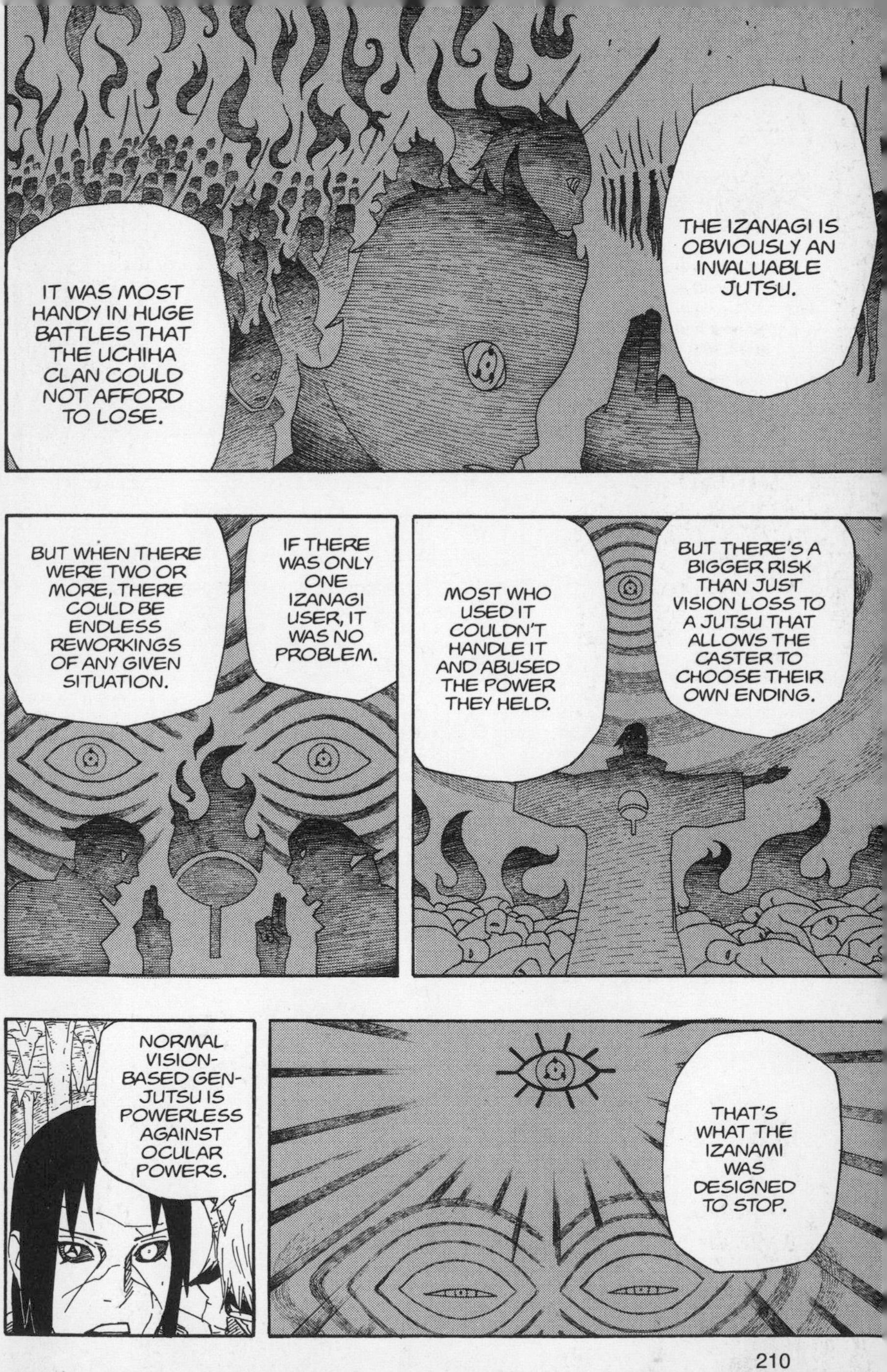
THE IZANAGI IS OBVIOUSLY AN INVALUABLE JUTSU.
IT WAS MOST HANDY IN HUGE BATTLES THAT THE UCHIHA CLAN COULD NOT AFFORD TO LOSE.
BUT THERE'S A BIGGER RISK THAN JUST VISION LOSS TO A JUTSU THAT ALLOWS THE CASTER TO CHOOSE THEIR OWN ENDING.
MOST WHO USED IT COULDN'T HANDLE IT AND ABUSED THE POWER THEY HELD.
IF THERE WAS ONLY ONE IZANAGI USER, IT WAS NO PROBLEM.
BUT WHEN THERE WERE TWO OR MORE, THERE COULD BE ENDLESS REWORKINGS OF ANY GIVEN SITUATION.
THAT'S WHAT THE IZANAMI WAS DESIGNED TO STOP.
NORMAL VISION-BASED GEN-JUTSU IS POWERLESS AGAINST OCULAR POWERS.

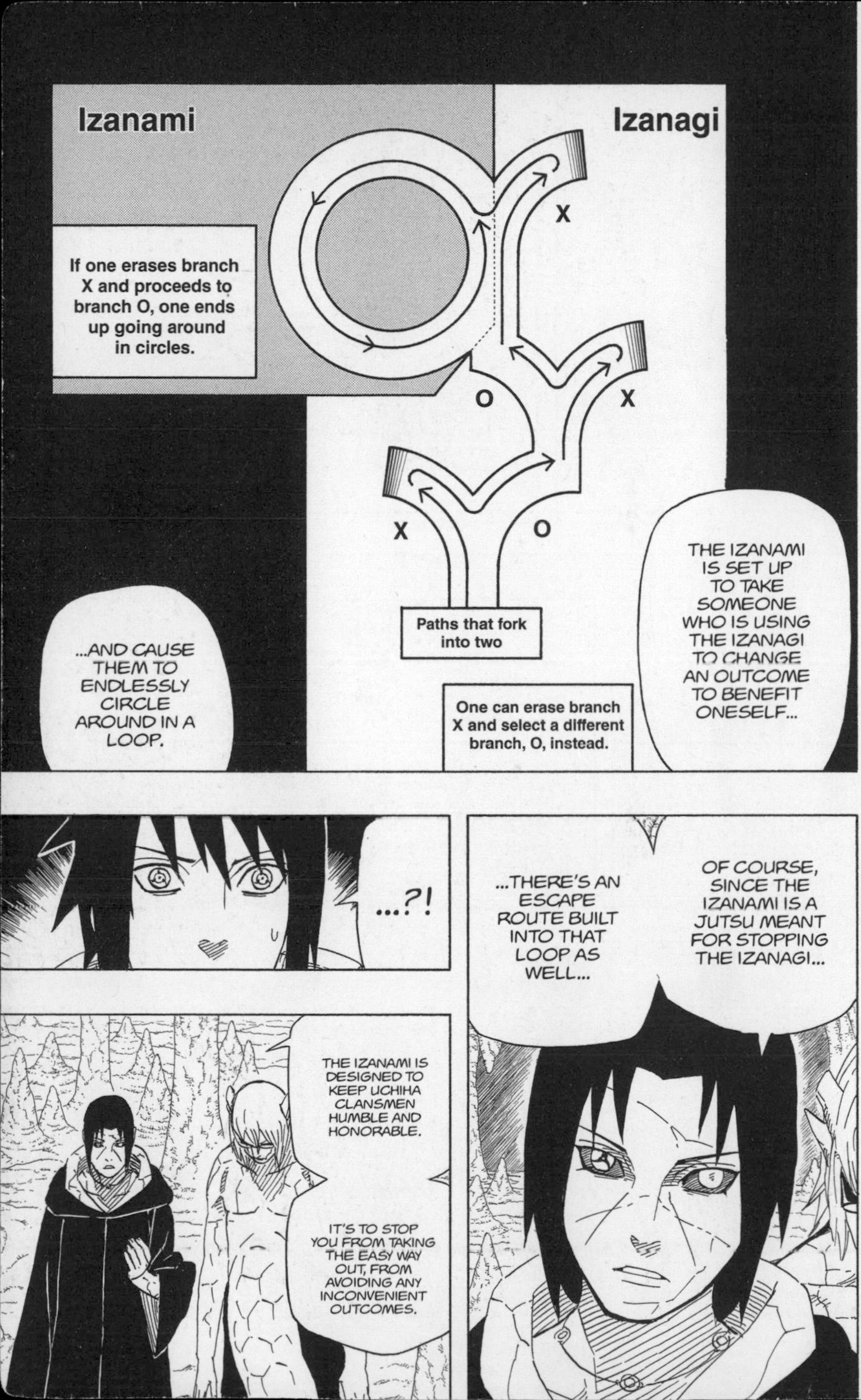
THE IZANAMI IS SET UP TO TAKE SOMEONE WHO IS USING THE IZANAGI TO CHANGE AN OUTCOME TO BENEFIT ONESELF...
Izanagi
X
X
O
O
X
Paths that fork into two
One can erase branch X and select a different branch, O, instead.
Izanami
If one erases branch X and proceeds to branch O, one ends up going around in circles.
...AND CAUSE THEM TO ENDLESSLY CIRCLE AROUND IN A LOOP.
OF COURSE, SINCE THE IZANAMI IS A JUTSU MEANT FOR STOPPING THE IZANAGI...
...THERE'S AN ESCAPE ROUTE BUILT INTO THAT LOOP AS WELL...
...?!
THE IZANAMI IS DESIGNED TO KEEP UCHIHA CLANSMEN HUMBLE AND HONORABLE.
IT'S TO STOP YOU FROM TAKING THE EASY WAY OUT, FROM AVOIDING ANY INCONVENIENT OUTCOMES.

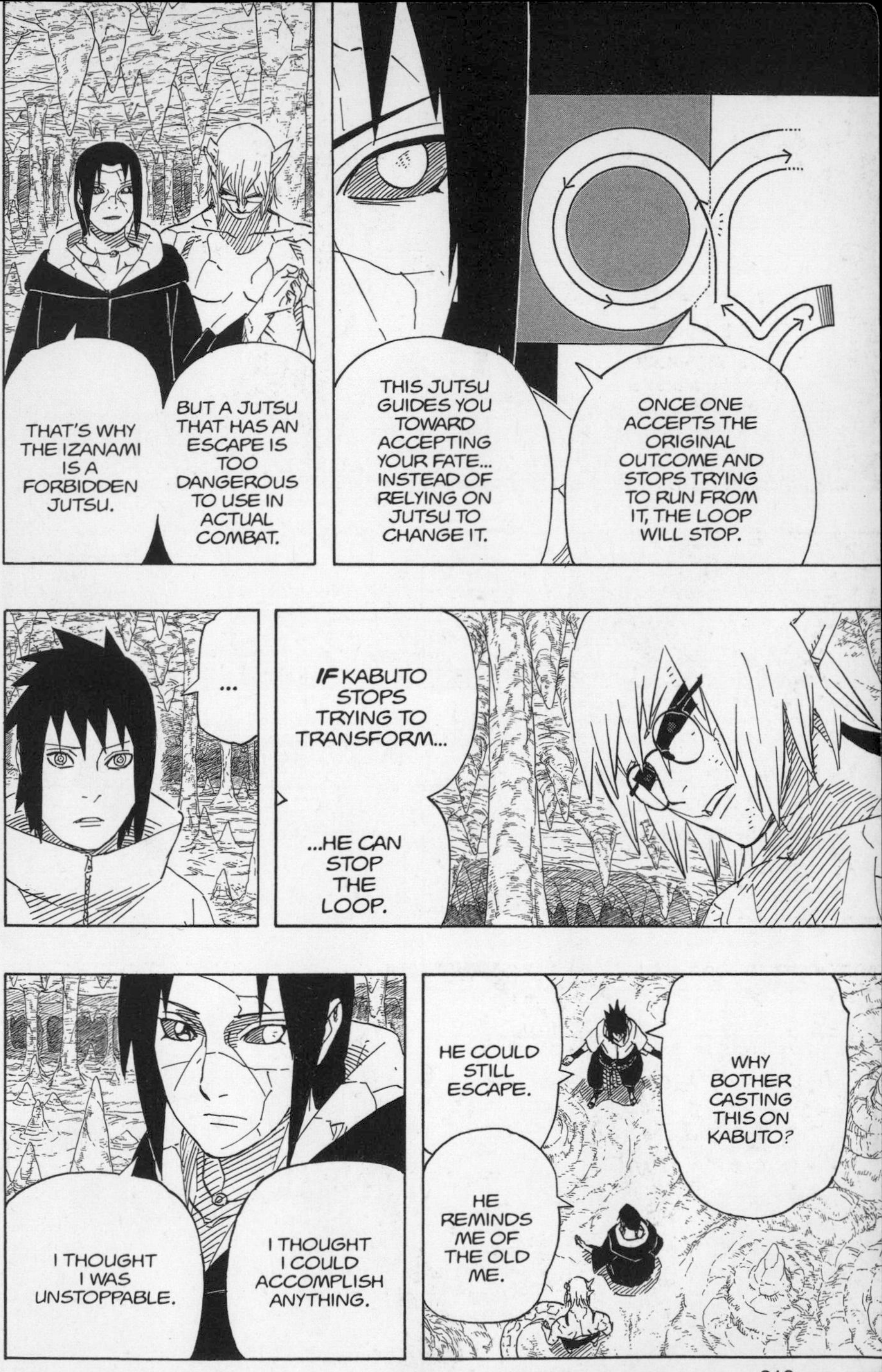
ONCE ONE ACCEPTS THE ORIGINAL OUTCOME AND STOPS TRYING TO RUN FROM IT, THE LOOP WILL STOP.
THIS JUTSU GUIDES YOU TOWARD ACCEPTING YOUR FATE... INSTEAD OF RELYING ON JUTSU TO CHANGE IT.
BUT A JUTSU THAT HAS AN ESCAPE IS TOO DANGEROUS TO USE IN ACTUAL COMBAT.
THAT'S WHY THE IZANAMI IS A FORBIDDEN JUTSU.
IF KABUTO STOPS TRYING TO TRANSFORM...
...HE CAN STOP THE LOOP.
...
WHY BOTHER CASTING THIS ON KABUTO?
HE COULD STILL ESCAPE.
HE REMINDS ME OF THE OLD ME.
I THOUGHT I COULD ACCOMPLISH ANYTHING.
I THOUGHT I WAS UNSTOPPABLE.

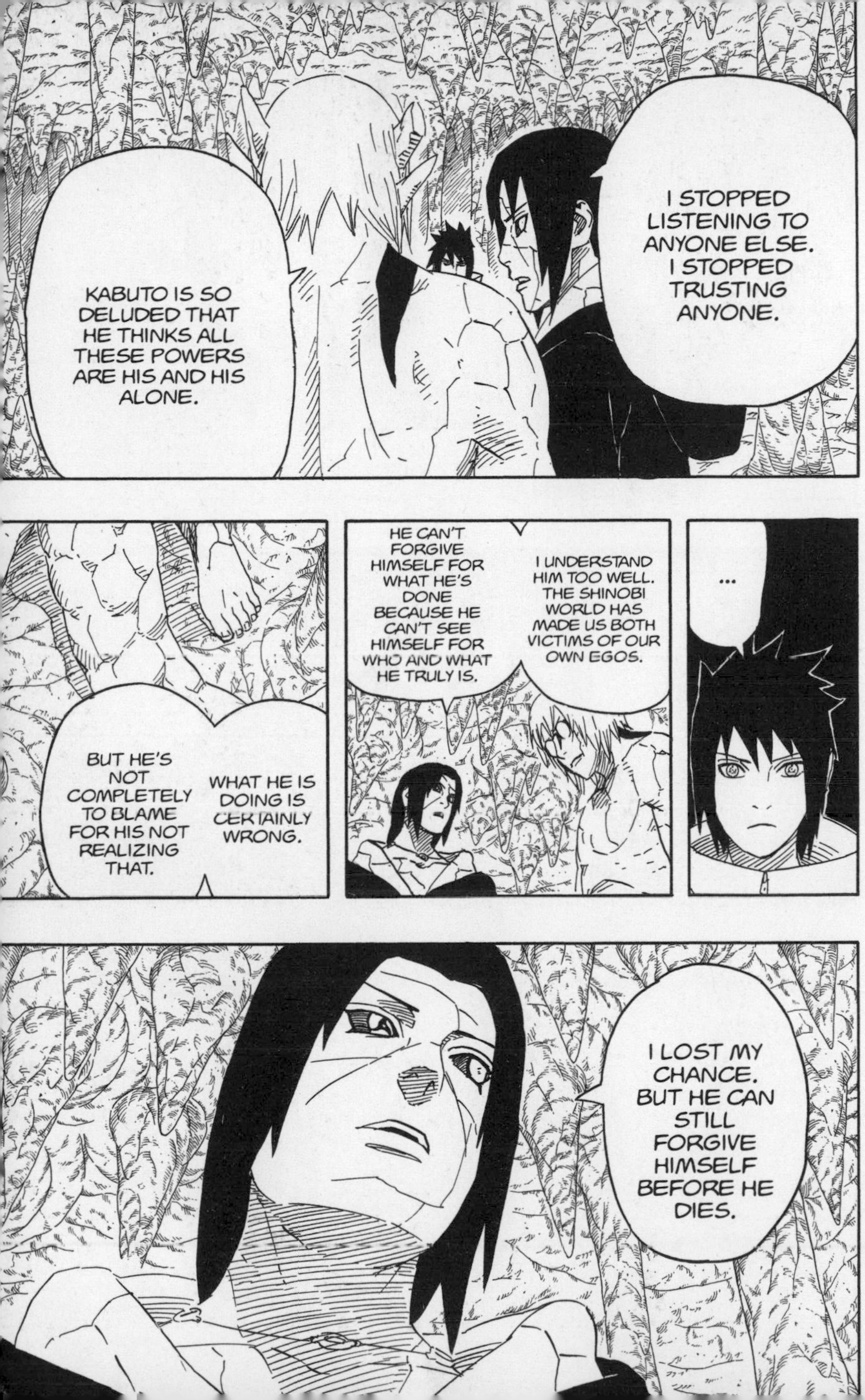
I STOPPED LISTENING TO ANYONE ELSE. I STOPPED TRUSTING ANYONE.
KABUTO IS SO DELUDED THAT HE THINKS ALL THESE POWERS ARE HIS AND HIS ALONE.
...
I UNDERSTAND HIM TOO WELL. THE SHINOBI WORLD HAS MADE US BOTH VICTIMS OF OUR OWN EGOS.
HE CAN'T FORGIVE HIMSELF FOR WHAT HE'S DONE BECAUSE HE CAN'T SEE HIMSELF FOR WHO AND WHAT HE TRULY IS.
WHAT HE IS DOING IS CERTAINLY WRONG.
BUT HE'S NOT COMPLETELY TO BLAME FOR HIS NOT REALIZING THAT.
I LOST MY CHANCE. BUT HE CAN STILL FORGIVE HIMSELF BEFORE HE DIES.

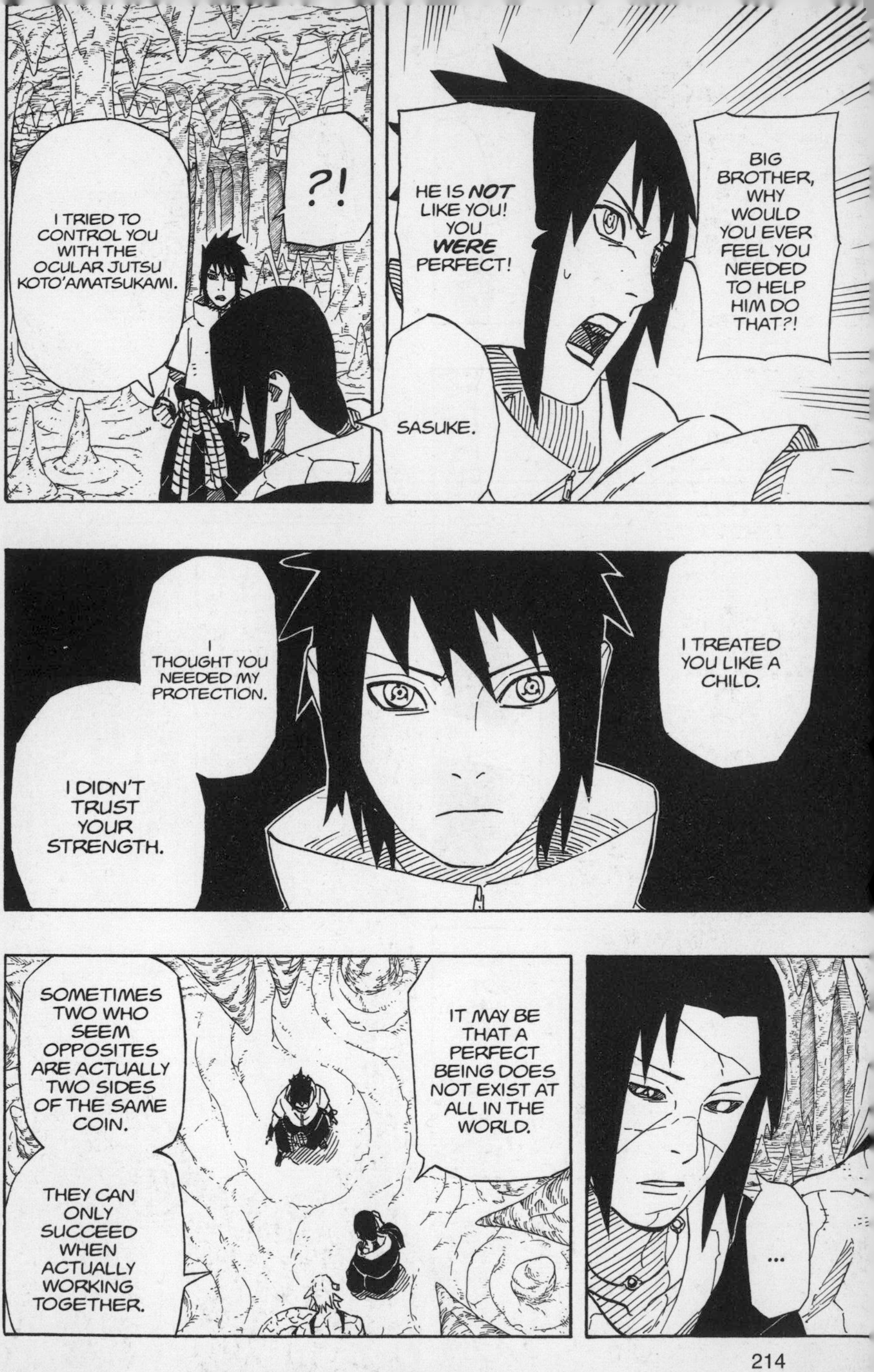
BIG BROTHER, WHY WOULD YOU EVER FEEL YOU NEEDED TO HELP HIM DO THAT?!
HE IS **NOT** LIKE YOU! YOU **WERE** PERFECT!
SASUKE.
?!
I TRIED TO CONTROL YOU WITH THE OCULAR JUTSU KOTO'AMATSUKAMI.
I TREATED YOU LIKE A CHILD.
I THOUGHT YOU NEEDED MY PROTECTION.
I DIDN'T TRUST YOUR STRENGTH.
...
IT MAY BE THAT A PERFECT BEING DOES NOT EXIST AT ALL IN THE WORLD.
SOMETIMES TWO WHO SEEM OPPOSITES ARE ACTUALLY TWO SIDES OF THE SAME COIN.
THEY CAN ONLY SUCCEED WHEN ACTUALLY WORKING TOGETHER.

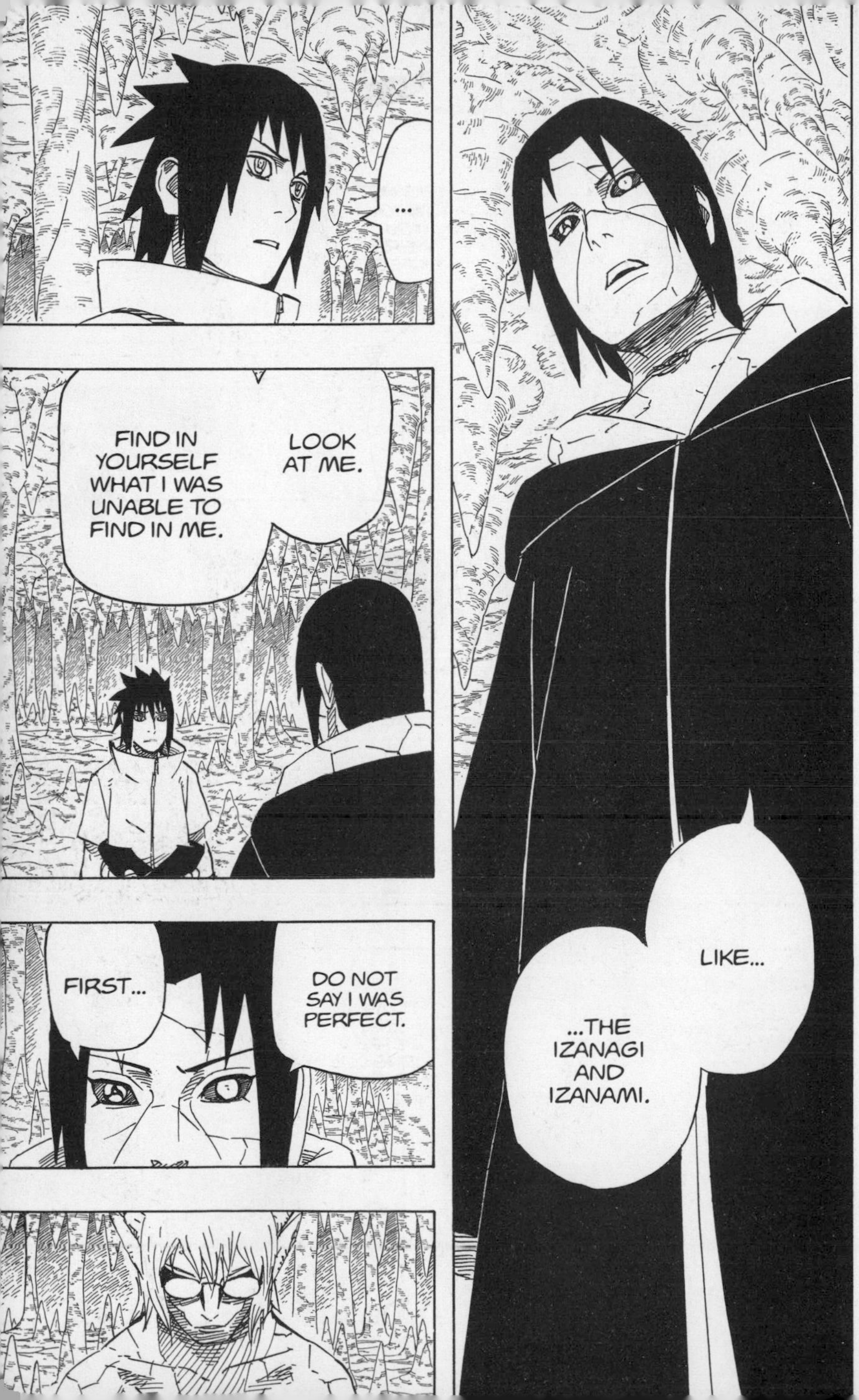
LIKE...
...THE IZANAGI AND IZANAMI.
...
LOOK AT ME.
FIND IN YOURSELF WHAT I WAS UNABLE TO FIND IN ME.
DO NOT SAY I WAS PERFECT.
FIRST...

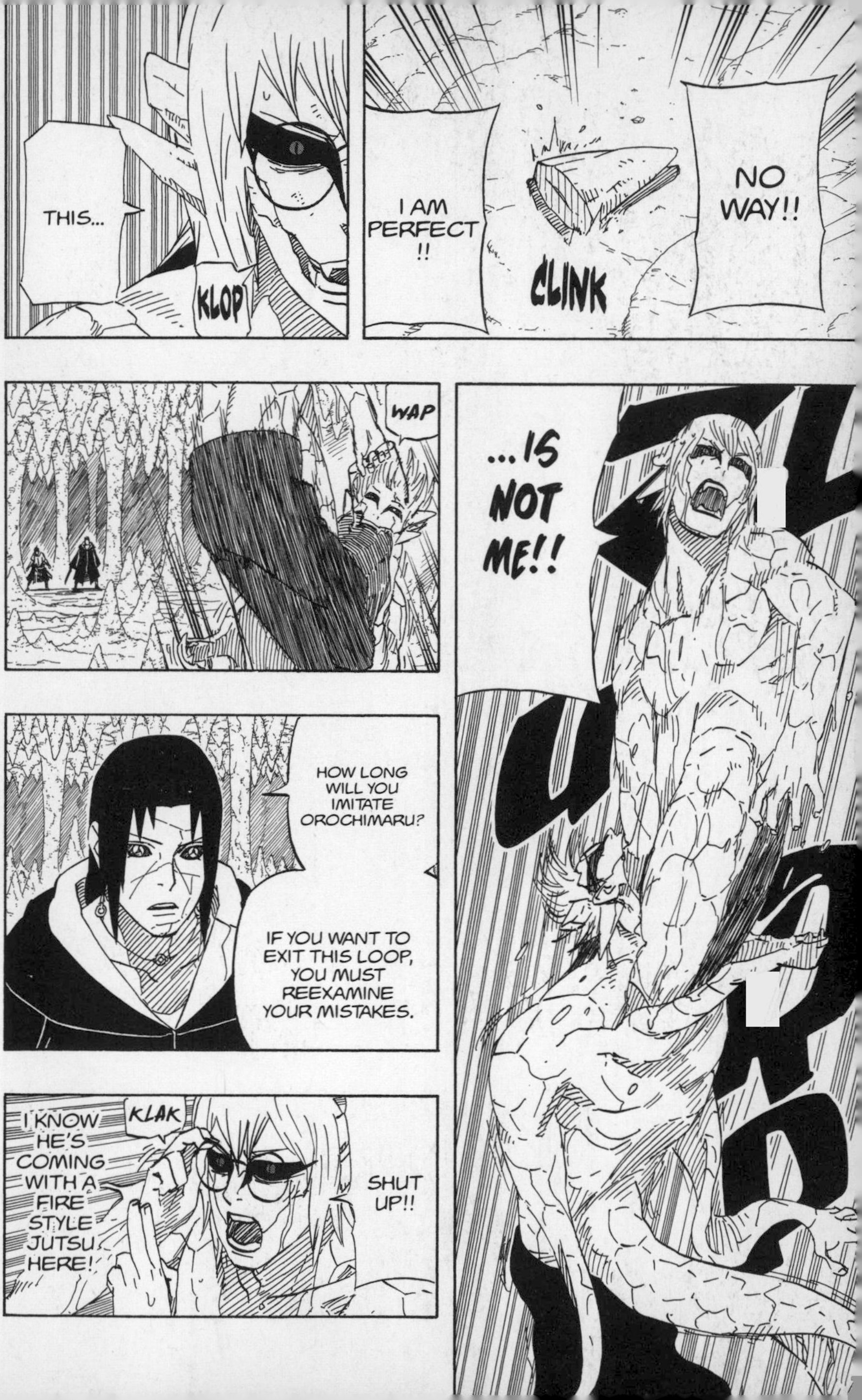
NO WAY!!
I AM PERFECT !!
CLINK
THIS...
KLOP
...IS NOT ME!!
WAP
HOW LONG WILL YOU IMITATE OROCHIMARU?
IF YOU WANT TO EXIT THIS LOOP, YOU MUST REEXAMINE YOUR MISTAKES.
SHUT UP!!
KLAK
I KNOW HE'S COMING WITH A FIRE STYLE JUTSU HERE!

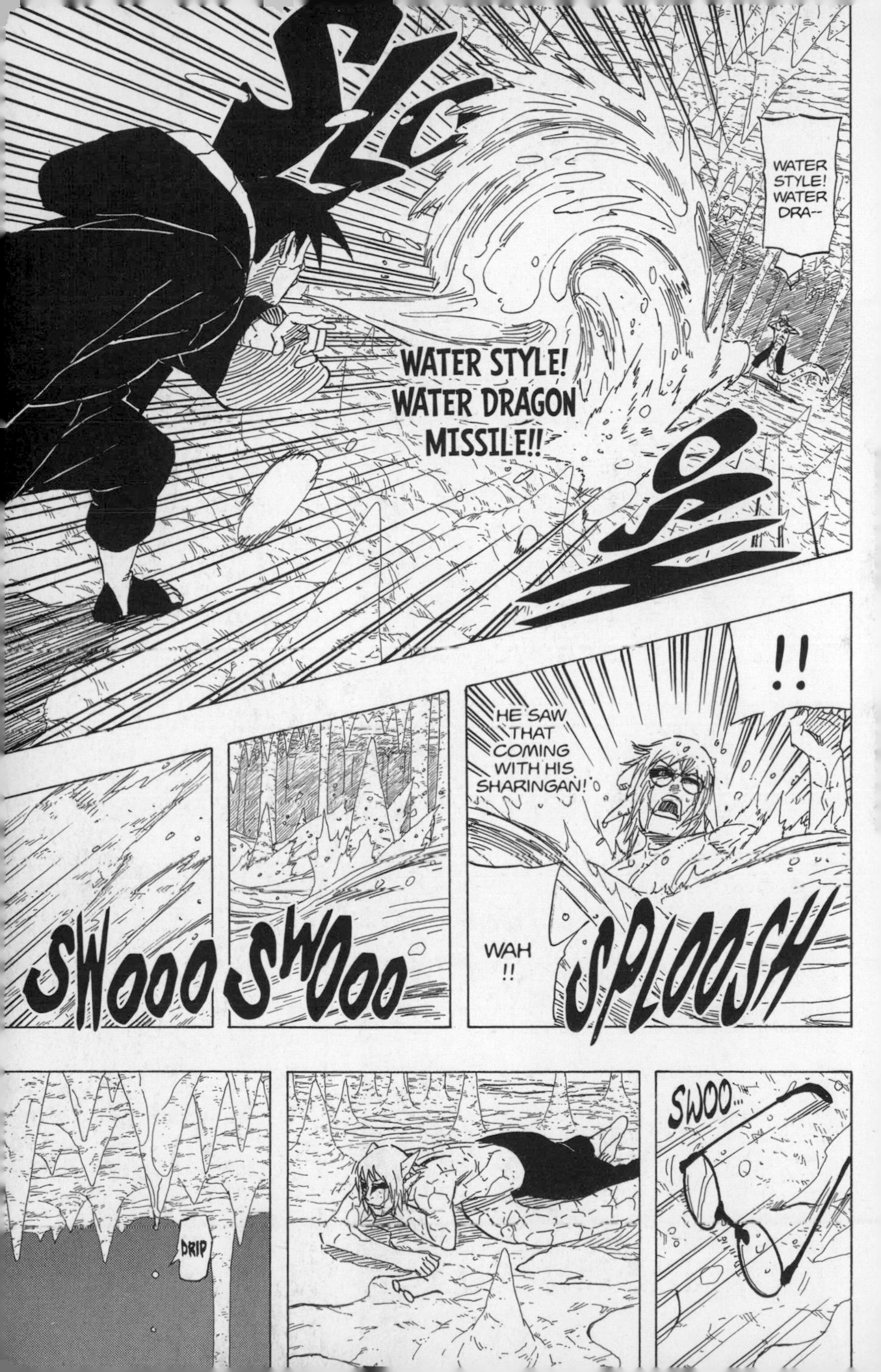
WATER STYLE! WATER DRA--
WATER STYLE! WATER DRAGON MISSILE!!
!!
HE SAW THAT COMING WITH HIS SHARINGAN!
WAH !!
SPLOOSH
SWOOO
SWOOO
SWOO...
DRIP

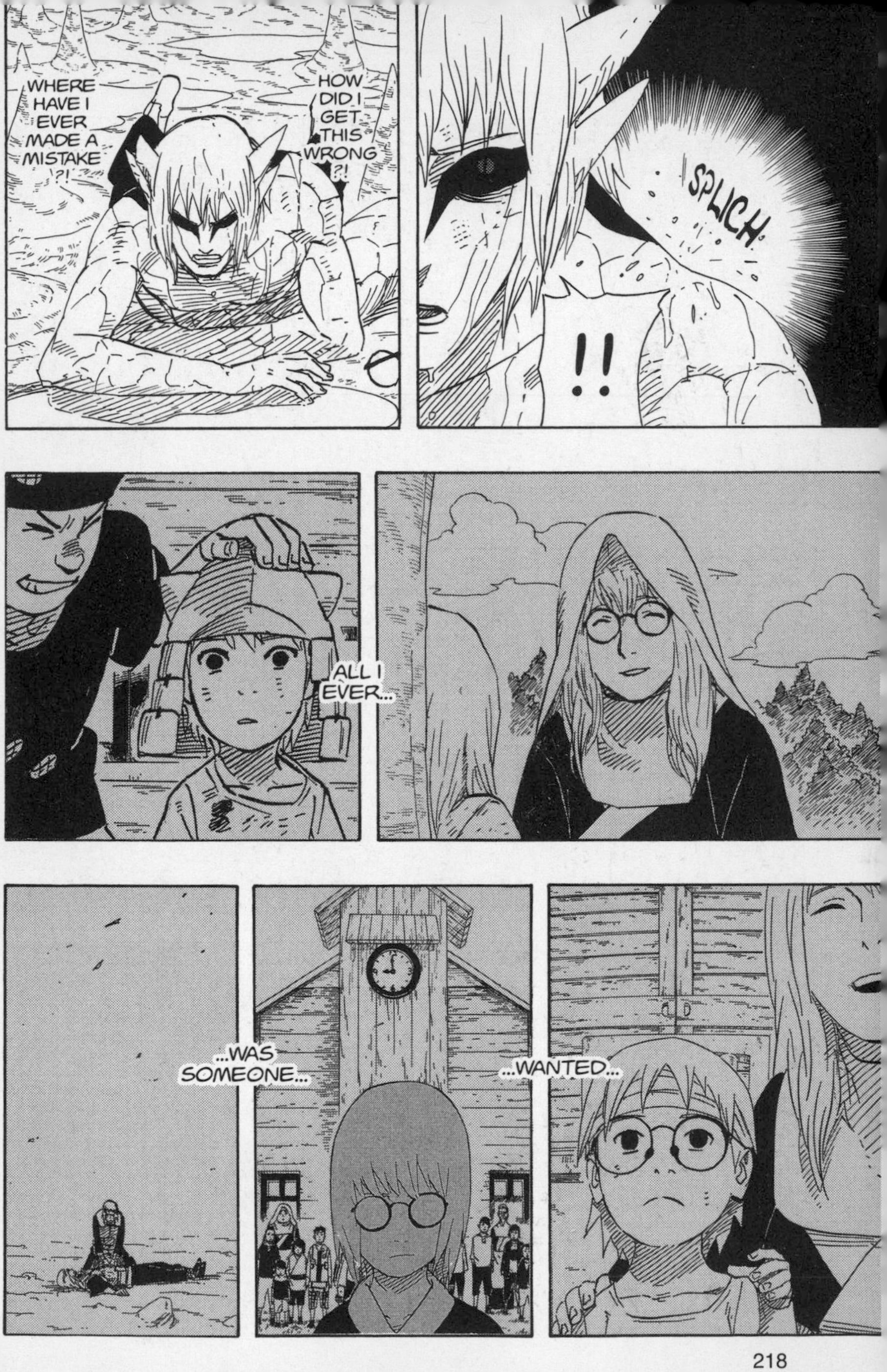
SPLICH
!!
HOW DID I GET THIS WRONG ?!
WHERE HAVE I EVER MADE A MISTAKE ?!
ALL I EVER...
...WANTED...
...WAS SOMEONE...

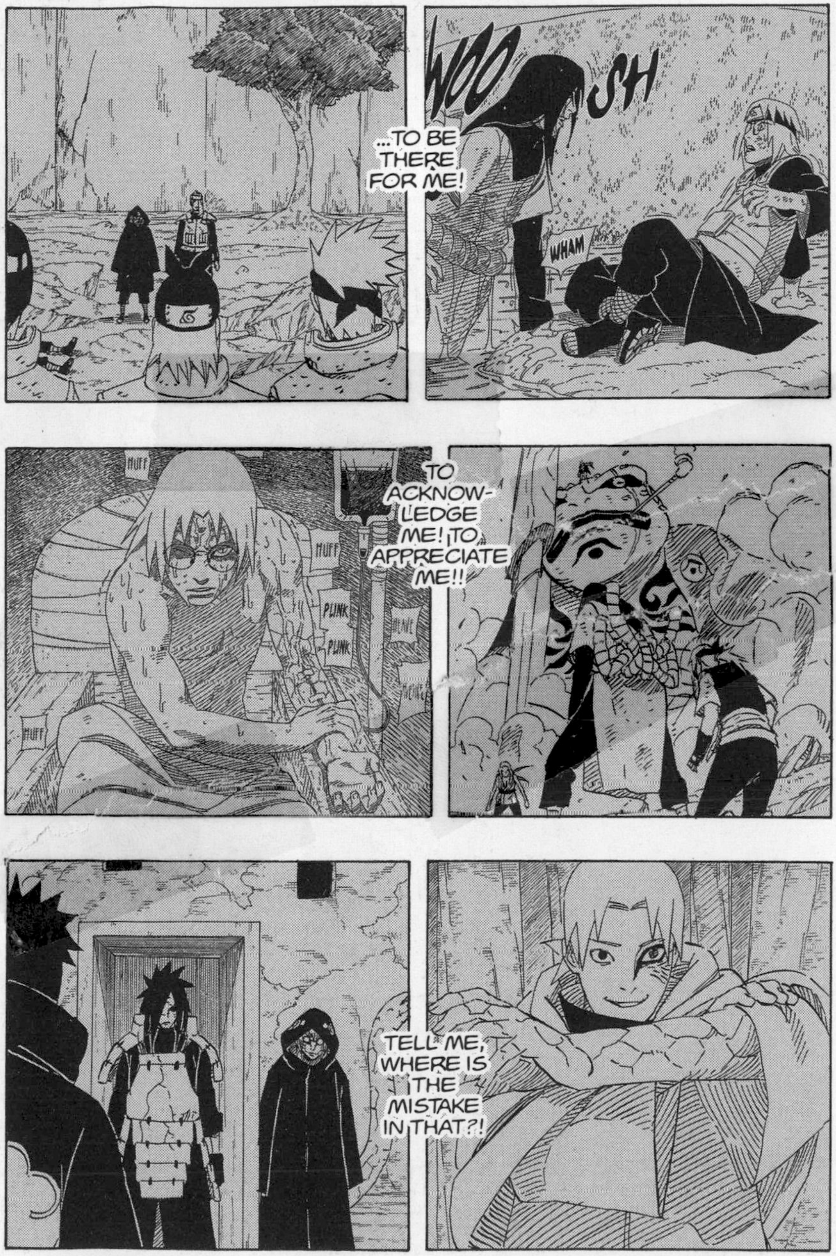
WOOSH
WHAM
...TO BE THERE FOR ME!
TO ACKNOW-LEDGE ME! TO APPRECIATE ME!!
HUFF
HUFF
PLINK
PLINK
HUFF
TELL ME, WHERE IS THE MISTAKE IN THAT?!

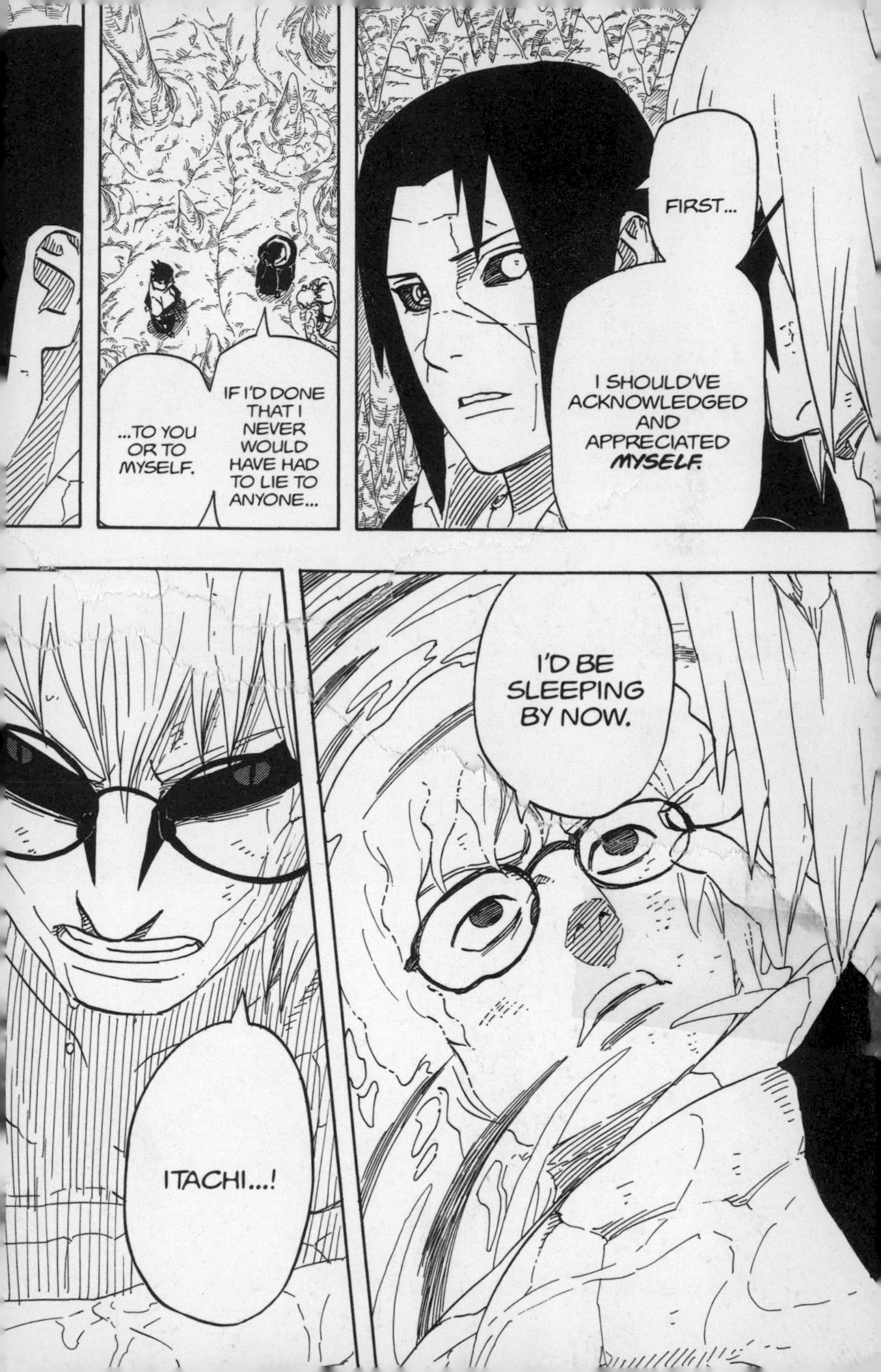
FIRST...
I SHOULD'VE ACKNOWLEDGED AND APPRECIATED *MYSELF.*
IF I'D DONE THAT I NEVER WOULD HAVE HAD TO LIE TO ANYONE...
...TO YOU OR TO MYSELF.
I'D BE SLEEPING BY NOW.
ITACHI...!

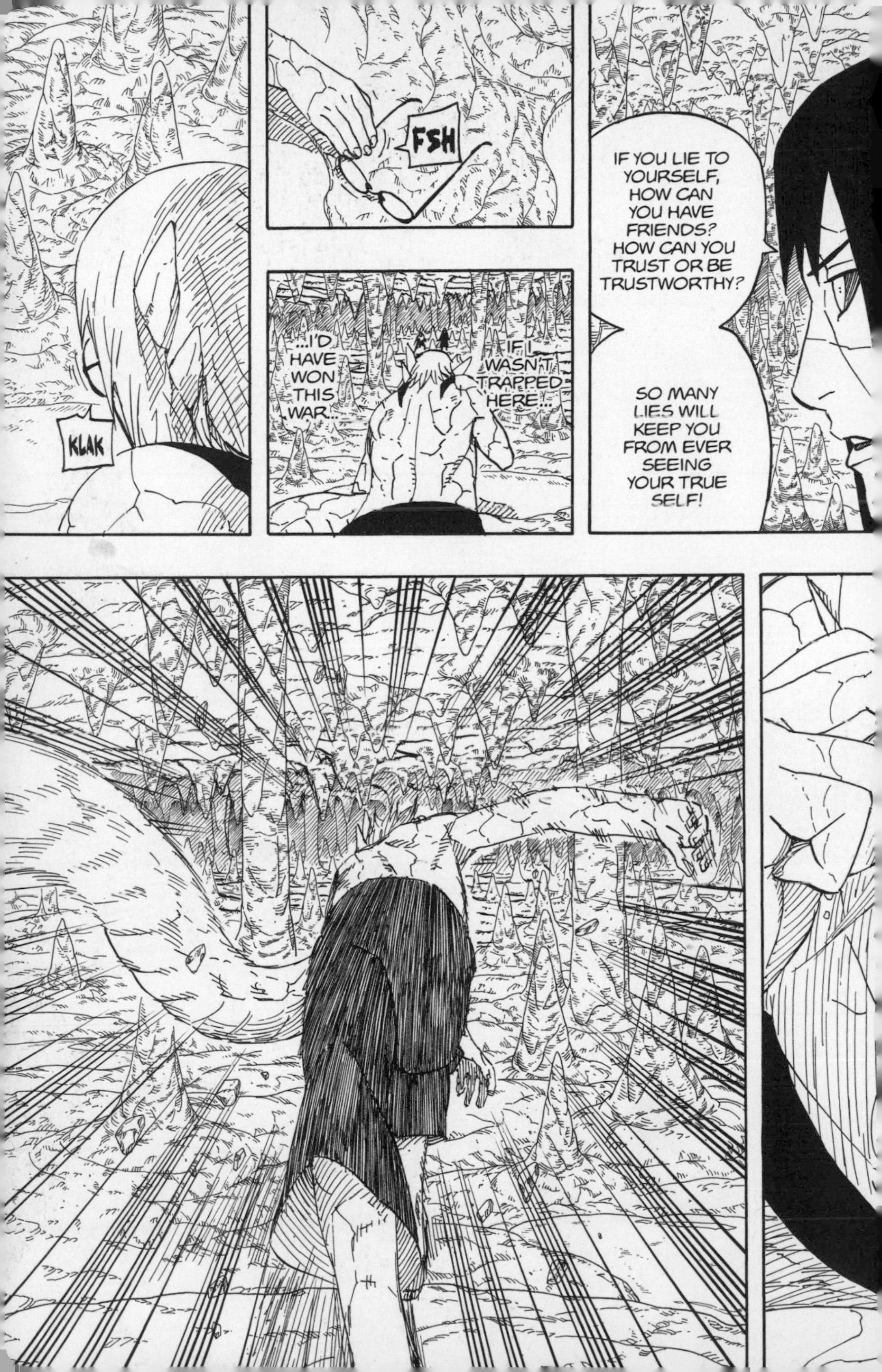
IF YOU LIE TO YOURSELF, HOW CAN YOU HAVE FRIENDS? HOW CAN YOU TRUST OR BE TRUSTWORTHY?
SO MANY LIES WILL KEEP YOU FROM EVER SEEING YOUR TRUE SELF!
FSH
IF I WASN'T TRAPPED HERE...
...I'D HAVE WON THIS WAR...
KLAK

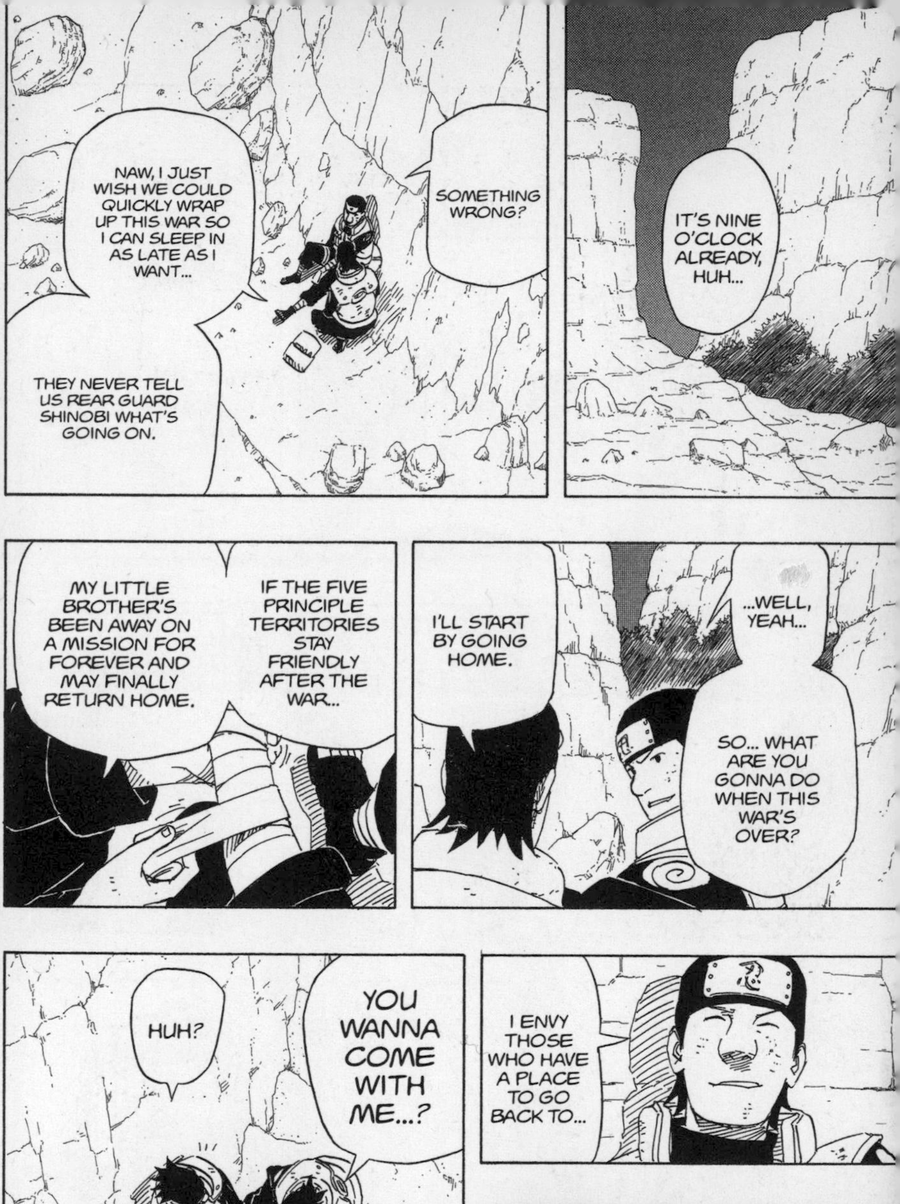
IT'S NINE O'CLOCK ALREADY, HUH...
SOMETHING WRONG?
NAW, I JUST WISH WE COULD QUICKLY WRAP UP THIS WAR SO I CAN SLEEP IN AS LATE AS I WANT...
THEY NEVER TELL US REAR GUARD SHINOBI WHAT'S GOING ON.
...WELL, YEAH...
SO... WHAT ARE YOU GONNA DO WHEN THIS WAR'S OVER?
I'LL START BY GOING HOME.
IF THE FIVE PRINCIPLE TERRITORIES STAY FRIENDLY AFTER THE WAR...
MY LITTLE BROTHER'S BEEN AWAY ON A MISSION FOR FOREVER AND MAY FINALLY RETURN HOME.
I ENVY THOSE WHO HAVE A PLACE TO GO BACK TO...
...
YOU WANNA COME WITH ME...?
HUH?

SHONEN JUMP MANGA EDITION

NARUTO

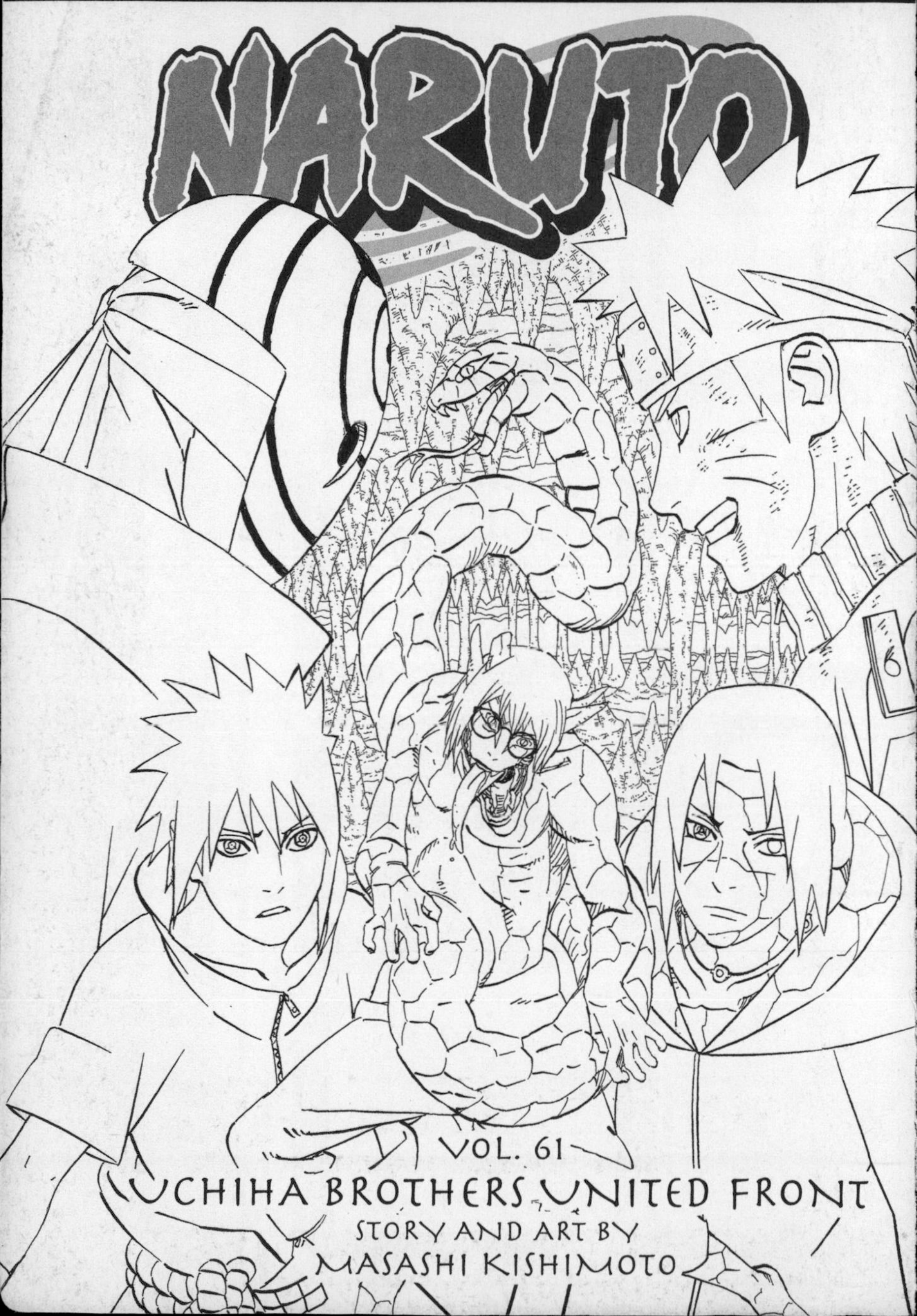

VOL. 61

UCHIHA BROTHERS UNITED FRONT

STORY AND ART BY
MASASHI KISHIMOTO

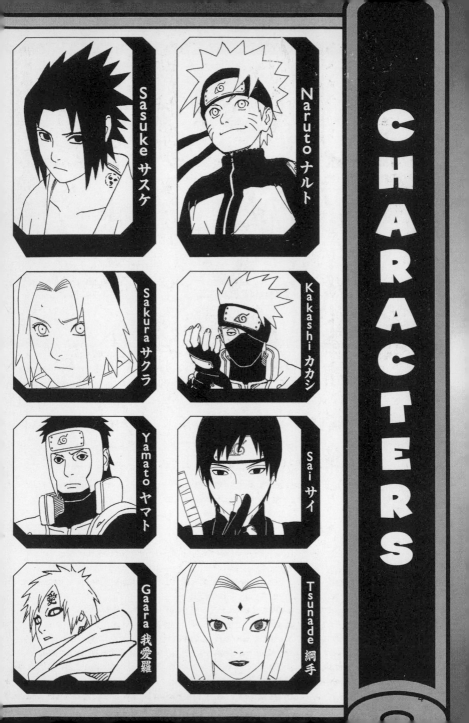

Sasuke サスケ

Naruto ナルト

Sakura サクラ

Kakashi カカシ

Yamato ヤマト

Sai サイ

Gaara 我愛羅

Tsunade 綱手

CHARACTERS